THE
RELENTLESS
REVOLUTION

The

RELENTLESS

REVOLUTION

A HISTORY OF CAPITALISM

Joyce Appleby

W. W. NORTON & COMPANY   New York • London

Manufacturing by RR Donnelley, Harrisonburg, VA
Book design by Dana Sloan
Production manager: Anna Oler

ISBN 978-0-393-06894-8

W. W. Norton & Company, Inc.
500 Fifth Avenue, New York, N.Y. 10110

W. W. Norton & Company Ltd.
Castle House, 75/76 Wells Street, London W1T 3QT

Book Club Edition

I dedicate this book to my son, Frank Appleby,

who has been an unfailing source of comfort, knowledge,

humor, and enthusiasm

CONTENTS

ACKNOWLEDGMENTS

◆

W RITING THIS BOOK was actually fun, and even more pleasurable were the many conversations I had about capitalism with Flora Lansburgh, Jim Caylor, Linn Shapiro, Perry Anderson, Ruben Castellanos, Bruce Robbins, and Lesley Herrman. I had a band of readers to whom I am deeply, deeply indebted. Jack Pole brought to the reading of *The Relentless Revolution* a welcome and profound knowledge of history. David Levine, another fellow historian, was my toughest critic, but he generously praised the parts that he liked and always encouraged me to press on. Ware Myers gave me the kind of crisp advice you'd expect from an engineer with intellectual leanings. Susan Wiener, a poet and writer, read the book with sympathy and the sharpest eye for errors grammatical, syntactical, and orthographic that I have ever known. Carlton Appleby pushed for clarity and precision. My dear friend Ann Gordon brought her care for the English language to my prose. Several colleagues—Margaret Jacob, Robert Brenner, Peter Baldwin, Nikki Keddie, Fred Notehelfer, Stanley Wolpert, Jose Moya, Mary Yeager, and Naomi Lamoreaux—contributed valuable expert knowledge. My nephew, Rob Avery, saved me from making several errors about computers, as Seth Weingram did for the arcane world of finance. Karen Orren listened and read with her usual acuteness. I was fortunate in having Steve Forman as my editor at Norton, for he was a shrewd, yet sympathetic, reader of my text. My son, Frank, to whom I have dedicated this book, read each chapter with critical insight. What was even more helpful, he shared his expansive knowledge with me and never tired of talking about capitalism. Through the kindness of Peter Reill and the Center for Seventeenth- and Eighteenth-Century Studies, I found Vic

Fusilero, the finest research assistant I have ever had. It's rare that some-one not only gives you an idea for a book but persists in convincing you to write it, but such is the case with Michael Phillips. After interviewing me for his radio show many years ago, he decided that I should write a book on capitalism, and so I have. I am grateful to all these friends. I may have to claim my mistakes, but I am certain that I would have had to claim a lot more without these superb readers.

THE
RELENTLESS
REVOLUTION

1

♦

THE PUZZLE

OF CAPITALISM

LIKE A GOOD detective story, the history of capitalism begins with a puzzle. For millennia trade had flourished within traditional societies, strictly confined in its economic and moral reach. Yet in the sixteenth century, commerce moved in bold new directions. More effective ways to raise food slowly started to release workers and money for other economic pursuits, such as processing the sugar, tobacco, cotton, tea, and silks that came to Europe from the East and West Indies and beyond. These improvements raised the standard of living for Western Europeans, but it took something more dramatic to break through the restraints of habit and authority of the old economic order. That world-reshaping force came when a group of natural philosophers gained an understanding of physical laws. With this knowledge, inventors with a more practical bent found stunning ways to generate energy from natural forces. Production took a quantum leap forward. Capitalism—a system based on individual investments in the production of marketable goods—slowly replaced the traditional ways of meeting the material needs of a society. From early industrialization to the present global economy, a sequence of revolutions relentlessly changed the habits and habitats of human beings. The puzzle is why it took so long for these developments to materialize.

Most of the marvelous machines that transformed human effort began with simple applications of steam and electricity. How many people had watched steam lift the top off a pan of boiling water before someone figured out how to make steam run an engine? Couldn't someone earlier have begun experimenting with lightning? The dramatic success of eighteenth- and nineteenth-century innovations compels us to wonder why human societies remained fixed for millennia in a primitive agrarian order. How can it be that brilliant minds penetrated some of the secrets of the cosmos but couldn't imagine how to combat hunger? The answer that the times were economically backward is of course semantic and doesn't really help us pierce the conundrum of great civilized accomplishments in the face of limited economic productivity.

Starting with these questions, I am going to explore the benchmarks in capitalism's ascent, looking at how this system transformed politics while churning up practices, thoughts, values, and ideals that had long prevailed within the cocoon of custom. This is not a general study of capitalism in the world, but rather a narrative that follows the shaping of the economic system that we live with today. Nor does it cover how various countries became capitalistic, but rather concentrates on those specific developments in particular places that gave form to capitalism. My focus is on economic practices, of course, but it can't be stressed too much that capitalism is as much a cultural as an economic system. A new way of establishing political order emerged. People reversed how they looked at the past and the future. They reconceived human nature. At a very personal level, men and women began making plans for themselves that would once have appeared ludicrous in their ambitious reach. Tucked into this account will be an examination of how different societies have responded to the constant challenges ushered into their lives during the past four centuries.

If we were to visit ancient Florence, Aleppo, and Canton, we would be astonished by the rich array of foods and goods for sale in their vast bazaars, souks, and markets. We would marvel at the beauty of their churches, temples, and mosques, as well as the merchants' elegant city houses and the country homes of the nobility. We would discover a population of talented artisans, knowledgeable statesmen, shrewd traders, skilled mariners, and energetic people everywhere. Yet they all were in thrall to an economic system so limited in size and scope that it could barely feed them. They accepted as normal that they would regularly suffer from drastic shortages of all kinds of goods because it had always been so.

Scarcity in Traditional Society

Traditional societies around the globe were built on the bedrock of scarcity, above all the scarcity of food. Whether in ancient Egypt or Greece, Babylonia or Mongolia, it took the labor of upwards of 80 percent of the people to produce enough food to feed the whole population. And because farmers often didn't even succeed in doing that, there were famines. All but the very wealthy tightened their belts every year in the months before crops came in. The fear of famine was omnipresent. Hungry subjects tended to be unruly ones, a fact that linked economic and political concerns. The worry about famines, which most adults shared, justified the authoritarian rule that prevailed everywhere. Few doubted that those vulnerable to food shortages needed to be protected from the self-interested decisions that farmers and traders might make about what to do with the harvest if they were left to themselves.

To prevent social unrest, rulers monitored the growing, selling, and exporting of grain crops. Where there were legislatures, they passed restrictive laws. Hemmed in by regulations, people had few opportunities to make trouble—or undertake new enterprises. Most manufacturing went on in the household, where family members turned fibers into fabric and made foodstuffs edible. Custom, not incentives, prompted action and dictated the flow of work throughout the year. People did not assign themselves parts in this social order; tasks were allocated through the inherited statuses of landlord, tenant, father, husband, son, laborer, wife, mother, daughter, and servant.

Despite the great diversity of communities around the world, they conformed in one way: Their population grew and retrenched like an accordion through alternating periods of abundance and scarcity—the seven fat and seven lean years of the Bible. You can see this "feast or famine" oscillation in the construction record of European cathedrals. Most of these magnificent structures took centuries to complete, with a spate of years of active building followed by long periods of neglect. When there was a bit of surplus, work could resume, only to be succeeded by stoppages during times of acute scarcity.

If we could go back in time, we would probably be most surprised by the widely shared resistance, not to say hostility, to change. Novelty has been so endemic to life in the modern West that it is hard for us to fathom how much people once feared it. The effects of economic vulnerability radiated throughout old societies, encouraging suspicions and superstitions as well as justifying the conspicuous authority of monarchs, priests, landlords, and fathers. Maintaining order, never a matter of indifference to those in charge of society, was paramount when the lives of so many people were at risk.

The wealth of the Western world has created something of a safety net against global famine, but there are still societies whose powerful traditions echo those of premodern Europe. Through our engagement with the Muslim world we now also recognize the hold of ideas about honor, the separation of male and female roles, the importance of female virginity, and the submersion of each person's desires into the will of his or her community. Recent terrorist attacks have prompted many Westerners to hope that improved economies might otherwise engage the young men who carry out the violence. More jobs would certainly be welcome, but such a response bears the traces of our capitalist mentality. What we don't sufficiently weigh are the powerful ties of shared rituals and beliefs and how threats to them affect people. Men and women in traditional societies see our concern about efficiency and profits as fetishes. These preoccupations of ours are as distasteful to them as they were to men and women in sixteenth-century Europe.

Capitalism's Distinctions

The word "capital" helps define my tack on this historical cruise. Capital is money destined for a particular use. Money can be socked away in the mattress for a rainy day or spent at the store. Either way, it is still money. It becomes capital only when someone invests it in an enterprise with the expectation of getting a good return from the effort. Stated simply, capital becomes capital when someone uses it to gain more money, usually by producing something. We can add an "ism" to "capital" only when the imperatives and strategies of private investments come to dominance as they did first in England and the Netherlands, next in Western Europe, and then in the American colonies. Outside these areas, capitalism moved next to Eastern Europe and Japan. In our own day capitalist practices hold sway through most of the world.

Capitalism of course didn't start out as an "ism." In the beginning, it wasn't a system, a word, or a concept, but rather some scattered ways of doing things differently that proved so successful that they acquired legs. Like all novelties, these practices entered a world unprepared for experimentation, a world suspicious of deviations from existing norms. Authorities opposed them because they violated the law. Ordinary people were offended by actions that ran athwart accepted notions of proper behavior. The innovators themselves initially had neither the influence nor the power to combat these responses. So the riddle of capitalism's ascendancy isn't just economic but political and moral as well: How did entrepreneurs get out of the straitjacket of custom and acquire the force and respect that enabled them to transform, rather than conform to, the dictates of their society?

Many elements, some fortuitous, had to be in play before innovation could trump habit. Determined and disciplined pathbreakers had to persist with their innovations until they took hold well enough to resist the siren call to return to the habitual order of things. It's not exactly a case of how small differences can have large impacts through a chain of connections. The better simile would be breaking a hole in a dike that could not be plastered up again, after letting out a flood of pent-up energy. But breaking that hole required curiosity, luck, determination, and the courage to go against the grain and withstand the powerful pressures to conform.

Just as the capitalist system has global reach today, so its beginnings, if not its causes, can be traced to the joining of the two halves of the globe. Europe, Africa, and Asia had been cut off from the Americas until the closing years of the fifteenth century. Even contact between Europe and Asia was confined to a few overland trade routes used to transport lightweight commodities like pepper and cinnamon. Then European curiosity about the rest of the world infected a few audacious souls, among them Prince Henry the Navigator. Prince Henry never left Portugal, but he funded a succession of trips down the west coast of Africa. Merchants, enticed by a trade in gold and slaves along the western Africa coast, increased the number of voyages. Soon Portuguese ships were rounding the Cape of Good Hope on their way up the east coast of Africa. By the beginning of the sixteenth century, the Portuguese had established strongholds on both African coasts and across the Indian Ocean to the Indian subcontinent itself. Simultaneously another Portuguese, Ferdinand Magellan, leading a Spanish expedition, circumnavigated the globe in 1517.

Seventy years before these Portuguese voyages, a Ming dynasty emperor sent out seven great expeditions from China. Led by Zheng He, who must have been a brilliant commander, the expeditions involved more than twenty-seven thousand sailors and two hundred vessels, the largest of them weighing fifteen hundred tons. (Columbus's first voyage, by contrast, involved a crew of eighty-seven and three ships weighing no more than one hundred tons.) From China these flotillas sailed through the East Indies, past Malacca, Siam, Ceylon, across the Indian Ocean, and down the east coast of Africa, possibly going as far as Madagascar. Sailors grew herbs on the ships' broad decks and managed to return from Africa with a couple of giraffes. Greatly aided by the magnetic compass, the Chinese voyages advertised the technological sophistication of the Chinese. Yet after three decades the expeditions stopped.

After Bartolomeu Dias rounded the Cape of Good Hope in 1488, dozens of similar caravels followed in his wake, bringing Europe into continuous contact with the East Indies. The seafaring Portuguese had only whetted the appetite of European adventurers. This shift in European travel to Asia, starting overland from Italy, to countries on the Atlantic Ocean had profound consequences. In the next century, Spain, Portugal, France, England, Sweden, Denmark, and the Netherlands permanently eclipsed the commercial dominance of the Mediterranean countries. The Atlantic became the new highway for world travelers, leaving behind the city-states of Genoa and Venice.

In these different responses of equally capable Chinese and Portuguese mariners we have one of history's great riddles. Why the retreat of the Chinese and the Europeans' rush to "see the world"? The Chinese had long demonstrated more interest in trade than men in Portugal, so monetary motives don't help us. Looser political control probably enabled many more Portuguese to act on their own impulses, even if royal purses were needed to bear the expense of the first exploratory voyages. In the absence of certain knowledge, we are free to rush in and tell stories that confirm our biases. Western storytellers have emphasized the intrepidity of their explorers, the readiness of Europeans to move away from their customs. Such explanations of the differences in the societies of East and West won't bear up under serious scrutiny. The story is more interesting than that.

Clearly it was not a lack of knowledge, wealth, or skill that kept the Chinese from maintaining contact with the Occident. What might it have been? On the practical side, the greater prosperity of Chinese merchants who had established commercial relations throughout the Indies might have checked any interest in going farther afield. Perhaps the Ming emperors lost interest in African countries when they discovered them to be, in most regards, inferior in science, art, and craftsmanship to theirs. Belief in the utter superiority of the "Heavenly Kingdom," as they styled it, predominated in Chinese culture. And why not? In ancient times, in an example of engineering wizardry, a Chinese innovator was able to cut a long trench through granite mountains to control floods by alternating bonfires and baths of cold water to crack the rocks.[1] The many examples of technical ingenuity and scientific achievement that highlight Chinese history point to a superior level of excellence in education. What didn't take place in China was a continuous path of developments, each building on its predecessor. Nor did the Chinese share the evangelical imperative of European Christianity, giving explorers some moral authority to search for converts among foreigners. A lot of "mays" and "mights." We'll never really know, but we can appreciate the significance of these contrasting responses.

The Dutch, French, and English quickly followed the Spaniards to the New World to carve out their piece of this unexplored area. As contemporaries quickly realized, almost everything, at least the things that Europeans wanted and couldn't grow themselves, grew in the tropics. As they moved from exploration to exploitation, European adventurers began looking for a source of labor to cultivate the new crops for export back home. The Portuguese had been trading in African slaves since Henry the Navigator's first voyages and soon began shipping enslaved men and women across the Atlantic. Unlike most of the native tribes in the New World, Africans were accustomed to the disciplined work of mining and farming. Aboriginal Americans made poor slaves; they often simply died of despair when chained to work. By the middle of the seventeenth century, with escalating demand, French, Dutch, and English merchants had entered an intense rivalry with the Portuguese to dominate the slave trade.

These voyages had an incalculable impact on Europe and Africa. The new demands for labor created modern slavery, an institution far crueler and more inhumane than the slavery of biblical times. Over the course of the next two and a half centuries, close to twelve million African men and women were wrenched from their homes and shipped to the New World to work first for the Spanish mines and ranches and then on the sugar, rice, coffee, and tobacco plantations that the Spaniards, Dutch, French, Danes, Swedes, and English created throughout the Western Hemisphere. The sea-lanes of the Atlantic gave access to this new source of labor.

The Trailblazer

In view of this spectacular activity across the globe, it may seem a bit perverse for me to pinpoint the beginnings of capitalism in one small island kingdom in the North Atlantic. Yet only in England did these dramatic novelties produce the social and intellectual breakthroughs that made possible the emergence of an entirely new system for producing goods. A series of changes, starting in farming and ending in industry, marks the point at which commerce, long existing in the interstices of traditional society, broke free to impose its dynamic upon the laws, class structure, individual behavior, and esteemed values of the people. Although thousands of books have been written about this astounding phenomenon, it still remains something of a mystery.

Visiting the Vatican Museum several years ago, I was struck by the richness of life captured in fourteenth- and fifteenth-century paintings there. They were full of plants, furniture, decorations, and clothing! I couldn't help but contrast these lavish depictions of everyday life with plain feaures of England. How counterintuitive that this poor, cold, small, outlandish country would be the site of technological innovations that would relentlessly revolutionize the material world! In the early twentieth century the historian Arnold Toynbee thought he had found the key to all development in the formula of "challenge and response." The English might have been challenged by their very lack of distracting luxury. Toynbee's hypothesis didn't hold up under rigorous scrutiny, but there may still be an element of truth in it.

For generations, scholars concentrated on eighteenth-century industrialization to mark the beginning of capitalism. They labeled it the Industrial Revolution. This is understandable because the spectacular appearance of factories filled with interfacing machinery and disciplined workers so visibly differed from what had gone before. But this is to start an account of a pregnancy in the fifth month. Critical changes had to take place before these inventions could even be thought of. But which ones and for how far back?

How deep are the roots of capitalism? Some have argued that its beginnings reach down into the Middle Ages or even to prehistoric times. Jared Diamond wrote a best-selling study that emphasized the geographic and biological advantages the West enjoyed. Two central problems vex this interpretation: The advantages of the West were enjoyed by all of Europe, but only England experienced the breakthroughs that others had to imitate to become capitalistic. Diamond's emphasis on physical factors also implies that they can account for the specific historical events that brought on Western modernity without reference to the individuals, ideas, and institutions that played so central a part in this historic development.[2]

David Landes entered the lists of scholars recounting the "the rise of the West" with an explanation that blended many climatic and cultural factors without providing a narrative of how they interacted to transform Western society. Alfred Crosby, in his assessment of this question, stressed a change in Europeans' fundamental grasp of reality. In the thirteenth century they adopted a quantitative understanding of the world that promoted mathematics, astronomy, music, painting, and bookkeeping. While presenting a fascinating account of technical achievements, Crosby's insistence upon intellectual changes leaves society and politics in a conceptual limbo. Deepal Lal goes back even farther in time to the eleventh century, where he finds the roots of the "Great Divergence" in papal decrees that established a common commercial law for all of Christendom.[3]

The Latin motto *post hoc, ergo propter hoc* reminds us that because something happened before something else, it is not necessarily a cause of the following event. The emergence of capitalism was not a general phenomenon, but one specific to time and place. People who take the long-run-up view of the emergence of capitalism note factors like the discovery of the New World, the invention of the printing press, the use of clocks, or papal property arrangements. These were present in countries that did not change their economic ways. Logically, widely shared developments can't explain a response that was unique to one country. What the myriad theories about how the West broke with its past do have right is that there were many, many elements that went into capitalism's breakout from its traditional origins. It is also important to keep in mind that a succession is not a process. A process is a linked series of operations; a succession is open to interruption and contingency.

European Divergence

There was nothing inevitable about the English moving from the agricultural innovations that freed up workers and capital for other uses to a globe-circling trade and on to the pioneering of machine-driven industry. It's only in retrospect that this progression seems seamlessly interconnected. But it wasn't. This appearance reflects a human tendency to believe that what happened had to happen. It is important to break with this cast of mind if we are to understand that capitalism is not a predestined chapter in human history, but rather a startling departure from the norms that had prevailed for four thousand years. Nor did commerce force capitalism into being. There have been many groups of exceptional traders—the Chinese, Arabs, and Jews come to mind—but they were not the pioneers of either the Agricultural or Industrial Revolution. We could say that a fully developed commercial system was a necessary, but insufficient, predecessor to capitalism.

To say that capitalism began in England is not to suggest that the explorations of the Portuguese and Spanish did not have an impact on the history of capitalism. These staggeringly bold adventures of the fifteenth and sixteenth centuries opened up minds and pocketbooks in England as elsewhere. But the examples of Spain and Portugal bolster the case for England's exceptionalism. Despite sallying forth in successive expeditions, neither country modified its aristocratic disdain for work or indifference to the needs of merchants and artisans. Everything that was remarkable about Portuguese and Spanish voyages got folded back into old ways. What differed in England was that a sequence of developments never stopped. And they attracted commentary, debate, and explanations. This intellectual engagement with the meaning of economic change blocked a reversion to old ways of thinking. Novel practices and astute analysis of them are what it took to overturn the wisdom of the ages. Many countries had brilliant episodes in their history; sustaining innovation through successive stages of development distinguishes England's performance.

Of course to start at any date is arbitrary. All historical developments have antecedents, some going back centuries. Each cut of the historian's ax into the layers of the past proves that the roots of modern society are very deep. Yet the seventeenth century brought fundamental alterations to England, and contemporaries became acutely and astutely aware of them. At its beginning a venerable social order existed to keep in place established precepts, prerogatives, and regulations. A century and a half later capitalism had gained critical momentum against the regime of status, stasis, and royal control. From the risky ventures and trial-and-error methods of large and small entrepreneurs emerged successes so resounding that there was no turning back. Changes became irreversible and cumulative. Growth turned into development, not just expansion, but getting more from less. Capital would never again be scarce. Indeed, the Dutch became the financiers of Europe with the savings accumulated during their heyday as the world's greatest traders.

The "rise of the West" is a very old theme in history books, one that, alas, has produced many invidious comparisons between the West and "the rest." I certainly do not want to contribute to the hubris that this historical tradition has fostered. I think that a careful reader of this book will note the emphasis on the unusual convergence of timing and propitious precedents in my explanation of how capitalist practices became the new social system of capitalism. Focusing on England may seem a bit old-fashioned, but the latest scholarship confirms that England was the unique leader.

Recently a stimulating debate has erupted around the proposition that Europe wasn't so different from the rest of the places on the globe before 1800. Kenneth Pomeranz has written a provocative study that details how parts of Asia enjoyed a standard of living in the eighteenth century similar to that of Western Europe. Only with nineteenth-century industrialization did there occur that "great divergence" that led to European hegemony, in his view.[4] Pomeranz's study has had a salutary effect, promoting new research and forcing a searching reevaluation of old opinions. His argument for "global economic parity" concentrates on material factors like life expectancy, agricultural productivity, and interregional trade. Intangibles like the public's receptivity to change and the flexibility of the government responses get little of Pomeranz's attention. Nor does he consider how various developments interacted with one another, either enhancing or discouraging successful innovations. At the cultural heart of capitalism is the individual's capacity to control resources and initiate projects. England's great and unexpected success forces us to look for the invisible influence at play that we might otherwise overlook.

Measures of well-being taken at one point in time don't say much about the direction or momentum behind different economies. Many times in the past, countries have flourished for a while only to fall back to an earlier level. Only in England after the sixteenth century did the initial, enterprising successes lead steadily to other innovations.[5] There, mutually enhancing economic practices escaped the confining channels of custom and gained leverage as blueprints for change. This fact impresses not as evidence of national superiority, but rather of how much contingency and fortuity played in the genesis of capitalism. In stressing the singularity of England, I am also emphasizing how surprising it is that this revolutionary new system of capitalism emerged at all.

England advanced economically just as it was being torn apart politically. During the seventeenth century, constitutional and religious conflicts turned into open rebellion and then civil war, followed by a republican experiment, itself brought to an end by the restoration of the monarchy. This period of divided authority coincided with the formation of a unified, national market for the country. Either because of, or despite, the protracted political turmoil, innovators and interlopers were able to defy venerable regulations about how the grain crop should be raised and marketed. When the political arrangements of 1688 restored political stability to the country, the new economic practices were firmly in place. So well established were they that old-timers complained of their being treated as customary.

Economic Change and Analysis

Most economists, when they think about history, take their cues from Adam Smith. His *Wealth of Nations* was the first great account of the economic changes England had witnessed in the two centuries before 1776, when it was published. Smith placed economic development in a long sequence of progressive steps that had evolved over time. This interpretation of the history of capitalism as moving forward effortlessly has produced the greatest irony in the history of capitalism, an explanation of its origins that makes natural what was really an astounding break with precedent. This view also depends upon people already thinking within the capitalist frame of reference. According to Smith, capitalism emerged naturally from the universal tendency of men and women to "truck and barter." In fact it took economic development itself to foster this particular cultural trait. Smith turned an effect into a cause. For Smith and his philosophical colleagues, economic change had slowly, steadily led to the accumulation of capital that could then pay for improvements like the division of labor that enhanced productivity. No cultural adjustment had been considered necessary because underneath all the diversity in dress, diet, and comportment beat the heart of economic man—and presumably economic woman.

Because the full elaboration of economic developments in England took place over two centuries—almost seven generations of lived experience—it was possible to imagine it as the evolutionary process that Smith described. But in continental Europe industrialization came with brutal speed. Men and women were wrenched from a traditional rural order and plunged into factories within a single lifetime. Karl Marx, observing this disruption in the middle decades of the nineteenth century, could not accept the English evolutionary explanation for the emergence of capitalism. He believed that coercion had been absolutely necessary in effecting this transformation. Marx traced that force to a new class of men who coalesced around their shared interest in production, particularly their need to organize laboring men and women in new work patterns.

Separating poor people from the tools and farm plots that conferred independence, according to Marx, became paramount in the capitalists' grand plan.[6] He also stressed the accumulation of capital as a first step in moving away from traditional economic ways. I don't agree. As Europe's cathedrals indicate, there was sufficient money to produce great buildings and many other structures like roads, canals, windmills, irrigation systems, and wharves. The accumulation of cultural capital, especially the know-how and desire to innovate in productive ways, proved more decisive in capitalism's history. And it could come from a duke who took the time to figure out how to exploit the coal on his property or a farmer who scaled back his leisure time in order to build fences against invasive animals.

What factory work made much more obvious than the tenant farmer–landlord relationship was the fact that the owner of the factory profited from each worker's labor. The sale of factory goods paid a meager wage to the laborers and handsome returns to the owners. Employers extracted the surplus value of labor, as Marx called it, and accumulated money for further ventures that would skim off more of the wealth that laborers created but didn't get to keep. These relations of workers and employers to production created the class relations in capitalist society. The carriers of these novel practices, Marx said, were outsiders—men detached from the mores of their traditional societies—propelled forward by their narrow self-interest. With the cohesion of shared political goals, the capitalists challenged the established order and precipitated the class conflict that for

Marx operated as the engine of change. Implicit in Marx's argument is that the market worked to the exclusive advantage of capitalists.

In the early twentieth century another astute philosopher, Max Weber, assessed the grand theories of Smith and Marx and found both of them wanting in one crucial feature: They gave attitudes to men and women that they couldn't possibly have had before capitalist practices arrived. Weber asked how the values, habits, and modes of reasoning that were essential to progressive economic advance ever rooted themselves in the soil of premodern Europe characterized by other life rhythms and a moral vocabulary different in every respect. This inquiry had scarcely troubled English economists or historians before Weber because they operated on the assumption that human nature made men (little was said of women) natural bargainers and restless self-improvers, eager to be productive when productivity contributed to their well-being.

Following Smith, economic analyzers presumed a natural human psychology geared to ceaseless economic activity. Weber challenged this assumption with a single line: "A man does not by nature wish to earn more and more money, but simply to live as he is accustomed to live and to earn as much as is necessary for that purpose."[7] Weber began with an interesting phenomenon to explore: the convergence of economically advanced countries and the Protestant religion. He concluded that "the spirit of capitalism," as he called it, could best be treated as an unexpected by-product of the Protestant Reformation of the sixteenth century. Examining the forms and sensibilities of Catholic Christendom against which the reformers had rebelled, Weber detailed how Protestant leaders taught that true Christians served God everywhere. They intruded their strenuous morality into every nook and cranny of customary society, using the scalpel of rationality to cut away the accretions of popish religion. It was the morality and rationality that Puritans brought to the world of work, Weber indicated, that had transformed the habits of people. Puritans invested work with a religious quality that aristocrats had denied it. Protestant preachers produced great personal anxiety by emphasizing everyone's tenuous grip on salvation. This promoted an interest in Providence in which believers scrutinized events for clues of divine intentions. This intense examination of ordinary life turned prosperity into evidence of

God's favor. All these factors, Weber said, inadvertently made men and women agents of economic development.

Driven to glorify God in all callings, cut off from the ceremonial comforts of a ritualistic religion, the Protestant became the archetypal modern man and the foe of tradition. Weber put his finger on what was wrong with all previous discussions of capitalism's history: They started with the unexamined assumption that men and women rushed to throw off the old and put on the new. Projecting their contemporary values upon those in the past, analysts spent little time examining people's motives because they were certain that they would naturally respond positively to the prospect of making more money even if it involved attitudes that they had never had or activities that appeared abhorrent to them. Reasoning on this assumption, they had removed all of the central puzzles about how capitalism had triumphed in the West.

Weber rejected out of hand the existence of Smith's natural propensity to truck and barter and criticized Marx for assuming the existence of a market mentality before there was a capitalist market. Smith made everyone a capitalist driven to seek self-improvement through the material rewards of the market. With this dependable human endowment, capitalism would emerge in the fullness of time. Marx invented a cadre of profit-driven men clairvoyant enough to imagine a world that had never existed. Weber labeled Smith's ceaseless economic striving a peculiar form of behaving that had to be explained, not taken for granted.

Influences on This Study

These powerful thinkers—Smith, Marx, and Weber—have greatly influenced all subsequent analysis of capitalism. As a scholar I have long been fascinated by how economic development has changed the way we think about our material world and ourselves as well as the way we work and live. While I have learned from all these master theorists, I have been most influenced by Weber because of his emphasis on contingency and unintended consequences in the formation of capitalism. His respect for the roles that cultural and intellectual traits play in history appeals to me as well. I should also place myself on the contemporary ideological continuum. I'm a left-leaning liberal with strong, if sometimes contradictory, libertarian strains. I have always had a keen interest in progressive politics, and I believe that we are ill served by the conviction that capitalism is a freestanding system untouched by the character of its participants and the goals of particular societies. Mechanical models of the economy that emphasize its autonomy purport to be disinterested, but they actually diminish our capacity to think intelligently about the range of choices we have.

I first started teaching in 1967 at San Diego State University, where I became interested in the history of capitalism through a circuitous route. All the American history instructors there used the same book in our introductory course. It was a collection of readings that demonstrated the origins of modern social thought through a succession of major texts from the sermons of Puritans who settled New England, through Thomas Hobbes's *Leviathan*, John Locke's *Second Treatise of Government*, Smith's *Wealth of Nations*, Thomas Paine's *Common Sense*, *The Federalist Papers*, and onward.

Teaching is a great revealer of one's ignorance. Everything seems to fit together while one is taking notes from someone else's lecture. When the task of making sense of the past falls on you, gaps and non sequiturs stand out like hazard lights. The glaring anomaly I quickly discovered dealt with definitions of "human nature." A term introduced to eighteenth-century public discourse, our ideas about human nature go unexamined because they spring from the commonsense notions of our society. Yet our understanding of human nature grounds just about everything else we believe, whether about politics, the workings of the economy, friendship, marriage, or child rearing. The problem that popped up in my teaching was how to account for the radical change in descriptions of human nature during the course of the seventeenth century. In the early selections in our textbook, the Puritan sermons and Elizabethan plays described men and women as thoughtless and capricious, if not usually downright wicked. Yet fast-forward a hundred years, and assumptions about basic human traits had changed dramatically.

The new view of men and women can most easily be found in Smith's *Wealth of Nations*. Yet Smith took his opinions about human nature for granted. Listen to him: "The principle which prompts to save is the desire of bettering our condition, a desire which tho generally calm and dispassionate, comes with us from the womb, and never leaves us til we go into the grave." He speaks of the "uniform, constant, and uninterrupted effort of every man to better his condition."[8] Where, I wondered, had Smith got this view of people as fundamentally rational and self-improving? Certainly it bore little resemblance to the characters that Shakespeare created or to Puritan conviction that "in Adam's fall did sin we all." Being in England for a year's sabbatical, I became a permanent fixture at the British Museum, where I began reading in a new genre, the writings about commerce that began appearing in pamphlets, economic tracts, broadsides, and advice books from the 1620s onward. Following this paper trail through the rest of the century, I discovered abundant clues about the break with conventional opinions about human nature. I saw that most authors tangled up their policy recommendations with assertions about human tendencies or what they often called the natural order of things.[9]

Capitalism as a Cultural System

Economic systems do not exist in isolation; they are intimately and crucially intertwined in their country's laws and customs. Capitalism, even though it relies on individual initiatives and choices, is no different. It impinges on society constantly. Social mores channel desires and ambitions. Social norms help determine family size, and family size influences population dynamics. Neither the landlords, nor laborers, nor merchants, nor manufacturers were—or are—purely economic actors. They all had complex social needs and played many different roles in society as parents, subjects, neighbors, and members of a church, political party, or voluntary association. We could consider contemporary entrepreneurs, corporate managers, bankers, and large shareholders of stocks and bonds as now constituting something of a capitalist class with common interests in their financial well-being, particularly protecting capital from taxation and enterprises from regulation. Yet these men and women are not just capitalists. They're parents, athletes, gun owners, Catholics, evangelical Protestants, members of AA, lovers of the good life, naturalists, environmentalists, and patrons of the arts.

One of the principal arguments of this book is that there was nothing inexorable, inevitable, or destined about the emergence of capitalism. So why make such a big deal about this? Why insist that the seeds of capitalism were not planted in the Middle Ages or that a capitalist mentality was not hardwired in human beings? Why? Because those notions aren't true. The powerful propulsive force of capitalist ways, once a breach with tradition had been made, is largely responsible for giving an aura of inevitability to their arrival on the human scene.

Societies that are resistant to capitalist ways today appear unnatural. Yet Europeans actually deviated from a global norm. Another important point: We should not make the first capitalist transformation a template for all others because that course of events could never be duplicated. Nor did countries that adopted a capitalist system, after England had shown the way, have to have the same qualities needed for the initial breakthrough. The same holds true for countries becoming capitalist today. Copying is not the same as innovating.

Because capitalism began in England with the convergence of agricultural improvements, global explorations, and scientific advances means that capitalism came into human history with an English accent and followed the power trail that England projected around the globe in the eighteenth and nineteenth centuries. This meant that the market economy retained a bit of foreignness for those for whom English and, by extension, capitalism are second languages. For England's neighbors and rivals, there was little choice but to imitate what the French in the eighteenth century called the English miracle. Other societies have elaborated their own variants of capitalism, often trying to protect certain customs and habits from capitalist imperatives. The people of Africa, the Middle East, India, and the East Indies had capitalism thrust upon them as Western Europeans arrived to exploit their resources. Still others, like the native people of North and South America, retreated into their communities when Europeans threatened their way of life and they were made strangers in their homelands.

Appreciating that capitalism is a historical development and not a discovery of universal principles brings clarity about one thing: The experience of the first capitalist country was unique. The range of possibilities for other countries remains to be discovered. Because capitalism as an economic system impinges upon the whole society, each country has and will transform its values and practices in its own way. The roles of culture, contingency, and coercion, so critically important in the history of capitalism, should not be obscured. Not only has the market changed with every generation, but the possibilities for capitalist development have been and still are many and varied.

In its forward thrust, capitalism acquired champions who insisted on the natural quality of capitalism. All cultures are natural in that they draw upon inherent human qualities and there are many potentialities planted in the human breast. Not all human qualities are called into play in every culture. Culture is a selecting mechanism, choosing among the diverse human skills and propensities to fashion a way for people to live together in a specific location at a certain time. A growing field in biology, epigenetics, studies how particular environments activate certain genes in human beings that can then be passed on to their progeny. Without the environmental trigger, the gene remains inert. This suggests that there is a very intricate interchange between our biology and our culture, one that goes well beyond the familiar nature-nurture relationship. All people may be self-interested, but what interests them depends a lot upon the society in which they have been reared.

Our present method of analyzing economies obscures their entanglement with society and culture. Professional economists analyze capitalism with mathematical precision. Building mathematical models to explain how markets behave, they tend to ignore the messiness that any set of social relations is bound to produce. All the economists' precise projections assume ceteris paribus—all other things remaining equal—but they rarely do. Philosophers use the word "reify" to indicate when a concept is being talked about as a real thing rather than as a way of talking about something. Economists talk about their subject as though it were a unitary thing rather than a mixed bag of practices, habits, and institutions. I am conscious of this danger and want to avoid skating too close to reification. When I make "capitalism" the subject of a sentence, I will be thinking of capitalists as those who use their resources to organize an enterprise or a cluster of business and corporation operators devoted to producing for a profit.

All these definitions of mine make for dull reading, but clarification is worth a little boredom. I further want to distinguish between those historical developments traceable to capitalism and those that have existed in tandem with older systems. People blame capitalism for social ills that have long caused great misery. The Four Horsemen of the Apocalypse— oppression, war, famine, and devastation—come to mind. Unattractive personal motives, traits like greed and indifference to suffering, are often projected onto capitalists. Greed is as old as Hammurabi's code. It could be said that capitalism is the first economic system that depends upon greed— at least upon the desire of bettering one's condition, as Smith said. So, in a way, capitalism is damned for its honesty. But greed can also disadvantage an entrepreneur. Capitalists have been and still are greedy, but the distinctive characteristic of capitalism has been its amazing wealth-generating capacities. The power of that wealth transformed traditional societies and continues to enable human societies to do remarkable things.

Capitalism has left few areas of life untouched. The most startling has been its influence upon women. It upended women's lives in two long waves, the first abusive, the second liberating. Women in the early years of each country's industrialization were swept up from their cottages and villages and dumped onto factory floors for twelve- to fourteen-hour days of muscle-wrenching tedium. Such long hours of labor were previously unneeded and not demanded.

The second wave began in the nineteenth century with techniques for limiting pregnancies. The correlation between an improved standard of living and lower fertility rates has held up everywhere and has always benefited women. Today in the homelands of capitalism, couples are not even having enough children to replace their nations' populations. Women have joined men in almost every profession and niche of the work force. Birthrates are still falling, and slowly marital roles have begun to adjust to accommodate families with two working parents.

Exploitation is not distinctively capitalist, but wealth generating is. Yet because of its economic power and global reach, capitalist exploitation almost qualifies as a distinctive characteristic. One cannot celebrate the benefits of the capitalist system without taking account of the disastrous adventures and human malevolence that this wealth-generating system has made possible and sometimes actually encouraged. Capitalists and the governments that became sponsors of capitalist endeavors cannot be held responsible for fomenting the human catastrophes predicted in the Book of Revelation, but lots of ills in modern times must be included in its history, especially those intrinsic to its success. The inventions that led to the Industrial Revolution drew heavily upon fossil fuels, coal at first and then oil. This greatly expanded the ambit of production, freeing economies from the limitations that land for growing food and producing timber imposed. Over time the relentless revolution increased the exploitation of natural resources and the accompanying degradation of the environment. "Can the globe sustain these capitalist successes?" has become an urgent question.

Capitalism has produced some enduring tensions, evident from the sixteenth century onward. Where the extremes of riches in a society of scarcity were usually tolerated, capitalism's capacity to generate wealth made salient, and hence open to criticism, inequalities in the distribution of economic and political power. Similarly, government interference was acceptable when the society was at risk of starving, but no longer so when the system seemed to function better when its participants had the most freedom. This very lack of government regulation in market economies enhanced chances for cycles of boom and bust, as we know so well today. These issues will continue to surface through the history of capitalism. Finding just solutions to the problems they cause remains the challenge.

Most decision making in the capitalist system lies with those who have access to capital. Since these ventures almost always involve employing men and women, entrepreneurs depend upon others for labor. Workers in turn depend upon employers for the wages that support them and their families. Once separated from land or tools, ordinary men and women had no resources with which to earn their daily bread and so had to go out and sell their labor. But the way we talk about jobs doesn't always make clear this mutual dependence. The adjective "free" as in "free enterprise" serves the ideological purpose of masking the coercion in capitalism. People may be free to take a job or not, but they are not free from the need to work as long as they wish to eat. Employers are not under the same existential restraint. Today all the "frees"—trade, enterprise, markets—have become so saturated with rhetorical overtones that I shall use these terms with care and then mainly to avoid the monotonous repetition of "capitalism."

Clarity about the nature of the capitalist system could enable us to make wiser policy decisions. Recognizing that capitalism is a cultural, not a natural, system like the weather might check those impulses in American foreign policy framing that assume that becoming like us is a universal imperative. Nor is the market a self-correcting system, as its apologists argue. Ideological assumptions about the autonomy of economics make it hard for us to recognize that the market serves us, not just as individual participants but as members of a society desirous of paying workers living wages, providing universal health care and good schools, as well as making humanitarian outreaches to the world. At a critical moment in the journey of capitalism to dominance, the importance of cultural influences and social considerations was dispatched to a conceptual limbo. We need to drag them back into the light.

In this book, I would like to shake free of the presentation of the history of capitalism as a morality play, peopled with those wearing either white or black hats. Even though every history is always suffused with moral implications, historians don't have to take sides. Still, they have to recognize how morals influence what people did in the past. Economists like to treat their subject as a science and minimize the moral overtones of wealth distribution, but neglect of people's powerful sense of right and wrong is an evasion of reality. How could it be otherwise when economic life touches so closely our values and, by extension, our politics? With a better understanding of capitalism, people in democracies can play a much more positive, vigorous role in shaping economic institutions. To those who will disagree with my proposals in this history of capitalism, what I say may seem self-serving, so I present it as an intention rather than an accomplishment. You will have to decide which it is.

Before closing my introduction, perhaps my definition of "capitalism" is in order. Capitalism is a cultural system rooted in economic practices that rotate around the imperative of private investors to turn a profit. Profit seeking usually promotes production efficiencies like the division of labor, economies of size, specialization, the expansion of the market for one's goods, and, above all, innovation. Because capitalism is a cultural system and not simply an economic one, it cannot be explained by material factors alone. In the beginning, capitalist practices provoked an outpouring of criticisms and defenses. Competition buffets all participants in this investor-driven economy whether people are investing their capital, marketing their products, or selling their labor. The series of inventions that harnessed natural energy, first with water and coal-fired steam in the eighteenth century, made economic progress dependent upon the exploitation of fossil fuels. Coal and oil once seemed without limit, but today they have become scarce enough to make us ask if our economic system is sustainable.

My challenge is to make you curious about a system that is all too familiar. That familiarity, joined to the notion that there is something inherently capitalistic in human nature, has obscured the real conflict between capitalism and its economic predecessors. Capitalist practices represented a radical departure from ancient usages when they appeared upon the scene in the seventeenth century. Because they assaulted the mores of men and women in traditional society, it took a very favorable environment for them to gain a footing. After that, the capacity of new capitalist ways to create wealth induced imitation. And the impertinent dynamic of "more" sent entrepreneurs from the West around the world in search of commodities along with the laborers to produce them. They carried with them the engines for the relentless revolution that capitalism introduced.

2

◆

TRADING IN NEW

DIRECTIONS

WHILE THE SPANISH were linking the Old with the New World following Columbus's voyage to the Caribbean, the Portuguese were
bringing together the ancient trades of the Atlantic and Indian oceans.
Commerce in the Indian Ocean after the conquests of the Arabs and
Mongols had already joined the landmasses of Asia, India, North Africa,
and parts of Europe by the end of the thirteenth century. Now they were in
contact with northwestern Europe and European settlements in the New
World. The vast East Indian trading network, organized by the caliphate
in Constantinople, circulated spices, luxury fabrics, and precious woods.
The Spanish sent home gold, silver, and indigenous foods from the New
World. After being separated for millennia, the peoples of the earth were
finally in touch with one another. Or more precisely, the curious, exploitative, and adventurous Europeans got in touch with them.

As Muslim traders pushed farther and farther to the east, their faith
had spread to China, India, the Malay Archipelago, and the Philippines.

Arresting the spread of Islam gave the Portuguese a religious motive for pushing beyond the Cape of Good Hope. When Tunisian traders on the Malabar Coast asked crew members of Vasco da Gama's pioneering voyage of 1498 what had brought them so far, they were told, "Christians and spices." Their evangelical spirit actually materialized in quite a few Japanese converts, who began to produce handsome pieces of devotional art for sale. These, along with translucent tortoiseshell bowls crafted in India and ivory spoons that African artists decorated with carvings of animals, displayed how quickly local crafts became part of global commerce.[1]

The spices, fabrics, and perfumed woods of the East Indies stimulated the imagination and taste buds of Europeans, not to mention their wanderlust. Bland foods turned into delicious repasts with the addition of cinnamon, cloves, nutmeg, and especially pepper. With salt and sugar rare and expensive, most people had to content themselves with tasteless meals. The thrill of seasoning sent Dutch, French, and English trading companies throughout the Indies to establish trading outposts. Going by sea made it much easier to carry heavy cargo than overland.

Since the time of the Roman Empire, Europeans had had some contact overland with the Orient, but famines and epidemics could wipe out commercial connections for decades. Arab traders were often successful in rupturing the European trade routes as well. It took experienced merchants like the Venetian family of Marco Polo to carry on this hazardous trade. The lateen-rigged ships and recently discovered sea routes gave Europeans a cheaper, safer way of establishing what turned out to be permanent contact by sea.

Four years after Dias made his way to the Orient, Columbus's pioneering route to the New World triggered another round of explorations. These voyages took Europeans to the islands and continents of the Western Hemisphere and to the discovery of just how large the globe really was. Educated people had long known that the earth was round, but they had no idea of its circumference. The conquests of Mexico and Peru gave Spaniards access to Aztec and Incan mines as well. Gold and silver extracted from these mines began pouring into Europe. Far more important, the ships crossing the Atlantic brought animals and plants that dramatically transformed the societies on both sides of the ocean. What has been called the Columbian exchange completed the biological and botanic homogeneity of our planet.[2]

Alas, germs lethal to the inhabitants of the New World were part of that exchange. The arrival of newcomers in the Western Hemisphere triggered an unintended holocaust, for the Europeans carried with them lethal microorganisms against which the native population had no protection. Exposed to these Old World diseases with no immunity, the entire population of Arawaks on San Domingo died within a generation. This deadly phenomenon repeated itself over and over again from the Arawaks in the sixteenth century to the Chamorros of the Marianas in the seventeenth century to the Aleuts in the Pribilof Islands in the eighteenth century—whenever New World people encountered Europeans for the first time.

The many ships under the direction of merchants, pirates, and naval commanders breached forever the isolation of the peoples of North and South America while they awakened the curiosity of thousands of Europeans. Immediately dozens of engravings were printed to slake the curiosity of Europe's small reading public. At first, old lithographs depicting the Garden of Eden were trotted out and reprinted, but gradually more accurate depictions of the people, animals, and plants encountered in the New World began to circulate. A whole new chapter in the history of curiosity began.

The seaborne trade that followed the great discoveries of all-water routes to the East and West Indies fitted very well with traditional European society. The noble virtues of command, mastery, ardor, aggression, and military prowess were in full display and very effective in intimidating and subduing people who were similarly impressed by manly feats of valor. Like the Spanish exploits, those of the Portuguese appealed to the aristocratic spirit with its love of military escapades. Afonso de Albuquerque exemplified the noble Iberian adventurer. Connected to the Portuguese royal family by illegitimate descent, he began his career fighting Muslims in North Africa. At age fifty-three in 1506, he sailed a squadron of ships around the Cape of Good Hope, gaining permission to build forts by helping local rulers secure their power. In 1511, he conquered the great emporium of Malacca for the king of Portugal.

In the rough-and-tumble of trade, conquest, and colonization, Albuquerque found himself imprisoned or shipwrecked more than once. At the insistence of his government, he laid an unsuccessful siege to Aden in 1513, becoming the first European to ply the waters of the Red Sea. Angered by the Egyptians, Albuquerque contemplated laying waste to the country by diverting the course of the Nile! On his return voyage after taking Ormuz in 1515, he died at sea. Commanders like Albuquerque had more in common with medieval Crusaders than modern merchants, as his sobriquet, "the Portuguese Mars," suggests.

The Spanish conquests had a similarly aristocratic and military cast. Ardent, fearless adventurers like Christopher Columbus, Hernando Cortés, Francisco Pizarro, Juan Ponce de León, and Ferdinand Magellan planted the Spanish flag from the Canaries to the Philippines. Blocked in their effort to reach the fabulous riches of the East by a westward route, the Spanish began to explore the land they had discovered. The Spanish crown moved in quickly after Columbus's exploratory voyages to establish settlements throughout the Caribbean. After the conquests of the Aztecs and Incas in Mexico and Peru in the first half of the sixteenth century, the Spanish fell into a gold mine—many gold and silver mines. Better at coercing labor than organizing it, they used the native people to work for them. When they proved resistant, the Spanish began to import African slaves from Portuguese slavers. From their fortified city of Havana in Cuba, the Spanish treasure fleets crossed the Atlantic twice a year, directing to a specie-starved Europe a steady stream of precious metals. Later they established a trade between Acapulco on the west coast of Mexico and Manila in the Philippines, carrying silver west and returning with silk to be transshipped to Europe. Ten percent of this bounty from the New World went straight into the royal coffers.

The spectacular discoveries of Portugal and Spain prompted the pope in 1494 to suppress any incipient rivalry between the two Catholic monarchies on the Iberian Peninsula. He divided the world between them! The pope recognized Spain's claim to the Western Hemisphere, except for Brazil, which a Portuguese expedition headed for India had run into by mistake. Portugal gained the western coast of Africa and points east along the route to the Indian Ocean where it had set up several provisioning stations. Spain got the rest. But even the pope could not inhibit this rivalry. After Magellan discovered the Philippine Islands in the 1560s, the Spanish began to settle Manila, demonstrating that the world being round, there was a need for two boundary lines. The Portuguese were finally able to thwart subsequent Spanish intrusion into the East Indies. Originally the Spanish concentrated on establishing encomiendas, large estates in the New World, to exploit native labor while the Portuguese developed trade in the Indies. With the establishment of sugar plantations in Brazil in the late sixteenth century, the two empires came to resemble each other.[3] From 1580 to 1640 they shared a monarch.

The countries on the Iberian Peninsula were Europe's trailblazers. Both of them established fortified settlements in their new outposts and insisted upon dominating trade. The Spanish enjoyed a monopoly for a century before other Europeans arrived to challenge their dominance, and the Portuguese imposed monopolies wherever they could. Initially these events represented nothing more than new wrinkles in the old, traditional fabric of European society, but their success had profound implications. Reaching the Orient by ocean changed the geopolitics of Europe. It moved the levers of world trade from the Mediterranean Sea to the Atlantic Ocean, which washed northwestern Europe. Between the sixteenth and eighteenth centuries, the momentum of trade and conquest passed from Portugal and Spain to the other countries with access to the Atlantic: the Netherlands, France, England, Denmark, and Sweden.

The Limits of Trade

The exchanges at the heart of trade have had religious, practical, romantic, and political overtones. Potlatches in the northwestern corner of the North American continent circulated possessions through gift giving. Kings secured desired goods and services through dues and taxes, and conquerors extracted tribute, but commercial exchanges, with their dependence upon money, middlemen, and bookkeeping, have exerted the most lasting influence.

Passing goods through bargaining has been around since the first human settlements in the Mesopotamian Delta in the fourth millennium B.C.E. Yet ingrained prejudices against merchants had confined commerce to a narrow social space before the eighteenth century. Merchants were associated with making money rather than with sitting as judges, leading armies, heading diplomatic missions, writing poetry, which the nobility did, or feeding the people, as peasants did. Commercial work was important but sullied those who did it.

Aristocrats not only looked down on those in commerce but encouraged qualities absolutely opposed to traits supportive of economic development. They cultivated leisure along with contempt for those who worked for a living. They lived off rents and other privileges and spent this money buying items to grace their persons, tables, and estates. Often they spent more than they received in rents and dues, creating an enduring, sometimes hereditary indebtedness from unpaid bills. They got away with this profligacy because few storekeepers or artisans wanted to incur the wrath of their principal customers.

Noble and gentry families were the celebrities of the premodern world. They contributed learning, taste, style, and their glamorous presence to major public celebrations. They were the only candidates for high positions at court, or in the military, or in the church. They had first claim to any economic surplus. Merchants could not effectively protect their interests because they lacked the power to do so. Time and time again they were done in by insecure titles to property, onerous taxes, or outright appropriation of their goods. Those who had their ruler's ear gave little thought to the consequences of these burdens. Still, since trading offered an alternative to taking by force what one wanted, it was considered a civilizing force.

Those in the highest ranks of society in, say, sixteenth-century Europe inherited their positions, which gave to family major importance. It was not "what you did" but "who you were" that mattered. Far from being ashamed of their inherited status, men and women of gentle birth celebrated their lineage as evidence of a divinely sanctioned order. Domination was their birthright. Even in those places like the sixteenth-century Italian city-states of Venice, Florence, and Genoa or Amsterdam, where an urban oligarchy ran things, aristocratic values commanded great respect. Society recognized three groups: the clergy, the aristocracy, and commoners. People then believed in natural inequality in a world divided between the special few and the ordinary many. They found proof of hierarchy in nature when they looked at the animal world with its lions and mice. The strong sense that this was the proper order, implanted as children were growing up, was as convincing to them as our beliefs are to us.

The reason to keep separate the ancient practice of trading from the novelty of industrial production in a history of capitalism is to fix our attention on those changes that brought into being capitalism. Trade itself is not one of them. Merchants got rich, when they did, by buying low and selling high. Sometimes they were lucky enough to get a windfall or to be able to take advantage of fortuitous shortages. The wealth from capitalism came from something else, profits from producing things. It took great capital to introduce machines into production processes, but they generated even greater profits by producing things more efficiently. The capital invested in machinery made investors rich because the machines enhanced the productivity of the workers employed. The creation of great wealth distinguished capitalism from preceding economic systems, but so did the reorganization of labor and the enlargement of the pool of consumers to buy the new products. The earth-spanning commercial networks that Europeans began laying down in the sixteenth century vastly increased the places where capitalists could send their goods. When capitalism acquired its momentum, investors didn't stay put in Europe. They followed the trajectory of Europe's trading empires.

The significance of expanded trade routes and partners could not possibly be overstated, but the key point to make about trade in a history of capitalism is that it had existed for centuries before capitalism and would have continued to flourish without it. Because we can see the obvious connections between the sixteenth-century voyages to the Orient and the New World, we're tempted to connect it seamlessly to the eighteenth-century invention of the steam engine and the emergence of full-blown capitalism as though the one followed the other inexorably, but there is no inevitability in life. Nor do we ever have a very good sense of what the future holds for us. In the middle of the seventeenth century, when new trades were opening up, there was no reason for people to expect that a succession of marvelous machines would alter modes of work that had prevailed for millennia or that a fresh description of human beings and their social nature would soon supplant the traditional wisdom that had long guided people.

European Domination

Before the arrival of the Portuguese, the common attitude of all the different participants in East Asian commerce, diverse in ethnicity and religion, had been that the sea belonged to no one. This changed with the arrival of the newcomers. Albuquerque's king showered him with titles after he had secured control of the Malabar Coast, Ceylon, Malacca, and Ormuz. Portugal achieved naval supremacy in the Indian Ocean after defeating an Egyptian fleet in 1509. When China, which possessed the only other strong naval power in the area, withdrew from the field of contest, the Portuguese controlled most of the trade until the arrival almost a century later of the Dutch, French, and English, who were equally bent on monopolizing whatever they could hold on to.

The Ottoman Empire was probably more advanced than Portugal in many ways, but Portugal had the advantage of swifter, more maneuverable ships. When they encountered an on-again-off-again hospitality in Malacca, where they sought spices, they turned to force, using their military superiority to take advantage of the chaotic rivalry among rulers in the Malay Archipelago. For those interested in naval warfare, the new Portuguese tactics are fascinating. Previously ships had really been carriers of soldiers. They would fire some guns in combat but mainly maneuvered to get their men on their opponents' decks. The Portuguese eschewed this approach. They turned their ships into seaborne gunnery platforms from which they pounded the enemy, never fearing a direct attack because of their ships' capacity to sail against the wind.[4]

It took a combination of gold, silver, and force to dominate the spice trade, but the Portuguese succeeded in doing so, laying down a new law of the seas in the East, even if they never entirely monopolized their lucrative trades.[5] For a short time Portugal, a nation of a million people, succeeded in imposing its will upon the Chinese, Arabs, and Venetians who had long plied these waters. They carried European tools and weapons to Africa, silver and gold to China, Chinese goods to Japan, and spices and silks back to Europe. On both coasts of Africa, the Portuguese established fortified towns where they could store goods and refit their ships: Mozambique and Mombasa on the east, Elmina and Luanda on the west. From spices to slaves, they conducted business around the world through some fifty settlements that they defended against all comers.

Rarely have such great riches fallen into the laps of rulers with so little effort on their part. The extraordinarily lucrative spice and silver trades promoted extravagant royal habits. In both Portugal and Spain taxes were high, and the distribution of wealth followed the traditional pattern in which the few indulged their taste for grandeur and the many penurious peasants and workers struggled to survive. Two powerful kings, Charles V, the grandson of Ferdinand and Isabella, and his son, Philip II, who ruled Spain from 1556 to 1598, knew exactly what they wanted to do with this seemingly endless flow of bullion. They would wage war against the Turks, French, Italians, Protestants, and even popes in order to establish their hegemony in Europe and protect the supremacy of Catholic faith, now challenged in the East by the Ottoman Turks and in Europe by Protestants. They also needed money to quell rebellion in their own empire, for the people of the Netherlands had begun a protracted revolt for independence in the 1580s. A heretical queen ascended the throne in England. The joining of the crowns of Portugal and Spain in 1580 made Spain more politically powerful, even if economically it was stagnating.

Spanish shipbuilders flourished with the new demand for oceangoing vessels. Spain's woolen industry also prospered under royal favor, but the royal bureaucracy battened off most of the merchants, manufacturers, and farmers through a steady diet of customs, tolls, and taxes. The Spanish kings' pervasive fear of heresy led them to curtail the travel of their subjects during most of the sixteenth century. Bans on the importation of books obstructed the free circulation of ideas as well as enterprise. The Spanish aristocracy resisted change, and the crown stifled new industries with onerous regulations and taxes. Spanish industry reached its high-water mark in 1560. After that the demand for the goods of English, French, and Dutch artisans and traders, who had been supplying Spanish consumers, took off while Spain's cities became as barren as its land.

The appeal of enterprise could not overcome the aristocratic contempt for commerce that permeated the society. Spanish hidalgos, those elegant gentlemen, used their considerable political influence to protect their way of life. They put ceilings on domestic prices that cut domestic profits while encouraging cheap imports from abroad. This of course undercut their own artisans. The monarchy was equally indifferent to Spanish farmers, whose crops were at risk every winter, when the highly valued merino sheep moved from the northern mountains to the warmer south. State-mandated trails existed to keep the sheep from trampling nearby fields. But the Mesta, the guild of shepherds, ignored complaints, and the king, a great beneficiary of the taxes that the wool trade generated, failed to enforce the laws.

In a general history of this era, Spain and Portugal would get a great deal of attention, but this is a brief history of capitalism, to which they contributed little. Neither at home nor in their settlements did they move beyond the conceptual universe of hidalgos, honor, and heroic deeds. Don Quixote, created by Miguel de Cervantes in 1605, epitomizes the qualities that spelled economic failure for the Spanish. Perhaps his mistaking a windmill for a mighty opponent was Cervantes's way of saying that Spanish gentlemen, mired in the past, couldn't even recognize this benign source of energy for productive work.

We are so used to listening to the upbeat story of progress that it is only with difficulty that we can imagine a different narrative, one that is truer to the past than the future. What happened to Spain and Portugal was not dissimilar to the earlier arrests of prosperity in the Roman, Asian, or Islamic worlds. This was what had always happened: short-lived bursts of energy followed by inevitable decline as yet another ascendant power failed to vault the limits held in place by its resources, its institutions, and its internal contradictions. These tales of empires, rising and falling, spawned a strong sense that history was cyclical and that change brought catastrophes more often than sustained accomplishments.

Portugal and Spain did not fail at what was important to them, and their empires lasted longer than those of other imperial powers. What is striking is how little their amazing exploits in navigation, explorations, and trade changed their societies at home. Spain could halt the expansion of Islam when it defeated the Turks at sea near the Greek city of Lepanto in

1571 (at which Cervantes fought), but they could not or would not tolerate a restructuring of their societies.

Formal and informal warfare became intense and brutal in Atlantic waters. As early as 1564 Spain began to convoy its gold and silver fleets from the New World to the House of Trade in Seville. The convoys, leaving the Americas in April and August, continued for a century. The English too organized convoys once the tobacco grown in its Chesapeake settlements grew valuable enough to attract raiders. Europe's endemic warfare lent some legitimacy to attacks on the high seas because all countries issued what were called letters of marque—licenses—to the owners of vessels to arm them for the purpose of capturing enemy merchant ships. As long as two countries were at war, as was much of the time, privateers were part of the nations' armed forces. Dutch, English, and French privateers repeatedly raided Spanish settlements, and they lay in wait for straggling ships in the Spanish silver convoys, twice capturing the entire fleet. Not yet in possession of their own colonies, these countries chipped away at the profits of the trailblazers.

The most famous privateer in the English world was Sir Frances Drake, who repeatedly attacked Spanish settlements and ships in the Caribbean. On one occasion he seized Santo Domingo, freeing the slaves, burning the city, destroying the ships in the harbor, and receiving a handsome sum after returning the city to the Spanish. His audacity in sailing to the Pacific around Cape Horn in 1572 to attack the unarmed Spanish silver fleet going to the Philippines thrilled the English public, whose queen, the Protestant Elizabeth, had long been a target of the Spanish king. When war between the Spanish and English broke out, Drake once again was in business as a privateer. Leading fleets of two dozen ships, he raided up and down the north coast of South America, known as the Spanish Main. Another pirate, Henry Morgan, mobilized dozens of ships and thousands of buccaneers in his attacks on Spanish possessions in the Caribbean. He was arrested for breaking the peace, but the outbreak of a new war won him a reprieve, a knighthood, and command of England's new colony of Jamaica.

On occasions like this when Europe's warring powers signed peace treaties, many of the licensed privateers like Morgan became pirates, taking out after merchant ships without the cover of royal licenses. Drake, like the Portuguese sailors who commandeered the trade in the Indian Ocean, represented more of the old order than the new. Sixteenth-century pirates took advantage of the new trades to the Orient and New World and adopted the superior designs for boats, but these adventurers would have been recognizable to the Phoenicians who plied the Mediterranean in ancient times. The trade in silks and spices from the East Indies enticed pirates because one such prize would pay the outfitting cost of an entire voyage. Turkish pirates preyed on ships in the Mediterranean, though the pashas of Tripoli later found it more rewarding to exact tribute in formal treaties. Piracy also flourished in the Red Sea, Indian Ocean, the Strait of Malacca, and the South China Sea, but especially in the Caribbean because of the allure of the gold and silver carried home by the Spanish.

Jumping ahead for a minute, we can see that as the volume of legitimate trade increased, the sober, solidly middle-class side of commerce asserted itself. Merchants got tired of losing valuable cargoes to pirates and having to pay high insurance premiums even when they didn't lose their ships. The great trading companies began agitating for protection from the random seizures of their goods. The celebrated career of Captain Kidd is exemplary. Hired to protect English East Indian vessels in the Red Sea in 1696, William Kidd, who operated out of New York, figured that he could make more money becoming a buccaneer. He scuttled his own ship, took one that was flying French colors, and began seizing the very ships that he had been hired to protect. Finally the government listened to the merchants. Captured when he returned to New York City four years later, Kidd was tried, convicted, and sent back to London for execution to publicize official intolerance of piracy.[6] Governments were now charged with making the seas safe for legitimate commerce. When Edward Teach, who terrified sailors in the Caribbean, where he marauded as the pirate Blackbeard, turned honest, the colonial governor of North Carolina colony married him to his fourteenth wife!

What Spain and Portugal did most significantly was to open up doors for their neighbors. The baton of economic development, if we can so consider it, passed to France, Holland, and England. Informally, they had entered these trades as pirates and smugglers because profits from the East and West Indies trade made those risky occupations worth pursuing. By the beginning of the seventeenth century, the French, Dutch, and English governments had chartered legitimate trading companies to challenge the Spanish monarchy that now controlled both Iberian empires. The stakes were high. As Sir Walter Raleigh, another Englishman entranced by the New World, shrewdly observed, "Whoever commands the sea commands the trade; whoever commands the trade of the world commands the riches of the world and consequently the world itself."

The Atlantic Ocean became the principal freeway of the trading universe that was fast becoming global in scope. First Spain and Portugal, then the Netherlands, France, and England benefited from easy access to the waters that carried European traders in all directions. The great losers in this geographic repositioning were the Italian city-states, the Turks, and other Muslims who had operated in the complex commercial network of the Indian Ocean. Up until the first half of the sixteenth century Venice had sent a fleet of merchants to trade with England, which had virtually no navy or merchant marine. All that changed when the English formed their own trading companies and sent ships around the world. Closed out by the Dutch from the spice trade centered in Indonesia, the English East India Company, chartered in 1600, established settlements at Surat, Bombay, Calcutta, and Madras. By the eighteenth century it had succeeded in taking control of most of India. The winners of this European intrusion into the Far East narrowed down to England and the Netherlands.

The Impact of Civil War

English and Dutch success invites a closer look at what was going on in these countries politically. While it might not have appeared a blessing at the time, both England and the Netherlands fought wars for greater national self-determination at the same time that they were challenging Spanish and Portuguese domination in the New World and East Indies. The Dutch fought for independence from the Spanish Hapsburg Empire over an eighty-year period. In the Netherlands there was greater wealth than in any place in Europe after the Dutch won their freedom from Spain in the late sixteenth century, officially recognized in 1648. But that wealth did not translate into the successive organizational and technological changes that characterize capitalism as a system. The Dutch grew fat and happy and complacent without following the English path toward progressive improvements. Indeed, its backward neighbor Belgium, which stayed within the Hapsburg Empire until the nineteenth century, industrialized first. Riches were not enough in these early decades of capitalist development to pry open the doors of a closed society in Spain and Portugal; Dutch prosperity did not translate into continued innovation.

From the 1620s through the 1680s, the English government was in turmoil. A king was executed, a Parliament dismissed, another king restored, and a hereditary succession rejected, ending with the so-called Glorious Revolution of 1688. Although these were primarily political conflicts, economic issues helped define the opposing sides. The king was the largest landholder in England, so his income could vary with good and bad times like that of other landed families. But the king, thanks to his unique prerogatives, had other sources of income, like payments from grants of monopolies, patents, and company charters. The most lucrative "gifts" he could sell were licenses for the exclusive public control of a product, a trade, or even a government service, like the inspection of tobacco or collection of customs.

King James I found in the granting of monopolies a particularly facile way of increasing his income. As one scholar reported, in the early seventeenth century a typical Englishman lived "in a house built with monopoly bricks . . . heated by monopoly coal. His clothes are held up by monopoly belts, monopoly buttons, monopoly pins. . . . He ate monopoly butter, monopoly currants, monopoly red herrings, monopoly salmon, monopoly lobsters."[7] The holders of monopolies had the exclusive right to sell these items and charged as much as people would pay for them.

Such a lavish sale of privilege would have been a burden at any time, but with the growth of internal and external markets, monopolies distorted the whole pattern of trade. Even the nobility became attracted to commercial ventures, especially if they involved colonies that would enhance the prestige of England.[8] The more the English rulers attempted to extract money in unconventional taxes, grants, and patents, the more economic issues got pulled into parliamentary debates. Defenders of royal prerogatives exuded the confidence of carriers of an old commercial tradition, appealing more to sensibilities than to economic reasoning. Men close to power continued to evoke the old ideal of subordinating economic activities to social solidarity, but fresh disputants were finding their voices and a new vocabulary for talking about harvests, rents, trade, and taxes as part of a new economic order.

In England the king came to represent adherence to tradition and the use of arbitrary power. Monopolies and closed corporations shared in the opprobrium of all things royal. In the wrangling over monopolies and other economic ills, a large swath of the English elite with seats in Parliament—improving landlords, members of trading companies, clothiers—discovered their common interests. Economic grievances transmogrified into political issues. With gross simplification it could be said that even if the forces behind economic development didn't cause the English Civil War, the conflict assured that they would eventually triumph.

Civil unrest in the seventeenth century, because it lasted so long, weakened the political authority requisite for policing economic restrictions. It's one thing to have a law—even a venerable law—on the books and another to be able to enforce it in the face of powerful incentives for evasion. With the leaders of England's political and religious institutions distracted by the long civil unrest, entrepreneurs strengthened internal transportation systems, marketed colonial products, and turned London into a great emporium. After this thirty-year period during which authorities were elsewhere engaged, many defended defiance of restrictions as good for the country. With less formal direction, an informal system of cooperation had prevailed. Once some restraints were removed, the subsequent commercial buoyancy earned more supporters for freeing up economic life. In the Netherlands and England, merchants and manufacturers ended up with a greater share of political power and a louder public voice than they had before.

After the Dutch achieved independence, they established a loose confederation with each province headed by a regent who was usually a prominent merchant. This decentralized blend of political and economic power put government squarely behind the commercial interests in the Netherlands. Only the northern provinces of Holland and its neighbors, which were largely Protestant, gained independence. More than offering protection to traders and manufacturers, Dutch leaders devised new supports for their economy with free ports, secure titles to land, efficient processes for settling lawsuits, the teaching of bookkeeping in schools, and the licensing of agents to sell marine insurance.

The Dutch as an Economic Model

In their struggle to hold on to the Spanish Netherlands, Spanish troops had destroyed Antwerp, whereupon its famous bankers simply moved north to Amsterdam. As a magnet of payments as well as of goods Holland became Europe's financial center. The Bank of Amsterdam, established in 1609, offered interest rates less than half those available elsewhere. Again flexibility triumphed as the Dutch developed credit arrangements for every circumstance and customer. Even the spurned Spanish monarchs turned to the bankers of their erstwhile possessions to borrow money. Over time the Spanish monarchy became so indebted to Dutch financiers that the famous silver fleet convoyed across the Atlantic sailed directly to Amsterdam. Those largely Catholic provinces that remained in the Hapsburg Empire later formed themselves into an independent Belgium.

Everyone marveled at the prosperity of the Dutch. How could a couple of million people packed into cities and towns along the North Sea defy all odds and grow rich? The backbone of their trade was a humble fish, the herring. Herring could be easily dried, and as an all-season source of protein in a protein-short world, it was in great demand. One contemporary estimate concluded that the fishing industry with its hundreds of boats employed half a million Dutchmen and women, twice as many as in agriculture and almost as many as those in crafts, retailing, and finance. Guilds closely controlled the fishing industry, making sure that fishermen observed the government standards of quality. During the first half of the seventeenth century, more than a thousand Dutch ships carried grain from the Baltic countries, exceeding the English by thirteen to one.[9] In England, Dutch success started a cottage industry of pamphlet writing to explain it.

Shipbuilding also flourished in the United Provinces of the Netherlands. Boatwrights created the flyboat, a flat-bottomed seagoing barge well designed for carrying heavy cargo like herring, timber, and grain. From their perch on the North Sea the Dutch reached out across the Atlantic to the colonies of the New World, down the west coast of Africa, into the Mediterranean, and around Cape Hope to the East Indies. Beginning with a few basic commodities for transshipment like herring, iron, timber, grain, and salt, Dutch merchants branched out to everything that the world's population wanted to sell or buy. They built a fleet that was larger than all the boats plying the waters under the flags of Portugal, Spain, England, France, and Austria combined.[10]

Daniel Defoe, the author of *Robinson Crusoe*, shrewdly described the Dutch as "the Middle Persons in Trade, the Factors and Brokers of Europe. . . . They buy," he continued, "to sell again, take in to send out, and the greatest Part of their vast Commerce consists in being supply'd from All Parts of the World, that they may supply All the World again."[11] But the Dutch were not just traders; they were also accomplished craftsmen. They finished the products that other countries grew or mined, and they benefited handsomely from the value that they added to goods. They took raw wool and turned it into dyed draperies; they transformed timber into wainscoting for the dining rooms of the rich; they made fine paper for the printing presses that abounded in their country; they rolled tobacco into excellent cigars. They even constructed a network of canals to carry goods and passengers that confirmed their ability to fund and organize complex projects. The sailing vessels moored at their wharves looked like so many moving forests; their quays and warehouses spilled over with crates, tubs, barrels, and packages, with cranes moving back and forth to unload silk from China, grain from the Baltic, coal from Newcastle, copper and iron from the mines of Sweden, salt from Spain, wine from France, spices from India, sugar and tobacco from the New World, and timber from Scandinavia. The slaves they took from West Africa to sell in the New World were never brought home.[12]

Needless to say, the aristocrats in the societies abutting the Netherlands spoke with disdain of a people so devoted to making money. In their eyes the Dutch were crude, greedy, and cursed by bad manners. The men and women of the Netherlands were notoriously frugal; they were also devoted to their homes. They supported hundreds of artists and artisans who engraved, designed, and crafted adornments for themselves and their houses. Dutch artists contributed a whole new genre of painting depicting ordinary people at ordinary tasks. Without noble patrons, the arts found new sponsors in the growing prosperous middle class that also supported engravers, book designers, and musicians. With artists like Rembrandt and Vermeer, the Netherlands had little to be ashamed of when it came to culture.

The Portuguese too felt the sting of Dutch commercial assertiveness. They claimed to be lords of the "conquest, navigation, and commerce of Ethiopia, India, Arabia, and Persia," but Dutch sailors who had served on Portuguese ships brought back home descriptions of this vast trading empire. They also reported that Portuguese control was not as effective as their titles suggested.[13] An even more egregious insult came when the Dutch occupied the richest part of Brazil between 1635 and 1644, an invasion the Dutch paid for by seizing the Spanish silver fleet.

Like most Dutch trading ventures, the first one to Java was financed cooperatively by a group of diverse investors. Despite an awkward maiden voyage, this Dutch fleet of three ships returned with enough pepper to cover its costs. The rivalry among Dutch merchants launched a dozen more ventures in the next decade. This led the States-General to form the Dutch East India Company in 1602 with monopoly trading privileges west of the Strait of Magellan and east of the Cape of Good Hope. It also received the right to exercise sovereign authority in the name of the Dutch Republic. Though impressive, such a charter was actually a hunting license; it would be in the waters and islands of the East Indies that the Dutch would have to make good their claims. Twenty years later a Dutch West India Company was chartered with a commercial monopoly in West Africa and the New World. Like its model, the company was granted the quasi-governmental powers of maintaining an army and navy, making war within its ambit of operation, and assuming judicial and administrative functions in its region.

Within one generation the Dutch had established themselves as the dominant power in the Malay Archipelago. With breathtaking efficiency, they supplanted the Portuguese, driving them back to a few fortified positions, which they held until the twentieth century. The Dutch East India Company had to fight off the English in Amboina, putting to the sword ten traders in a dramatic gesture of their serious intention to be the only European power in the area. The English moved on to India. The Dutch also engaged in the intra-Asian trade. They bartered local goods for pepper to be shipped to China and Japan for luxury goods and gold or silver, much of which was sent back home to finance more outbound voyages.[14] Strong population growth in China and elsewhere enlarged this trade, though like European countries, Asian regions suffered from repeated famines.

Now commanding the center of the spice-producing islands, the Dutch won over most of the indigenous rulers, who fought among themselves with great ferocity. The company established its headquarters in 1619 on Java, conferring the old Germanic tribal name of Batavia on the Javanese city that they had destroyed while capturing it. The archipelago included dozens of sovereign states that often interfered with the control the Dutch wished to exert, so what began as an aggressive commercial policy became a program of conquest. By 1670 the tasks of subduing local rulers had been accomplished. Still, the profits from the spice trade were so high that Chinese and European rivals rarely gave up trying to corner a bit of the market, muscling in on the trade of pepper, sugar, coffee, tea, silk, and textiles. Still, the Dutch East India Company enjoyed a monopoly of trade with Japan from the middle of the seventeenth century to the middle of the nineteenth century as well as on the commerce in cloves, mace, nutmeg, and cinnamon.[15]

A self-perpetuating urban oligarchy oversaw the domestic and foreign commerce of the Netherlands. Once independence was secured, the regents managed to push those Catholic aristocrats left over from the Hapsburg era back into their medieval castles. The regents and their fellow merchants ran a dozen thriving cities. Those with trading interests in the Netherlands wanted to hold at bay also those religious leaders who were more concerned with the enforcement of orthodox beliefs than with the commercial benefits of toleration. And they succeeded. The regents, in deference to the polyglot nature of commerce, extended hospitality to all comers; they rushed to facilitate trade across ethnic and religious lines.

Holland became an intellectual center, offering refuge to dissenters, freethinkers, and a raft of cranks. The book trade flourished, fostered by the high rate of literacy in the Netherlands as well as the freedom to publish writings banned in surrounding countries. Of some one hundred thousand people living in Amsterdam, a third of them were foreigners: Portuguese, Jews, Belgians, and refugees from all over Europe. Artisans seeking religious freedom added their skills to the rich reservoir of crafts already present. People in the seventeenth century loved the metaphor of the beehive. The Netherlands truly fitted the metaphor, attracting artists, writers, philosophers, and artisans, who all prospered from the cross-pollination of ideas and talents. But this particular honeycomb was never chaotic, for the regents, the rulers of the Netherlands, cherished order almost as much as profit.

Trade and Society

Because sixteenth-century trade created new wealth and reached deeper into the countryside with its monetary exchanges, it had a more pervasive impact than had earlier commercial enterprises. The flood of silver that the conquistadors stole from the Incas and Aztecs precipitated a century-long inflation in Europe. This inflation didn't fall, like the rain that Shakespeare's Portia described, impartially on everyone. It hurt those with fixed incomes, like landlords tied to old leases. Wages too lagged behind price rises, but inflation gave a boost to entrepreneurs. The profits of merchants in the East Indian trade were enhanced too. Merchants from England, France, and the Netherlands sailed forth on their yearlong voyages with goods and currency to pay for them and returned to find their cargoes of silks, precious stones, spices, and perfumed woods selling at substantially higher prices than when they left.

In England, trade burgeoned within an aristocratic society headed by a royal family. Unlike Spain, where the hidalgos disdained anyone connected with trade and used their influence to keep tradesmen in their proper place, many an English gentleman was attracted to profit-seeking ventures. The established order in England was hierarchical and open at the same time. There was a fluidity in society not found elsewhere.

Another unusual feature marked the English nobility: Only the firstborn son inherited the family title whether that title be duke, count, marquess, or baron.

Where Spain, Portugal, and France had an aristocracy of blood, the English nobility was narrowed to a single male line. The eldest sons carried the family title, and his siblings were considered commoners. The lines between titled nobles and other members of the elite were loosely drawn. Winston Churchill, for instance, was the younger son of the Duke of Marlborough, but still a commoner. Another striking contrast between England and France lay in the concept of derogation, in which a nobleman in France could lose his title by engaging in trade, unlike in England, where a large contingent of the aristocracy took an interest in economic investments without any risk of losing status.

The joint-stock trading companies were a financing novelty that appealed to a wide variety of people with money. Borrowed from the Italians, this form of corporate enterprise was unknown in Spain or Portugal. Unlike the merchant companies composed of active traders, members of a joint-stock trading company subscribed to a certain number of shares in the company. For the English gentleman or woman here was a chance to become a part of a profitable venture without taking an active part in it. Dozens of such joint-stock companies, with royal charters, were pushing out the boundaries of interregional trade.

Members of the English aristocracy showed a decided preference for companies that established colonies or pioneered trades that would enhance England's status in the world. Commerce had champions in the highest circles of society, and the House of Commons included merchants among its members. Because of this, English law changed faster than the glacial pace set elsewhere. The protection of private property, secured in England centuries earlier, became flexible enough to include the new forms of intellectual property, like inventions. The 1624 Statute of Monopolies established that patents for new devices would be granted for fourteen years, striking a balance between the inventor's reward and the public's access to useful devices. The law recognized new forms of property like company shares to encourage investors to risk their money.

A peculiar dynamic of the emerging world commerce revealed itself most strikingly in England's first colony, that fragile outpost of European life established by the Virginia Company on the far side of the Atlantic. With Spain as their example, the investors expected to realize rich profits in gold and silver and, if not that, in spices, sandalwood, and pearls. Each shareholder had a vote in the company's annual meeting in London, and all paid for their shares in installments. As it turned out, the initial investment of men and equipment sent over in 1607 was quickly exhausted. The colonists at Jamestown found little of value to send back home. Failure followed failure; the death rate was appalling. Shareholders stopped paying for their shares. The company turned to a lottery to raise more money and began distributing the one asset it had, land. At this juncture, one of the colonists, John Rolfe, who is remembered as the serious young Englishman who married the Indian princess Pocahontas, successfully hybridized a tobacco strain, which he christened Orinoco. Orinoco was good enough to compete with the much-esteemed Spanish leaf.

Rolfe's hybrid triggered a boom. Throughout the 1620s tobacco fetched between two to three shillings a pound, a price high enough to encourage Virginia Company shareholders to pour money and men (along with a few women) into their plantations. Newcomers and surviving colonists scrambled to plant more tobacco. The volume of exports surged from fifty thousand pounds in 1618 to more than three hundred thousand, eight years later. Cultivation spread along the tidal rivers emptying into the Chesapeake Bay. When the inevitable oversupply followed this boom of demand-driven expansion, prices dropped to one twenty-fourth the price of good Virginia leaf in the 1620s. Busts, caused by decentralized decision making from overly confident profit seekers, were to become a permanent feature of capitalism. But an upside followed this downer.

A whole new crowd of consumers could afford to buy tobacco at the cheaper price. Here is a wonderful example of the unintended consequences of pioneering enterprises. The increased demand for tobacco to chew or smoke created an incentive to cut production costs in order to take advantage of this larger body of consumers who would buy if the price were low enough. Within a few years the planters had found a way to serve it.

Not to be outdone by the Portuguese, Dutch, and English, a bold and tenacious Frenchman, Jean de La Roque, backed by the French East India Company, single-handedly wrested the trade in coffee away from the Middle East, where coffee had been grown exclusively for centuries on the mountain slopes of Ethiopia and Yemen. De la Roque took more than two years to complete his voyage from the Red Sea to around the Cape of Good Hope. Despite the time, going by sea, he cut transportation costs considerably. Coffee in the seventeenth century ranked as a luxury because of its high price, but a luxury the Europeans longed to indulge themselves in. Within the next decade, coffee trees were sent to France's island of Martinique and French Guiana. The Dutch started growing them on Java, the Spanish in Colombia, and the Portuguese in Brazil, which today exports almost a third of world production. Thriving in all these places, coffee dramatically fell in price. Like tobacco, many Europeans could now afford this aromatic, caffeinated way to start the day.[16]

When ordinary people joined their social superiors in the pursuit of the pleasures of consumption, their numbers changed the character of enterprise. Retrospectively we can see that this boom-and-bust cycle unintentionally widened the market for new goods. Investors responded to the profits of the boom; ordinary people, to the opportunity of the bust. The increase in the volume of goods when ordinary people became consumers meant enormous augmentations in the wealth and power of those nations and persons who participated successfully in supplying the new tastes. Society also had to learn to accommodate a push from below. Always much more than an economic system, capitalism persisted in Europe in changing mores and values however deeply embedded they once had been. This adaptability was to become a critical factor in the spread of capitalism beyond its homelands in the West.

Unintended and Unexpected Consequences

During the sixteenth century and into the seventeenth, while Europeans were experiencing their Renaissance, the Mughal court of India was flourishing, as was the Ming dynasty in China. The Ottoman caliphate still hoped to control world trade along with European land, as evidenced by its menacing Vienna with an army. Both European Christians and Ottoman Muslims found the styles of each other exotic and appealing. Decorated Italian cut glass vases and lacquered boxes could be found among the possessions of a Persian aristocrat. The techniques for working up art and ceramics themselves came from Syria and Iraq. Islamic artists copied the naturalistic style and oil paintings they saw in Europeans' royal portraits. Traditional Islamic patterns of flowers and birds appeared in European books and boxes for centuries after contact. Sometimes the cultural messengers were missionaries; sometimes, merchants.[17] As Europe was becoming more secular, religion increased its hold in the Islamic world, so this exchange of techniques and sensibilities had a vastly different impact.

One more unintended consequence colored the early history of both Virginia and capitalism. The company went bankrupt, and the king turned Virginia into a royal colony. Many of the original shareholders were left with patents to land that had been issued in lieu of dividends. When in the middle decades of the seventeenth century Virginia had settled down into a self-sufficient economy with steady profits from the annual tobacco crop, these shareholders brought out their patents, stuffed away in trunks, and applied for grants of land with them. They often sent out a young relative along with some money to set up a plantation. Virginia got a new infusion of capital just as it was beginning to switch from reliance on the labor of indentured servants to the purchase of slaves.

France, along with England and the Netherlands, had profited from the profligacy of Spain and Portugal. French artisans supplied buyers from the Iberian Peninsula with the finest cloth, leatherwork, printing, furniture, and wine. Like England and the Netherlands, France had sent out explorers and settlers to the New World fast on the heels of the Spanish. At that time France had the largest European army and grandest royal court. Most contemporaries considered it the world's preeminent power. Yet the country's glories associated with the Sun King, Louis XIV, at the end of the seventeenth century became its weaknesses under his successors.

Maintaining imposing royal establishments drew heavily on France's resources. Being both powerful and placed cheek to jowl with rivals got French kings into wars of dynastic and religious ambitions. England benefited from its island geography. During the course of the seventeenth century it acquired a powerful navy, which supported trade a good deal more than could an army however splendid. In the next century English shipyards at Portsmouth were the largest workplace in the country and an important consumer of coal and ironmongery.[18] It was said that Louis XIV would have spent more on a navy could he have reviewed it before the ladies of the court the way that he did his magnificent army. From such seemingly irrelevant factors economic advantages disappeared or accrued.

Both the crown and the French nobility lived off the taxes and rents levied on the peasants, most of whom could not produce enough to feed their families in bad years, much less invest in new farming techniques. With more sons and daughters to provide for during the sixteenth-century spurt in population, many rural families divided their properties into ever-smaller morsels of land. This morselization of property made almost inevitable the degradation of farming in much of France. Only intervention from the government saved the country from several severe famines.

The effects of France's backward agriculture radiated throughout the economy. Kings awarded their favorites special perks, such as the right to charge a fee to cross a bridge much like that which the billy goat in the fairy tale possessed. The holder of this privilege could bequeath it to his heirs. Over time, tolls for roads, bridges, canals, and towpaths accumulated, making it slow and costly to ship food from region to region. In a country as climatically diverse and large as France, harvest failures would not occur everywhere, but the fact that there was food elsewhere in the land didn't help the hungry, because distribution was clogged by these seignorial privileges. Transporting grains from one region to another became a herculean task, unless the government strongly intervened to save lives. France had nothing like England's unified internal market, where goods passed freely once the king's patents of monopoly had been abolished during its Civil War. France's truly byzantine transportation arrangement wasn't limited to food shipments. The industrial sector suffered as well because harvest failures pushed up the price of food, leaving the people without money to buy clothing or house furnishings.

The splendor of the French court rose on the backs of the impoverished peasantry. Fear of the wrath of this destitute people influenced decisions at court. The king's ministers considered any reforms in agriculture too risky to implement. The one time a minister tried, his opponents blamed his innovation for the subsequent bad harvests. In this institutional strait-jacket the old regime persisted until the end of the eighteenth century, when it came tumbling down in the French Revolution. France remained powerful economically and politically with impressive manufacturing enterprises in textiles, furnishings, wines, leather goods, and printing, but this sector could never grow larger than 20 percent of the economy because it took at least 80 percent of French workers to produce food for the whole country.

The more successful Dutch economy depended upon peace. When fighting for its independence during the sixteenth century, the Dutch navy had been ferocious in its attacks on the Spanish, but with independence finally gained, the burghers of the Netherlands designed their boats for speed and cargo capacity. They carried very light armament. This fact did not escape the attention of the French and English. The famous Dutch flyboats made a most attractive target. Both neighbors—the English three times, the French once in consort with the English—provoked war with the Netherlands in the middle decades of the seventeenth century. They seized the vessels of the Dutch East India Company and disrupted those herring fisheries off the coasts of Scotland and England that formed the backbone of the Dutch commercial empire. While the Netherlanders retaliated with great skill and ferocity, the superior size of France and England won out. During the last war the Dutch prevented a French invasion of Amsterdam only by opening the dikes that held back the waters of the North Sea. In attacking the United Provinces, France and England used their coercive power to win commercial concessions, much as the Portuguese had done in the Indian Ocean. Evidently in the minds of European rivals what could not be gained through competition might yield to violence. Though by no means unable to defend themselves, the Dutch came out of these wars chastened by their vulnerabilities.

Even though the Netherlands surpassed England in wealth and the reach of its trading prowess during most of the seventeenth century, its economic development hit a plateau in the eighteenth century. Instead of pressing on to new levels of development, the Dutch became the great financiers of other countries' ventures and follies. The American colonists turned to them when they needed money for their war for independence. The Dutch, so inventive in craftwork and commerce, did not become technological pioneers. It took a century before they followed others into industrialization. Even their neighbors the Belgians, who did not succeed in breaking away from their Spanish overlords until 1830, pushed ahead of the Dutch. The Belgians' abundance of iron and coal played a critical role in their industrialization, making more salient the importance of natural resources to capitalist development.

Dutch success as Europe's shipper, finisher, and banker may help explain their industrial backwardness. Many a Dutchman or woman found ways to enjoy the good life as a rentier. As was the case with so many successful merchants, many in the Netherlands turned their attention to acquiring status and enjoying the good life by investing in land or becoming bankers, or doing both.[19] What the Dutch had succeeded in doing was to push to the outer limits the profits from commerce. After many generations of expanding prosperity, their ruling class began to ossify, but not before dazzling the rest of Europe with the wonder of riches created from nothing but hard work and ingenuity. While never becoming poor, Holland and its sister provinces declined relative to their neighbors. Though still thriving in the eighteenth century, they were left behind in the relentless, ceaseless search for new developments that have marked the history of capitalism.

Explaining things that didn't happen, but might have happened, is always a challenge. Why the arrest in forward movement, innovation, and changes in investment? Were the Dutch, as their critics claimed, smug, complacent burghers with little interest in striking out in new directions once they had found their comfortable niche? Or were there other inhibitors of economic development? One fact does seem relevant. The Dutch never freed themselves of those most ancient of all limitations, food shortages and the fear of famine that accompanied them. Dutch farmers were wizards of agricultural techniques but could produce on the land available to them only two-thirds of the amount needed to feed the people each year. This shortfall made the Dutch crucially dependent upon others. And interestingly, this vulnerability seems to have stifled their imagination more than it caused them hunger. They remained attached to a provisioning mentality that prized security above risk taking.

I began this chapter by noting that commerce had existed for centuries before capitalist practices appeared and would have continued to flourish without that development. I wanted to break the connection in most people's minds between the discovery of the New World and the emergence of capitalism because capitalism was not an extension of trade. It required a different set of attitudes and skills. Although the term "commercial capitalism" is frequently used, it misleads by giving the impression that commercial capitalism merged into full-blown capitalism. That didn't happen in many countries, as the experience of Spain and Portugal, even France and the Netherlands attests to. The connection fails on this record alone.

One of the reasons that commerce could not transform, as opposed to influence, the world's economies is that it involved too small a part of the working population. Farming absorbed upwards of 80 percent of a country's workers, year in, year out. Changing this proportion would revolutionize an economy—or at least make it possible to do so. Yet the explorations and trading that began at the end of the fifteenth century did do something remarkable: They linked Asia, Europe, North America, and South America closely to one another. Now the world's countries could not totally escape the impact of events thousands of miles away. A perfect example of this is the conversion of China's monetary systems to a silver standard that doubled the value of silver worldwide in the early sixteenth century. With this switch came a surge in the production of silver destined for China. Manila galleons brought new foods from the New World, helping to feed more Chinese. As China's population grew, so did the demand for silver, which served for money on all the linked continents.[20]

The novelties from European trade in the East Indies and the New World promoted new commercial institutions, created a fresh group of entrepreneurs, and stimulated the imagination of contemporaries. Public discussions ensued that analyzed these economic novelties. Fresh intellectual interests, enhanced by a new vocabulary, became crucial to the modern transformation of traditional countries. Many mechanical devices and institutional procedures became useful to entrepreneurs without themselves being causes of the emergence of capitalism. The invention of movable type made printing cheaper, promoting a book trade that carried news of explorations throughout Europe. The Greek astrolabe and compass proved a great aid to navigating the waters of three oceans. Italian double-entry bookkeeping enabled merchants to keep better track of their profits. All these improvements contributed to industrial enterprise, but they didn't cause capitalism to appear; they were propitious factors in its development. Capitalism required a different social dynamic and innovations that changed how food was grown and goods produced.

Because traditional mores were thoroughly embedded in the literature, laws, religious rites, work rituals, and habits of people, they didn't suddenly collapse; they crumbled slowly. Governments continued to regulate many occupations outside of farming. Statutes and edicts specified the proper procedures in the producing and selling of woolens, the Central European manufacturing sector. In the cities, guilds limited the number of workers in enterprises like making paper, printing books, working leather, and crafting tools. Overseas merchants had restrictive charters. Both England and the Netherlands secured political systems more open to commercial interests during the seventeenth century. The English government remained strongly aristocratic, but much of that aristocracy entered enthusiastically into new enterprises. More important, it sponsored many agricultural improvements that would determine how many workers and how much money would be available for other economic ventures.

3

CRUCIAL
DEVELOPMENTS IN
THE COUNTRYSIDE

ALL ECONOMIES BEGIN with food production. We know this, but not intuitively. The array of goods at our ubiquitous malls dulls our sense of what scarcity might be like. Famines are things that occur in other, distant lands. Yet they were once as common as the bad weather that caused them. Despite the handsome buildings constructed in the Middle Ages, the universities founded, the wars funded, Europeans—along with the rest of the world—often did not have enough to eat. The very rich might have plenty in the months before the first harvests came in, but most people had to tighten their belts, hoping that the carrots and turnips they had laid down the last fall would not mold, nor a late frost delay spring planting.

There were few ways to preserve food in those days. During the lean months farmers would be hard pressed not to eat the animals wintered over for spring breeding or the seed reserved from the grain harvest for next year's planting. Dying from starvation was not common, but it loomed as a possibility when harvests fell short. With the benefit of hindsight, we can see the absolute necessity of producing more food with less labor if countries were ever to support other economic pursuits because only the restructuring of farming could free up workers and investment funds needed for, say, industry.

Scarcity exercised a pervasive influence in premodern societies. Public authorities kept a weather eye on each year's harvest as it came into the granaries to be stored for the coming year. Officials were always on the lookout for farmers who held their grain off the market, hoping for a rising price, or who sold part of it to brewers without permission. Fear of famine promoted pervasive oversight. The growing and marketing of grain were enmeshed in a skein of regulations. Each country's laws reflected the authorities' fear of famines and the riots they provoked. Every step in the production of the wheat, barley, oats, or rice—those precious grains that composed the staff of life—came under surveillance.

The great triumvirate of marketing evils in English law—engrossing, forestalling, and regrating—were all felonies. What were these heinous acts? Buying up large quantities of foodstuffs and holding them off the market, waiting for a better price, and then retailing them to others. These old statutes with their wonderfully archaic names, affirmed that the growing and marketing of grains were as much social as economic activities. Grain was not seen as a commodity to be moved through the countryside in search of the best price.

The farmer who grew grain, what the English called corn—be he tenant, freeholder, or landlord—did not really own the crop; he attended it during its passage from the field to the market. He could not store it, he could not move it to a distant market, nor while it stood in the field could he sell it to a middleman. Rather he had to load up his cart with the grain not needed in his household and proceed to the nearest market. There he offered his harvest to his traditional customers. Similarly, the miller who made the flour and the baker who worked it up were constrained to push the finishing process along in an orderly fashion to its final form as a loaf of bread, selling at a price set by the local assize court.

Even today hunger is a heartrending reality for millions. Reporting on famines in the Central African Republic a few years ago, the *New York Times* described a farmer who let his wife take the last of their millet to make a porridge to keep them all alive. Most people probably don't realize that the grain that goes into bread or beer is the same as the seed for next year's crop of wheat or barley. With persistent dearth, the temptation to eat the seed set aside for the coming season often becomes impossible to resist, as with the farmer in the Central African Republic, with dire consequences for the future.

Seeking to appreciate, rather than disturb, nature, people in traditional societies felt awe and reverence for their social arrangements, whereas modern men and women often think about reforming them. The daily philosophy of acceptance and resignation not only acted as a balm for pain, but encouraged respect for the spiritual stamina that enabled people to endure hard times. The stability imposed by authority staved off many bad consequences, but it also inhibited fresh thinking. The tedium of constant worry bred a kind of lethargy. Only by entering imaginatively into the old order that preceded capitalism can we appreciate the struggle it took innovators to change it.

Moving from the moral economy of sustaining society to that of promoting development was not accomplished in a single century. The sensibilities of contemporaries in the sixteenth century had not been formed in a commercial world. The ethos codified in the Tudor statutes regulating wages, poor relief, and the harvesting of grain rested upon powerful assumptions underpinned by God's injunction to Adam to work by the sweat of his brow and by Amos's direful castigations against those who "swallow up the needy."

The salient features of the biblical economy were sufficiently congruent to the ordering of labor in sixteenth-century Europe to command belief: The world could be made fruitful through labor; labor came to man as both a punishment and a gift. As a gift, it tied human society to God's charity. As a punishment it forever harnessed men and women in the common work of sustaining life and doing God's will. Biblical texts explained this social order, infusing the daily round of tasks with a divine rationale. If the poor tenant found himself ground down by a cruel landlord, the pain of privation could be relieved by the lesson in Proverbs "Rob not the poor, because he is poor: neither oppress the afflicted in the gate: For the Lord will plead their cause, and spoil the soul of those that spoiled them."

There was little that was private in the lives of rural or urban workers. Masters hovered over servants. Guilds controlled merchants and artisans. There were hundreds of these monopolistic occupational organizations, those of merchants being the most prestigious. To scan a list of artisans' guilds is to get a picture of manufacturing when the hand—or *manus*—actually did it. There were guilds for shoemakers, bakers, dyers, stonemasons, carpenters, and even white stationery makers. Highly regimenting, the guilds protected the privileges of their members against outside competition. They also regulated prices and made sure that quality standards were maintained. Boys entered trades as apprentices and moved on to become journeymen; a few became masters of their own establishments. Girls normally served as housemaids under the strict supervision of a mistress. In Europe, neither group was allowed to marry until they were well into their twenties.

The obsession with order in premodern times had its roots in the limited economic horizon that prevailed and had prevailed through all time. Concerns about each year's harvest of grain provided the principal justification for government control of most aspects of everyday life. The propriety of political control went unquestioned, especially among the propertied. People didn't think of limited food production as a problem to be addressed; rather it was seen as a part of the cosmic order, an unalterable feature of human life. The annual round of activities that produced food belonged to a venerable round of duties and rights designed to protect society from famine, a goal made all the more vivid by everyone's experience of hunger. Countries were often called commonwealths because of everyone's shared stake in survival.

Military powers like the Romans in antiquity and the Arabs in the eighth century were able to support large armies not because they knew how to produce enough food to feed the soldiers but rather because they could extract food from their conquests. The Spanish used their might in a similar fashion in the sixteenth century. When famine threatened, the Spanish took the grain crops from their possessions Sicily and Naples and

let the Italians starve. No people before the seventeenth century ever succeeded in altering the grim statistic that some 80 percent of the population had to farm to feed the rest. And the designation of feeder or fed was
imposed by authority.

Agriculture as opposed to getting food by hunting and gathering made
possible sedentary societies four centuries before the birth of Christ. The
slaves, serfs, and laborers stuck to their hoes because even the primitive
cultivation of crops yielded enough food to sustain them and the social
superstructure raised on their backs. The surplus from their harvests and
livestock went to pay royal households, religious establishments, armies,
and a small coterie of merchants and artisans living in the interstices of
society. Culture emanated from the few powerful and presumably talented,
wise, and learned. Many societies in the past enjoyed prosperity, but none
escaped the threat of famine by significantly improving the output of their
agriculture.

A Growing Basket of Consumables

Geography, climate, and indigenous animals pretty much dictated what
would be put on the table in premodern times. Grains, salted meat, and
root vegetables carried people through the winter in cold climates. Lambs
were slaughtered in the spring, beef throughout the year, but usually when
the animals were young because of the high cost of keeping them alive.
Good hunters plucked birds from the sky before they flew south. Well-
off farm wives could afford to keep rabbits and chickens and sometimes
bees. Families ate their homegrown fruits and vegetables through October. Then apples could be turned into cider. No one wanted salted fruit,
and few fruits or vegetables can be successfully dried, so any excess per-
ished because the sugar necessary for preserving them would have been
expensive. Hops and barley went into beer unless the harvest was so lean
that the law stepped in and forbade sales to brewers. New World maize—
or what we call corn—and potatoes came into some European diets in the
middle of the seventeenth century. And then there were sunflowers. Introduced from the New World, they were grown widely from the middle of
the sixteenth century. Their grand height was turned into a contest. A gar-

dener in England reported a sunflower fourteen feet high, passed by one in Madrid at twenty-four feet and another reported from Padua at a hard-to-believe forty feet. By the eighteenth century someone had patented a device for extracting oil from the sunflower seeds.

Discoveries of water routes to the East Indies and the New World added variety to European dinner tables. They also dealt a blow to the venerable belief that human history went in cycles without anything really new occurring. Along a broad front of topics from geography to theology, the existence of life at the antipodes proved by the explorations of the fifteenth and sixteenth centuries compelled intellectual reassessments as well as practical attention. Even more arresting, the joining of the Old and New Worlds made possible a global exchange in plants, animals, human practices, and—alas—germs. Before that, the people of the Western Hemisphere had been sealed off from the rest of mankind; after 1492 a new biological homogeneity began to emerge with profound consequences for the world's people.[1]

Everything about the New World seemed strange to the Europeans. They had never seen reptiles as large as the iguana, and they puzzled that there were not only no horses or cows in the New World but also no four-legged animals larger than a fox on the islands of the Caribbean. The explorers and conquerors missed the familiar trees of Europe, but they marveled at the exquisite flowering plants of the Caribbean, later determined to number more than thirteen thousand. Horses, cattle, and uninvited rats throve in their new habitat. Hernando de Soto led a four-year expedition across the southeast of the North American continent. With many of his provisions on the hoof, he trekked across what is now North Carolina, Tennessee, Alabama, and Arkansas, leaving behind a host of European pigs to propagate in the New World. Conquistadors, given vast tracts of land, began to raise cattle while the horse made its way north, transforming the culture of the Plains Indians.

On his second trip Columbus brought seeds for all the Spanish fruits and vegetables that he hadn't seen on his first visit to the Western Hemisphere. Veritable "Johnny Appleseeds," the Spaniards acted quickly to exchange the flora and fauna of the two worlds. Spaniards and Portuguese introduced bananas, lemons, oranges, pomegranates, figs, dates, and coconuts, the latter found in the Philippines. From the New World, Europeans got a great variety of squashes, not to mention cocoa and tobacco. The range of European vegetables and fruits was far greater than those in the Western Hemisphere, but a few New World staples like potatoes, beans, and corn were to have a major impact on food-short Europe because the New World vegetables could be grown in places inhospitable to the grains Europeans depended upon as their principal source of nutrition. For instance, corn could grow where it was too wet for wheat and too dry for rice, and it yielded twice as much food per acre. These New World crops with their differing soil and weather needs usually acted like so many insurance policies against famine.

The potato was richer in calories than grains and could thrive on very small plots. Even more remarkable, potatoes yielded two to three times more bushels per acre than wheat or barley. They could be stored through the winter and didn't demand much in the way of cultivation. People are amazingly resistant to changing their diet, slow to adopt strange foods, however beneficial. But the harvesting bounty of the humble potato won over the Irish, who began cultivating it at the end of the sixteenth century.

Potatoes had several advantages that rarely come into play now. They could be grown at high altitudes, helping the Spanish feed the miners of Potosí and enabling Chinese peasants to flee government tax collectors by moving into hill country.[2] When invading armies burned crops to the ground, potatoes remained hidden in the earth. In China, Poland, and especially Ireland the potato's bounty translated into earlier marriages and more children. When an airborne blight struck potato plants in 1846, 1848, and 1852, Ireland lost an eighth of its population from starvation or disease—one million of its eight million people. Whole families died in their cottages; corpses were found in the fields. The devastation, acerbated by British trade policies, sent another quarter of Ireland's men and women to the New World.

The greatest New World contribution to the feeding of Europe came from the sugar produced in the islands of the Caribbean. Columbus brought sugarcanes from Portuguese Madeira on his second voyage. The Portuguese brought sugar cultivation from São Tomé off the West African coast to their New World colony of Brazil in the early sixteenth century. Quickly exhausting the gold deposits on Santo Domingo, settlers turned to the production of sugar as a surer source of profit. Spanish colonial administrators helped by making available sugarcanes and the slaves to cultivate them. An intensive kind of agriculture, usually involving work gangs of slaves, sprang up quickly. Unknown in the European world of family-based farming, these factories in the fields were the first examples of highly capitalized agriculture. Farm work, always drudgery, became brutal when the workers were enslaved and beaten to work harder. The sex ratio in the sugar plantations was often as high as thirteen men to one woman. Sugar was instantly popular in Europe. Soon the English, Dutch, and French seized Caribbean islands of their own during the seventeenth century to exploit this new and lucrative crop.

We all know the appeal of sugar in our candies, cookies, cakes, and coffees, but we've lost an appreciation of the critical role it played in the European diet. Sugar did more than furnish calories and sweetness; it made possible storing fruits and vegetables throughout the year. There were only three ways to keep food before artificial refrigeration: salting it, preserving it, or drying it. Sugar was the essential ingredient for preserves. Before a nineteenth-century German chemist showed how to extract sugar from beets, people had to import it from those tropical areas where sugarcane flourished. Its desirability and rarity did for the islands of the West Indies what oil later did for the Middle East: It gave them a monopoly of a commodity whose demand continued to climb for two centuries.

While the trade in exotic spices, luxury fabrics, and precious metals from the East and West Indies added great variety to the lives of well-off Europeans, they only slowly penetrated the closets and tables of ordinary men and women. Cities had grown, and trade among European countries had greatly increased, but in the rural areas men and women, their children and servants continued to work as they had for centuries, tilling the soil, cutting timber, and caring for livestock. People did not assign themselves parts in these agrarian activities; rather these responsibilities were allocated through the inherited statuses of landlord, tenant, cottager, and laborer. Supplying the food, fabric, and shelter for survival occupied the time of the whole family with a strict gender division of labor persisting. Customs, not incentives, regulated the flow of tasks that followed the calendar. Mix in a little ignorance, isolation, and superstition, and you can see that changing this order would involve a complicated choreography of incentive, innovation, and pure chance.

It took two hundred years before the volume coming from Caribbean plantations lowered the price of sugar enough to bring this wonderful ingredient into most people's pantries. In 1750, 1 percent of calories in the English diet came from sugar; by the opening of the twentieth century it was 14 percent. The prospect of high profits suppressed any qualms about enslaved labor. Sugar became one more item in the expanding inventory of goods that knitted European countries together in an intensifying round of material exchanges. From the Baltic countries came grain and lumber, from the Dutch came dried herring and the goods their merchants collected around the world, from the Iberian Peninsula olive oil, wine, and fine merino wool, from Italy wine and fruit, from France luxury fabrics and wine, from England wool, metal tools, and foodstuffs. Within the web of international commerce, those countries with access to the Atlantic enjoyed a distinct advantage.

The rich ate vast amounts of meat, fish, and fowl while the poor had to content themselves with a monotonous fare of bread. In northern England and Scotland not even wheat was available; the poor ate oats while everywhere members of the upper class enjoyed a great variety of dishes. A surviving household account gives us a record of what a nobleman served on the feast of Epiphany. His 450 guests ate 678 loaves of bread, 36 rounds of beef, 12 mutton, 2 calves, 4 pigs, 6 suckling pigs, 1 lamb, numerous chickens and rabbits, as well as oysters, lingcod, sturgeon, flounder, large eels, plaice, salmon, swans, geese, capons, peacocks, herons, mallards, woodcocks, larks, quails, eggs, butter, and milk along with wine and 259 flagons of ale.[3] If we compare it with the monotonous diet that some 80 percent of the society ate, we see the difference in material comfort that status conferred. In this world of scarcity there were some who enjoyed abundance.

Agrarian practices, dignified through centuries of experience, organized by shared habits, backed by authority, knitted together communities through routines, shared tasks, rituals, and celebrations. An idealization of the rural way of life has even persisted through three centuries of modernity. Many Europeans still farmed together in common fields in the sixteenth and seventeenth centuries. The least efficient farmer set the pace; community plots maintained strict schedules for planting and reaping. After harvesting, the villagers had to agree on a time for letting their animals graze on the remains of the crops left standing in the fields. While most villages also contained freehold farmers and prosperous tenants, their lives were also deeply entwined with those of their neighbors. The stability of this way of living had built a mighty wall of hostility to change. Even where families farmed separately, there were many restrictions on the use and disposition of land as well as complications in titles and the right to sell or bequeath one's land.[4]

Population Growth and Agriculture

The rhythms of birth and death set the tempo for the expansion and contraction of population. In good times, people had more children—or more children survived. Over time the bulging demand from the new generation pushed up the price of food, which in turn encouraged some farmers to reach out and cultivate plots of marginal fertility. The higher prices that came from greater demand made it possible to extract a living from land that normally was too poor to trouble with, but as a strategy to sustain a larger population this one was doomed. Eventually the yield declined, and the enlarged population was even more vulnerable to famine. Europe and other parts of the world regularly went into these demographic cycles of growth and decline. Diseases killed people as well, often working in tandem with the debilitating effects of hunger. And then there were the casualties of war, made worse by armies battening off the countryside. The Thirty Years' War, which lasted from 1618 to 1648, led to a 35 percent drop in population in Germany, bringing to an abrupt end the population growth of the previous century.

A few simple economic truths reigned supreme. Abundant food lowered prices; food shortages forced prices up. Population growth increased demand, and demand raised prices. With population decline both the price of grain and the acres in cultivation went down. Because premodern farmers didn't produce enough grain and livestock to keep their families from want, the fear of bad years was ever present. It discouraged investment and increased dependence upon authority. Better to salt the money away for lean times ahead; better not to offend those who could help in grim times. With such precarious harvests, people were at the mercy of the weather. In situations like these, fatalism reigned. Only when agricultural productivity increased would bad weather become less a matter of life and death and people be willing to entertain a belief in men and women's capacity to control their destiny.

European population had seesawed between growth and decline for centuries. It hit its nadir after the Black Death swept across the continent in the fourteenth century. Fleas on rats stowed away in the caravans coming from China carried the bubonic plague to Europe, where almost one-half of the people died within four years. Permanent cycles of the plague's return kept population low for the next century. Only very slowly did the death rates drop.[5] These sustained losses of people led to a general economic retrenchment. With fewer consumers and those scattered across the Continent, it became too costly to transport goods. Many trading connections snapped. But fewer people often meant better times for the survivors, who could garner higher wages or wrest better leases from landlords forced to compete for tenants. It was this paucity of workers that prompted Portuguese traders to sail down the west coast of Africa to buy enslaved men and women to bring back to Lisbon.

With a decline of population, people abandoned the settlements that had grown up around marginal land tilled in response to the earlier growth of population. In England more than four hundred villages and hamlets ceased to exist in the second half of the fifteenth century. At the beginning of the sixteenth century European population began to bounce back from the Black Death, but the number of Europeans did not pass the benchmarks set in the first century until the middle of the eighteenth century. The seesaw of growth and retraction returned. Population, which had grown in the sixteenth century, declined in the next century, but a new plateau emerged in the 1740s. This one became a permanent launching pad for the population growth we are still experiencing. After that, the retrenchments stopped, though continental Europeans suffered some famines in the early nineteenth century.

At the end of the eighteenth century Thomas Robert Malthus, with these realities well in mind, published his famous *Essay on Population*. In it, he exposed a catch-22. He started with a simple hypothesis about population growth: People would have more babies if food were plentiful, and this happy outcome would lead inevitably to dearth in the future. As he pithily put it, "The power of population is so superior to the power in the earth to produce subsistence for man, that premature death must in some shape or other visit the human race."[6] All this was because population grew exponentially: If two parents brought six children to adulthood, they could soon have thirty-six grandchildren, a sixfold increase. Agriculture, if it expanded at all, did so slowly and arithmetically—two plus two, not two times two—as more acres were added to production or yields grew larger. A 10 percent increase in cultivation would add ten bushels of grain to an initial one hundred, not nearly enough for the new mouths to feed. Hastening the return of dearth, the new tillage also would be inferior to that already tilled, for people farmed the good land first, moving to marginal land only when demand pushed up prices.

The implications of Malthus's theory startled: Reproduction could be counted on to wipe out any abundance that big harvests ushered in. In short, good times created bad times. For Malthus, it would take the grim reaper with his train of disease, dearth, and disaster to reestablish an equilibrium between people and food. Malthus was reacting negatively to the optimism swirling through European intellectual circles after the French Revolution, so he was not about to entertain hope that people might cut down on their insistent copulation. He recognized the possibility that having fewer babies would stave off famine but gave no credence to men and women's willingness to control their fertility. No Enlightenment, in his opinion, could rewrite these inexorable laws of population growth and decline. He did acknowledge in subsequent editions of his essay that England was fortunate in having so many horses (the English loved shooting and hunting). The horses created a firewall against famine, Malthus said, since they could always serve for food in desperate times. And of course there was also their output of manure, so precious to farmers.

Like many prophets, Malthus was right ... about the past. He published in 1798 on the cusp of two dramatic developments that are central to the history of capitalism: the limitation of family size and the steady growth of harvests after two centuries of mutually enhancing agricultural improvements. England and the Netherlands had already broken through the age-old limits on productivity by the end of the seventeenth century. Even so, Malthus saw clearly that population growth was the uncaged tiger in early modern societies, which is where our story begins. His grim figures, by the way, gave his young contemporary Charles Darwin a key idea. If all species had to struggle to feed themselves, then nature had initiated a war of all against all, leading the Darwinian enthusiast Herbert Spencer to coin the phrase "the survival of the fittest."

After World War II scholars became interested in the centuries-old accordionlike oscillation of European population because it seemed to contain some clues about "the rise of the West." For historians, their "Mount Everest" became explaining how countries in the West had thrown off the fetters of poverty and ignorance and marched into a modern era of their own creation, one that set them apart from other places as well as their past. For a long time, scholarly attention focused on foreign trade, urban growth, and the development of industry to explain the West's divergence from its past and other contemporary societies. It finally became apparent that something was missing from this narrative, for money and workers could not move into industry unless farmers produced more food to feed them. This meant that change, if it was to be lasting, had to come in the most conservative and populous sector of the society, the countryside.

Wishing to confirm or disconfirm Malthus's strictures about human reproduction, demographers found ways to investigate the population dynamics of the past with more precision. They pored through extant registers of marriages, births, and deaths that parish churches kept and through the statistics recorded by governments. With family reconstitution forms and painstaking effort, they charted the dates of weddings, christenings, and burials. Cumulatively, these records yielded statistics on the average age at marriage, the typical interval between births, and the life expectancy for men and women and their children.[7] Aided by computers, historical demographers were able to plot rates of fertility and mortality. Meticulously filling in family reconstitution forms for hundreds of communities, they discovered patterns for whole countries and regions.

An arresting discovery emerged from this work: The majority of men and women in Europe married at a late age, around twenty-six and twenty-seven for men, twenty-four and twenty-five for women. This stood in stark contrast with the early age of marriage among the Chinese and Indians, whose men and women got married near the age of puberty and subsequently moved in with the families of the husbands or wives. Even in southern Europe, extended families lived together. Quite the contrary in England, most couples had to establish separate households before they could marry. This custom acted as a population check. If a third of a woman's fertile years passed by before she married, she would have fewer children. The fact that a man could not marry until he could support his wife explained how this pattern of late marriage was maintained. Acquiring a plot of land usually depended upon the death of the father, a reality that linked mortality and fertility. But the age of marriage proved flexible. Later, when there were other industrial jobs for men, the age of marriage dropped two or three years. Still, it remained much higher for European countries than elsewhere.

These findings indicated why famines in Europe had never been as severe as in other parts of the world and why they disappeared first in England. Late marriages were most marked among the poor, whose adolescence was spent in apprenticeships and as farm servants. Among members of the propertied classes, concerns about heirs to continue the family lines were paramount. The wealthy married off their pubescent girls and boys because there was money to support young newlyweds. Parents could arrange—and canon law permitted—marriages among boys and girls as young as eight and nine, but this was not typical, as had long been thought. Romeo and Juliet were the exception, not the rule, and ordinary people always had to bide their time before they could marry.

The high price of food still had to be lowered if people were to break out of the vise of food shortages that had long set limited economic horizons, but this demographic indicator showed how European countries succeeded in limiting family size. New efficiencies in farming had to release workers and capital from the agricultural sector as well as bring down the cost of food for there to be any breakout from the vise of scarcity—a very tall order. The bookkeeping of a London baker in the early seventeenth century gives us a look at food costs relative to income. He paid three dollars in wages each week, while feeding the thirteen people in his household—wife, children, journeymen, apprentices, and maidservants— cost him twelve dollars. Food took four-fifths of his total outlay. A small firm today that covered the meals of its eight employees would spend less than a quarter on food.[8]

How Food Costs Limited Economic Development

With something like 80 percent of the people engaged in raising food, there were too few extra laborers and too little money to support many other enterprises. Whatever surplus accrued to those who worked the soil generally went to taxes for the ruler, rent for their landlords, and tithes for the church. Instead of acquiring income from enterprise, the members of the middle and upper classes—royal officials, landlords, and clergymen— were supported by the extractions in taxes and rents from those who worked the land. Others—merchants, lawyers, bankers, tradesmen—lived off the spending of the recipients of taxes, tithes, and rents. There could be no increase in demand for manufactured goods or even for the commodities brought from faraway lands without changes in food production because there was no money to spend on them. To make the point, the percentage of the population in farming in Europe of the sixteenth century was similar to that of Europe during the time of the Roman Empire.

Food costs strictly limited the funds available to buy such luxuries as leather goods, decorative objects, spices, cutlery, carriages, furniture, fabrics, and books. Bad harvests pushed up the price of grains, curtailing purchases further. Meat, for instance, left the table of the poor for years on end in times of dearth. People would postpone new purchases until better times returned, adding an uncertainty to the prospects of those who made those postponed purchases. Even if money had become more abundant, growth in commerce or manufacturing had another obstacle, a lack of people to work outside the farm. Expanded production depended upon having men and women available to work in these enterprises, but the demand for laborers in farming came first.

This state of affairs had several consequences. It encouraged people to save money for the proverbial rainy day. It also meant that luxury consumption was confined to the very small percentage of the society with disposable income—no more than 15 percent. To get out of this box, farmers had to learn how to produce more food with fewer hands. New methods of farming would have to sustain larger and larger harvests to remove the fear of famine that inhibited investments in other enterprises. The price of food would also have to continue to drop to enable people outside the gentry and the urban rich to buy manufactured and imported goods. To further complicate the picture, these requisite changes for a permanent escape from scarcity had to start in rural communities known for their fidelity to custom.

The incentive for change must have come when food prices began to rise in the early sixteenth century. With more mouths to feed pushing up the price of grains, the improvements that the Dutch pioneered became attractive despite the risk of doing something differently. The influx of New World gold and silver caused a century of inflation period, but cereal prices rose even faster. In England a number of propitious factors converged to promote reform of the old agrarian order. The relationship between landlords and their tenants was flexible enough to permit the adoption of new practices. Landlords, their tenants, and freeholders began imitating the techniques that farmers in the Netherlands had shown to be successful.

The catastrophe of the Black Death had an impact on the structure of landholding throughout Europe. In Eastern countries, landlords turned their tenants into serfs, while in Western Europe many families escaped tenancy altogether and acquired land of their own. In England there were many independent farmers—yeomen or freeholders—along with tenants farming large tracts of land. English landlords succeeded in breaking their customary low-rent leases that lasted the lifetime of the tenant. They acquired the power to adjust rents to the price levels of the grain and livestock their tenants produced. With fixed obligations, the tenants too could plan better. Many entered into arrangements in which, for instance, they specified improvements in cropping in return for long leases that would enable them to share with their landlords in the benefits from their expenditures of time and money. In France, landlords used different tactics to increase their incomes; they squeezed their tenants with fines, feudal dues, and labor services.

Higher prices from a rising population during the sixteenth century encouraged landlords in Europe's Baltic bread basket to move onto neglected land and bring in larger crops to export. Again, growth brought the old scissors movement of more workers lowering the price of wages and the same population growth raising demand for food along with the price of it. The wealthy flourished for a time. In the long run, food production could not keep up with the insistent demand from new mouths to feed. In the short run of fifty years, rising grain prices created a powerful incentive to find ways to get bigger yields. Most landlords in most places preferred to stick to their ingrained ways, but enough opted to try new ways to increase harvests to set Europe on the course of transforming its agricultural system.

All Europe gained from the intensification of trade during the sixteenth and seventeenth centuries.[9] More ships and carts were carrying more goods between countries, meaning that if harvests failed in one region, imports from other parts of the Continent could sometimes make up the loss. Urban population grew faster than rural areas, so city fathers began to store grain against future crop failures, particularly in the Netherlands, which always fell short of feeding its people. Spain depended upon northern European countries for wheat, copper, tin, wood, hemp, linen, and high-quality textiles, and for a while many Spaniards had the money to buy them. Naturally this increase of money chasing goods led to inflation. But interestingly, the cost of food went up faster than that of other commodities. Inflation came from an excess of people as well as of silver.

Having a natural source of water, European farmers did not have to depend on irrigation, as did those in China and the Middle East. Setting up the canals, sluices, and waterwheels for irrigation was a costly business that only the government or the well off could afford. This fact probably limited the number of possible innovators there to officials or the rich, often the most conservative members of society because they have the greatest investment in the status quo. Still, parts of China enjoyed both growth and greater wealth for a long period until population growth overwhelmed its capacity to respond in the middle of the eighteenth century.

Dutch Farming Improvements

On land wrested from the tidal incursions of the North Sea, the United Provinces were the wonder of Europe, especially after they secured their independence from the Spanish at the end of the sixteenth century. They extracted tons of herring from the seas that lapped at their shores and then created the world's largest merchant fleet to ship this wonderful source of precious protein to their European neighbors. In Flanders, farmers reclaimed wasteland that was usually too sandy to nourish grains by planting flax and hemp, the crops that produce linen and rope (not to mention marijuana). These plants had the advantage of leaving behind fibrous stalks that could be plowed under to bulk up the sandy soil. Elsewhere the Dutch drained marshland to create more acres for tillage. They also experimented with clover, a weed that had been around forever. Evidently someone's close observation showed that clover, like many legumes, actually left nitrogen in the soil. Turnips too became a new crop, one that could be grown in the summer and stored for winter feed for animals. This innovation led to bigger animals and more manure for the hungry soil.

Agriculture throughout the world was woefully unproductive because cropping drained the land of its fertility. The traditional remedy for soil exhaustion was allowing land to become fallow to recapture its fertility, but this took a third or a quarter of acres under tillage out of production. Farmers could also restore fertility by adding nitrogen to the soil. Their principal source of this came from animals that unfortunately had to be fed to stay alive and defecate, taking even more land away from producing food for the people. Breaking through this bind of declining soil fertility took a bundle of mutually enhancing practices. Fortunately Dutch farmers had been experimenting with possible improvements for many decades.

Some farmers in the Netherlands realized that they could abandon the old medieval practice of leaving a third of the land to lie fallow each year. This move increased the number of tilled acres by a third. Instead of the fallow rotation, they divided land into four parts, rotating fields of grain, turnips, hay, and clover each season. Not only did this increase the number of tilled acres by a third, but the clover fed livestock after it had enriched the soil with its nitrogen deposits. The virtuous circle of growth replaced the vicious circle of decline. When some landlords and farmers responded to the possibility of becoming more productive, they were taking the first permanent steps away from the age-old economy of scarcity.

English farmers copied the Dutch and succeeded in making their agricultural base feed more and more people with fewer laborers and less investment. Unlike the Dutch, the English had enough arable land to grow the grains that fed the people as well as their livestock. The Dutch could not produce what was needed to get their people through a year. With their profits from trade, they could store grain, but this lifesaving program got more and more expensive.

At the beginning of the seventeenth century England contained almost six million people and more than one million horses. The horses could deliver the power of eight to ten men, adding to the wind, water, and coal that English industry could call upon for energy.[10] With many different types of soil, the possibilities of improving fertility varied. Rich but heavy clay soil could be lightened with sea sand and ground seashells if farmers lived near enough to the sea to cart them home. Farmers could dig in marl and limestone. Sandy soils were enriched through planting legumes and clover, which left behind nitrogen, the vital enhancer of all soils. Farmers also began to tether animals in fields for nature's most efficient delivery of manure.

While some English farmers copied the Dutch four-field rotation, others adopted up-and-down husbandry. In this routine, a farmer would crop his best land for three or four years and then put it in pasture for another five, during which time the animal manure and nitrogen-fixing crops would rebuild the fertility necessary for growing grains again. As in the Dutch system, land was no longer left fallow but always growing some crop, whether for animals or humans. Every element on the farm was put to some use; every hand, given new tasks. These innovations made urgent a farmer's attentiveness because of their interlocking qualities. Both the Dutch and English began to flood meadows to warm the soil in winter and extend the growing season. Over the course of the century all these improvements raised the seed to yield ratio, the labor to yield ratio, and the land to yield ratio. Or more simply, they led to bigger harvests from fewer acres, less labor, and fewer seeds.

Doing things differently when the subject is the staff of life took courage, imagination, and careful attention to detail. In the familiar and rather mindless narrative of progress, the assumption is made that all that was required for change was to mix opportunity with the natural human drive for self-improvement. Then people, the account goes, would seize these ingenious ways to bring prosperity to the countryside. This would be true only if traditional farm families and landlords thought like venture capitalists today. They didn't, and many factors kept them from doing so. Novelty frightens those used to following custom. Taking risks could make the difference between having enough to eat or not having enough.

One more factor worked against the adoption of these new techniques: The biorhythms of premodern men and women were not attuned to sustained labor. People were used to suffering from want and many other discomforts but not to exerting themselves for long stretches of time day after day. Human beings do not naturally labor long hours. Raising grain crops the old way required intensive work at planting and harvesting time. In between these seasons there was lots of leisure time. The Christian calendar even encouraged work-free days with dozens and dozens of feast days, almost a hundred a year if Sundays are included. Working hard is a capacity that has to be developed, usually through rigorous, early childhood training. Fear of punishment and tenacious oversight can change habits, but only slowly. It is also clear that some people are more attuned to laboring strenuously for a perceived purpose than others. What became critically important to breaking out of the old agrarian order was making it easier for those who were receptive to exerting themselves in new ways to do so. Being what economists call a rational economic actor didn't make a lot of sense for landlords or tenants when there were so many more customary ways to spend money and risks outpaced rewards.

English Agricultural Improvers

The new wave of improvements moved England beyond the seven-fat-year, seven-lean-year phenomenon. This time, rather than collide with the familiar blocks to permanent change, gains were made secure. Over the next three and a half centuries, the percentage of farmers in northwestern

Europe passed from around 80 percent to some 3 percent of the population. Two groups in England had largely freed themselves from institutional constraints on change. They were freehold farmers and landlords
who had succeeded in replacing low fixed rents with leases reflecting
market prices. These were the probable innovators. The landlords would
have to succeed in finding cooperative tenants since few of them farmed
their own acreage. The amount of land in the hands of the nobility and
gentry varied greatly throughout England, as did the ability of landlords
to coerce their tenants into adopting agricultural reforms. A few nobles
so hated badgering their tenants that they turned to other economic areas
like mining. Together the improving landlords and freeholders probably
came to control about 60 percent of the arable land in England. The king,
landowners whose customary tenants enjoyed fixed rents, landlords who
had no taste for managing their estates, and poor cottagers held the rest of
the arable acreage in the country.

Improving landlords and freeholders could add to their holdings
by buying land that came on the market because of an owner's death
or financial troubles. They could respond quickly to price incentives
because they were well off enough to gamble on change. Their success
with improvements brought them the money to buy more land. The government took a hand in promoting agricultural improvements as well,
granting pensions to experts to publicize utilitarian plants and demonstrating to farmers how to raise them. Manuals on farming went through
successive cheap editions at the same time that literacy was increasing.
Over the long haul the returns on improvement cut down the sense of
risk felt by those watching from the sidelines, removing one of the disincentives to change.

The records don't allow us to know which group—the improving landlords or the improving freeholders—played the stronger role in turning
English agriculture from a largely subsistence, village-based system to a
market-driven regime of private farms. Since the size of the farm had little
influence upon whether or not to adopt the new techniques, we might
turn to the cultural and personal qualities that prompted innovation.
Roman advice books describe the best dung as being the tread of the master's boot. Writers in the seventeenth century repeated that bromide again

and again. If true, this may have given the advantage to the owner farmer over the landlord who had to induce his tenants to learn new skills. Only a very efficient manager could save all animal waste, convert his fields from pasture to tillage, rotate grain crops, grow soil enhancers like clover, flood meadows, and keep his children and servants at their various tasks.

The greatest force working for the adoption of improvements sprang from their conspicuous success in producing larger harvests. Because improvements got results, the trailblazers, few and scattered across the countryside, acted as catalysts for change. Abandoning fallow periods immediately brought more acreage under the plow. When enough people invested their resources in productive improvements, they forced others to imitate them or suffer. Enlarged harvests precipitated a drop in the prices of grains. The improvers could still profit because they had larger yields, but those landlords and farmers who had not enhanced the fertility of their soil or adopted better cropping methods would be wiped out by the persistent decline in prices. Slowly the mechanism of the market built a momentum for improvement.

The countryside's most salient division became that between those who engaged in improvements and those who didn't—whether they were farmers, tenants, or landlords. It was not between landlords and their tenants per se. Nor did self-interest exercise a consistent influence because in times of dramatic change it was difficult to know wherein one's interests lay. The market was hard on those who wanted to stand still; its price dynamic rewarded the provident and improving and punished those resistant to change or out of touch. The future is always unclear, and capitalism's reliance upon individual decisions made it even more difficult to imagine, much less know, what would be the results of cumulative decisions.

These may sound like innocuous statements, but they challenge the Marxist position that the conversion of agriculture from primitive reproduction to enhanced productivity began with farsighted landlords who coerced their tenants into commercial leases with rents set in response to harvest yields that exposed tenants to the competitive forces of the market.[11] In this analysis tenants are assumed to have resisted cooperating with their landlords' improvement plans because they feared becoming dependent on the market and losing the independence that fixed rents gave them. But there is no way that anyone could have predicted the results of initiating improvements or what dependence upon the market would entail. These are retrospective observations. Nor was it possible to imagine that adopting a few experiments in agricultural technology would start a train of unique developments leading to a total restructuring of the economy. Pointing to landlords as the agents of change makes them more prescient and disciplined than they were.[12] There is no evidence that landlords, as a group, initiated the crucial changes in agriculture or that farmers and tenants were loath to embrace them on their own.

I believe that the reverse of the Marxist position is true: that new social relations were the consequence, not the cause, of the transformation of English farming. The changes themselves took place over five or six generations of experimentation and resistance, during which time there would have been a slow, untidy sorting out of the successes and the failures in all strata of the old agrarian order, from cottagers to great lords. Innovations certainly redistributed agricultural income. They delivered profits to those who undertook them and reduced returns to the landlords, farmers, and tenants who did not. This sequence of developments slowly rearranged hundreds of rural communities.

Many a gentry family tumbled from casual indebtedness to forced liquidation of estates. Tenants who did not have secure leases lost their holdings. Bad luck, sickness, or insufficient planning could push them into the ranks of cottagers—those with a house and small garden plot—or, worse, of itinerant laborers. The records indicate that some freeholders prospered even as their numbers grew smaller over the course of the seventeenth century. The most successful moved into the gentry while others lost their independent footing altogether. The market in its own impersonal and seemingly inexorable way increased both rich and poor and changed the array of options for many in the middle.

Priming the Pump of Capitalism

Improved agricultural techniques didn't stop at enhancing harvests; they upended the old agrarian order. Producing for the market, with all of its practical adjustments, replaced a settled way of life, guided by tradition and inherited status. What Marx and his followers got right was the coherence of a new class of owners determined to use its influence and money to secure policies that favored its interests. Ironically, this complicated social rearrangement began to be seen as a natural process. Part of the improving landlords' campaign to free themselves of the old restraints, encapsulated in the laws against engrossing, forestalling, and regrating, was rhetorical. Disputants and pamphleteers began talking about producing for the market as a natural system resistant to political tampering.

Continued, abundant harvests had another intellectual impact. They made it possible for people to feel less threatened by change, less subservient to nature, less inclined to accept authority. We might put it this way: In an emergency our psychological template is different. We're anxious and fearful. We accept the authority of a leader; we do as we are told. Premodern society had always lived with a sense of teetering on the brink of disaster. The fading of that fearfulness made way for more optimistic assessments of the future and more positive estimates of human capacities. Men and women relaxed a bit.

By the middle of the seventeenth century both population and prices had leveled off in England, only to begin a climb again after 1730. The world's population had expanded and contracted over three millennia, but from that eighteenth-century benchmark it has continued to the present. Unlike the old accordion pattern that had characterized previous European population fluctuations, the increase in people this time laid a new basis for future growth with each cohort forming a larger springboard from which world population still soars. Food supplies were to be severely strained from time to time, but instead of shrinking, they expanded to sustain new levels of population. The twenty million Frenchmen Louis XIV ruled in 1700 became the forty million Frenchmen who couldn't be wrong in 1914. English population grew at an even faster clip. And in England's North American colonies—that catch basin of surplus men and women from northwestern Europe—the number of people doubled every twenty-five or so years.

Since officials started keeping systematic records for agricultural output in England only in 1860, the numbers I'm giving here are guesstimates from the account books farmers kept and records from litigation over leases. In 1520, when almost 80 percent of the English population worked the land, 100 families could produce enough food in a regular season to feed 125 families. Those 25 extra families constituted the country's military, clergy, and royal officials as well as retailers, mechanics, merchants, and artisans. From 1600 onward fewer and fewer hands were needed in English farming. In 1800 only 36 percent of adult male laborers were working in agriculture, and those farm families grew the food for their own and 60 other families. This meant a fourfold increase in those who composed the political, clerical, and commercial sectors of society. In the next half century the farming population dropped to 25 percent of the whole. At the same time other countries in Europe would have had between 60 and 80 percent of their men and women still working on the farm while the populations of France, Germany, Italy, Spain, and the Netherlands grew by the same amount.[13] France did not have the market integration in the middle of the nineteenth century that England had achieved by the end of the seventeenth century.

We need to take a last look at the traditional agrarian world in order to understand the outrage that the new agricultural practices elicited. Farming had been organized around villages, most of which contained large common fields with strips of land on which villagers could sow and reap. While each villager farmed his own strip, decisions about when to plant, when to harvest, and when to glean were made collectively. The weak and the irresponsible were knit into the same web of responsibilities with the able and industrious. The countryside was also peopled by cottagers who had one or two acres for growing food and keeping poultry. They got by through working on the farms of others, as did servants on yearly contracts and casual day laborers. By the beginning of the sixteenth century, private farming had pretty much replaced the old open fields, regardless of the law, but the old ideal lingered on as a—well—ideal.

As food prices kept climbing, it grew more and more attractive to consolidate what was left of the communal strips into separate, private farms. Because the government was so heavily invested in preventing food shortages, such enclosures required parliamentary statutes. As the word suggests, enclosures enclosed what had previously been open. During the first half of the sixteenth century, when wool prices were high, some English landlords had turned their arable land into sheep runs. These enclosures cast tenants out of their holdings. They then became the "masterless men" who walked the roads looking for work and food during the Elizabethan period. Although frowned upon and much criticized, these enclosures continued until wool prices fell again. Enclosing to create private farms for grain tillage, which was done mainly in the seventeenth century, had a different social impact. These enclosures actually created jobs and produced more food, so they didn't make government officials anxious. They looked like a better management of cropland, the matrix from which all other economic activities sprang.

The coordinated tilling, weeding, and reaping of the common fields had created patterns of work, play, and ceremony that reinforced the corporate life of the village. Enclosure disentangled each person from this network of community obligations and activities. It permitted individuals to organize their own resources and brought in its train greater disparity between the poor and the prosperous. The awareness of a common fate faded when the principal producers became single families rather than a group of villagers coordinating their round of seasonal tasks.

Unlike many other changes, the consolidation and hedging of once open fields were conspicuous. And they drew commentary. For moralists, community farming was worth maintaining because it taught men and women their duties to one another. But by the mid-seventeenth century advocates of new farm techniques had vigorously challenged this argument. They were impressed by the productivity gains achieved when the farmer had the flexibility to lay down pasture or plant grain, flood meadows, and follow his own crop rotation. The disputants evoked different ideals. Cherishing the poor and cultivating brotherly love were pitted against using one's own wits, foresight, discipline, and intelligence to enhance the bounty of nature.

Two ministers in the 1650s traded pamphlets that explored with great passion these options. The Reverend John Moore started the exchange with a full-throated attack on enclosures: they turned husbandmen into cottagers, undoing them because they could not care for their families on tiny plots. They encouraged indifference to the poor that amounted to not loving Christ. Responding anonymously, the Reverend Joseph Lee agreed that not caring for the poor was a sin, but tenants and freeholds would be better able, after enclosure, to contribute to the relief of the poor. The gain in productivity was the virtue of enclosure. As Lee explained, "the monarch of one acre will make more profit thereof, then he that hath his share in forty in common." While arguing on the basis of advantage, Lee also strongly suggested that people had the right to do what they wanted rather than be shackled to an idea of corporate well-being.[14] Similar battle lines were to be drawn over and over again as contemporaries wrestled with economic practices that had no sanction in the Bible and little connection to community traditions.

Equally concerned with reknitting the old social fabric, the English Poor Laws passed at the end of the sixteenth century reaffirmed society's commitment to feed its members and look to their need for work. It established two overseers of the poor in each parish, the basic unit of local government. Every English man, woman, and child was entitled to relief from his or her birth parish when in need. Parish officials made dead certain that applicants were eligible before giving them any relief. One overseer of the poor encapsulated the gist of the law: "work for those that will Labour, Punishment for those that will not, and Bread for those that cannot."[15] These laws established the community's responsibility either to give outdoor relief or to provide facilities for indoor care. The law grew in importance as more and more people, once settled in villages, became impoverished cottagers or migratory laborers during the long process of change from open fields to enclosed, private farms.

We can get something of a handle on the dimensions of poverty in England because a civil servant named Gregory King compiled a detailed list of his country's social categories at the end of the seventeenth century. He drew up lists that numbered, among others, those who were baronets, shopkeepers, persons in the law, and vagrants.[16] Scholars have pored over and amended King's fascinating enumerations ever since. One startling fact in his summary is that more than half the English had to turn to some form of charity to get through each year. That group had probably been larger a century earlier, when roving bands of beggars and vagabonds alarmed the propertied. Such fears prompted standards for all labor contracts and wrote into law the ideal of a settled population in which each worker had his superior. Employers were bound to keep their wage servants for at least a year and to observe statutory limit in wages.

Improving agriculture had thrown many out of work, but it also enabled more people to survive. Historical demographers happened on to a critical benchmark in English economic history when they reconstructed rising and falling grain prices along with rising and falling births and deaths. They learned that after the terrible harvest failures of 1648–1650, spikes in prices were rarely accompanied by more deaths. Though food costs could skyrocket from time to time, dearth stopped turning into disaster. By 1700 English annual output in agriculture was at least twice that of any other European country and continued so until the 1850s.[17]

Englishmen and women did not know that they had crossed a barrier that divided them from their own past and from every other contemporary society. Yet they had. After the middle of the seventeenth century famine no longer threatened them. Chronic malnutrition lingered on for the bottom 20 percent of European population, not completely disappearing for another century. Agricultural productivity, combined with the purchasing power to bring food from other places in times of shortage, had eliminated one of the Four Horsemen of the Apocalypse from England's shores. A powerful reason for maintaining the strict social order had unobtrusively disappeared, leaving behind a set of social prescriptions whose obsolescence would slowly be discovered. Nothing could have so dramatically distinguished England from the rest of Europe with its last general famine in 1819, not to mention the rest of the world, which still wrestles with failing food supplies.

Despite the dislocations of the Agricultural Revolution, it improved everyone's life chances. Inland trading in foods and other goods became denser. A single national market, the largest, free trading zone in Europe, took shape. This countrywide commercial network created another bulwark against famine because rarely did crop failures hit all regions at the same time. Now there were the connections—transportation, middlemen, and means of payment—to ship food anywhere there was a dearth. If the poor couldn't pay for food, the government did. The formation of a national market reflected more than a good road system. It gave proof of farmers' willingness to ship their harvests outside the local area. They did so, but not always happily. One contemporary lamented, "[W]e had once a kind of Market in every Parish and could utter most of our Commodities at home. We were not then forc'd to carry our Corn God knows where, deal, with God Knows whom, sell for God knows what, to be paid God knows when."[18]

England and the Netherlands were the only European countries to enhance their capacity to feed their people in the first half of the seventeenth century. A half century later they were the first countries to increase population and income at the same time. When we turn to the rest of Europe, we see the enormous difference made by agricultural improvements. In Europe the protracted fighting of the Thirty Years' War and a spate of storms and freezing temperatures wreaked devastation from Russia to Ireland. Agricultural practices in Italy and Spain remained static. Population growth only exacerbated declining agricultural productivity in Germany, Austria, Hungary, and the Balkans.[19] Farther east landlords in Russia and Poland had been able to tie their peasants to the land through a regime of serfdom that removed incentives to improve agricultural routines. Those landlords in the Baltic who had responded to rising food prices by bringing more land into cultivation proved so indifferent to the peasants' welfare that they shipped grains to garner profits in foreign markets at the expense of those starving at home.

In France, where farmers had access to information about Dutch improvements and soil and climate conditions were similar, no such improvement took place for another century. The depopulation of the Black Death had given the French peasantry a firmer hold on their land, but they were subject to numerous legal burdens. When population began to rise in the sixteenth century, the survival of more heirs meant that family plots had to be divided. This morselization of holdings left families struggling to survive on too few acres. France also lacked what England had in abundance, a network of rivers and canals to carry grain shipments. A byzantine maze of feudal privileges overlaid the French countryside. So difficult was the transportation of goods from one region to another that Frenchmen and women in one part of the country could almost starve to death when there was abundant grain in another.

While the French had a strong presence in trade and manufacturing, their agriculture stagnated. The misery of the peasantry only grew as noble landlords and the state siphoned off more and more money from their meager returns. French landlords had little leverage to change the farming techniques of these penurious peasants, but they could and did revive old feudal privileges to extract more money from them as prices rose. The king also exacted higher and higher taxes from the peasantry, even while he was protecting them from aggressive landlords.[20] Not until the French Revolution at the end of the eighteenth century would there be any meaningful reform of the so-called ancien régime.

Traveling across Spain and France in 1787–1789 on the eve of the French Revolution, Arthur Young, an ardent English agricultural improver, reported his astonishment at the neglect of farming in Spain and the poverty in France. Noting that the poor went without shoes in one province, Young put his finger on a problem that still plagues economies. Widespread poverty struck at the root of national prosperity, he noted, because only the poor can consume in numbers sufficient to sustain other trades.[21] The double role of workers had become salient to him. Keeping their incomes low made goods cheaper while at the same time limiting the market for those goods. In both Spain and France, Young criticized the intrusion of government, noting that in France, ancient privileges clogged the circulation of all goods, even grains in time of famine.

Being able to feed more people more cheaply with fewer workers released workers for other occupations and left more money in everyone's pockets for purchasing pottery, utensils, Indian cottons, books, and a range of leather goods from shoes to saddles. When English farmers went from feeding six additional families to meeting the needs of thirty, they underwrote a stunning transformation in productivity. The steady increase of food output also introduced a new measure of certainty in people's lives. After a generation without famines, spenders and investors could shed the caution associated with fear and begin to take a few risks with their savings. There is no direct connection between more effective farming and the ingenious engineering of new machines that ushered in a new age in manufacturing. The Agricultural Revolution could not produce the inventions central to industrialization, but without its bounteous harvests, those inventions would have been confined to that small part of the economy not dedicated to growing food for the whole.

Unlike the earlier quickening pace in commerce, the production of more food with less money and fewer workers released the vital resources of people and capital for a variety of other economic activities, some of them previously unimaginable. Among the welter of revolutions in the early modern centuries, that in agriculture is the one with the most profound consequences. Yet this revolution is often slighted in studies because it was not as conspicuous as the glamorous trade in spices, porcelain, and textiles or the marvelous parade of machines that advertised the "rise of the West" and its industrial might.

Village life stayed the same for those who inherited their parents' places, but their redundant siblings lost those prescribed roles in life. Displaced by irreversible changes, they took to the roads, searching for work in nearby towns, or sought out forests and upland meadows where they might establish themselves as squatters. The commercialization of farming increased the number of men and women who worked for wages. Once uprooted from the traditional agrarian order, they lost their village status and were forced to join a class of workers in a modernizing society where patrons were few and employment was uncertain. Some became part of a migratory, seasonal work force. Many moved to London, a few no doubt catching hold of an opportunity created by a maturing commerce and a developing industry. Others traveled in a constant search for work, their feet following the course of economic expansion.

Henceforth the people of England could be divided between those whom the changes of the century dislodged and those who stayed put. Their experience was the harbinger of what awaited the entire European peasantry in the ensuing decades. Millions of these men and women would cross the Atlantic to establish a European beachhead in North and South America while their sisters and brothers became part of an emerging proletariat. Present-day famines remind us of the complex challenge of feeding a society. They also make us aware of how an agricultural revolution made capitalism possible.

4

---◆---

COMMENTARY
ON MARKETS AND
HUMAN NATURE

THE EAST INDIA COMPANY began importing colorful calicoes and ginghams at the end of the seventeenth century. After spending lifetimes wearing heavy wools and linens, ordinary Englishmen and women reacted with enthusiasm to this opportunity to wear light, bright fabrics. Their response so surprised observers that some of them waxed eloquent on the benefit of material desires. "The Wants of the Mind are infinite, Man naturally Aspires, and as his mind is elevated, his senses grow more refined, and more capable of delight," one wrote, going on to connect these aroused tastes with a tendency to work harder to be able to spend more. An important component of capitalism's triumph over the traditional order came from getting people to change their minds about fundamental values. Their world had been held together by a coherent set of ideas that did a pretty good job of describing the way things worked in a world of scarcity. The distribution of praise and disapproval in songs, sermons, and old sayings kept people in their proper places. Since we learn social prescriptions while we're growing up, we rarely give them much thought later on. Studying how they function is the province of sociologists and psychologists. But in a history of capitalism they cannot be ignored because capitalism relied on people's acting differently: taking risks, endorsing novelty, and innovating. The calico craze epitomized this switch to a new way of being in the world.

Traditional society is structured around statuses, permanent places in the social structure like that of a nobleman or commoner. Social classes came in with capitalism and refer to groups distinguished by their wealth or lack of it and their relation to the economy. The spirit of enterprise ran athwart traditional social norms in conspicuous and profound ways. For instance, in modern society the hope of enjoying a richer life is one of the principal inducements to economic innovation whereas the hierarchy of inherited statuses clogged the path of anyone wishing to rise in society. Statuses were inherited and bore no relation to merit. Being absorbed in making money gave offense to gentlemen who considered such ambitions vulgar. Gentlemen didn't strive; only servants rushed around doing things. Classes congealed around work, those who employed others and those who were employed. In the United States today almost all consider themselves to be in the middle class. Then the middle class, or bourgeoisie, referred to wealthy merchants, doctors, and lawyers who did not do manual labor but were not part of the gentry or nobility either.

Without force, people will change behavior only when they understand why they should and then only slowly. Usually it takes a new generation or two to grow up with the fresh ideas. The major reason that societies change slowly is that novelties must be incorporated into culture forms, and this is the work of expression and discussion. By that I mean that people need to take stock of innovations, assess their impact, search out the meaning for their lives, and determine how other facets of their community will be affected. The proponents of an entrepreneurial economy came up with explanations to facilitate the kinds of social transformations they were pushing for. Those most involved in change speak out first, and then the more articulate members of society weigh in. While this seems obvious when spelled out, few accounts of the emergence of capitalism deal with the absolutely essential task of nurturing values supportive of the new system. It's as though people think that because economies are about material things, only material forces operate in it when in fact economies involve human beings who don't do anything without an idea in their heads.

Before institutions change, advocates and opponents of policies have to thrash out the pros and cons of the alternatives much as the Reverends Lee and Moore did about enclosures. Capitalist values could not be imposed by authority because the genius of the new entrepreneurial economy was individual initiative. These unknown people made the critical choices on their own. The poor could be indirectly coerced through their need for food and shelter, but the system gave even them more latitude in choosing where and how to work. Words like "new," "improved," "profitable," and "interest" acquired cachet at the same time that the evident disruption of old patterns of living and working provoked cries of anguish and anger. Those who enjoyed high status differed on whether to accept reforms or maintain old ways. The power to persuade became a mighty weapon in the ensuing contest of world views.

A New Economic Discourse

During the two centuries in which England's market economy took shape, there was a vibrant press, originally nurtured by the religious and constitutional disputes of the seventeenth century. When evidence of the new wealth-making possibilities became conspicuous, contemporaries began to seek explanations, and they found it easy to publish their ideas about what was happening to the traditional economy. Often they wrote to justify their particular interests as active participants in the market. Some analyzers were "hired pens," pleading the case of the overseas trading companies or of domestic manufacturers. Moralists often wrote to lament the sinful selfishness of individuals who flouted old rules designed to protect the poor. Quite unexpectedly to almost all who watched the marketplace, many—though by no means all—ordinary men and women responded positively to new opportunities. This demonstration of a capacity to think for themselves and act in their own interests surprised their social superiors because it had long been assumed that simple farmers or small-town traders didn't possess the imagination to act outside prescribed routines.

Slowly receding was the world of scarcity, where the country's labor and resources were committed to replacing one year's consumption with another year's production. There was still widespread suffering from wants of many kinds. One respected expert, writing at the end of the seventeenth century, conjectured that half the English population required assistance to get through each year, having to rely on the countrywide tax-supported system of relief.[1] In no way generous, outdoor relief did make it easier for innovating employers to fire or displace workers since local governments had in place ways to provide for those in want.

Soon those watching the novel phenomenon of economic development put into circulation descriptions of how people behaved in their market transactions. They started to depict men and women as having an inherent disposition toward the producing, selling, and buying that drove the market's expansion. These observations, scattered in pamphlets, how-to books, broadsides, and learned tomes, many of them written by such luminaries as John Locke, Isaac Newton, and Daniel Defoe, converged on the universal appeal of making money. The initiatives of ordinary people, such as floating a meadow to gain a head start on spring planting or carrying locally made cheese to a distant market, mattered most. This no longer appeared as peculiar conduct; being responsive in their commercial dealings was treated as a newly discovered human capacity. Even as sober a witness of the human scene as Locke indulged in a futuristic fantasy when he wrote that if everyone worked, the world's work could be done routinely in half a day.[2]

Every piece of advice about exchange rates, wages, rents, and account balances called on new notions about how men and women reacted to choice. Instead of human impulsiveness, these observers of England's pulsating economic rhythms began to describe participants as calculating costs and weighing benefits. After several decades of such observations, a preponderance of commentators came to believe that there was a uniform response from market bargainers. People could be counted on because they counted their interests. By the mid-eighteenth century Samuel Johnson could casually comment that "there are few ways in which a man can be more innocently employed than in getting money."[3] A decisive cultural shift had clicked into place.

At the end of the eighteenth century, the intellectual effort to understand the phenomenon of capitalism found its Aristotle in Adam Smith, whose *An Inquiry into the Nature and Causes of the Wealth of Nations* appeared in 1776. Smith presented a brilliantly detailed explanation of the causes of the unparalleled wealth in Great Britain. (After the Scottish and English crowns were joined in 1706, England was called Great Britain or the United Kingdom.) Building on the new conception of human beings as responsibly pursuing their own interest, he advocated a system of "natural liberty" because he thought that the "invisible hand" of the market would function better if left free of most regulation.

With few opportunities to choose among options, men and women had appeared as fickle, impulsive, and given over to their passions. From the Christian point of view, they were also bathed in sin. With such a picture of human nature, it would have been a form of madness to leave them free to do as they wished with their resources. The new truths about how people behaved in their market transactions underpinned Smith's recommendations. Smith himself seemed unaware that his immediate predecessors had dramatically upgraded human nature while observing the new market economy. The ideas had been around long enough for him to take them for granted. More significantly, these new assertions had acquired the status of universal truths, something Edmund Burke affirmed when he wrote Smith that "a theory like yours founded on the nature of man, which is always the same will last, when those that are founded on his opinions, which are always changing, will and must be forgotten."[4] What a seductive idea: an invariant human nature.

In England all this was played out in the public arena, where pamphlets were written, speeches reported, and disputes advertised with a significant proportion of the population attentive. The country had become highly homogenous during the course of the seventeenth century. It had one monarch, one language, one established church, a single legal system, and a vigorous press. As local farmers and artisans had moved in ever-wider circles, a national market emerged. London itself best expressed England's unity. With more than half a million inhabitants in 1690, it was Europe's largest city and still growing rapidly. Some 10 percent of the five million English people lived in London.

The pattern of London's growth contains some fascinating features. With a high mortality rate, it required at least eight thousand outsiders moving in annually to sustain its growth. Since mobility was highest among the unmarried, we can presume that most of the men and women who came from other towns, villages, and hamlets were young. This churning through England's metropolitan center had a countrywide effect. One scholar has calculated that more than one-sixth of the English had lived in London sometime in their lives. Coming into contact with London—the seat of government, matrix of enterprise, and center of public sociability—spread ideas, cultivated tastes, and stimulated wants.[5]

The debate over economic change might have remained an elite affair had not the Civil War with its ferocious battles over religion widened the catch basin of readers and discussants. The religious dissensions of the sixteenth and seventeenth centuries had spawned a large and diverse group of writers. The English were getting used to public discord. Like other European societies, a censorship system was in place, but unlike them, it was rarely enforced. Economic tracts were not particularly censorable anyway. What was important was the existence of many writers and even more readers accustomed to getting involved in public discussions. The settlement of the seventeenth-century political discord gave England a constitutional monarchy. All English persons received important guarantees for their person and property in the pathbreaking Bill of Rights of 1689. The licensing law through which publications could be censored was allowed to lapse, and the Bank of England was founded. The first promoted the circulation of ideas, and the second the circulation of money, both lubricants of innovation. Equally important, a new upper class with a mainly progressive attitude toward economic development solidified its power.

England came out of its "century of revolution" with significant economic and political gains. The century began with a king who believed he had a "divine right" to rule and ended with a constitutional arrangement that placed sovereignty in the balanced power of king and Parliament.

Although the upper class longed for stability, it could not suppress the strong antiauthoritarian strand that now entered popular culture. Awe of authority had greatly diminished during the past three generations. Just think of this remarkable set of novelties: a king who got his crown only by giving his subjects a bill of rights, an aristocracy whose members showed a decided interest in commerce, entrepreneurs who expanded the realm of enterprise, young people who moved about the country with ease, and a capital that vibrated with contentious conviviality. Reviewing this is not to praise the English, but to point out the social environment necessary to enable capitalists to push aside a venerable social order.

The novelty of all these novelties tested people's capacity to understand the invisible force in their lives. References to the spirited debates about commerce and money in England appear only obliquely in most studies of capitalism. For instance, in comparisons of China and England, scholars rarely give any attention to the public discussions that economic change provoked in seventeenth-century England. The Netherlands fostered freedom of expression and actually printed more books than the English, but Dutch publications on economic topics were rare and usually issued by the government. Elsewhere in Europe vigorous censorship stifled the emergence of a reading and talking public. Everywhere there was fear of disorder.

The hustle and bustle of profit-directed enterprise were not congruent with the aristocratic emphasis on taste and leisure, what Edmund Burke called "the unbought grace of life." The aristocratic ethic that dominated European societies—indeed societies all over the globe—looked unkindly on unmannerly striving. Napoleon Bonaparte was not complimenting England in the early nineteenth century when he called it "a nation of shopkeepers." It took persuasive advocates to make capitalism accept-able, even tolerable. Only in England did entrepreneurial advocates make their case persistently and publicly. The intensification of trade triggered a public discussion that led to fresh ways to imagine the economy. The effects of these English debates about the economy were intellectual and moral. They had to do with comprehension and analysis, critiques, and arguments, but they forced the disputants and their audience to rethink fundamental values.

Self-interest drove most authors to take up their pens. Changes in economic life had unsettled lots of people. Those who lost out were quick to complain about the innovations while the successful innovators wrote to point out why the novelties were good for the country. Tracts written by manufacturers coalesced around prescriptions for disciplining employees. Trading companies—particularly the English East India Company—hired writers to defend practices that went against conventional wisdom, like exporting bullion. Agricultural reformers published advice books. Interlopers in established trades urged the liberation of economic endeavor in their pamphlets. A few statesmen entered the fray to provide a bigger picture of what was going on. This serious and sustained examination of private enterprise led to a reconceptualization of economic matters. Such factors are too elusive to be quantified, but they were absolutely crucial to whether or not English institutions adjusted peacefully to the dynamics of capitalism. In pitting the private against the public and the personal against the moral, economic writers had to create a new ethic.

Assessing Employers' Responsibility to Their Workers

In 1994 the World Bank held its annual meeting in Madrid. Spain's most popular radio personality, Iñaki Gabilondo, in a rather perverse gesture, sent a reporter out to find out what the men and women waiting outside a church for a free Christmas dinner thought of the gathering of financiers in their city. They greeted the interviewer's introductory question with derisive laughter. When he convinced them of the seriousness of his interest in their views, these recipients of free food eagerly ventured their opinions about the country's economic needs. Not surprisingly, the consensus was that companies should spend some of their profits to provide jobs for those, like them, who were down on their luck. And if they didn't do so voluntarily, the government should step in to give a hand to those who relied upon the business plans of the wealthy for their daily bread.[6]

Without realizing it, these Spanish mendicants put their finger on one of the oldest controversies in the history of capitalism: whether employers bore any responsibility toward their employees when they could no longer profit from their labor. Should they be able to dismiss them, like "fair-weather friends," when demand for the things that they produced had collapsed. In one form or another—think outsourcing today—this question has continued to pop up as economic initiatives first challenged, then rendered obsolete laws designed to make employers the protectors of their workers. For monarchs, the problem was particularly acute, for kings looked upon all their subjects as arrayed in a hierarchy of dependency in a commonwealth entrusted to them.

The issue got sustained attention in the 1620s, when English clothiers suffered from the effects of a glut of cloth in Europe. The expansion of English woolen exports in the previous decades had created employment for an increasing number of families. They represented a new category of workers whose jobs arose from international trade. The impulse of the clothiers was to stop making cloth until the market turned up again. This appalled contemporaries. People were used to dire consequences from bad weather, but the distress caused by market downturns seemed different, even if the suffering was the same. What could be tolerated from nature appeared intolerable as an employer's choice. From the standpoint of those officials charged with keeping order, the employers' antisocial response undermined the well-off's moral obligation to care for the sick, the weak, and the poor. The clothiers, wishing to conserve their capital, argued that retrenching for the present was the wisest course of action. If they spent it charitably now, there would be no stock to invest when the market turned up. At first the royal government responded positively to the poor's demand for protection, committed as it was to the subordination of private concerns to the well-being of the whole.

The issue didn't go away. A downturn in trade in the early seventeenth century stirred debate anew and led to a different outcome. This time the trade glut coincided with coin shortages and erratic exchange rates that plunged the country into a depression. Things got so bad that the king appointed a committee of merchants to study the situation. Its reports were subsequently published. The extent of the decay of trade discouraged the normal search for local bogeys or simple causes. Quite unexpectedly, the English government declined to restrain the clothiers. This was the most enduring consequence of this debate; henceforth the king and his advisers ceased thinking of turning back to a more contained economy in order to prevent the social disruptions that the ups and downs of international commerce caused.[7]

Out of the debate came a brilliant piece of economic reasoning from Thomas Mun, a major figure in the English East India Company. Mun broke free from thinking about the economy as a system directed by political rulers for social purposes. He argued persuasively that nothing the English authorities could do would bring back prosperity because buying and selling or sending coin abroad followed the transactions of private traders, not government fiat. Mun produced a model of trade as a coherent system of impersonal and largely autonomous interactions. England would get more specie solely if it sold more than it bought, he said. With a lovely flourish, he drove home his point: "Let the mere exchanger do his worst; let princes oppress, lawyers extort, usurers bite, prodigals waste . . . so much treasure only will be brought in or carried out of a commonwealth, as the foreign trade does over or under balance in value." And then he picked up his pen to add a bold assertion: "And this must come to pass by a necessity beyond all resistance."[8] We're used to believing in inexorable economic laws, but in 1621, when Mun wrote this, he was proclaiming that the economy was not under the control of the sovereign and hence not amenable to social demands.

Mun's writings contributed to the popularity of the balance of trade theory, the so-called mercantilist idea that a country's wealth came from being a better seller than a buyer. Actually Mun was making the more important point that money passively followed the exchange of goods through the circuitous channels laid out by the settling of trade accounts in international commerce. He didn't aim to explain the benefits of a favorable balance of trade but rather to scotch the paternalistic notion that a depression could be cured by official regulations of exchange rates. The mercantilist goal of achieving a favorable balance of trade, advanced by a variety of commentators, continued to dog economic discussions, even though its basic fallacies were exposed repeatedly. Primarily a political response, the obsession with England's balancing its trade—i.e., not buying any more than it sold—was cultivated by those who benefited from controlling domestic consumption.

The East India Company throve on spending at home and pushed for higher wages to enhance purchasing power. Manufacturers were concerned with exporting and wanted to keep wages down to keep their prices of goods low and competitive. The central mercantilist assumption was that the wealth of the world was a zero-sum pie. National enrichment came from getting a larger piece of the pie. Mercantilists also continued to give money a privileged place despite the obvious interchangeability of money and goods. Some form of mercantilist thinking always crept back into public discussion in times of national insecurity and economic instability and continues to do so.

Breaching the wall of paternalism in the 1620s with a ramrod of economic realism marked a significant moment in the history of capitalism. It indicated that men of commerce could persuade their social superiors—the aristocrats who sat on the king's Privy Council—of the wisdom of their recommendations. The advisers and pamphleteers had created a public arena for discussing economic relations. Had we not the examples of Spain and Portugal, we might not stress the significance of this cooperation between entrepreneurs and members of the landed elite. The Spanish king and his noblemen had run roughshod over merchants and artisans whenever they challenged aristocratic privileges. It represents another critical difference between England and continental Europe.

Mun was a contemporary of the famous philosopher Francis Bacon, often credited with moving seventeenth-century English natural philosophy toward the science of observation and analysis. Bacon was a great believer in facts as a master teacher. Study nature, he advised his contemporaries. Test your ideas, and you will learn because nature fights back. Bacon's bête noire was opinion—what today we might call ideology—because opinion promoted only heated conversations, never truth seeking. Empiricism gained a greater and greater hold on European imaginations, starting with Galileo's idea about the cosmos on to Robert Boyle's work on gases and Newton's on gravity. Speculation about unknowable and imponderable subjects began to wither. These philosophical advances strengthened an interest in developing testable hypotheses about the economy.

Discussions of Usury

On a more practical level, getting capital into the hands of people who knew how to invest it presented a major challenge to the promoters of economic development. Lending money for repayment with interest contravened the biblical injunction against usury. A deeply rooted religious rationale impeded the free use of one's money. Critics of commercial expansion drew heavily on the social vision embedded in the Old Testament in which money was considered sterile and could not be lent with the view of earning a return. For Jews the laws of the Pentateuch clearly evoked the goal of a Hebrew brotherhood.

The famous verses on usury in Deuteronomy explicitly denied legitimacy to the extension of credit for profit: "Thou shalt not lend upon usury to thy brother; usury of money, usury of victuals, usury of any thing that is lent upon usury: Unto a stranger thou mayest lend upon usury; but unto thy brother thou shalt not lend upon usury. . . ." The Deuteronomic injunction against usury was part of a moral code that sharply distinguished between acceptable behavior toward the members of one's community and toward outsiders. Unable to criticize commercial transactions that were hidden from public scrutiny, opponents clung tenaciously to the tie of charity binding rich to poor. They frequently quoted biblical assertions that men were properly one another's brothers.

The Catholic Church maintained that Christ's coming had erased the distinction between brother and other, going, as one author has described it, "from tribal brotherhood to universal otherhood."[9] Still, the laws of the Hebrew brotherhood became a part of canonical law, representing the church's stand against an unrestricted commercial economy. As in any simple prohibition, enforcement depended upon the unambiguous nature of the crime; commercial developments in the heart of Catholic Europe in the fourteenth and fifteenth centuries had eroded many of the distinctions that separated usurious from nonusurious practices. The imaginative evasions of merchants and the casuistry employed by clerical apologists had made a simple ban against charging interest difficult to enforce.[10]

Protestant theologians, from Luther to Calvin, moved away from a policy of enforcing Hebrew law as positive civil laws, preferring to rely on the promptings of Christian consciences. Usury was not to be condemned in all cases. Rather charity and the Golden Rule were to guide Christians. English lawmakers vacillated. In 1488 an antiusury statute proclaimed that all usury was to be extirpated and that anyone lending money at interest should forfeit one-half of the principal sum involved. Statutes during the subsequent reigns of Henry VIII and Elizabeth established a 10 percent ceiling, which was dropped to 8 percent in James's reign. In 1652 the maximum allowable rate was reduced to 6 percent, where it stayed for the rest of the century. By contrast, in the Muslim world, all forms of taking interest remained sinful, leading to numerous evasions. An unintended consequence of accepting usury was the transparency introduced into bookkeeping, once there was less to hide.[11]

Moralists made usury a symbol of all that was distasteful in the commercial world, where private gain was sought, treasure tolled, hard bargains were struck, and unlucky competitors ill used. Social and religious conservatives found in the usury issue the means to expose the dangers of a market economy. Not only was the rational pursuit of profit thus against the law of charity, but it flouted Providentialism by its implicit reliance upon self. There was a fundamental incompatibility of religion and the profit–oriented commercial activities, they asserted. In the seventeenth century, when the influence of the market became more pervasive, the issue of usury continued to draw fire from those totally antagonistic to the self-centered, calculating spirit of the entrepreneur, be he merchant, landlord, farmer, or manufacturer. Where much of the fifteenth- and sixteenth-century literature on usury had centered on the fact that money could not earn more money, economic changes weakened that line of attack. Money, as capital, had proved to be very fruitful. The enhanced productivity that followed investments in agriculture and industry justified the taking of interest to many, but this required a new line of argument.

In all this public discussion, a model of the market system, for which the Dutch provided a stimulus, was taking shape. Envy and wonder stimulated English observers to try to figure out how they might imitate the phenomenal success of the Netherlands. During the seventeenth century the Dutch extracted tons of herring from waters that washed on English shores, had the largest merchant fleet in Europe, drew into their banks

Spanish gold, borrowed at the lowest interest rate, and bested all comers in the commerce of the Baltic, the Mediterranean, and the West Indies. Dutch prosperity, like Dutch land, seemed to have been created out of nothing. The inevitable contrast with Spain, the possessor of gold and silver mines now teetering on the verge of bankruptcy, only underscored the conundrum of Dutch success.

The Netherlands represented a kind of anti–fairy tale. The rags-to-riches heroes of medieval folklore invariably found pots of gold or earned fortunes through acts of valor. Elfin magicians, fairy godmothers, and subdued giants were the bestowers of great wealth. Spanish exploits in the New World had been entirely in keeping with this legendary tradition. The conquistadors had won the fabled mines of the Incas and Aztecs with their military prowess. Even the less glamorous triumphs of the Portuguese conformed to the "treasure" image of getting wealthy. Venturing into uncharted oceans, they had bravely blazed a water trail to the riches of the Orient.

The Dutch, on the other hand, had made their money in a most mundane fashion. No aura of gold and silver, perfumed woods, rare stones, aromatic spices, or luxurious fabrics attended their initial successes. Instead their broad-bottomed flyboats plied the waters of the North Sea in an endless circulation of European staples. From this inglorious foundation the industrious people of the Low Countries had turned their cities into the emporiums of the world. The Dutch were the ones to emulate, but to emulate was not easy, for the market economy was not a single thing but a complicated mix of human activities that seemed to sustain itself.

The first step in economic reasoning was the isolation of key variables like value, profit, and various rates from the social activities in which they were enmeshed. This step in analysis is the most difficult because it requires that we not be distracted by the lively details of the actual. In addition, seventeenth-century men and women were used to thinking of a social whole like the king and his kingdom, not of the parts that interacted within it. The Dutch can be credited with pushing English thinkers toward analysis.

Goaded by a curious mixture of jealousy and admiration, English commentators from the first to the last decade of the seventeenth century took their questions about the market to the Dutch example. It provided a means of observing the buying, selling, producing, lending, and exchanging of goods, independent of personal and political considerations that had often veiled the purely economic aspect of these acts. Sometimes just pointing to the Dutch could overturn a policy. When Parliament revoked penalties for the export of foreign coin in 1663—a restriction that had reflected the mercantilist goal of increasing the country's bullion—the fact that the Dutch allowed specie to move freely in and out of the country without harm alone convinced the members of Parliament.

Dutch accomplishments inspired some Englishmen with a zeal for the right ordering of trade, while they prompted those with a more speculative bent to search for the secret spring of the new market economy. Analyzing the Dutch economy encouraged the creation of an abstract model of the market and hastened an appreciation of the unseen forces at work in it. With the widening of the market, uniform and known prices replaced the face-to-face bargaining of the local market. Like gravity (which Newton was to explain in 1687), aggregate demand represented power exercised from a distance, motion through a void. As the ultimate consumers moved farther and farther away from the producer, the steps linking production and consumption became more obscure and more in need of clarification. The predominance of foreign trade in the Dutch economy made these links accessible for investigation.

In the Dutch example there were challenging contradictions between appearances and reality with puzzling divergences between expectations based upon established truths and what actually happened. Without mines, how did the Dutch come to have plenty of coin? With few natural resources for export, how could the Dutch engross the production of other countries? How did the Dutch have low interest rates and high land values? How were high wages maintained with a burgeoning population? How could high prices and widespread prosperity exist simultaneously in the Low Countries? Throughout the middle decades of the seventeenth century the Dutch were formidable rivals to English merchants and sources of raw data of incalculable value.

By the end of the period key assumptions about market relations had entered the public discourse in a way that decisively influenced all subsequent social thought. The discrete facts of buying and paying, employing and earning, producing and selling were woven into a single economic paradigm susceptible to sustained inquiry, challenge, and adjustment. Central to the efforts to analyze market relations was the conviction that there existed a determinable order. But this was not a political order to be presided over by a ruler; rather it was an ordering from the consistent behavior of men and women in their market transactions.

In denying the power of the sovereign to control commerce, analysts did not suggest that individual market decisions were random or idio-syncratic. Instead they searched for the relevant cause-and-effect rela-tionships, assuming a uniformity operating at all levels. This in turn led to the conviction that anarchy was not the inevitable alternative to external control. Gone from discussion was the old description of the impulsive nature of human beings found in literature, replaced by a description of market participants as self-interested, calculating, and rational. Old words were given new meaning. If you were to look up words like "career," "indi-vidual," "expertise," "interest," and "manager" in the *Oxford English Dic-tionary*, which records changes in meanings over the centuries, you would find that "career" referred to horse races well into the nineteenth century and that "individual" was not applied to persons until the seventeenth century.

Members of the East India companies entered the list of disputants in order to defend their practice of exporting specie, which continued to be suspect as long as people considered a store of bullion the only form of wealth. The company offered a stellar example of how to make money in defiance of convention. Only piracy was more profitable than its first voy-ages, which returned a 200 percent profit. Then the company settled down to annual payments of more than 20 percent for the next century. Because its customers in the Orient didn't want much that Europeans had to sell, company ships took out coin to pay for their purchases.

Demystifying money had been one of the intellectual goals of Thomas Mun's pamphlets, but it wasn't an easy job, for it went against a powerful hoarding instinct. It flouted the widely held belief that the whole point of foreign trade was to amass bullion. How could England benefit from reducing its stock of gold and silver? Since domestic consumption took from the store of English capital, how could it be healthy for the kingdom? Better to sell English goods to foreigners and take in their gold. In the regime of scarcity that had long prevailed, this made sense. Given traditional consumption patterns, it probably was better to hoard than to spend. The nobility and gentry were extravagant, and the poor spent just to keep body and soul together. Neither contributed to the kingdom's wealth. But with new consumers buying new goods, wealth could be created at home. Money and goods were fungible. Sometimes people wanted money, and sometimes products. Societies were no different.

The balance of trade explanation of how nations grow wealthy had highlighted production and left in the shadows the role of consumption. Its verities were challenged when the maverick spirit of fashion revealed its power to change behavior. The English East India Company set off a nationwide craze for printed calicoes when it began bringing in cheap Indian cottons. By 1690 the taste for chintz, calico, and muslin had reached epidemic proportions. What began as an inconspicuous use of cotton for suit linings gave way to a craze for printed draperies, bedspreads, tapestries, shirts, and dresses.[12] The names of the new fabrics betray their origins: "Calico" is a city in India; "chintz" is Hindu for "variegated"; "seersucker" comes from the Persian word for "striped"; and "gingham" is Malayan for "striped." After generations of confinement in wool and linen clothing, the English public went wild for the new colors, designs, and textures. Even more important, delight in the new fabrics slid quickly down the social ladder, placing workingmen and women in a new light as consumers. But therein lay the rub. If people bought cottons, they would scale back on their purchases of wool and linen, the mainstays of the English cloth industry. The East India Company dispatched English artisans to show Indian textile makers how to design patterns to English tastes, while the clothiers worked at home with some success to get the government to ban the import of most Indian fabrics.

It was evident to all eyes that the colorful Indian fabrics adorned the bodies of servant girls as well as their mistresses. Under the sway of new consuming tastes, people spent more and somehow found the means to do so. Suddenly the commercial importance of the domestic market hove into sight. The elasticity of demand, as the economists would say, became apparent. Emulation, love of luxury, vanity, or just a taste for beautiful things began to look like positive human drives—at least for the economy—because they got people to work more so that they could spend more. Considering the susceptibility of young people to trends and their bulging numbers in London, their consumption pushed in new directions that would fully flower with industrialization.[13] It was exactly this spectacular display of new consuming tastes that had triggered a positive discussion of the role of consumption in economic development. In retaliation, the clothiers did not hesitate to evoke the old balance of trade theory with its zero-sum pie assumption about world wealth and its "beggar thy neighbor" policy prescriptions. They stressed the difference between individual consumers' preferences and the good of the whole economy.

One effusive observer of the new taste in Indian cottons dwelt on the fact that man's "wants increase with his wishes, which is for everything that is rare, can gratify his senses, adorn his body, and promise the ease, pleasure, and pomp of life." Another pamphleteer, taking issue with those who lamented the popularity of imported luxuries like East Indian calicoes maintained that they were not the source of sin but rather "true Spurs to Virtue, Valour and the Elevation of the mind, as well as the just rewards of Industry."[14] Biblical injunctions against the love of luxury were being overlaid with a secular enthusiasm for economic development.

Defenders of the East India Company came to the fore with explanations of why domestic consumption benefited the nation in contradiction to mercantilist ideas about saving at home and selling abroad. "The main spur to trade [English writers like metaphors about horseback riding], or rather to Industry and ingenuity, is the exorbitant appetite of men, which they will take pain to gratify, and so be disposed to work, when nothing else will incline them to it, for did men content themselves with bare necessaries, we should have a poor world."[15] The advocates of free enterprise were in the vanguard when they circulated these opinions. Undergirding them was the dawning realization that entrepreneurs could make money from laborers if they could change their habits and get them to earn more by working more regularly. This kind of optimism went against the grain of conventional upper-class ideas about ordinary people and their bad habits. Countering these assumptions was very much in the interest of the East India Company, which exported bullion and imported goods for domestic consumption.

Enthusiasm for spending may sound like an anticipation of Madison Avenue rhetoric, but it was a message carrying a potent association of desire and discipline. When men and women wanted something enough, they would work harder to get it. This notion led some writers to the conclusion that if wages were higher, then the poor could spend more on clothes and furnishings and thereby increase the consumption of the very goods that they manufactured. These observations suggested that consumption might actually fuel economic development, a truly radical idea for the time. Members of the elite had looked down on the poor for too long not to resist these assertions about their newly discovered capacity to stimulate the economy. After all, thinking that ordinary men and women were wayward, idle, and crude had long justified the social control of the lower classes by their social superiors.

In fact Englishmen and women earned much higher wages in 1700 than laborers in the rest of Europe and around the world. They also ate better. A study of the average caloric intake of eighteenth century Europeans showed that England alone was able to feed 80 percent of its people enough food so that they could put in a full working day.[16] Contemporaries were not inaccurate when they described an urban scene of well-fed people, bulging shopwindows, and bustling workaday comings and goings. England had a large and growing working class capable of buying the new crockery, calicoes, cutlery, and cheap printed pictures now available to them. This large body of domestic consumers fueled England's commercial expansion and a richly elaborated material culture dependent upon the market.

Ordinary men had created the infrastructure for a national market. Overseas trade linked this internal commerce to an expanding world trade. New attachments to objects, a raging delight in novelties, and the pleasures of urban sociability bespoke a deep engagement with the material world that made spending seem more beneficial to the economy than did parsimony. Average wages had gone up because men and women were moving out of low-paid farm work. They were also working more hours a week, evidence of demand for their labor. The number of feast days celebrated as holidays dropped considerably, while the old favorite of workingmen, the irreverently named St. Monday devoted to sobering up from weekend drinking, yielded to the desire for higher wages.[17] During the eighteenth century the average number of workdays moved from 250 to 300.

The popularity of cheap-priced cottons alarmed woolen manufacturers, who used the balance of trade theory to explain what was wrong with spending good English coin on fancy Indian chintzes. They had long banked on the depiction of the economy as a kind of giant joint-stock trading company that worked cooperatively to lay up a hoard of bullion. When the conflict of interests between manufacturers and merchants came out in the open, the quality of analysis improved. A slew of pamphleteers mocked the stupidity of mercantilist notions. Defenders of the East India Company pointed out that any law that restricted the English to purchasing domestic goods would force them to pay more than necessary for their needs. Consumers' having rights was a totally novel idea, at odds with conventional wisdom. Soon some reconceived the economy as an aggregation of self-interested men and women who were both producers and consumers. Commonplace to us, these comments were extremely radical because they undermined the aristocratic conviction that there was an enormous, unbridgeable chasm between ordinary people and themselves.

The idea of men and women as consuming animals with boundless appetites capable of driving the economy to new levels of prosperity excited the imagination of dozens of writers, but they were entrepreneurs, not moralists. The proposition that the wealth of nations began with stimulating wants rather than with organizing production robbed intrusive social legislation of a supporting rationale. Once advocacy of freeing trade became attached to a new explanation of economic growth, the earlier commercial wisdom of carefully managing trade to ensure high prices came under challenge, a century before Adam Smith's explanation of why freedom was better than control in matters economic.

Popular responses to fashion revealed that some demand was elastic. If demand was elastic, then growth and prosperity required attention to people's tastes and desires. Even the wastrel was saluted as a benefactor to society, for if he personally went bankrupt, his spending helped others, as could not be said about the miser. Going behind the new tastes, writers began to explore the human motives regulating personal spending and discovered a human dynamic and a market mechanism that undermined the static, bullion-oriented mercantilist view. The promoters of free trade wrote rhapsodically about the pleasures of shopping with a "the more the merrier" inclusiveness. But it must be noted that unlike the impulsive creatures who peopled Shakespeare's plays, the new English consumers had to discipline themselves to hard work before they could enjoy their fancies. Then appeals to desire would replace the need for restraint and vigilance. In just these many ways did capitalism bore away at an age-old social ethic.

In the eighteenth century writers began talking about human nature, a term that had recently been coined. "Everyone from the peasant to king is a merchant," said one commentator. This was social promotion rather than social leveling, for evidence of new spending habits gave the laboring class a boost toward importance, long denied them. Society was used to rewarding people according to merit and inherited status. Accepting, even admiring the market's rewards meant going along with an impersonal system that operated through the collective actions of egocentric participants. It would take a long time before the old belief in natural inequality yielded to a commitment to equality, but the first steps were being taken at the end of the seventeenth century.

A Crisis in English Currency

Another breakthrough in English thinking about economics came in a crisis over money. Of all the novel elements in the new world of enterprise and exchange, none caused more headaches than money. A lot of diverse meanings crowd into that word. Money had always been a store of wealth, but now it had become the lubricator of distant market exchanges. Money was also cash, the means of instant gratification. And money was—well—money—that is, gold and silver minted into legal tender with the imprimatur of a monarch's guarantee of amount and purity.

Thinking about money can cause vertigo. For instance, it's confusing to keep in mind that gold and silver had a value that differed from the value of gold and silver after it had been turned into coin. In England the mint ratio—that is, the face value or denomination of a certain quantity of silver—was too low. Silver in coins was undervalued. This created an incentive to melt them down and export the silver to Europe to receive a higher price as bullion. Exporting English coin was illegal, but it was widely recognized as a common, if felonious, practice. This created a shortage of coin. It came at a bad time, for the government was at war with France and needed to send regular shipments of money to the Continent to pay soldiers' wages and buy supplies for England's allies.

The enhanced value of silver abroad promoted a further fraud. Some scofflaws discovered that they could clip off the edges of their hammered silver shillings, melt down the clippings, and send the silver abroad to sell while passing off the shillings to others. Strangely, clipped coins circulated as easily as shillings as unclipped ones, which made little sense. As the gravity of the shortage became more severe, attention focused upon the money mechanism itself. How was this slippery medium of exchange to be corralled if it wasn't understood in the first place?

In 1695 the king's ministers addressed the twin problems of the shortage of coin and the battered condition of the remaining silver shillings. They sought the advice of the treasury secretary, who composed a report that was a model of monetary analysis. As long as bullion was worth more by weight than coin, silver in bulk would never be brought to the mint for coining, he told them. It would be like bringing a one-pound chicken to a store to be turned into a halfpound package of chicken parts. Rather the opposite would take place: Coin would be melted down and shipped out as bullion, illegalities notwithstanding. The problem of the clipped coins presented a different problem. After decades of clipping, the coins themselves contained a lot less silver than they were supposed to have. A new milling process could give the coins fluted, unclippable edges, so the treasury secretary recommended reminting all the silver coinage circulating in England with 25 percent less silver, which would mirror the actual value of most shillings in circulation at the time.

The crisis over money brought to the fore two surprising facts: The exchange value of money did not depend wholly upon its silver content, and the exchange value of silver differed according to its form—that is, whether it was coin or bullion. Discussions about the money mechanism usually lead to glazed-over eyes, so I'll move quickly beyond mint ratios and official denominations to the political battle that the coin shortage precipitated. Noble and gentry landlords still had a big say within the ruling class of England, and they wanted to avoid a devaluation of the currency. New coins with a lower silver content would lead to some inflation, a boon to their rent-paying tenants but not to themselves. Realizing this, they sought more advice about a recoinage.

They turned to the great philosopher John Locke, who took an interest in economic subjects, especially when they touched upon political matters. Locke rejected the treasury secretary's reasoning and insisted that silver had a natural value that lawmakers and kings were unable to change. There was only one source of value in coin, he said, and that was its silver content. Any change of denomination would be a fruitless fraud. Shillings were but silver in another guise. Coins had only their intrinsic silver value; the monarch could not create an extrinsic value by turning it into a coin. He was wrong, but confident, as only a philosopher can be.

Those familiar with Locke's political philosophy will realize that Locke had a great deal at stake in this debate. In his explanation of how people formed governments, he had asserted that the use of money arose in the state of nature. Because people gave an imaginary value to gold and silver, it became useful as a store of value. This meant that property had been created before government, a key point in his argument for limiting its power. Money, the essential mechanism for commerce, arose naturally and was not dependent upon anyone's authority. Silver coins couldn't be more or less valuable than silver bullion because the ruler didn't have the power to enhance the value of a natural thing. In creating government, people had acted to protect their life, liberty, and property, and they chose government as a convenient means to do that. Locke gave the English a naturalistic theory of political obligations wrapped around an inaccurate description of the money mechanism.

More than three hundred pamphleteers, including Isaac Newton and Daniel Defoe, entered the ensuing debate over the proposed recoinage. The issue was whether or not the clipped coins should be reminted with the official silver content or lowered to match the devaluation by chisel.

Sharply divided, the antagonists carried the conceptualization of money to a new level of sophistication. Locke's opponents—for the most part merchants and entrepreneurs—started with the facts on the ground, as it were. Coining silver added value, as was evident when people accepted clipped coins as easily as they pocketed unclipped ones. The monarch under whose authority the coins were issued *had* added extrinsic value to the intrinsic value of silver by turning it into legal tender.

Practical rather than philosophical, many of these writers broke free of Locke's dogmatic position. They accepted the definition of money as a medium of exchange, separable from precious metals. Reversing Locke's cause and effect explanation for the rise of money, they said that the utility of having a medium of exchange prompted the use of gold and silver, not an imagined value making gold and silver useful as currency. Money was valued because it was useful, not because men in the state of nature had given it an imaginary value. One writer mocked Locke for pretending "that the Government had no more power in Politicks than they have in Naturals."[18] He hit the nail on the head; Locke was saying that government could no more affect the value of money than it could halt rainstorms. But Locke was far from the last theorist to claim that economic relations were natural rather than political.

Drawing more polemical conclusions, other critics pointed out that Locke "extends his care to creditors and landlords, not regarding the cases of tenants or debtors; men for this four or five years last past, have borrowed many thousand pounds in clipped money, but he notes no unreasonableness or injustice in compelling them to pay such debts again in heavy money, perhaps of twice the weight."[19] Such a clear statement of the interests involved in the case called attention to the differing impact of deflation upon those with money and their dependents. Expressed so publicly, this charge threatened to undermine the perception of the king's advisers as reasoning impartially for the good of the whole.

Locke had the worst argument in this controversy but the greatest influence. When Parliament finally acted, it decided that the clipped coins would be brought in and reminted at the old standard. The disaster predicted by Locke's opponents was fully realized. The reminted silver did not provide England with a good currency; much of it was quickly melted down and sent abroad as bullion. The halving of the number of silver coins in circulation caused a drastic deflation. Landlords and creditors reaped the benefits. The shortage of money pressed especially hard on the poor, who rioted in some towns. Even the government had difficulty paying its soldiers.

The fact that the clipped silver coins passed at face value even with a quarter to half their silver clipped away suggested the possibility that other things might be used for money. If money's status as legal tender counted most, then it should be possible to find gold and silver substitutes. Writers began to tout various schemes to increase currency through paper issued by land banks.

Economic Development in a New English Regime

The year 1689 had brought Mary and her Dutch husband, William, to the throne of England, an event that precipitated the first of many wars with France. The animosities behind these wars had an economic impact, triggering a retreat from European trade and the raising of tariffs. The new king had to accept restrictions on his prerogative and worse—or better, from the people's point of view—would henceforth share power with Parliament. In one stroke the English had limited and centralized national authority in the new sovereign, the king in Parliament. Both achievements boded well for enterprise. Five years later Parliament founded the Bank of England, a quasi-public institution to receive the tax revenues, lend to the government, and issue bills of exchange that could pass as currency.

Collecting taxes in most European countries was the occasion for protracted haggling between the central governments and the various local provinces, states, or counties within them. The monarchs spent their income as they saw fit. After the Glorious Revolution, uniform rates applied across the country and Parliament monitored how the king spent tax revenues. The new transparency in tax collecting and budgeting enhanced certainty and predictability, both important to enterprise. The rhetoric on free markets often stresses risk taking, which of course is imperative, but investors care about protecting capital and will do almost anything to cushion risks. England's constitutional monarchy and national bank did both. In 1712 Parliament created a national postal service. By 1715 trade statistics were available to guide policy making.

A dashing Scottish speculator, John Law, founded the first bank in France and used that establishment to raise funds for the development of part of French Louisiana. Calling it the Mississippi Company, Law issued bank notes for the development of thousands of square acres in the New World. The government's confidence in Law led to his gaining such privileges as those of minting coin and collecting revenue. People almost rioted in their eagerness to buy his company shares, but Law didn't know when to stop issuing them. Their oversupply brought about a spectacular crash, and the Mississippi Company became the Mississippi Bubble, a new term to describe the sudden inflation and equally sudden deflation of an object of value, be it a certain kind of investment, tulips, or real estate.

Law knew how to dazzle people with the prospect of future riches. Successes like his in the 1720s appear repeatedly in the history of capitalism, pointing up the psychological component of the profit motive. In France what might have been a cautionary tale became a hypercautionary one. The government wouldn't tolerate paper money for another seventy years. Even in England it soured people on paper money and its use as an economic stimulant. A new orthodoxy congealed. The supply of money, the philosopher David Hume maintained, had nothing to do with prosperity, which depended upon real things in the economy, like shops, stores, and factories. Any increase in money would only produce inflation. This became the classic, academic position throughout the nineteenth century, articulated by David Ricardo and enshrined in the elegant writings of John Stuart Mill.[20]

The Dutch had actually created the first modern banking system, one that pioneered bills of exchange backed by gold in the bank vault. They also started the first stock exchange and worked out a way to lend money on the collateral of real estate, a forerunner of our mortgages. But it was not until the early nineteenth century, when the Netherlands acquired a king, that the Dutch developed a centralized taxing system. Even then they couldn't audit the budget of their new king. Matters were even more byzantine in France, where the monarchy had to negotiate with powerful provinces to set tax rates. At the same time, French tax exemptions covered whole provinces as well as most of the nobility. Taxes fell on the poor, whose poverty limited revenues. Not being able to raise sufficient revenue finally stopped the government in its tracks.[21]

The Bank of England became the most important financial institution of the eighteenth century. Sure of its power to repay the loans because of its publicly stated taxes, British financiers willingly lent to the government. Managing the public debt meant that the directors of the Bank of England were privy to the details of the government's borrowing and its tax stream. With that knowledge it was easy to keep interest rates low by assessing the risk. These facts, perhaps more than any others, made possible Great Britain's triumph in most of the eighteenth-century European wars (the American Revolution was an exception). The Bank of England stabilized the capital markets, which were playing an increasingly important role as enterprises became more costly. The British government levied higher per capita taxes than any other European country, but the people got their money's worth in services and stability. Even the Royal Navy worked hand in glove with British enterprise, convoying home both the tobacco and sugar fleets.[22]

From these late-century debates emerged a strong sense that the elements in any economy were negotiable and fluid, the exact opposite of the stasis so long desired. Sometimes money was better to have than goods; other times the reverse. Investments in land and trade tended toward an equilibrium, one pamphleteer explained, for "the mutation frequently happens; the money man today is a landed man tomorrow; and the landed man today becomes a moneyman tomorrow; every man according to his sentiments of things turns and winds his estate as he . . . fancies will be most advantageous to him."[23] Actually to be a landed man in England conveyed a social status that would never be accorded the "moneyman," but the pamphleteer conveyed accurately the new appreciation the English had for pragmatism in commercial matters.

In England people ceased to think of the market as a place for face-to-face bargaining and commenced to speak of it as an unseen entity comprising thousands of transactions. Throughout the century, writings on prices, demand, and trade policies reached an impressive level of sophistication. Money, food, and land lost their special status, homogenized by reference to prices and rates. The uniformity attributed to human beings when they were bargaining undercut in subtle ways the widespread belief in natural inequality. It would be awhile before the guardians of morals and fixed ranks would have to yield to the most popular idea of interchangeable market participants, but writers on the economy had established a beachhead for the coming invasion of commercial logic. Nobody aimed to change social values. That happened through the process of responding to new experiences. The expertise of the English in economic analysis gave them an advantage that neither the Dutch nor the French, their closest competitors in wealth making, had. Nowhere else had the old order been rejected intellectually as thoroughly as in England. There was little abstract discussion of the market in the Netherlands, and French economic thinkers concentrated on developing government fiscal and monetary politics rather than let business interests have their own way.

Fresh Economic Thinking

Since the late seventeenth century Louis XIV's famous controller-general Jean-Baptiste Colbert had made the French government an integral part of business planning. It actively promoted new technologies, established administrative structures to deal with industry and labor, and generally offered advice on how to enhance profits, not always with happy results. Two generations later the drastic need to improve France's capacity to feed its people inspired a new group of economists with strong connections to the monarch. Taking the name "physiocracy," which meant "the rule of nature," these analysts gave to agriculture a special quality that bordered on the mystical. They asserted that all value arose from land. Hence all taxation should fall on this economic foundation.

Perhaps nothing reveals how closely theories are tied to social realities than the French case. The English had succeeded in producing abundance while actually freeing farmers from legal restraints. Saddled with an absolute monarch, the physiocrats believed that only the king's authority could get the country to do the things necessary to match the economic development of England, their greatest rival. Unlike Colbert, the physiocrats wanted more freedom for farmers, merchants, and manufacturers, but government assistance from public officials like themselves was needed to help market participants help themselves.[24]

Getting a moribund monarchy to reform the country's agriculture was a daunting effort, but the physiocrats pushed ahead. In their many pamphlets, they urged the diversion of investments from manufacturing and trade to farming.[25] Correctly noting the benefits in Great Britain coming from a free trade in grain, they made that, along with a single tax, their rallying cry. In the 1770s, when the baron de Turgot became the king's principal minister, he liberalized by fiat the domestic market in grain. Nature was not on Turgot's side; bad harvests undermined his effort and played right into the hands of his many opponents. In the end the physiocrats, despite their friends in high places, were too few, too theoretical, and too weak to overcome institutional resistance to all forms of change within old regime France.

Retrospectively, we can see that the physiocrats were attempting to do by command what English entrepreneurs had done for themselves by taking advantage of lax law enforcement to weave together local commercial connections into a national market. The larger point is important. Self-assertive individuals did the innovating in England whether they were improving farmers and landlords, joint-stock trading company managers, interloping merchants, cheese mongers, or professional lenders. They had no larger vision, and they bungled as often as they hit their mark. It often took several generations of trial and error to fashion an optimal operation, but English economic ventures succeeded not only in producing impressive results but, even more important, in demonstrating the unexpected social benefits of allowing men and women to make their own self-interested choices.

While slower, the way capitalism actually came into being was more enduring because it educated and changed ordinary people as it expanded. Change by authority is dependent upon the ruler or group. Those endowed with political power can find other interests or have successors who do not share their goals, as was demonstrated by the Ming dynasty emperor who sent out Zheng He to explore the east coast of Africa. This point having been made, it is well to add that once capitalism had emerged as the dominant economic system, capitalists acquired power as a new class of entrepreneurs that used its power to suppress labor unrest. They left untouched the old master-servant laws that were highly prejudicial to workers as well as laws that interpreted labor organizations as felonious conspiracies. Capitalism didn't eliminate oppressive upper classes. It just changed the basis upon which they stood. The ladders for social mobility were spread about the landscape more generously, but those without capital suffered as had those without inherited status earlier.

In England, mercantilism came back into favor in the eighteenth century, but in actual practice, most enterprises had already escaped legal restraints. Mercantilists took advantage of the fierce international rivalries of the eighteenth century to argue for applying high tariffs to imports to strengthen the national industries and, not so incidentally, to help manufacturers by using higher prices to discourage purchases of foreign goods, usually described as luxuries. It was perhaps this crusade that led the philologist Samuel Johnson to comment that patriotism was the last refuge of the scoundrel! Mercantilists might have shaken their heads in disbelief that self-seeking men and women could establish order in the market, but they didn't have much success convincing others.

Upper-class conservatives could slow the rate of change, and the poor could invoke a higher law of charity, but the momentum was with private enterprise. When food prices skyrocketed, as they still did when harvests failed, there was much talk of a commonwealth in which the concerns of the vulnerable had first priority. In the end, long-term relief came in the form of improved agricultural techniques. The laws against engrossing, forestalling, and regrating stayed on the books until the end of the eighteenth century, but they fell into desuetude as those marketing food crops did pretty much what they wished with the abundant harvests they had learned to produce.

Certain intellectual developments that were critical at the threshold of economic change became less important after capitalism had become established. Japan offers an instance of this. In 2006 Japan adopted for the first time a jury system. The idea of amateur participation in the judicial system ran so counter to deep-rooted prejudices against questioning authority that the government had to launch a massive public relations campaign to teach men and women how to behave on a jury. Few Japanese wanted to challenge others or give vent to their own opinions in public, the very stuff of jury deliberations. Such cultural traits may not appear as inhibitions of economic advance, but they would have been at the outset. By contrast, at the end of the seventeenth century, Englishmen and -women were already habituated to vociferous, public debates on everything from salvation to the bad manners of the poor. Questioning authority proved critical to getting novelty accepted. Once capitalist practices had been established for all to see, authorities might adopt them, as did Japan in the late nineteenth century. The initial reform of economic institutions proved to be a messy, noisy, contentious business. Nobody knew exactly what was happening. Copying a finished product can be orderly, even predictable.

In addition to intellectual openness, the elusive quality of trust played a critical role in the early years of capitalism. Almost everyone who has studied trade in its first flush of expansion has commented upon how hard it was for merchants to trust distant agents and customers. Sending their wares and payments through labyrinthine networks of commerce often seemed like playing the lottery. Typically, European merchant firms sent their children, cousins, and in-laws as agents to Tenerife or Batavia or Port-au-Prince to watch out for the family interests. England had some conspicuous advantages in laying a foundation of trust because the country had a pretty homogenous population of close to six million. While people in different regions spoke dialects, English was a lingua franca. The various doctrinal disputes among Protestants and between Protestants and Catholics had pretty much disappeared into conformity to the Church of England by the end of the seventeenth century. Periodicals carried news from one region to another. The king in Parliament, meaning the monarch and members of the House of Lords and the Commons, spoke for the whole. People took property disputes to court increasingly throughout the eighteenth century. The English were a litigious people, but they trusted their institutions to adjudicate their interests fairly.

The English Civil War had divided the elite, but when William and Mary took the throne, a new and more pragmatic generation had taken over direction of the country. English laws had long protected property, but after 1689 "the rights of Englishmen" became a rallying cry for the English as well as their North American colonists. While the upper class supported draconian laws for crimes against property, and Catholics and dissenters were excluded from holding office, Englishmen and -women mingled more freely across lines of class and status than their peers elsewhere. Sharing opinion in print took much of the poison out of conflict and made possible the emergence of a consensus about religion, the economy, and the constitutional balance between king and Parliament. These things provided deep underpinnings for trust. The English shared the same prejudices and pride, and somehow these shared convictions even taught them to trust foreigners.

Economics as a discipline acquired a certain cohesion with Adam Smith's masterful *Wealth of Nations*. Throughout the nineteenth and twentieth centuries, economics, like other studies of society, became a profession. The subject acquired enough precision to lay out its major theorems in algorithms and stochastic statistics. I am deeply suspicious of this precision when it is applied to anything larger than a single rate or measure. A country's economy is embedded in its culture, which embraces a hotchpotch of qualities at play in collective life. "At play" is the right phrase here, for the culture of everyday life is composed of lively sensibilities, convictions, expectations, aversions, taboos, secret pleasures, transgressive acts, conventional attitudes, and forms of politeness. Such disorder would never fit into an equation. Social science predictions generally carry the caveat that they will hold ceteris paribus—"if all else remains equal." But all else rarely remains the same.

Many scholars do not believe that capitalism existed until there were concentrations of capital in industrial plants with a new proletariat as the work force. The term for them is synonymous with industrialization. For others, capitalism is as old as the first civilization when men and women stored wealth for some future enterprise. I think capitalism began when private investments drove the economy, and entrepreneurs and their supporters acquired the power to bend political and social institutions to their demands. For England this had happened by the end of the seventeenth century. Those who promoted the market economy were greatly aided by a public discourse about how nations grow wealthy. Efficiency, ingenuity, disciplined work, educated experimentation all became part of a new ethic. While these new ways of looking at the world of work had to coexist for a long time with the older values that stressed status, stasis, and communal obligations, the ideal of productivity finally became dominant. Where earlier talented young men might have aspired to be courtiers or even clergymen, as the eighteenth century opened, careers in manufacturing, finance, retailing, and foreign trade beckoned.

There can be no capitalism, as distinguished from select capitalist practices, without a culture of capitalism, and there is no culture of capitalism until the principal forms of traditional society have been challenged and overcome. But it must be said—and is not often enough said—that the mores of a more traditional organization of society do not die out with the dominance of capitalism. Rather they regroup to fight again with new leaders and new causes. Any history of capitalism must contain the shadow history of anticapitalism, sometimes carried out in the name of a new theory, but often as a reexpression of values that prevailed before the eighteenth century.

In describing in great detail how the capitalist system supplanted a venerable, established order, I want to stress the difficulty of such a development. I want readers to resist the temptation to bring capitalism onto the historic stage as something inevitable, because it was not. The number of societies today that won't make the attitudinal and practical adjustments required of an industrial economy should reinforce this point. Social institutions, like the family, religious faith, or types of political regime—autocratic or anarchic—can exert great independent influence on economic decisions. Taking hold in the West was a way of talking about economic relations that assumed that economic progress was inexorable, and capitalism a force not to be blocked, but the irregular patterns of development during the past four centuries indicate that some traditional societies have found the power to put the brakes on changes that threaten their way of life. The variety of arrangements in the world today—even within capitalist economies—cautions against talking about universals and uniformities that might occur in the natural world but rarely do in the social realm.

Capitalism was never just an economic system. It impinged on every facet of life and was itself influenced by every institution or identity that shaped its participants. It created new cultural forms, stimulated new tastes, and introduced a whole new vocabulary for discussing the impact of private enterprise on the welfare of the society as a whole. In time traditional ways of acting and thinking lost their controlling power. They became options, to be chosen as matters of taste. A different, dominant ethos took shape, not so much making people freer as turning economic freedom and individual rights into values considered fundamental. Once its amazing power to generate wealth was detected, most countries, at least in the West, wanted part of the action. When capitalism emerged in eighteenth-century England, it was relatively easy for other countries to copy English innovations. They could also discriminate between what they wished to copy and what they found distasteful in the modernizing dynamic of. French capitalism was not exactly like the English original, or German capitalism a replica of how the French adapted this enriching economic system to their ways.

5

THE TWO FACES OF

EIGHTEENTH-CENTURY

CAPITALISM

B EFORE THERE WERE factories under roofs, there were factories in the fields. As with oil in the twentieth century, sugar could only be produced in a few favored spots, such as Brazil and the islands of the Caribbean. And again like oil, it was in demand everywhere. The lure of profits from raising such a precious commodity drew Spain's European rivals to the tropical parts of the New World, where they developed an intensive kind of agriculture, using slave labor. Over the course of three hundred years, eleven million African men and women were shipped like cattle to the Western Hemisphere. Although England dominated the trade during its heyday in the eighteenth century, France, Portugal, Spain, Denmark, and the Netherlands participated in the traffic in human beings. This is the ugly face of capitalism made uglier by the facile justifications that Europeans offered for using men until they literally dropped dead. Hypocrisy, they say, is the homage vice pays to virtue. In this case, hypocrisy left a bitter legacy. To assuage consciences over such a massive injustice, Europeans made invidious racial comparisons that have outlasted slavery by more than a century.

A much more benign, even awe-inspiring chapter in the history of capitalism paralleled the brutal days of the sugar plantations. Starting in the eighteenth century, a succession of ingenious men discovered how to make natural forces push, pump, lift, turn, twirl, smelt, and grind all manner of things. There was never any thought of importing slaves into Great Britain, but the high cost of workers' wages proved to be a powerful incentive to find alternative sources of energy.

This gave a push to inventors who began a technological saga that has only accelerated with time. Drawing on seventeenth-century scientific experiments in hydraulics and hydrostatics, these pioneer engineers designed mechanical slaves, machines that could harness energy. Isaac Newton's brilliant calculations of how gravity kept the planets in place prompted a new respect for human reason. As Alexander Pope wrote:

> Nature and nature's Laws lay hid in Night;
> GOD said, Let Newton be! And all was Light."

Thomas Newcomen, Richard Arkwright, and James Watt demonstrated that lesser mortals could take the Promethean fire from Newton and build engines that could work a lot harder than human beings and their animals.

These two phenomena—American slave-worked plantations and mechanical wizardry for pumping water, smelting metals, and powering textile factories—may seem unconnected. Certainly we have been loath to link slavery to the contributions of a free enterprise system, but they must be recognized as twin responses to the capitalist genie that had escaped the lamp of tradition during the seventeenth century. Both represented radical departures from previous practices. Take farming. Growing food had long been the province of each country's peasantry. Peasants' work was hard and demeaning, but families embedded in village customs did varied tasks of raising and preparing food. Sugar plantations began de novo, without rural traditions, using laborers wrenched from their homes to work like robots in military-style routines growing a single exotic crop.

Tapping into the energy of fossil fuel changed forever the relation of human beings to their natural environment. Inventiveness wasn't new, but the scope of the steam power was. People had created elaborate waterwheels, windmills, fountains, bellows, guns, and dams, but they had never before penetrated the secrets of physics or devised ways to use those secrets to manipulate natural forces. The amount of power that could now be generated and the diversity of uses to which it could be put transformed production processes everywhere. Like that of the sugar plantation, their potential for generating profits accounts for the invest-ment of time and money that people were willing to put into developing steam power. Both took concentration of capital, breaking ground for a new sugar plantation costing considerably more than setting up a cot-ton factory. This capital investment became the major feature of the new economic order. Perhaps even more significant to the workingmen and women at the time, both factories in the fields and factories under a roof introduced work routines that required long hours of disciplined labor. Employers had always preferred hard work to easygoing habits, but their considerable investment in slaves and equipment turned that preference into an imperative.

Politics in the late seventeenth century altered the history of capital-ism by changing the European trading patterns. Fierce dynastic rivalries strained relations between Great Britain and France, France and Austria and the Netherlands, Spain and Great Britain, France and Russia and Spain, as well as some Italian states. Various combinations of these coun-tries went to war against each other eight times between 1689 and 1815 for a total of sixty-three years.[1] One major consequence of these hostilities was a sharp reduction in the intra-European trade that had grown sub-stantially in the previous two centuries. Neighboring Great Britain and France, in particular, turned from each other as trading partners toward their overseas holdings. The wars themselves made raising revenue urgent, so heavy import tariffs became the order of the day. The various European colonies in the New World were expected to complement the economic needs of the mother country.

The persistent warfare among European powers created a kind of catch-22. The warring countries needed the riches they extracted from Asia and the New World to support their wars, but the intense competition for control of these lucrative trades triggered more bellicosity. France and England confronted each other in five different spots around the globe: over cotton and silk in India, slaves on the west coast of Africa, sugar plantations in the Caribbean, Indian alliances in the Ohio River valley of the North American continent, and furs in the Hudson Bay area. James Fenimore Cooper commented wittily on this rivalry in *The Last of the Mohicans* when he observed that the French and English armies in North America were forced to travel long distances in order to fight each other.

Because of its centrality to the sugar trade, the slave trade was the most hotly contested European venture on the face of the globe. The numbers themselves shock one into an awareness of its significance. Between 1501 and 1820 slavers took 8.7 million Africans in chains to the Western Hemisphere; between 1820 and the final abolition of slavery in Brazil in 1888, 2.3 million more were sent. A total of 11 million men and women came from Africa to the New World colonies in comparison with the 2.6 million Europeans who crossed the Atlantic in the same period. Over one hundred thousand separate voyages brought this human cargo, 70 percent of them owned by either British or Portuguese traders.[2]

Sugar was one of capitalism's first great bonanzas; its successes also revealed the power of the profit motive to override any cultural inhibitions to gross exploitation. Slavery was old. Egyptian slaves had built pyramids; Roman ones, bridges and aqueducts. What capitalism introduced was sustained and systematic brutality in the making of goods on a scale never seen before. It's not size alone that distinguishes modern slavery from its ancient lineage in Greece and biblical times; it's also race. Slavery then often had an ethnic component because slaves were taken as the captives of war, but never a consistently racial one. When the Portuguese brought back captured Africans to work in depopulated Lisbon starting in the fifteenth century, the trade didn't differ much from the commerce in slaves that the Arabs had been conducting for several centuries throughout central and eastern Africa. A hundred years later, something new had been added to this commerce in human beings: They were integrated into an expanding production system. Those sent to the Caribbean were put to work in gangs planting sugarcanes, chopping weeds, cutting the harvest, and crushing the canes in the mills that turned out molasses and sugar. The very size of the trade promoted warfare in Africa in order to meet the new demand for slaves.

The Spanish, who were the first Europeans to arrive in the New World in search of gold and glory, would have been happy to use indigenous people to labor for them. Europeans did that wherever they could. But that was not to be, for the native people of the New World were peculiarly vulnerable to European diseases. So isolated had they been from the rest of the world's people that they didn't even have the same range of blood types as Asians, Africans, and Europeans, who had been mingling for many centuries. The joining of the Old and New Worlds caused an unintentional genocide as tribe after tribe in the Western Hemisphere died from the diseases that Europeans brought with them, leaving but a "saving remnant" of the indigenous population of North and South America.

Historical demographers put the pre-Columbian population at 90 to 110 million, with 10 to 12 million living north of Mexico. Measles, smallpox, pleurisy, typhus, dysentery, tuberculosis, and diphtheria actually wiped out whole tribes. Repeated exposure to new diseases culled the indigenous population down to a tenth of its original size. People sickened and died with astounding rapidity. Without knowing what caused disease—germs weren't isolated until the nineteenth century—no one understood the phenomenon. Indians sustained a profound psychological blow as they watched their own die while their conquerors survived. No less ignorant of the cause, Europeans tended to see God's hand in saving them while destroying their pagan enemies.

A New Source of Labor

The Spanish, and later the Portuguese, tried to enslave the survivors, with limited success. Columbus had even sent 500 captured Indians back to Seville in 1495. In the early decades of the sixteenth century a succession of Spanish conquistadors moved onto the islands of the Greater Antilles, forcing the native people to pan gold and raise food for them. One of the witnesses of the bloody conquest of Cuba in 1511 was Bartolomé de Las Casas. In a long career as priest, historian, polemicist, Dominican friar, and bishop of Chiapas, he became the Indians' greatest defender. It was Las Casas who suggested that the Spanish import African slaves as a way to protect the indigenous people. He argued that Africans were better prepared to work than the Indians who, he said, had not yet reached the same stage of civilization.[3] From his suggestion came one of the most lucrative plums of Caribbean commerce, the asiento, a contract that Spanish officials awarded for an annual supply of slaves and European goods. The first one, signed in 1595, gave the Portuguese the exclusive rights to land 4,250 slaves annually at Cartagena. In 1713 the British secured the asiento in the peace treaty ending the War of the Spanish Succession.

While the Spanish used Indian and African slaves in mines, cattle ranches, and food-raising farms, the profits that sugar garnered paid for importing slaves. Pioneer agronomists in India had domesticated the sugar plant more than two thousand years earlier. It took more than a millennium for the sweet foodstuff to reach the Mediterranean. There Venetian merchants took control of the European market for it.[4] Italians learned how to grow sugar successfully in Sicily, as did the Arabs in Ethiopia and on Zanzibar. The technique for processing sugar through cane-crushing mills came from the Arab world as well. The Portuguese no doubt picked up this know-how after invading Ceuta in Morocco just a few years before colonizing Madeira, its island possession off the Moroccan coast. In short order they experimented with growing sugar there and in the Azores, Cape Verde Islands, and São Tomé, all this in the fifteenth century. The Spanish followed suit in their Atlantic islands, the Canaries.

What was startlingly new in Madeira and São Tomé was the Portuguese organization of slaves into strict divisions of labor.[5] Large numbers of workers had been collected under one roof before, but Portuguese sugar producers figured out how to coordinate the complicated tasks of crystallizing sugar from vats of boiling cane cuttings. Italian merchants had seized slavs (hence the name "slave") from Eastern Europe for work in the Mediterranean from the thirteenth through the fifteenth centuries while Arab merchants had enslaved more than a million Western Europeans from the sixteenth through eighteenth centuries. At first the slaves the Portuguese used were white, but once Portuguese merchants had begun regularly bringing home Africans, sugar growers switched to black enslaved laborers. The thousand Africans that the Portuguese brought back annually to Lisbon in the mid-fifteenth century grew to thirty-five hundred a century later.[6]

Good luck and good winds had given the Portuguese a large foothold in South America, Brazil. At first, they concentrated on exporting the famous brazilwood that produced red dye and gave Brazil its name. (Actually Portuguese priests had first called this vast region Holy Cross.) Forests stretched along the southeast coast and inland for several miles. The Portuguese relied upon the Tupi hunters and gatherers to extract the resources from the trees. This turned out to be a temporary labor force, for the Tupi refused to farm. They fled into the recesses of the forests or killed themselves when the Portuguese attempted to coerce them to work. It was more plunder than production, as one scholar commented, and when it was over, the Portuguese in Brazil turned to the sugar production that they had mastered closer to home.[7]

Breaches on the Spanish Lake

Nowhere is the profit-maximizing imperative of capitalism more in evidence than in the sugar sweep in Europe's New World colonies. Columbus carried sugarcane slips to the Caribbean on his second trip. Spanish authorities back home encouraged their cultivation, but the colonists themselves were more interested in precious metals. It was left to the Portuguese in Brazil to demonstrate the profits to be boiled out of sugarcane once you secured workers to do the drudgery. Sugar growing in Madeira and São Tomé gave the Portuguese a template for establishing plantations in the New World. Over the course of more than three centuries, Brazil imported almost four million slaves, the largest of any European outpost and more than a third of the total sent to the New World. Small wonder that Brazilians, looking out at the mountain in the harbor of Rio de Janeiro, could only see a sugar loaf.

While the pope made Spain accept the Portuguese presence in Brazil, the Council of the Indies in Seville had every intention of keeping the

Caribbean a Spanish lake. Alas, Spain's wars in the sixteenth century had exhausted both the country and the royal treasury, just at the moment when the French, Dutch, English, even the Danish were eager to enter the scramble for New World wealth. Nor could Spanish manufacturers supply the goods that their colonists wanted—surely not as cheaply as the Dutch and English, who were only too willing to smuggle tools, weapons, cloth, and food into the many port cities of the Spanish New World. Spain's effort to maintain monopoly control only attracted outlaws to the Caribbean. Soon the area was considered "beyond the line"—outside the norms of European civilization and its international treaties. Here Europeans accepted rapes, abductions, plunder, torture, attacks, piracy, and chicanery of every kind, all made the more debased by the inhumane treatment of enslaved Africans and Indians.[8]

True to their concentration on commerce, the Dutch wanted a toehold on the Spanish Main. Dutch West India Company traders moved from piracy to smuggling and finally to the occupation of Curaçao, off the coast of Venezuela, in 1634. Near Curaçao also was a source of salt, a precious food additive critical to the Dutch herring trade. The company had already established New Netherlands on the North American continent when it purchased Manhattan for goods worth roughly twenty-four dollars. With its natural harbor Curaçao became the center of the Dutch slave trade. With this gateway to Spain's mainland colonies, the Dutch entered the competition for the Spanish asiento.

The Spanish had paid little attention to the Lesser Antilles, the so-called Windward and Leeward Islands five hundred miles east of their headquarters on Santo Domingo and Cartagena. The English and French were only too happy to take possession of them, the French settling Martinique and Guadeloupe; the English, St. Christopher, Barbados, Antigua, Montserrat, and Nevis. English entrepreneurs began cultivating tobacco with white indentured servants on their islands; but white servants presented social problems, and the supply was uncertain. When their labor contracts ran out in four or five years, the freed men and women had to be given land or work. Far more attractive as a labor force were African slaves, if an export crop could be found to justify their purchase prices. Enter sugar.

France was continental Europe's richest and most powerful country, but French entrepreneurs had to contend with an unreformed absolute monarchy in which the capricious use of power threatened the security of their investments. Rather than an integrated market, the internal pathways of French commerce were clogged with tolls to be paid on roads and bridges while most of its peasants lacked the skills and investments to farm well. Yet in the New World the French learned how to produce sugar. The returns grew dramatically during the eighteenth century, but they reached only a small group of favored investors. Heavily taxed, New World sugar plantations postponed a fiscal crisis for the French monarchy until the end of the century.

The Dutch, French, and English not only intruded on Spain's Caribbean holdings but also challenged Portuguese slavers, mounting an aggressive campaign to break up the Portuguese monopoly of the West African slave trade. Considering the breadth of the coast from which slaves were bought and the diversity of African rulers to deal with, it was not difficult for latecomers to enter this lucrative trade. Europeans themselves did not penetrate sub-Saharan Africa until the nineteenth century. Rather slave cargoes were gathered at fortified castles or factories, often on offshore islands. Sometimes bands of freelancing armed Africans raided villages and sold their captives to all comers. Along thirty-five hundred miles of coastline from Senegambia to Angola, traders gathered slave cargoes that they sold for European goods. Slave sellers particularly favored guns with which to capture more men and women. Separated by sex for the voyage across the Atlantic, the captives were packed into ships, each person confined to a space of four square feet for a period of eight to twelve weeks. A typical voyage would carry 150 to 400 persons, 12 to 15 percent of whom usually died en route. Revolts broke out in about 10 percent of all voyages, almost always in the first weeks.[9]

By the end of the sixteenth century Europe's sugar refining center had shifted from Antwerp to London; the sugar industry in Sicily retrenched to meet only local demand. The English entered the slave trade with a monopoly firm, the Royal African Company, but by the end of the seventeenth century the time for monopolies had passed. Interlopers complained vigorously, and the trade was thrown open. Liverpool became its center as Nantes was France's. At its peak in the 1790s, a slave vessel left an

English port every other day. After England secured the Spanish asiento in 1713, it dominated the slave trade for a century, until reformers at home brought a stop to the whole awful enterprise.

Merchants in the English continental colonies, particularly those from Rhode Island and New York, participated in the slave trade along with the slavers that sailed from Liverpool. The northern British colonies also played a major role in provisioning the West Indian colonies, which imported almost everything rather than divert hands and land from producing sugar. They paid for their American colonial imports in molasses, which New Englanders took home and distilled into rum. Sugar went from being a luxury to a necessity in the kitchens of all but the poorest Europeans. The value of sugar imports alone was four times that of the entire commerce with Asian countries.[10] Every European country with access to the Atlantic Ocean joined the race for profits from a sweetener that tasted good in tea and puddings, and, more important, could preserve fresh fruits and vegetables all year round.

The sugar planters, who invested their capital in plantations, worked their slaves and land as hard as possible. They accepted the inevitable decline of soil in the pursuit of quick returns. So profitable was the crop and so cruel the plantation owners that they literally worked their slaves to death. The labor force in the Caribbean had to be replaced about every ten to thirteen years. Far from home, European entrepreneurs shed their manners and morality. Many owners left the management of their property to others. These absentee owners returned home to live in luxury. Few questioned the origin of their great wealth. In England about a dozen of these sugar nabobs sat in the House of Commons. Without their plowing money back into the plantations, the fertility of the soil dropped, creating opportunities to bring new plantations into the market. Brazil was important through most of the seventeenth century; Barbados peaked around 1690; Haiti and Jamaica, after 1700. The greatest slave revolt in history brought the heyday of St. Domingue to an end in the second half of the eighteenth century; Cuba prevailed throughout the nineteenth century. While Cuba dominated the sugar industry, slaves could be sold there for thirty times what they had cost in Africa.[11] Profits like that would always find takers.

Slaves in England's Continental Colonies

No European country began its explorations of the New World with the intention of bringing slaves from Africa to raise exotic crops for a worldwide market. The turn to slave labor in the three English colonies of Virginia, Barbados, and South Carolina offers a picture of how the transformation happened. Virginia, England's first colony, was settled in 1607 with the typical high hopes of finding gold and silver. After a decade of disappointment and hardship, tobacco saved the colony after a colonist had hybridized a leaf that could compete with the Spanish leaf. Smoking and chewing tobacco proved so popular in England that this demand triggered a boom back in Virginia. Anyone with access to land planted tobacco.[12] The decentralization of decision making, characteristic of the free enterprise system, led to overcropping, and soon there was a glut of the "filthy weed." When prices dropped precipitously, tobacco came within the budgetary reach of thousands more consumers. A fresh opportunity opened up: making a profit at the new low price by learning how to cut costs.

Slavery was not essential to raising tobacco. English indentured servants and family farmers had been growing it for several decades, but using slave labor was an alluring alternative for the wealthier planters. A Dutch vessel had brought a score of slaves to Virginia in 1619, but at that early date investing in slaves was not attractive. A few decades later a number of settlers arrived with sufficient cash to establish themselves on larger plots of land. The English king had promoted the slave trade in part to keep the freewheeling Dutch out of their North American colonies. Now English slavers could supply Virginia planters with slaves directly from Africa at a good price. A final inducement to switching from English indentured servants to African slaves came from the fact that servants, after completing their labor contracts, threatened to become an unruly underclass. Governor William Berkeley described the situation when he lamented: "Oh how miserable is that man who must govern a people six parts of seven are poor, in debt, discontented, and armed!" Slaves were more expensive than servants, but they remained in bondage until death and could be kept under better control than ex-servants.[13]

When healthier conditions lowered the initially high mortality rate in Virginia, slaves became a better buy than white servants. Virginia now had the makings of a planter elite, men with resources to set up slave-worked plantations. At the same time the mother country began a very lucrative business exporting tobacco to the Continent. A leading Virginia churchman complained about Virginia's lack of clergy and was rebuked by the British attorney general with "Souls! Damn your souls, make tobacco." The 10 percent black population in the first decade of the eighteenth century moved quickly to its 40 percent plateau. By then the British navy was convoying home an annual tobacco fleet of three hundred ships. Meanwhile poorer folks moved out of the Tidewater to the Piedmont area, Maryland, North Carolina, or the inland valleys, where they could farm on a smaller scale, putting in a few acres in tobacco to pay for blankets, tools, and utensils.

Barbados went through a similar transformation when sugar cultivation replaced mixed farming. When men with the means to buy land, slaves, and machinery for growing and processing sugarcane arrived, the poorer settlers looked for another home in the New World. South Carolina received a charter in 1663, triggering a Barbadian exodus of whites and blacks north to the American continent. South Carolinians too started with a mixed economy. Their slaves introduced the open grazing familiar to Africans, but all this changed with the introduction of rice as an export crop. The Africans, especially those who came from the Sierra Leone area, where rice cultivation had long been practiced, understood the elaborate water and special cultivation that rice required. They also identified native herbs with which some poisoned their masters.[14] As with sugar and tobacco, rice produced enough profits to attract wealthier settlers who could afford to buy slave labor. By 1720 there were two African slaves for every English settler in South Carolina. As the Virginia planters had done when they adopted slave labor, the Carolina planter elite passed draconian laws controlling every aspect of slave behavior to still their fears of a slave rebellion.

When American independence brought an end to British subsidies for tobacco, rice, and indigo, the American South was lucky enough to find a new cash crop in cotton. Eli Whitney's cotton gin, invented in 1793, made profitable the short-staple cotton that could be grown throughout the region. Soon the crop spread west to Alabama, Mississippi, and Louisiana, embedding slavery in the economy of the new nation. By 1815 southern planters were sending 17 million bales of cotton to the mills of Lancaster and Manchester. By 1860 this total had risen to 192 million bales, and the slave population had quadrupled to almost four million black men, women, and children.

The Caribbean and American South constituted the underbelly of capitalist expansion with the cruel exploitation of foreign laborers to produce drugs for newly addicted European consumers. The range was impressive. In 1714 the French introduced coffee from Yemen, whence it spread to Haiti and regions in Central America. The Aztecs had drunk cocoa cold and spiced. With sugar available, both cocoa and tea became popular drinks in Europe. Though the Chinese were the greatest producers of tea, it was also grown in the Caribbean. With the exception of sugar, all these crops were drugs. Even sugar, one might say, could be addictive, and of course, fermenting the molasses that gushed from sugarcane vats soon turned into rum. All these intoxicating novelties had been inaccessible to Europeans, whose climate prevented growing the exotic crops of the tropics. European governments also liked these taste enhancers and mood alterers because they could load them with "sin" taxes.[15] Moralists complained about their spreading popularity, but their scolding lost traction as the value of individual liberty rose. After all, desire had proved a mighty stimulus to steady work habits when people were left free to choose from the cornucopia of goods available to them.

A Labor System That Demanded Rationalizations

The survival of slavery over four centuries compels our attention. What was there in European culture that permitted such atrocities as were committed against Africans as well as the indigenous populations of North and South America? For one, the level of cruelty everywhere in the world at that time made slavery less unusual. A nineteenth-century parliamentary report, for example, coolly described the superiority of adolescent girls over mules for the task of pulling coal carts through the narrow passages of mines. The callousness shown African men and women reflected some of the harsh treatment of all dependents. And then there is that amazing capacity of human beings to justify what they want to do.

As with our reaction to the starving millions today, "out of sight is out of mind" prevails. A very small percentage of the European population had any contact with slavery. This probably accounts for the milder form of slavery in the American South, where master and slaves lived cheek by jowl. In British America, unlike Latin America with its many mulattoes and mestizos, race became the handle that defenders of slavery seized to legitimate their holding men and women in perpetual bondage.

Capitalism twisted relations among the races in a particularly ugly way. The reason for this is obvious and obscure at the same time. Capitalism began as a system of production, fueled by an insatiable drive for profit. Places around the world with natural resources attracted investors. These Europeans could bring with them their capital, but not the laboring men and women required to extract or grow those far-flung resources. Instead they had to rely on workers where the resources were, meaning the mobilization of Asians, Africans, Arabs, or Native Americans—people of color. Abroad European entrepreneurs organized labor to their own advantage, usually with the help of local potentates who were bought off. Europeans judged the new workers by their speed in adapting to their work habits. They were usually found wanting. Europeans filled their letters back home with laments about the laziness and dirty habits of those on whom they depended for labor.

Rationalizations of slavery alert us to the guilty conscience that hovered over the system. Sometimes scholars make European prejudice against Africans appear as prompting enslavement rather than as furnishing excuses after the fact. Once slavery was in place, there was every inducement to disparage Africans. Their black skin evoked the pejorative imagery and expressions associated with blackness: black devil, black market, blackguard. A wonderfully circular reasoning kicked in as well: The unattractive personal traits that slavery instilled in children and their parents—indolence, insolence, sluggishness, lethargy—were exactly the qualities that were used to justify enslavement. By the end of the eighteenth century a new commitment in Europe to liberty and equality had doomed slave labor, though it was not until 1888 that the last Western country, Brazil, ended it. And nobody wanted to talk about it. A twentieth-century English historian wryly commented that the slave trade appeared in their history books only in connection with its abolition.

Scholars have argued that slavery in the Iberian colonies operated more benignly because the Portuguese and Spanish were accustomed to the institution and had incorporated slavery into their laws. Their long association with North African Muslims had brought them into sustained contact with people of color. In addition, the Catholic Church adamantly insisted on converting slaves. Portuguese slavers routinely baptized their cargoes before they set sail. The church sanctioned slave marriages, but the Protestants did not. Spanish and Portuguese rules set out very specific terms by which an enslaved person could regain her or his freedom, and custom, law, and religion encouraged masters to manumit their slaves. Slaves also had access to the courts as witnesses and litigants.[16]

There was an accompanying toleration of the many mixed race children in their settlements. One contemporary called blacks and mulattoes "the hands and feet" of Brazil because they did all the work in their communities. Reflecting the attitudes of the hildagos at home, whites considered labor debasing. A foreign traveler said of Argentina that Negroes were the most intelligent people he met because they were the craftsmen, builders, farmers, miners, transporters, cooks, nurses, and general laborers. "If it were not for slaves," he said, "it would not be possible to live here, for no Spaniard, no matter how poor, will do any kind of work."[17]

A closer examination of the records indicates that the exploitation of slaves in Brazil and Cuba was extreme, even though Portuguese and Spanish colonists mixed socially more easily both with Native Americans and enslaved Africans. More significantly, slaves survived better in Anglo-American colonies than Latin American ones. The pattern of natural population growth was stronger there. An astounding two-thirds of the descendants of African slaves live in the United States, though it had received less than 6 percent of the total number taken from Africa![18] Several factors account for that: More women were brought to the continental colonies. The higher birthrate suppressed the number of African imports, and the climate was healthier. Three-quarters of all blacks worked on plantations with fewer than fifty slaves, in contrast with the West Indies, where work forces normally numbered in the hundreds. The system was still brutal, but less debilitating and more racist.

A more significant question for this history is how important was the Atlantic slave system to capitalism. At the very least it generated enormous wealth, most of which was repatriated to the countries of the European investors. Up until the end of the eighteenth century, the New World was the biggest depository of British and French funds overseas. Their colonial trades employed hundreds of thousands of their fellow countrymen, though like the Africans, these men suffered greatly from the insalubrious conditions at sea and in the West Indies. Half the British soldiers stationed in the Caribbean lost their lives there. The mortality rate among crew members of all slavers was even higher. Most investors in the sugar islands were absentee landlords who avoided at all costs this deadly zone. In 1789 the British Privy Council reported that a total of fifty thousand whites, mostly men, lived in their island colonies alongside slightly fewer than five hundred thousand slaves and some ten thousand freed men and women of color.[19]

One thing we can say for certain is that the use of slave labor produced no sustained economic developments in South America, the West Indies, the American South, or Africa itself. The Atlantic system declined as swiftly as it had flourished. More like a footprint left in the sand, the whole elaborate structure of sugar making disappeared after abolition. Slavery persisted longer in the United States, but the story was the same. The market value of American slaves on the eve of the Civil War was almost three billion dollars, a sum greater than the value of all manufacturing and railroads in the United States. Four years later the South lay in ruins. The damage from war and a twelve-year military occupation depressed the southern economy until well into the New Deal.

Great Britain abolished slavery in its colonies in 1833, the French in 1848, the Dutch in 1863, Spain in 1886, followed by Brazil two years later. Neither abolitionists nor sugar nabobs expected the near collapse of West Indian sugar production when the enslaved men and women were free, but they voted with their feet and moved to small family farms away from the scenes of their wretched past.[20] Efforts to convert slavery into a kind of peonage in Jamaica in 1867 produced a violent revolt that was brutally suppressed while in the American South a rigid system of segregation ordered the relations between blacks and whites until the middle of the twentieth century.

The abrupt decline of plantation production suggested to some scholars that the abolition movement had been prompted by a decline in Britain's sugar industry rather than by moral outrage.[21] In the sixty years since that thesis was propounded, historians have demonstrated that in fact both imports and exports from the British West Indies were on the rise when Parliament passed the statute abolishing the slave trade. In the ensuing years, Britain spent millions on naval squadrons to patrol the waters of the Atlantic and Caribbean to prevent other countries from importing slaves—something of a Sisyphean task. Notwithstanding these efforts, more than two million more slaves were sent to Cuba, which was reaching the apex of its productivity in the middle decades of the nineteenth century. When Parliament abolished slavery, the market for sugar was still growing.

Industrial Inventions

Spelling the end to the Atlantic slave system brings us back to another eighteenth-century chapter in the history of capitalism, the one that took place back in England when technological wizards transformed the world of work. There used to be a joke that only the best graduate students were told that there had been no Industrial Revolution. The problem with the concept is lodged in the word "revolution." It implies both dramatic change and suddenness. Only the dramatic change part of the phrase fits what actually happened in nineteenth-century Great Britain, for the industrial innovations covered under the rubric of revolution took more than a century to be conceived, designed, tested, and adjusted, as had been the case with the earlier Agricultural Revolution. Then even more time elapsed before the new machines were applied to spinning, weaving, making dishware, firing bricks, working up iron, and transporting cargoes and people on rail and water.

"Industrial Evolution" would be a much better term for the genesis of the machines designed to do the heavy lifting for men and women. The phrases that we use in talking about human evolution—"the unvarying operation of natural laws," "replications," "random variations," "waste," and "survival of the fittest"—fit better here. All these came into play in the perfecting of the steam engine. Like evolution, the sequence of steps leading to the completion of any particular machine was not optimal, but with enough time, satisfactory models emerged. Since I doubt very much that my "Industrial Evolution" will catch on, I shall use the term, "Industrial Revolution," hoping that my readers will remember that the pace of transforming the world of work was measured.

A change in the European political order proved propitious for industry. Trade patterns shifted away from intra-European to colonial commerce because of the fierce rivalries between Britain and France during the eighteenth century. This led nations to promote processing raw materials at home, where they kept rivals at bay while creating a lot of jobs in refining sugar and rolling tobacco. Colonies were ideal sources for raw materials and good customers for manufactured items. And they had to obey—more or less—the laws laid down by the mother country. The English Navigation Laws specified that sugar and tobacco had to be shipped directly to Great Britain, just as any items the colonies might import from Europe had to be landed first in British ports. The British cut back on imports of linen from German and Holland and of wine from France. Port became the favorite drink because of the exceptionally good diplomatic relations between Britain and Portugal. Of course other countries retaliated with their own protective legislation. These were the policies that Adam Smith decried in the *Wealth of Nations*. Calculating the cost of maintaining British colonies, he argued that the country's best trading partners were its closest neighbors.

A lot of economic developments enhanced the possibility for an Industrial Revolution, though none of them can be seen as a cause per se. Conditions make things possible for causes to work, but they cannot cause anything. First and foremost were the dramatic agricultural changes that cut in half—from 80 to 40 percent—the number of men and women working in agriculture. The Dutch and English had long been manufacturing in innovative ways, but until they were capable of improving the productivity of their farmers, manufacturing remained a minor part of the economy. The redundant workers from rural England eventually became the proletariat of the industrial age. And not only workers were shed from farming. Expenditures went down as well, leaving money to invest elsewhere and to purchase goods other than food. A century of profitable trade had built up and dispersed capital throughout England.

More specifically, two major economic realities in England put a premium upon finding laborsaving devices: high wages and the very cheap cost of coal. Wages being high in England seems counterintuitive in view of the many men and women no longer needed in the fields. Still, English workers got paid substantially more than elsewhere in Europe—much higher than in other parts of the world. This can be attributed to the leveling off of population growth during the seventeenth century and the expansion of other kinds of employment. Many of the redundant workers stayed on in the countryside and became part of the putting-out system where clothiers brought raw wool to cottagers whose families washed, fulled, carded, spun, and wove it into cloth. Master craftsmen in England also did much of the country's ironworks in their own homes through much of the eighteenth century.

In this domestic system, employers paid by the piece. The head of the house set the hours, the pace, and the conditions of work. Mothers were at the spinning wheel; fathers at the loom with children—depending upon their age, sex, and dexterity—doing other tasks in the operation that took sheared wool from the backs of sheep and turned it into bolts of cloth.[22] A step in turning much of the old rural population into a modern working class, the putting-out system also led to an increase in family size. Not having to wait for a piece of land to farm before starting a family, cottagers could marry earlier, thanks to an expanding industrial economy. Their earlier marriages pushed up the birthrate.[23]

It was during the decades that English agriculture was shedding workers that London began its ascent to preeminence among European cities. Its population of roughly 400,000 in 1650 had grown to 575,000 by 1700, 675,000 at 1750, and 800,000 by 1800. By comparison, when London passed up Paris, France had a population six times that of England. With a higher rate of deaths than births, London took in a steady flow of men and women from the countryside, estimated at 8,000 to 10,000 a year. One scholar has estimated that 1 adult in every 6 spent some time in London.[24]

The city's merchants hired seamen, dockworkers, warehousemen, and the caulkers, sailmakers, brass fitters, and ropewalkers that kept their ships afloat. Importing raw materials paid off in good-paying jobs processing sugar, coffee, tobacco, and tea, not to mention gin, which became a favored drink in the eighteenth century. Higher wages meant that an increasing number of workingmen and women were able to buy the goods coming from England's workshops. Unlike many capital cities throughout the world, London was not filled with bureaucrats and courtiers but rather with the participants of a great emporium. Its vitality was visually demonstrated when fire destroyed the city in 1666 to be rebuilt with astounding speed by private investors.

Still one more economic factor contributed to the complex of incentives and facilitators of the Industrial Revolution. England had been favored with vast and readily accessible deposits of coal. Once the country's forests had been depleted, the price of charcoal rose sharply, and people began switching to coal for fuel. Coal was a godsend to industries that required lots of heat like glassblowing and brickmaking. Replacing coal for wood as a source of carbon took pressure off the land as well. With cheap coal, the English could build their houses with brick, further unburdening the land. Timber could be saved for shipbuilding and the framing of structures, though increasingly it was imported from Sweden and shipmaking outsourced to the American colonies. Coal converted into coke fired the blast furnaces that cast iron for weapons, tools, and building structures. The new industrial processes didn't just produce faster; they vaulted the limits that land and the food and fuel it produced had heretofore placed on what could be produced.[25] While fossil fuel was so cheap and abundant with a population relatively small, there was little thought of what mining and burning it would do to the planet over the course of a couple more centuries.

The wildly popular calicoes and muslins from India pointed to a strong home market for cotton. Its fibers could be handled mechanically more easily than those of wool or flax, if ways were found to do it. Finally, the growing reliance on coal in an array of industries made apparent how worthwhile it would be to take advantage of its cheapness to create artificial energy.[26] This combination of high wages and cheap fuel in eighteenth-century England created a strong incentive to develop ways to substitute the expensive for the cheap, more fuel for less human labor or put more simply, to invent machines using fuel that could vastly increase the output of human laborers. It was this concept that had eluded manufacturers. It has been said that every element of a modern automobile existed when Leonardo da Vinci lived at the end of the fifteenth century, save the concept of an engine that could turn heat into work by burning fossil fuels.[27]

A Scientific Revolution

Not all the desire in the world can produce a new idea. As the saying goes, "If wishes were horses, beggars would ride." Because we know that a handful of inventors developed some marvelous machines, we are tempted to believe that if we can supply a motive for them, we have explained why they stepped up to the mat. But machine designing requires more than a good motive and, in this case, more than talent. Thomas Savery, Thomas Newcomen, and James Watt went beyond adding ingenuity to experience; they drew upon knowledge that had not previously been known. Technology met science and formed a permanent union. At the level of biography, Galileo met Bacon.

In 1632 the Italian Inquisition forced Galileo Galilei to abjure his belief that the sun is the central body around which the earth and other planets revolve. Having already had a long and distinguished career as a mathematician and astronomer, Galileo had conceived accurate laws of motion and improved the refracting telescope before he was silenced. He had also infected an English contemporary. Francis Bacon, though a lawyer and judge, was enraptured with Galileo's observations and his inductive reasoning. In his *Advancement of Learning*, written to promote the acquisition of useful knowledge, Bacon argued that experiments, not theories, were the linchpins of the new science that was taking shape across the European continent, though it would be more accurate to call it natural philosophy, for the term "scientist" was not commonly used until the mid-nineteenth century.

Objective knowledge became the great desideratum, to be gained through forming hypotheses about forces in nature and then designing experiments that could test the hypotheses. Bacon had heard a lot of sounding off in his long career at court, so he had come to value facts over opinions. Nature, he said, talks back, by which he meant that if someone's opinions about the order of things were false, experiments would not substantiate them. Opinions, on the other hand, continued circling unabated because there was usually no way to disconfirm them. Bacon endorsed the wide dissemination of the new knowledge. This too was a departure, for knowledge had long been treated as a body of secrets to be passed on to a select group. The practice of openly sharing observations and analyses widened the ambit of investigation. Published findings acted like a magnet, bringing the filings of curiosity from all over to bear on particular problems.

Across Europe the finest mathematicians and philosophers engaged with Galileo's agenda about the laws of motion, and of optics, and the use of models. Throughout the seventeenth century scientific curiosity fermented, especially in England, but was evident in Germany, Italy, the Netherlands, and France as well. From two Englishmen, Isaac Newton and Robert Boyle, came the experiments that were going to have the greatest impact on industrial inventions. Newton was born the year, 1642, that Galileo died; Boyle was fifteen years old at the time. A succession of seers followed.

The reigning paradigm in natural philosophy had come from Aristotle, who had lived twenty centuries earlier. Aristotle described the world through the dichotomy of matter and form. While his work was astounding in its breadth, it described and defined things in nature rather than explain them. The behavior of matter differed according to its essence or form; the four basic elements of air, water, earth, and fire conveyed the qualities of dry, wet, cold, and hot. Heavy objects fell to the ground because it was an inherent quality of their heaviness. Newton's theories about the operation of gravity introduced an entirely new principle into the operation of matter. Heavenly bodies as well as those on earth were subject to gravitational pull. More than mere principles, these laws could be expressed mathematically. They could be demonstrated, though only a handful of people could do the math at the time Newton's *Principia* was published in 1689.

Aristotle had also said that nature abhorred a vacuum. Responding to this Aristotelian challenge, Galileo experimented with suction pumps. Robert Boyle, working with his air pump and bell jar, demonstrated conclusively the existence of a vacuum that meant that the atmosphere had weight. Because of the open character of English public life, knowledge moved from the esoteric investigations of natural philosophers to a broader community of the scientifically curious. The fascination with air pressure, vacuums, and pumps become part of a broadly shared scientific culture that reached out to craftsmen and manufacturers in addition to those of leisure who cultivated knowledge. Religious toleration, the free circulation of ideas through publications and discussions, and the easy mixing of ordinary citizens with members of the educated elite created a broad receptivity to these theories about the world that were overturning centuries of learning.[28]

Galileo had been defeated by authority, the authority of the church, but slowly a new authority was being created, that of a community of philosophers who read one another's writings, copied one another's experiments, and formed a consensus of experts. England was much more hospitable to this new mode of inquiry than was the Vatican. The Royal Society, founded in 1662, promoted and protected experimentation. In the Baconian spirit of producing useful knowledge and probably to justify its royal support, the society initially surveyed farming practices across England. It sponsored as well a study of the use of the potato as food. Far more important, it brought together in the same room the people who were most engaged in physical, mechanical, and mathematical problems. Its members soon discovered how difficult it was to turn useful "knowledge" into useful practices, but they did initiate a lecture series that took this knowledge to the provinces, where others might actually figure out how to make it useful.[29]

Of course none of this would have had any impact on the world of work where people sweated near blast furnaces and toiled at weaving looms had not the physical laws they studied affected the actions of lifting, pushing, and rotating. The two important discoveries for the invention of the steam engine, the pivotal innovation of the century, were the existence of a vacuum and the measuring of air pressure. And even this knowledge might have remained locked up in air pumps and bell jars had there not been a diffused conviction, since Newton wrote that nature could be made to work for human beings, that its forces could be understood and controlled.

On the Continent, where the Catholic Church was strong, Newtonian thought was suspect, treated almost as occult. Even in England, churchmen feared that too much study of nature might lead men and women to become materialists, the eighteenth-century equivalent of atheists. But in the Netherlands and England, little note was paid to these objections. Men whom we might call tutors to the world wrote books simplifying the physics that went through many editions in several languages. A participatory society had taken form with a plethora of civic organizations, self-improvement societies, bookstores, periodicals, pubs, and plays. There were popular guides to Newton, even ones written for children, and they found a ready audience. A teenage Benjamin Franklin, visiting London to learn the mechanics of printing, discovered Newtonian physics. About the same time, a young man destined to be the signature philosopher of the Enlightenment, Voltaire, spent three years in England and pronounced Newton's theory a human triumph.[30]

The Church's opposition to learning the new physics added another charge against France's old regime among critics like Voltaire. France, bogged down with so many problems throughout the eighteenth century, came late to industrialization, but its intellectuals were fascinated by both Newtonianism and its application. Denis Diderot and Jean Le Rond d'Alembert published in 1751 a magnificent encyclopedia that wedded the speculative with the practical. The editors, both philosophers, visited dozens of workshops to write the seventy-two thousand entries about the useful arts, ranging from clockmaking to centrifuges. From it, Adam Smith apparently picked up his famous description of the division of labor.[31] Diderot and d'Alembert's encyclopedia was but the grandest of a genre that had already found publishers in England who foresaw the appeal of conveniently organized sources for technical information.

Enough curiosity existed in England to sustain fairly expensive adult courses on the new physics. Coming to the capital from the province, Thomas Paine availed himself of such classes, which later paid off when he designed an iron bridge. Young men circulating through London distributed the most sophisticated ideas of the age through the country. Soon itinerant experts were offering lecture series in Leeds, Manchester, Birmingham, and lesser towns. They lugged with them hundreds of pounds of air pumps, orreries, levers, pulleys, hydrometers, electrical devices, and models of miniature steam engines. With these instruments they could demonstrate Newton's laws of "attraction, repulsion, inertia, momentum, action, and reaction."[32] Mechanics' institutes started with the specific goal of teaching working men how the new machines actually worked and—significantly—why.

The Inventors and Their Inventions

The pervasiveness of human inventiveness around the world demonstrates that no country, race, or continent has a lock on it. The Arabs and Chinese made critical advances in sciences long before Europeans. They also developed complicated hydraulic systems. In sub-Saharan Africa craftsmen skillfully mined and made artifacts in gold, copper, tin, and iron. Pre-Columbian Mayans, Incans, and Aztecs constructed impressive buildings without the benefit of iron or wheels. Examples like these tell us that it is not a civilization's superior intelligence that led to the Industrial Revolution, but rather the propitious linkage of technological curiosity to economic opportunities and a supportive social environment. Put simply, it took intelligence and knowledge operating in a society that offered incentives for applying both to production processes. The ambience also had to give scope of action to individuals to experiment. Or more accurately, authorities did not have the power to divert inquiring minds from areas of inquiry and did not punish by law or through prejudice people who undertook innovations that would disturb the traditional workplace.

Two pioneering blacksmiths, Thomas Savery and Thomas Newcomen, were the first to exploit the new knowledge of atmospheric weight, using it to force steam to run an engine. Effective in pumping water from mine shafts, Newcomen's 1705 invention also pumped life into a number of unprofitable colleries. Those in the know advised mineowners, who might be the Church of England, an Oxford college, or noblemen whose land had mineral deposits, to buy a steam engine. Around the same time Abraham Darby figured out how to use coke, a solid derivative of burning coal, instead of carbon from wood in blast furnaces. In a nice symbiosis, his steam engines used coal under their boilers and were used to pump water from the mines that were producing the coal. As with so many other inventions, it took almost a half century before cast iron could be made easily with coke, using the pumping action of steam engines to blast air into the furnaces.[33]

Newcomen's steam engine replaced both waterwheels and bellows in mining and ironmaking, the first of an endless succession of substitutions. The machines were profligate with fuel, but England had a lot of coal. It did mean that steam engines had to be used near the coalfields in the center of England. Economists call this concentration of enterprises around coal deposits the economies of agglomeration. By that they mean that workshops, if they are clustered together, will be able to draw on a pool of skilled laborers, specialized services, and raw materials at lower prices, an unintended and beneficial consequence of what was really a limitation.[34] By 1800, sixteen hundred Newcomen engines were in operation in England; one hundred in Belgium; and forty-five in France. The Netherlands, Russia, and Germany had a few; Portugal and Italy, none.[35] Something new was needed to make steam engines economically viable in places where coal was scarce, but in the meantime the success of Newcomen's machines in solving the drainage problems of coal mines turned England into Europe's principal mining center with 81 percent of its tonnage.

James Watt, a Scottish instrument maker, entered the picture when he was given a Newcomen engine to repair. This encounter inspired him to become a mechanical engineer. Though largely self-taught, Watt drew on the knowledge from the savants he knew in Glasgow. He remained an avid reader and book collector throughout his life.[36] Experimenting with the precision of a laboratory scientist, Watt puzzled over the terrible waste of steam during the heating, cooling, and reheating of the cylinders in Newcomen's engines. For this problem, he designed a condenser to send the exhaust to a separate, but connected, chamber. He patented this invention in 1769. Like the use of steam as a force to move objects, the condenser drew upon a basic property of nature, in this case atmospheric pressure. Through a long career of making steam engines and training steam engineers, much of it spent at his factory in Birmingham, Watt continued to work on his design, transforming it, as one scholar recently noted, from "a crude and clumsy contraption into a universal source of industrial power."

The average capacity of Watt's late-eighteenth-century models was five times that of waterwheels, and they could be located anywhere.[37] A horse could expend ten times more energy than a man. Watt started with that statistic to specify a unit of artificial energy. One "horse power" measured the force needed to raise 550 pounds one foot in a second, or about "750 Watts." Among those industrialists who saw the possibilities of the steam engine was Watt's son. Assiduously guided through mathematics and physics by his father, the young Watt applied himself to designing engines for ships, as did a cluster of Americans eager to find a way to carry passengers and freight up the Hudson and through the lower Mississippi rivers in the first decade of the nineteenth century. From steamships to railroads was an obvious next step, performed by George Stephenson in the 1820s. Watt and his partner, Matthew Boulton, turned out hundreds of engines for every conceivable manufacturing application, more than a thousand by 1819, the year of Watt's death. They fiercely protected their patents, and unlike the many inventors who earned little from their ingenuity, they prospered. The process for getting a patent often operated like an obstacle course. Even more surprising, Watt's contemporaries recognized the portentousness of his accomplishments.

Improved Textile and Pottery Making

The 1820s mark the beginning of the age of steam that changed the face of the earth—its atmosphere, biosphere, hydrosphere, and surface. A hundred years earlier, world population had begun the ascent that didn't peak until the end of the twentieth century. Prompted in part by the growing number of mouths to feed, bodies to cloth, families to shelter, factories to fuel the voracious appetite for fossil fuel went long unrecognized. Looked at retroactively, the cascading effects of thousands of unintended consequences from the successive technologies of industry were horrendous. It took another century and a half for people to realize that the effects of the collective actions of billions of rather small two-legged animals had actually blown through local and regional limits to become global. Statistics carry the message: Between the closing decades of the eighteenth and twentieth centuries, artificial energy made laborers two hundred times more efficient. One expert has calculated that global output grew fortyfold in the twentieth century alone.[38] But that is to get ahead of the story that gathered force during the nineteenth century with engineers constantly fiddling to improve the design of Watt's engine.

Making beautiful things also became easier with steam. Since the sixteenth century, Europeans had been importing porcelain from China. These delicately wrought and decorated pieces put to shame the heavy crockery that European potteries turned out. They also showed what it was possible to achieve. In the last quarter of the eighteenth century, firms in Sèvres and Limoges, France, and Staffordshire, England, took on the challenge of matching the quality of China ware. Josiah Wedgwood led this endeavor. Born into a potter's family, he grew up familiar with the casual organization of work in the potteries of Staffordshire. As in most crafts at the time, workers took off for wakes, weddings, fairs, and personal bouts of drunkenness. Hours were irregular, and the master potter, who typically had a shop with eight or nine journeymen and apprentices, was not much of a taskmaster. Every potter knew most of the maneuvers that turned clay into a pot, and with rare exceptions, they accomplished these tasks with indifferent success. A legendary figure in the history of industrialization, Wedgwood looked at these features as a challenge for reform.

Wedgwood approached pottery making like a scientist, an artist, and a taskmaster. He experimented with clay and quartz, blended metallic oxides, and invented the pyrometer to measure oven temperatures. He perfected a cream-colored earthenware that even the royal family used. His reputation grew from his genius at organizing his factory and molding his employees into expert craftsmen much as they molded clay into plates, bowls, and cups. Truly a visionary, Wedgwood imagined what would be ideal and then bent every effort to achieve it. Contrary to customary work routines in the potteries, he decided that his different lines would be produced in separate rooms and that potters, raised up to do every task, would instead concentrate on a single one. For producing colored ware in Wedgwood's factory, for instance, painters, grinders, printers, liners, borderers, burnishers, and scourers worked together in a single room, along with the modelers, mold makers, firemen, porters, and packers who belonged to all the divisions.[39]

Wedgwood took the mixed bag of humanity on his payroll and shaped it into a modern work force. He used bells and clocks to instill punctuality. Exact record keeping enabled him to identify and fine refractory employees. He introduced women into his plants, infuriating his male employees even though they were paid substantially more than the women. He had no tolerance for the easy work habits of his father's generation, but he did take care of his workers' material needs, paying them high wages, looking after their health, and building houses to replace the huts that they were used to living in.

Not long after Wedgwood opened up his new factory in the northwest of England, Empress Catherine the Great of Russia placed an order for a thousand pieces of his famous creamware. When he read that the empress wanted her plates and bowls decorated with beautiful landscapes as well as depictions of ancient ruins and magnificent houses, Wedgwood realized that he didn't have the artists to do this kind of work; nor would it be easy to train the ones he had. Somehow he was able to send 952 dishes to the empress. This close call with failure convinced him to start a school to train designers and decorators from an early age. Perhaps nothing demonstrates better his tendency to think in the long term than this willingness to shape adolescents into skilled craftsmen and women. Visitors to China had reported in amazement that seventy different pairs of hands worked on each plate issuing from a Chinese factory. The difference between Wedgwood's organization and this extreme division of labor in China was that while Wedgwood wanted quality, he insisted upon efficiency.[40]

In the closing decades of the eighteenth century, Wedgwood shipped tons of his creamware, black basalts, and jasperware to Poland, Denmark, Italy, South America, Germany, France, and the Low Countries. His was the standard of the day for style, artistry, glazes, material, and production facilities. When he installed steam engines into his pottery at the end of the eighteenth century, the modern ceramics industry was born. Wedgwood also helped spur England's canal-building mania in the last decade of the eighteenth century, giving early proof of the mutually enhancing relationship of industry and transportation.[41] Nature favored England with many rivers; canals enhanced their convenience.

Like the Staffordshire potteries before Wedgwood arrived on the scene, the English textile industry had clung to old production routines. Some workers were gathered in factories run by waterpower, but many men still worked at home with the help of their families and a few apprentices. Blacksmiths and clockmakers fashioned the tools with wood and a few iron parts.[42] It was an industry ripe for industrialization, and cotton was the fabric that held out the best hope of success. Its fibers were easier to work with than those of wool, silk, or flax, and its market was huge. The goal was to mechanize the movements made by the hands and arms of the spinners and weavers.

Four men, working independently, transformed textile making with their inventions of the spinning jenny, the spinning mule, and the power loom, all designed to speed up the process of turning wool into thread and thread into cloth. Their differing success epitomizes the mixed fate of inventors. Both James Hargreaves and Thomas Arkwright came up with the spinning jenny, a simple device that multiplied the spindles of yarn spun by one wheel. Once it was in operation, the number of additional spindles went quickly from eight to eighty. Hargreaves was a weaver, but Arkwright had better connections to backers and was able to set up a factory where he successfully brought six hundred workers, many of them women and children, under one roof. Edmund Cartwright, a country clergyman and graduate of Oxford, became absorbed with the weaving process after visiting a cotton spinning mill. A year later, in 1785, he patented a power loom that used steam power to operate a regular loom for making cloth. It became the prototype of the modern loom. Although Cartwright built a weaving mill, he went bankrupt. Samuel Crompton invented the spinning mule, which, as the name suggests, combined two inventions, the spinning jenny and the power loom.

He had to sell the rights to his mule because he was too poor to pay for the patenting process.

Steam power gave the British the competitive edge in textile making, particularly cotton. They could undersell almost all Indian and Chinese producers. The market for cotton was global, and England's fabrics were so cheap that they were able to break open many of the world's protected markets. The boom in cotton sales put a premium on dyes as well, most of them produced in the New World. Brazilwood delivered a red dye, as did the madder plant, which came from Turkey. Human inventiveness is wonderful; somehow someone discovered that the dried female body of an insect found on Mexican cactus, cochineal, could produce a brilliant scarlet color. It became part of the palette for dyeing cottons. Indigo, a beautiful shade of blue, originated in India. Before the age of chemical dyes, colors were hard to come by, and wearing brilliant shades of clothing signaled wealth. Eliza Lucas Pinckney, one of the few female innovators of the period, successfully experimented with the cultivation of indigo in South Carolina. Now both climates of the colony could produce something for the world market: the wetlands with rice and the drier upland with indigo. These brilliant dyes turned yet one more luxury into a pleasure enjoyed by shopgirls and their beaux. Ordinary people could now wear purple, once the color of kings, but not without raising eyebrows at first.

Steam turned textile manufacturing into the principal industry of the nineteenth century. Cotton could be grown in more places than sugar could be, but the places were still limited. Americans didn't start raising short-staple cotton until Eli Whitney invented the cotton gin in 1793. After that, demand became ferocious, growing twentyfold in fifty years. At last the mills of Manchester had a steady supply of cotton as settlers and their slaves moved into the virgin lands of Georgia, Alabama, and Mississippi. When the North successfully blockaded cotton shipments to England during the Civil War, Great Britain turned to Egypt, where the government had been promoting cotton production. Still later the availability of cheap power to pump water long distances made profitable cotton growing in China as well as parts of Arizona and California. But this is to get way ahead of the story of capitalism in the eighteenth century.

The Appearance of Factories

Workers had been long gathered in breweries, shipyards, blast furnaces, mines, and paper mills. With the industrialization of textile making and ceramics, the factory became the symbol of a new industrial era, though factory workers remained a minor part of the diverse work force of modern societies. The poet William Blake memorably called them "dark Satanic Mills." Those using waterpower dotted the English countryside, but most steam-powered ones clustered around England's coal deposits in the Midlands. Factories were dark, dirty, and dangerous places, slightly better for employees than were mines. Women and children worked alongside men in mines, moving coal by basketfuls through long, poorly ventilated tunnels. Whether powered by water or steam, factories brought to an end the autonomy of the family working together at home. Now owners or supervisors could monitor their employees' performances as they coordinated their routines, though kinsmen continued at first to work together in factory units. The increasing complexity of the machinery and consumers' insistence upon standard products made supervision more and more important.[43] Bringing their workers into one location, employers could impose twelve-hour workdays,which became the norm in the nineteenth century.

Wedgwood's success brought jobs to Staffordshire. His hometown grew fivefold during his lifetime, but other timesaving inventions threw men and women out of work. All the innovations dramatically altered the lives of workers. Taking the long view, economists can show that making goods cheaper usually ends up creating employment by releasing demand for other commodities. The pain comes in the short run, and many an English worker reacted to that pain with bitterness. In the second decade of the nineteenth century, Yorkshire laborers whose families had sheared sheep for generations smashed the shearing frames that were undermining their way of life. They took the name of an earlier resister, Ned Lud. These Luddites declared war on the machines that violated venerable work routines and banished comfort and conviviality from the workplace.

Actually woolen clothmakers in the west of England had earlier embarked on a serious effort to thwart clothiers from introducing the spinning jenny. Menacingly, this device could do the work of twenty spinners. These craftsmen had the advantage of a long tradition of regulation in the woolen trade, so they called upon Parliament to enforce laws that had been on the books for generations. After a decade of petitioning, lobbying, and pamphleteering clothmakers finally secured a parliamentary inquiry. These workers were fighting to retain an old and stable way of life; their employers, to enhance profits by saving labor costs. The workers harked back to once-honored rules that inhibited innovations; the manufacturers argued that the laws were archaic and self-defeating. It was a new twist on the much older wrangle between tradition and reform, continuity and change.

Parliament repealed the old statutes regulating the cloth trade in 1809. Two years later Luddite militancy animated thousands of laborers across a wide swath of England. While clothmakers were smashing stocking frames, farm workers attacked another invention, the mole plow used to make draining channels with a steel ball. As the name suggests, it created a track resembling that of a mole, the animal that raises the dirt slightly as it moves just below the earth's surface. The government sent an armed force of twelve thousand soldiers to quell the rural riots, a force greater than that which the Duke of Wellington took with him to Spain to fight Napoleon. Parliament followed up by adding frame breaking to the list of capital crimes, which already numbered in the hundreds. Over the century that spanned the Industrial Revolution there were more than four hundred instances of direct action against the pace and scope of workplace changes in Great Britain. The destruction of property evoked savage responses from landlords, manufacturers, financiers, and merchants, who exercised a firm control on the British government. Nowhere are that control and the values that underpinned it more conspicuous than during the Irish famine of 1846–1848. While hundreds of thousands of men, women, and children were starving, the Irish sent food to prosperous England because the laws prevented their feeding themselves from the product of acres owned by absentee landlords.[44]

Resistance to innovation continued sporadically well into the nineteenth century, going from machine smashing to the threat of insurrections. The Captain Swing demonstrations of the 1830s actually slowed the adoption of threshing machines. Fighting mechanization continued until the end of the nineteenth century among typesetters, sawyers, and those in the boot and shoe trade. Farm workers protested about more things than technical innovations, such as the use of Irish labor and how the Poor Laws were being implemented.[45] The atavistic nature of the workers' response is usually stressed to the neglect of their real grievances about hours, wages, and working conditions.

Technology is often presented as relieving drudgery when in fact the necessary coordination of industrial tasks, the constant noise, and ever-present fear of accidents made manual labor ever more unpleasant. High-pressure work became the norm, not just because of the operation of the machinery but also because machine owners wanted their capital investment to pay off every second. As mines sank deeper so did the danger from explosions, and all mechanized work filled lungs with contaminants.[46] Without representation in the production process, workers seized ad hoc means to be heard above the noise of clanking metal. They ran machines at the wrong speed. They neglected the tools that upended their work lives. As machines reduced the number of workers needed, the number of unemployed or underemployed increased. After several efforts to find alternatives to mechanization, the workers' associations settled down to mind the machines. There is scant doubt that men, women, and their children had to work under conditions far more onerous than their forebears.

From a historical perspective, these aggressive campaigns on the part of workers were very much a rearguard action, but in the immediate future, in which we all must live our lives, the protesters frequently won concessions. The public often sided with them because they had tradition on their side. Parliament took away the power of the justices of the peace to regulate wages, a legal protection that cut both ways for workers. The age of paternalism was giving way to the age of progress, an idea that had acquired a firm hold on the imagination of the British upper class. Few in the press represented the workers' side to the general public, though Adam Smith did comment shrewdly in *Wealth of Nations* that manufacturers never gathered for dinner but what they set the price of wages. While employers easily made informal agreements, workers, when pressuring for any concessions, fell afoul of the laws against conspiracies.

It would be another century before collective bargaining became part of the capitalist system and laborers would be able to enjoy the benefits of industrialization at both work and home.

The Intellectual Impact of Technological Change

People have their favorite English quality to account for England's industrial career—high wages and low fuel costs, secure title to land, agricultural improvements, low taxation, the rise of cities, and its scientific culture—but why not recognize how mutually enhancing all these elements were? Considering how unprecedented this succession of inventions was, it would have taken many factors, working interactively like genes with their feedback mechanisms, to achieve this revolution in production processes. Those who emphasize how financial incentives induced men to work on laborsaving machines take for granted a major component of England's advantages, that of fostering attitudes favorable to economic enterprise. Many of these can be traced to a retreat from the political turmoil of the seventeenth century.

What "the best and the brightest" of any generation choose as their lifework has a lot to do with the values they take in when they're young. Had James Watt been born in England a century earlier, he might easily have devoted himself to reforming the Church of England, though it's doubtful that such a career would have been climaxed with the placing of an enormous statue of him in Westminster Abbey as happened.[47] In the eighteenth century gifted young men poured their considerable talents into industrial inventions and sometimes earned fame as well as wealth. The fact that there were so many of them across several generations sustained industrial development. They also were cooperative competitors, eager to register their patents, but excited enough about the work to share hunches. And inventiveness ran in many a family like the Watts and Maudsleys.

During the eighteenth century it became apparent for the first time that innovation was the secret, if uncertain, spring behind capitalism. I say "uncertain" because there is no way to compel innovation. Certainly it can be encouraged, and evidently some cultures foster it more than others, but innovative ideas begin in the secret recesses of a particular person's brain.

What is astounding is the number of inventors who were self-taught. These were not the tinkerers who used their shop knowledge of how to use pulleys, gears, shafts, wedges, flywheels, and levers to improve existing machines, but rather genuine geniuses like Richard Roberts or John Mercer who taught themselves the scientific literature on mechanics. Roberts automated the spinning machines in 1825, an innovation that lasted until the twentieth century; Mercer pioneered processes for printing cotton, including mercerization, which gave tensile strength to fabrics.[48]

The Enlightenment in France and England

In the play of ideas that became so critical to the transformation of European society in the eighteenth century, France and England had a fascinating relationship. The British had entered the century with a new kind of society, one that had abandoned censorship and tamed political absolutism with a balanced constitution that distributed power among the king, the nobility, and commoners. (The House of Commons didn't exactly represent ordinary people. The accumulated wealth of its members exceeded that of the aristocracy, but it stood for the people.) In France, arcane laws bogged down would-be entrepreneurs. Laborers and peasants had privileges that frustrated economic development. Whether it was a province, the nobility, a heritable monopoly owned by an individual, or a corporation, large segments of the society were able to resist that dreadful thing called change.

A moribund French monarchy clung to its unchecked power until 1787, when an empty treasury forced the king to summon the old Estates-General. It hadn't met in almost two centuries and promptly converted itself into the National Assembly. That fatal step catapulted the country into revolution. And that's what it took to break through the fetters, red tape, licenses, and letters of incorporation—all the ancient Lilliputians—that had tied down the mighty giant that was France. During the nineteenth century the country played catch-up, and by World War I its per capital wealth matched that of Great Britain.

The radicalism of the French Revolution frightened most of the English, who, after several generations of prosperity, feared anything that would rock the boat. This conservatism affected all levels of society. For instance, after hearing that the scientist Joseph Priestley had expressed sympathy with the French Revolution in 1794, a mob destroyed his house. He fled to rural Pennsylvania. What a difference a century had made! Yet in many ways England had been responsible for the French Revolution. The French reading of English history, their study of Newton and Locke, and their personal discovery of the open, curious, ambitious, and industrious society of eighteenth century England gave birth to the idea that the old regime could be reformed, a more important thought than that it should be.[49]

The conspicuous changes in the built environment acted on the imagination as surely as the questions that philosophers posed. A peculiarly intense form of curiosity drew the countries of Western Europe along the path of innovation, which grew ever wider as people brushed aside customary practices. On this broad avenue of human inventiveness Europeans encountered themselves as the creators of their own social universe. There is no way to overestimate the reverberations of such a realization, so at odds with their religious traditions. The world, it seemed, was not a given to be studied and revered but rather a work in progress to be improved.

Two publications and one surprising document in 1776 had a critical impact on the history of capitalism: Adam Smith's *Wealth of Nations*, Thomas Paine's *Common Sense*, and the American Declaration of Independence. Smith wrote in part to free the economy from governmental intrusion. He described in great and convincing detail what he labeled the "obvious and simple system of natural liberty." Supporting his ideas about the economy was a model of human behavior that broke decisively with the traditional notions that men and women were unpredictable, capricious, and irresponsible. Reading his words will make the point: "The uniform, constant, and uninterrupted effort of every man to better his condition [is] the principle from which public and national, as well as private opulence is originally derived." Smith also maintained that the "principle which prompts to save is the desire of bettering our condition, a desire which though generally calm and dispassionate, comes with us from the womb, and never leaves us till we go into the grave."[50]

Just as Newton saw uniformity behind the dazzling diversity of planets, meteors, and stars, so Smith found consistency in the multifarious commercial transactions that made up the market. He described an economic universe that was not subject to the laws of the state but, on the contrary, subjected the state to its laws. The inventions that culminated in industrialization had hardly begun when Smith wrote, but there had been enough improvements for him to divine the future.

Integral to Smith's theorizing was the law of unintended consequences, an arresting insight of the Scottish philosophers that explained how acts could be willed by self-interested individuals but still turn out to be beneficial to a larger group. The most famous example of course was the invisible hand of the market that used competition to convert the profit motive into a force for good. As Smith explained, it is "not from the benevolence of the butcher, the brewer or the baker that we expect our dinner, but from their regards to their own interest."[51] Here was a concept that contributed to the strong impression that reality was often obscured by appearances. Smith was responding to the developments of his lifetime, 1723–1790, when it was still relatively easy for an ambitious young baker to get the money to set himself up to compete effectively with established competitors. Later the concentration of capital took a lot of the optimizing agility out of the "invisible hand."

Smith and his fellow Scots proposed a conjectural history of mankind that traced human society from hunters and gatherers to herders, then to sedentary farmers, and finally to commercial society. The discovery of indigenous peoples of South and North America still hunting and gathering helped anchor the Scots' hypotheses in observable facts. From this perspective, a slow process of progressive change, not the contingent events and powerful people written about in history books, propelled history forward. Smuggled into Smith's careful synthesis of economic facts were the propositions that human beings were consistent, disciplined, and cooperative market participants and that natural laws governed the realm of voluntary activities because these qualities were dependable.

The Scots asserted that human history didn't oscillate through cycles of change, as had been thought, but rather that cumulative, irreversible patterns of improvements were moving events in a new direction. Time carried with it development, not mere change. This realization altered Europeans' stance toward both past and future. The Garden of Eden had reminded Christians that they lived in a fallen state, and the Renaissance had extolled ancient Greece. The classical notion of cyclical change had linked human life to the observable cycles of birth and vigorous growth to maturity, followed by inevitable decay and death. Now, with time parceled out in dependable processes, sequential patterns, and irreversible trajectories, all the rivulets of human activity could be seen flowing into the great river of progress, though that term did not gain currency until the nineteenth century. The new script of development took over the imaginative space once devoted to the poignant story of inevitable degeneration. Fear moved aside to make room for hope.

Thomas Paine was one of hope's most successful propagandists. Paine wrote *Common Sense* for Americans after he had immigrated to Pennsylvania in 1773. He was an irrepressible iconoclast and a passionate fighter for reforms that would benefit ordinary men and women, not just their employers and landlords. To make his case, he attacked the whole idea of a balanced constitution in which the British maintained such pride. Paine denigrated the past when he wrote that the British constitution was "noble for the dark and slavish times in which it was erected." Quoting liberally from the Bible, he explained that kings had been sent to the Israelites as a punishment. He contrasted society—then a new word and concept—with government. Society came about through voluntary association and was a benefactor whereas government, though necessary, was an unpleasant punisher. Commerce Paine saw as an alternative to war in getting people what they wanted. He described it as "a pacific system" that worked "to cordialise mankind, by rendering nations, as well as individuals, useful to each other."[52]

When Paine wasn't writing incendiary tracts, he was working on a design for an iron bridge that was eventually built. He joined his radical political platform to an enthusiasm for economic progress. His targets were the vestigial injustices of an aristocratic society, not the new abuses of an industrial society. His writings influenced the history of capitalism not just because he helped push the American colonies out of the British Empire but also because he made the attack on tradition a popular cause.

Men like Paine admired the entrepreneurial economy because it was open to talents rather than reserved for those of inherited status. This remains true today, even if it is harder to get access to capital.

The threat from old enemies faded slowly—at least in the imagination. Paine continued to lash out at England's aristocrats while the new industrialists were consolidating much greater power than they had had. Ordinary laborers lost a lot of liberty in this era. In the nineteenth century factory owners, newly solidified into a powerful class, exercised control over them through their right to hire and fire at will and without cause. Making private property the premium social good, they rejected the idea that freedom is just as precious to workers as to themselves. Because it took laws to protect workers trying to organize on the private property of their bosses, owners have often treated workingmen's campaigns as attacks on liberty. For others, the protracted battle between labor and management over safety, wages, hours, and working conditions has called into question the linkage of economic and political freedom that once appeared unproblematic when capitalists were fighting against an entrenched landed class.

During the eighteenth century the cumulative effect of capitalist practices could clearly be seen as forming a system. Production was organized to return a profit rather than provide for the survival of the society. Individuals using their own resources made the decisions about how to use those resources without much interference from public authority. The sum of decisions became an economic reality of great significance in the setting of prices. Information coursing through an informal communications network in the form of prices or rates of interest or rents then influenced other participants' choices. Employers rather than craft customs organized the work to be done. Personal power accrued to those who made money through the impersonal workings of the market. The powerful hierarchies of the church and the landed class continued to exert influence but frequently had to yield to those with power in the economic realm.

We could say that industrialization had a foot in slavery when we follow its course in the United States. Then slavery played a strategic part in the transformation of the textile industry, the leading sector in both the American and British economies. In the nineteenth century the American North and South formed a compatible economic relation. Northern manufacturers supplied clothes, timber, and tools to southern planters, who concentrated their capital on producing cotton, which was the leading export for the nation for the first five decades of the century. Without the profits from southern slavery, the American economy would certainly have developed more slowly, but there would have been nothing inherently unprogressive about a slower pace.

The restrictions on the freedom of wage earners were often difficult to see, but the chains of slavery were only too visible. I began this chapter linking the exploitation of slave labor in the Caribbean sugar plantations with the inventions that led to the Industrial Revolution. Driven by the same profit motive and drawing on the same funds, both material and cultural, the two had similarities, but by the end of the eighteenth century, they had diverged sharply. Industrial innovations took place at home in the midst of one of the most fertile intellectual periods in history; slavery flourished out of sight, in remote and backward areas, but not quite out of mind. Sensibilities further divided them. At home the abundant proof of social progress of which the marvelous machines were part awoke the sleeping conscience that had made possible the Atlantic slave system.

The cause of furthering human rights sprang, as if from nowhere, to animate two generations of reformers in the eighteenth century.[53] Dozens of new propositions about men and women and their unfolding nature clamored for attention. The possibility—over time, the probability—of favorable change danced before all eyes in the abundance in the food stalls and the cornucopia of fabrics, china, books, tools, and trinkets shown off in shopwindows. Where once nothing had seemed more certain than that the past would endlessly repeat itself, now all awaited what would come next.

In the midst of this moral ferment a new spirit of humanitarianism infected the popular imagination in Western Europe. Curiosity created new commitments, and these inspired organizations that in turn launched political campaigns. Polemical pamphlets, memoirs of slaves, testimony from those involved in the trade pushed to the fore the vivid image of African men and women in chains. The contradiction between fighting for freedom while holding on to slavery was embarrassingly obvious to leaders of the American Revolution and their British opponents. They had after all justified their break with Great Britain on a universal right to "life, liberty, and the pursuit of happiness." Four years after the Declaration of Independence, the Pennsylvania legislature abolished slavery. Under the Articles of Confederation, Pennsylvania was actually a sovereign state, so it became the first government to demonstrate that an institution as old as the Bible could be ended peacefully through the action of a democratically elected legislature.

Every other northern state followed Pennsylvania into this new era. By 1801 the Mason-Dixon line, which began as a surveyor's line between Pennsylvania and Maryland, had become the symbolic division of free and slave labor in the United States. The gradual abolition laws of the northern states mandated freedom for those slaves born after a certain date once they had reached the age of twenty-five or twenty-six or twenty-eight. Even in the South, antislavery societies flourished until the 1820s, when profitable cotton cultivation sustained slavery for another forty years. Unlike the British with a statute that applied to their island possessions far from home, northerners freed slaves living in their midst. Far fewer slaves existed in the northern states than in the South, but it is estimated that enslaved men and women composed a quarter of the working population of Manhattan. When New York law denied legitimacy to holding human beings as property, it constituted the largest peaceful invasion of private property in history. It took the American Civil War to complete what Pennsylvania had begun with the passage of the Fourteenth Amendment to the federal Constitution in 1868. If one ever wondered whether ideas had any force in the workaday world, the campaign to end slavery should still any doubts.

Today there are fascinating experiments in capitalism shaping up around the world, but originally and for at least three centuries capitalism came from the West. Its momentum carried Europeans and their modes of operation around the world. Once capitalism was a full system with cultural values and social habits enhancing its power, it was poised to crush any opposition to its expansion. The qualities of Western Europeans—openness to novelty, aggressiveness, tenacity, ingenuity, and sense of superiority—became sharper under the grindstone of success. This is the Europe that the rest of the world knows, admires, and fears. It is also the culture that nurtured natural rights, democracy, and a humanitarian sensibility.

6

THE ASCENT OF
GERMANY AND THE
UNITED STATES

I N THE EARLY nineteenth century public attention was riveted upon
Napoleon Bonaparte's armies carrying revolutionary ideas across the
continent of Europe. But British industrialization gathering steam during the same years would be the more lasting revolution, building as it
did on two centuries of advances in agriculture and trade. An integrated,
modern economy was in the making. The benefits of Britain's technical
breakthroughs didn't materialize into higher standards of living until well
into the century, but the country's prosperity was pretty evident. Almost
two-thirds of its population had found jobs in manufacturing, retailing,
or transportation, swelling the urban population. London became the
glittering world capital of finance, trade, and fashion with a civil society
enlivened by association meetings, demonstrations, the theater, and popular magazines, big and small.

Even shorn of its continental American colonies, Great Britain retained its preeminence as a seaborne power with colonies in the Caribbean, Canada, Singapore, Australia, and India. Contemporaries captured its global reach when they observed that "the sun never sets on the British Empire." Industrialization was creating a new incentive for controlling raw materials that could be brought home to be worked up into finished goods. Its continental American colonies lost to an independent United States, Britain turned its attention to India, which enhanced the importance of its naval station in South Africa.

Yet this nineteenth-century chapter in the history of capitalism will not focus on British success but rather tell how Germany and the United States were able to pass Britain and take a commanding lead among world economies. It is in many ways a perverse tale, for Great Britain had established free trade and worked assiduously to bring other countries into the global commerce revolving around its banks and products. Germany and the United States fought the magnetic pressure Britain exerted by erecting tariffs to protect its industries, creating what Max Weber described as the "closed national state which afforded to capitalism its chance for development."[1]

Those who move into untrod territory rarely move straightforwardly. Without maps or visual cues, they wander about, running into cul-de-sacs and lingering around dry wells. Having gone where no one else has been, the innovator has less fear of competition. When others decide to follow the successful trailblazer, their trip is more direct. In the case of Germany and the United States, modernizing their agriculture and industry became part of a push to create a nation. Their forward motion announced that capitalism was not an English aberration but rather a new stage in world history. By the beginning of the nineteenth century people had begun to anticipate that there would be further changes, that the future would not mindlessly replicate the past.

The pressure Britain's neighbors (and rivals) felt to follow its lead was acute, for that most ancient of political strengths, military power, now depended upon industrial capacity. First Britain's challengers had to figure out how to get their hands on their marvelous machines, leaving them with little choice but to engage in industrial espionage. Societies that enjoyed sufficient isolation from the Western European center of wealth and war making could ignore British gains, and they did, unless they were drawn into the British Empire. Those closer could not.

Once Britain's spectacular new machines could be seen, it was possible to imagine replicating them. Such an appropriation had haunted private investors as well as British officials, but theirs was too open a society to be very successful at keeping secrets. The steam engines that revolutionized old ways of making tools and spinning cotton attracted spies from France, Germany, even Britain's quondam colonies in America. All these countries had the same task: to discover what was turning conventional artisanal shops into manufacturing plants of unprecedented productive power. Britain prohibited skilled workers to emigrate, but the French had actually persuaded close to a thousand factory operatives to emigrate over the course of the eighteenth century.[2] Nor could patented machines be exported legally, but the Germans smuggled in machines or bought them in Belgium. Americans with good memories inspected British plants and later copied them. Sometimes workers, slipping out of the country, duplicated in their new homes the lineups of machinery that had changed the face and pace of British manufacturing.

Many countries set up spinning mills, but England's success, it turned out, involved more than machines. The dexterity and efficiency of English managers and workers had to be imitated as well. And that was a question of culture, something a good deal harder to copy. No other country came close to matching England's output of textiles, the major product of the early Industrial Revolution. Even though wages everywhere else were considerably lower than they were in Great Britain, neither France nor Germany succeeded in exploiting that cost advantage. In 1811, 40 percent of all cotton spindles operated in Great Britain. Canada and the United States, which also had high wages, operated another 22 percent of the spindles, and the remaining 39 percent were spread through Germany, France, Russia, Belgium, Switzerland, Italy, Spain, Portugal, Austria, India, Japan, China, and Mexico! It was an amazing record, a triumph of machine design and worker expertise.[3] During roughly the same period, 1780 to 1830, English population doubled while its total industrial output increased by almost 300 percent—an astonishing growth rate especially since much of that time Britain was at war with France.

The inventiveness that began with a crude steam engine in 1701 continued without pause in Great Britain. By 1851 Queen Victoria herself was ready to celebrate the ingenuity of her people. With Prince Albert as sponsor, a great exhibition of "the Works of Industry" opened in a stunning building made of glass on an iron frame. Inside the Crystal Palace, visitors could examine thirteen thousand contrivances gathered from the world's collieries, docks, offices, kitchens, factories, and laboratories. The exhibition's implicit heroes were the "inventors," "artists," and "authors" who emerged as new romantic figures. The more enduring impact from such an arresting display of the fruits of industry came from a new perception of time. It began to seem that all mankind had been moving inexorably toward great technological achievement. Contemporaries in the nineteenth and early twentieth centuries were still so dazzled by the marvelous machines of their era that they could not imagine that their forebears hadn't been straining to get to the machine age as fast as possible.

History books began describing industrialization as a universal human goal. The past that used to enthrall Europeans, such as the glories of ancient Greece or the ardor of the Crusaders, slipped into the shadows. Writers treated those unlucky enough to have been born before the modern era with condescension. People spoke of industrialization as a destination, like a great city, toward which men and women had long been moving, even though they could no more anticipate what came after them than we can the events in the twenty-second century. This historical perspective didn't fade until the late twentieth century, when writers began to refer to "postindustrialism." Modernity having been reached, it became obvious that human life went on with new aspirations and concerns.

An inquisitive history of capitalism was slow to be written because inevitability hung over such transformations as those of horse-drawn railway cars in coal mines to railroad locomotives chugging across the world's continents. People found a name for this unabating improvement. They called it progress. Earlier "progress" had just indicated going from one place to another, as in "progressing across the countryside." Now it gathered new meanings. Progress flipped the value assigned past and future. Change no longer frightened; it confirmed progress.

Within twenty years of the Crystal Palace Exhibition Germany and the United States overtook the great pathfinder to take the lead in the insistent march of capitalism. The volume of American steam power passed that of Great Britain in 1850 and had far outdistanced it by 1870, with Germany following within a decade. To take the measure of steel production as another measure, the United States surpassed Great Britain in 1886; Germany did the same seven years later. Other indicators followed the same trajectory.[4] And Germans and Americans did more than belch out smoke and steam. They started a new wave of innovations in chemistry, electricity, and internal combustion machines. For the first time the front-runner that had astounded the world for two centuries lagged behind—not just in productive capacity but in innovation. Latecomers to industry had the advantage of newer equipment and untapped capital. Their farms were still shedding workers to meet the labor needs of industrialists. It may seem a bit perverse to drop Great Britain just as it reached the zenith of its technological achievements, but this history is following the relentless revolutions of capitalism rather than cataloging its various successes.

Germany and the United States are so unalike that their economic successes clinch the larger point: Once the key elements of industrialization were exposed, they could be adapted to different settings and cultures. The successful economic trajectory of two such dissimilar countries cautions against relying on one formula for economic success. But passing up the pacesetter took some special gifts. The United States was an obvious contender for economic preeminence. During its colonial tutelage to Great Britain, colonists had shown an impressive capacity to fit their economic ventures into the larger scheme of European commerce. Independence liberated them from Britain's prescribed channels, freeing their commercial smarts as well. Germany too possessed great assets for economic development if they could be dug out from the thick layers of tradition and inherited privilege. German strengths were both material and cultural: great natural resources, an educational system that fostered science and technology, and a work force proud of its skills and disciplined habits.

For the United States the push to advance economically became an intrinsic part of its emerging national character. Americans celebrated their enterprise and efficiency as a way to differentiate themselves from decadent, feudal Europe. Bereft of any strong aristocratic traditions, they valued audacious qualities, often exaggerating the grip of the dead hand of the past on countries abroad. At the first census of 1790, a population of almost four million men and women, mostly young and inured to work, lived on the edge of the most fertile land on the globe. On their way to this national domain, they would discover coal, iron, gold, and oil in great abundance. That first census also counted more than three-quarters of a million enslaved persons. The value of slaves soared with the invention of the cotton gin, which made profitable the short-staple cotton grown throughout the region. Any hopes spawned by the ideals of the Revolution that slavery might decline throughout the South died.

In 1789 the United States adopted a constitution designed to create a single nation from its thirteen semiautonomous states. In that same year Germany was more a name than a country. It referred geographically to more than three hundred separate kingdoms, principalities, and municipalities, including Austria. For the United States nationalism abetted economic development while in Germany the task of modernizing the many different German economies supplied the means for creating a nation. Americans suffered from having been colonies, accustomed to playing a subordinate role to the mother country. Germany bore the burden of fragmentation long after its neighbors—England, France, Belgium, the Netherlands, Russia, Spain, and Portugal—had acquired strong national identities. Nationalism resonated through the nineteenth century. Different as they were, both the United States and Germany embarked on nation building. This drive gave to economic endeavor a moral, romantic, and aesthetic appeal.

German nationalism owed a lot to the French Revolution and its Napoleonic aftermath. Napoleon had honed the revolutionary army into a mighty military force. He reformed institutions wherever he conquered, carrying his modernizing impulses along as his army marched across Europe in the first decade of the nineteenth century. He erased the Holy Roman Empire, which had tied together a loose confederation of German-speaking Central European states since 800. He formed in its place a confederation of thirty-nine states, including Austria. Napoleon's legacy and the name of that small town in the Austrian Netherlands where he met defeat would long be remembered.

After Waterloo, a coalition of European powers met in Vienna and created a peculiar entity called the Concert of Europe. The French Revolution's excesses had been so frightening that even former enemies cooperated to defeat Napoleon. The exhausted, participating countries in the concert basically used diplomacy to shuffle lands around to achieve some kind of balance of power. A century of hostilities made peace seem worth a few sacrifices. The British succeeded in getting the others to condemn the slave trade, but the major purpose of the concert was to calm the Continent down. There was no returning to the past, so the job of conservatives was to maintain the status quo that they had established. They blamed the radical ideas of the Enlightenment for fomenting the French Revolution. To them, the rallying cry of "Liberty, fraternity, and equality" represented an attack on religion, the family, and standing authorities. The lesson was clear: People needed an iron glove, and the hand within it had best be one attached to a distinguished heritage. The postrevolutionary conservatives didn't want to replace one set of ideas for a better one; they wished to eliminate ideas from politics altogether. Far better to rely on customs and customary habits of obedience.

On the other side of the learning curve, European liberals cherry-picked those novelties from the creed of the French Revolution that fitted well with their notion of reform. They detested Napoleon's megalomania but applauded his rationalization of the law. They championed natural rights and added to them a commitment to free trade and economic development. They also supported a broader suffrage to counteract the influence of the aristocracy newly empowered by Napoleon's defeat. Round two of the confrontation between stalwart defenders of the status quo and enlightened representatives took place in Germany. Only now it wasn't a contest between two sets of ideas but rather arm wrestling between liberals and the aristocrats who had engineered the Congress of Vienna.[5] Germany, especially the kingdom of Prussia, which gained two cities and the iron-rich Ruhr Valley, came out of this extended European trauma very much on the winning side. Still, like Italy, "Germany" represented an agglomeration of duchies, principalities, and independent cities.

Economic Development and German Nationality

It was crystal clear that the separate German states suffered economically from being a crazy quilt of states rather than a group under a national blanket. The 350 German principalities lacked uniform weights and measures, excise duties, road rights-of-ways, and commercial practices, not to mention currencies, banking institutions, and toll-free transportation. Rather than promote commerce, the autonomous cities acted as administrative centers for either the church, a university, or a princely court. Armies, especially in Prussia, commanded a large proportion of public funds, and everywhere administrative costs were bloated. While improvements in British agriculture steadily raised the people's standard of living throughout the eighteenth and nineteenth centuries, impoverished serfs still did the farming in most of Germany.[6]

The French had eliminated the old feudal dues that bore down on their peasantry in one spectacular night of legislation. Ending serfdom in Germany took a lot more time—in 1807 for Prussia, but not until 1832 in Saxony. In Prussia 65 percent of workers still tilled the soil, so restructuring rural landholding was tantamount to transforming the entire society. Looking enviously at agricultural gains in England and the Netherlands, where only 40 percent tilled the soil, Prussian landlords began to think that free labor might improve agricultural output. The government passed laws freeing all serfs while compensating landlords for their loss of income from fines and rents. The reform gave the land of those serfs who didn't have enough to farm effectively to the landlords as well. It will not shock modern readers to learn that landlords, who controlled the government, took hundreds of thousands of acres from these newly freed serfs, who were left to fend for themselves as agricultural laborers.[7]

When the transition from serfdom to free labor was complete, southwestern Germany retained its tradition of small farms. Even in Prussia, the number of farms doubled, going from fewer than a million in 1816 to more than two million in 1858. Those former serfs with enough land to farm worked for themselves while the great Prussian estates were now worked by landless workers. Not until the end of the century did harvest yields markedly increase.

German urban centers were hardly more advanced than the countryside. Guilds suppressed competition and retained the capacity to repel innovations until well into mid-century. Formidable obstacles prevented people, products, and ideas from moving about through these many jurisdictions. Only a common language and the memory of having once been together in the Holy Roman Empire supported the dreams of a united Germany, but that was enough for the leaders of Prussia, whose military made it the likely champion of unification. Prussia had the coal, iron, investors, and political will to sponsor economic development. Its leaders realized that the road to nationhood lay through commercial development even though the Junker aristocrats loathed the urban middle class that dominated commerce. Nothing for it; they needed wealth to maintain their army and its esteemed military traditions.

The potential for a great German nation centered in the kingdom of Prussia, which was bigger than the next three largest states of Bavaria, Hanover, and Westphalia put together. In a fascinating contrapuntal action between economic and political incentives, Prussia lured more and more German states into the Zollverein, the uniform, commercial union that it had started in 1817. Some entrepreneurs benefited from an expanded internal market and protection from foreign competition, but other regions suffered from competition, which their local tariffs had mitigated. Yet year by year the Zollverein grew, helped by Prussia's willingness to make financial sacrifices to gain the admittance of major states in the south. Economic improvements held out hope of herding the diverse German states into one national fold.

A new concept helped nudge German unity forward. Once economies had been viewed as strong or weak, but now, with England setting a fast pace away from former levels of productivity, people started talking about advanced and backward economies.[8] It was a startlingly new way of thinking about economic activities. Previous economies had simply involved the repetitive, age-old tasks of feeding the people, producing useful objects, and making their exchange possible. Economies now were expected to develop or bear the onus of being backward. "Backward" had a different ring from "traditional." The idea of backwardness exacerbated competition among Austria, Prussia, Russia, France, and England. This linear view of history as a progressive movement is so familiar to us that we can easily miss its initial impact. Before, military might have mattered most, especially in Germany, the ground for so much warfare. The high cost of maintaining a military establishment made the state's economic development critical to sustaining a position in the international order. With Great Britain continuing its industrial ascent, wealth creating and power exerting became ever more entwined.

Germany's large domestic market provided the stimulus for development. The great river arteries of the Rhine, Oder, Weser, and Elbe carried most of the commercial traffic with canals aiding navigation. Steamships appeared in the 1820s, followed by more canal building, but the most transformative invention for nineteenth-century Germany was the railroad. Not the horse-drawn wagons on rails that had been used in coal mines for a long time, but locomotive-driven railroads that pulled loads up and down hills, across great plains, and right onto the loading docks in port cities. All it took was laying down track, preferably with standard dimensions. Perfected by the English in 1830s, the railroad shrank the distances between places, people, and products, as measured by time, much as had lateen-rigged ships three centuries earlier. In Germany, as in the United States, canals became important complements to railroad transportation.

The German states sprawled across the center of Europe between the modernizing West of France, Belgium, and the Netherlands and the backward East of Russia, Poland, and the Balkan states still part of the Ottoman Empire. German railroads connected these halves of Europe. Their construction prompted the repair of decaying overland trade routes and stimulated the economies of Germany's neighbors—always a sound policy if a country has something to sell. The Zollverein expanded, as more German principalities chose to join, coinciding with a speculative boom in railroad building.[9] As so often happens with technology, one fruitful area stimulated another; railroad building supported German mining, metallurgy, and machine making. In France railroads radiated out from Paris; in Germany they linked industrial centers.

Unlike most underdeveloped countries today—to use the twentieth-century term that has replaced the unkind adjective "backward"—Germany had the capital to build railroads. Private bankers like the Rothschilds and Mendelssohns were a major source of investment funds. That they were Jewish firms enabled conservatives to inject the poison of anti-Semitism into discussions of economic problems. Other prominent private banking houses belonged to Huguenots. From a social standpoint bankers could be seen as outsiders, but their branches and connections in Amsterdam, Brussels, Paris, and London only enhanced their capacity to finance German industrialization. In this early period financial institutions were critical. Capital was not in short supply, but it was dispersed through a population untutored about investments.

It was imperative to Prussia to exclude Austria from any new arrangement so that it could dominate the future German nation. Otto von Bismarck, the great architect of the German nation, adroitly deployed the Prussian Army against Denmark, Austria, and France in a series of short wars that secured unification of Germany on his terms. By 1871 there was a new German Empire with the king of Prussia as emperor. The waxing Hohenzollern dynasty had pushed aside the waning power of the Hapsburg Empire, now reduced to Austria and Hungary. Once unification was achieved, Germany became the industrial giant of Europe. Bismarck had triumphed with his policy of "iron and blood" against what he rather dismissively called the "speeches and majority decisions" of his liberal opponents.

Germany had extracted a large indemnity payment from France in addition to taking Alsace-Lorraine as a victory prize from the Franco-Prussian War. The acquisition of the iron-rich Ruhr Valley triggered a large internal migration from the overpopulated eastern parts of Germany to the industrial West. The consequent prosperity created an exuberance that proved propitious for economic development. Again cultural differences proved influential. Germany's population, for instance, proved more mobile than that, say, of France, where partible inheritance kept younger sons at home waiting for a share of their parents' property. Germans also began crossing the Atlantic, to build new lives in the New World. Germany and Ireland accounted for 80 percent of the nine million immigrants who came to the Americas, mainly the United States, in the middle decades of the nineteenth century.[10]

Private Initiative in the United States

In the United States the elaboration of a commercial society took place under remarkable, and remarkably different, circumstances. Commercialization worked interactively with democracy to accelerate national development. Americans had paid dearly for their revolution in blood and debts, but 1789 brought to an end a long period of economic distress. Revived prosperity promoted the construction of roads, the extension of postal services, and the publishing of newspapers. The United States soon printed more newspaper issues than any other country in the world, regardless of size. The establishment of the new government under the Constitution coincided with this economic turnaround.

Treasury Secretary Alexander Hamilton thought Adam Smith's idea that an economy could regulate itself crazy. Perhaps this was because Hamilton knew that it had taken his authority and expertise to convert the revolutionary debt into an asset. This he accomplished by consolidating all the IOUs held against the state and federal governments. He then issued "stock" to pay them off and dedicated specific taxes to fund the interest on these issues. Investors quickly bought up the debt. Thanks to Hamilton's fiscal prowess, the United States became a safe place to store money. Most Europeans who bought Hamilton's stock invested the earned interest in the country's many private ventures. You could say that the United States became the financial community's first emerging market. At the same time, the European war that the French Revolution triggered put a premium on American foodstuffs. Its shippers became neutral carriers for the belligerents.

Competition and obstacles, if not overwhelming, have proven a great stimulus to economic development. Northerners, who since the seventeenth century had worked hard to find a niche in the world market, developed the institutions and personal traits that propelled capitalism while the planter elite of the staple-producing South rested on its laurels, or more precisely, on its handsome profits, first from tobacco and rice and then from cotton. The planters spent lavishly to maintain a genteel way of life and hid, as best they could, the harsh realities of their dependency on slave labor.

Owning slaves acted as a kind of insurance policy for their masters. Jefferson inherited 135 slaves when his father-in-law died in 1774, among them Elizabeth Hemings and her 9 children. When Jefferson died fifty-two years later, he owned more than 70 Hemingses. The value of slaves soared after Whitney's cotton gin made profitable the crop of the short-staple cotton that could be grown all over the South. Rarely has an invention come at a more opportune moment. Textile mills were proliferating in Great Britain and elsewhere. Southern specialization intensified their demand for foodstuffs, lumber products, and manufactured goods that the North could supply. Producing cheap shoes and clothes for slaves became a start-up venture for many a bootstrap entrepreneur.

Against the measurable wealth that slave labor created must be placed the immeasurable loss to the South of cultural capital in skills not learned, investment opportunities left undeveloped. Even less tangible was the enormous drain of the region's moral resources from defending a social system that others found increasingly indefensible. All of the northern states had found ways to gradually abolish slavery by 1801, and the U.S. Constitution provided for a ban on slave imports from Africa after 1808. With the expansion of the South's frontier, the price demanded for enslaved persons in the domestic market doubled within a decade. Soil exhaustion in Virginia and Maryland made it very tempting for planters to sell their stock in human beings.

The domestic slave trade represented the one great entrepreneurial activity in the South. With eastern land worn out from the overcropping of cotton, frontier openings became bonanzas. The biggest losers in this new era of southern expansion were the African Americans whose opportunities for manumission practically disappeared once their value rose. Men, women, and children were wrenched from kith and kin and force-marched to western Georgia, Alabama, and Mississippi, carrying the institution of slavery deeper into the continent. Before railroads arrived to promote long-distance trade, the internal slave trade represented the most important interstate commerce, a fact rarely mentioned in American history textbooks. By 1820 more than a million African Americans had moved beyond the boundaries of the original states to Alabama, Mississippi, and Louisiana.[11]

When Jefferson came into the presidency in 1801, he worked swiftly to democratize Hamilton's accomplishments, dismantling the Federalist fiscal program, reducing taxes, and cutting the size of the civil service. The United States got the best of two worlds with Hamilton's and Jefferson's economic programs. Hamilton dismissed the notion that ordinary people could use their money wisely and thus ignored the most protean element in the economy, but he won the confidence of investors at home and abroad. Jefferson, on the other hand, distrusted financiers and wanted to liberate working-class white men from the condescension of their superiors. His belief in limiting government power also had roots in the slaveholders' determination not to be harassed by the federal government.

Rejecting Hamilton's guidance of the economy from the center, Jefferson freed money and credit from national control and left it to the states and private corporations to supply the country with competing banks.[12] For the next half century the states, shorn by the Constitution of the power to block economic developments, took the lead in promoting them. They built an infrastructure of banks, roads, and canals while offering bounties, licenses, and charters for promising and unpromising ventures alike.[13] It is rather ironic that the judge whom the Federalists had appointed at the last minute to monitor the newly elected Jefferson, Chief Justice John Marshall, wrote stellar decisions against state-conferred monopolies and other breaches of contract that enhanced the scope of free trade and promoted commerce based upon competition rather than privilege, another Jeffersonian goal.

If the Constitution laid the bedrock of America's liberal society, the free enterprise economy raised its scaffolding. After its ratification, a new economic order took shape, erasing most traces of the one dominated by Great Britain. The elimination of imperial control over land and credit enabled thousands of operators to act on their plans with the financing of high hopes. Jefferson's commitment to decentralizing governmental power dispersed opportunity to rural America, which had the abundant brooks and streams to be converted into waterpower, the principal source of energy for American manufacturing for some decades. Fortuitously this centrifugal movement of initiative was accompanied by successful efforts to join the parts of the Union by roads and canals and, still later, telegraphy and railroads. Congress also promoted informal unity with its expanding postal service and underwrote the mailing costs of the country's proliferating newspapers.

Eager for farms of their own, a never-ending stream of Americans pushed west with confidence that they had a right to the land. Acquisitions from native tribes had to be bought, negotiated for, or wrested from those tribes that had lived there for centuries. Then the adjective "hostile" became linked to the word "Indians." Newspapers characterized the Native Americans' tenacious fight to save their ancestral hunting grounds as examples of savagery. The invaders justified their intrusion on the ground that the indigenous people had failed to improve the land or at least improve it in the European manner. Capitalism with its steady promotion of development gave a kind of specious justice to Americans' advance into the wilderness. Skirmishes and set battles between the invaders and defenders continued throughout the settlement of the Ohio and Mississippi valleys.

Nothing could hold back the tide of land-hungry men and women from the land that Americans had appropriated rhetorically much earlier. They called their first legislative body of 1774 the Continental Congress. When George Washington formed his first cabinet fifteen years later, he said that he wanted men "disposed to measure matters on a Continental Scale." After the War of 1812, Congress gave its veterans 160-acre bounties in land lying between the Illinois and Mississippi rivers. The westward movement of families away from eastern centers of authority and refinement accelerated. When land offices opened on the frontier, sales soared. Most veterans sold their patents to land speculators in eastern cities. Frontier communities sprouted up like daisies in a summer meadow. By 1815 annual sales of the national domain had hit $1.5 million and more than doubled four years later.[14] Producing food became the great enterprise of Americans. Moving onto better and better land throughout the century,

American farmers finally reached California, whose lush Central Valley remains today one of the world's greatest exporters of cotton, vegetables, cattle, poultry, nuts, and fruits.

American geographic mobility astounded foreign visitors, who wrote home about the undulating train of wagons snaking their way to Pittsburgh, whence they could raft down the Ohio. To these visitors, American society offered an ever-changing visual landscape as people moved, roads were graded, land was cleared, and buildings were raised in a reconfiguration of the material environment that went on without rest. Ordinary men had never before had such a chance to create their own capital. With cheap land, easy credit, and ready markets at home and abroad for their crops, they flourished. Some would break in new land and then sell it at a considerable profit when others moved to the area. Access to land meant maximizing family labor. One Ohio pioneer, finding that his hundred-acre farm did not offer "full employment" for his sons, plunged all his savings into buying enough land to absorb their full working capacity. Farmers not only thought in terms of capitalizing their labor but considered their sons' labor in those terms as well.

Although much of the land in Ohio was poorly drained, most chroniclers of the frontier remarked on its astounding yields. The returns from selling cotton abroad helped settle international debts, but the northern frontier pushed economic development toward building towns, hundreds of them. Four million families started new farms between 1860 and 1920. Farm mortgages became more common when state legislatures after the Civil War pushed mortgage rates below 12 percent.[15] Farming has been romanticized over the years, but many contemporaries considered farm work drudgery. One New Englander bemoaned the fact that there had been no factory jobs when as a boy he had to apprentice himself to a farmer. Some sons and daughters—particularly those with a scholarly bent—voted with their feet to leave the family farm and seek out jobs as schoolteachers, another expanding field.

With few exceptions, entrepreneurs came from outside the circle of wealthy colonial families. Drawn from a growing middle class distinguished by its work ethic and openness to new ideas, they borrowed from friends and family, invested their own sweat equity, and sank or swam with regularity. With such volatility, "panics" and "busts" came every score of years. The human loss in dollars and disappointments was significant, but the young economy was resilient enough to snap back. The lifting of colonial restrictions on manufacturing unloosed as well Yankee ingenuity. In the generation born after the Revolution many a poor boy discovered his talent for making clocks, buttons, industrial wire, textiles, shoes, hats, pianos, vulcanized rubber, and steam engines of various kinds. Eli Whitney, who invented the cotton gin, also originated the principle of interchangeable parts in manufacturing when he got a contract to build rifles for the army. Specialization offered commercial opportunities to whole communities. Wethersfield, Connecticut, for instance, annually sent to market one and a half million onions.[16] Levi Dickinson invented a broom from corn. By 1833 the townspeople of Hadley, Massachusetts, were producing half a million brooms a year. One English traveler noted that he had never "overheard Americans conversing without the word DOLLAR being pronounced." It didn't matter, he said, whether the conversation took place "in the street, on the road, or in the field, at the theatre, the coffee-house or at home."[17]

The market's opportunities came in new guises to new participants. The digest of patents put out by the first patent commissioner reveals the full sweep of commercial imagination. Because America's patent law was cheap and easy to acquire, ordinary people took advantage of its protection. As rural towns got connected to the national market through a system of roads, canals, and railroads, patent applications dramatically increased. Scores of ordinary Americans patented devices in metallurgy, chemical processes, hydraulic implements, machine tools, and household conveniences. Others only dreamed of inventions, like the pamphleteer who conjured up for his readers two-hundred-foot-high sails stretched across the length of a mile to capture and convert wind into power equal to two hundred thousand men![18]

After 1834 the U.S. Patent Office scrutinized applications for novelty and usefulness. While this move diminished the number of patents granted, it also proved a boon to unknown and underfunded inventors whose success in getting a patent acted as a vote of confidence in the invention.[19] Every idea that found material expression in a novel artifact proved just how wrong were the old-timers who invoked the past to predict that the world already had too many clocks, steam engines, stoves—you name it. Novelty, usually experienced as a break with the expectation of how things ought to be, became the most constant feature in the lives of Americans. After so many centuries of resistance to change, new products in the nineteenth century sometimes caught on just because of their novelty.

Freed from British restrictions, American merchants sent ships up the California coast, across the Pacific, and into the Indian Ocean. Elias Hasket Derby, America's first millionaire, made his money opening up markets in Russia and the Orient. Americans boat designers and shippers had the pleasure of beating out the English with clippers built along the New England coast. New York's Black Ball Line dominated the passenger and mail routes of the North Atlantic. Pushing the rivalry a bit further, American merchants began sending their clippers to China to deliver tea to the London market, prompting a great China race.

Alexis de Tocqueville, author of *Democracy in America*, saw enough of the economy to predict its upward trajectory. "Independence," he wrote, "gave a new and powerful surge to their maritime genius. . . . Today it is Americans themselves who carry home nine-tenths of the products of Europe. It is again Americans who bring three-quarters of the exports of the New World to consumers in Europe." Having noted that, he went on to explain how Americans could beat out Europe in shipping costs: "It's not because their ships were cheaper which they weren't. The wages of seamen were even higher," he stressed, going on to say, "[O]ne would seek in vain the causes of this superiority in material advantages; it is due to purely intellectual and moral qualities."

The European navigator ventures on the seas only with prudence; he departs only when the weather invites him to; if an unforeseen accident comes upon him, he enters into port at night, he furls a part of his sails, and when he sees the ocean whiten at the approach of land, he slows his course and examines the sun. The American neglects these precautions and braves these dangers. He departs while the tempest still roars at night as in the day he opens all his sails to the wind; while on the go, he repairs his ship, worn down by the storm, and when he finally approaches the end of his course, he continues to fly towards the shore as if he already perceived the port. The American is often shipwrecked, but there is no navigator who crosses the seas as rapidly as he does. Doing the same things as another in less time, he can do them at less expense.[20]

The profits from grain and cotton crops spread rapidly through the states, filling thousands of pockets with just enough money to finance new ventures whether it was moving to a good teaching post, starting a store, working up an invention, buying supplies for a frontier stake, venturing a cargo to the West Indies, buying a slave, or making a strike for one's own freedom from enslavement. From an accountant's point of view, young Americans were poor, reckless, and debt-prone; but a risk-taking genie had been let out of the bottle of parental constraint, and not all the prudence of the ages could stuff it back in. The democratic practices that rapidly, if unexpectedly, followed the establishment of the American Republic redounded to the benefit of young people. With the British gone and the colonial upper class deprived of its hold on political power, ordinary people could choose their own life goals and usually pursued them in the economy that Jefferson and his successors chose to leave unregulated.

Still, the United States, like most of Germany, was economically primitive by any modern standard. Until the end of the 1820s only those living on the nation's rivers could be sure of long-distance transportation and then only in one direction. Roads did not go very far inland and were impassable in rainy months. Most people lived in very simple houses, often of their own construction. Enslaved families crowded into barracks-like cabins. Olive Cleaveland Clarke, who grew up in western Massachusetts, remembered being seventeen before she saw her first carpets. She had to visit Northampton to make an acquaintance with a piano.[21] Musical instruments were scarce. Chester Harding, who later made a career of portrait painting, had never seen a picture of any sort until he was twenty-five. The Netherlands in the seventeenth century could boast of two million works of art.

Life expectancy was not high in the nineteenth century, age forty-five for those white women and men who successfully made it to age twenty.

For African Americans, the picture was much bleaker, life expectancy dropping as low as thirty-five. White women in 1800 bore an average of seven children; enslaved women, nine, each delivery posing a threat to the mother's health.[22] Such high fertility made for a youthful nation, with 58 percent of America's population under twenty in 1820, compared with 44 percent in 1899 and 27 percent today.[23] Wages, good by European standards, were far from bounteous when the cost of living is factored in. Food, clothing, and shelter took 80 percent or more of a worker's wages for the typical sixty-hour workweek.[24] In Europe food alone could eat up 60 percent to 80 percent of a family's weekly budget, depending upon the harvest. But people take their bearings from what has gone before them, not from future, unimaginable standards of living. And what Americans in the first half of the nineteenth century experienced was the steady improvement of their material environment: acres brought under the plow, steam engines applied in ingenious ways, rivers and streams dammed and sluiced to power mills, with miles of canals and roads cut through the wilderness.

Technology in Germany and the United States

The United States and Germany borrowed the technology in the basic industries of textile making and locomotive design from Great Britain. Using British designs as launching pads for innumerable modifications and ancillary inventions, both countries proved adept at perfecting the inventions that they acquired from Great Britain, as well as from Belgium and France. John Jervis's work on the railroad is exemplary of the process. Britain's locomotives didn't do well on sharp curves, so Jervis reconfigured them in a kind of inventive dialogue with his British mentors. By 1836 American manufacturers had stopped importing locomotives from Great Britain because they had domestic ones to buy. Similarly iron production got under way in the United States in the 1830s with blast furnaces that had to be redesigned from British models in order to make use of Pennsylvania's abundant anthracite coal. In the 1840s Americans got 80 percent of their pig iron from Great Britain; by 1856 domestic production had overtaken iron imports.[25]

Germany's abundance of coal, iron, and accessible capital translated quickly into railroad mileage. By mid-century the number of operating railroad miles had become a good indicator of economic development. Britain had close to ten thousand miles laid; Germany came next in Europe with 58 percent of that total; France with 29 percent, Austria-Hungary with 19 percent, and Italy and Russia with less than 1 percent.[26] The United States already had almost nine thousand miles, a figure that was to treble in the next ten years. Originally, the most efficient American lines were those private companies built because politicians guided publicly financed railroads to their home districts, however remote.[27] Unlike European countries, the United States had hundreds of miles of sparsely populated areas to cover in order to join the Pacific and Atlantic coasts. The American government became a major sponsor of railroad construction, providing incentives in land grants to railroad companies. Real estate speculations abounded as building the transcontinental railroad became awash in graft. Despite this, laying railroads became an important adjunct to nation building for both Germany and the United States.

By the last three decades of the nineteenth century the United States and Germany had nurtured the innovations that picked up the beat of economic development. Constant innovations didn't come without cost, because every improved device rendered obsolete its predecessor. Prodded by the lure of stronger sales and higher profits, backers of incessant inventiveness hurt established industries and firms. The early-twentieth-century Austrian economist Joseph Schumpeter captured the essence of capitalism, with his "creative destruction" of the old by the new.[28] Rarely has anyone so precisely hit the nail on the head, implying the consequences associated with both "creative" and "destruction." Less catchy is the economists' take on this, "early obsolescence," a phrase meant to indicate that commercial objects don't grow old; they just become obsolete when they are replaced by something better. Retrospectively we can see that innovation pushed the relentless revolution of capitalism, yet why or how one country or region grabbed the technological lead remains a bit obscure.

Telegraphy offers a fascinating example of the Ping-Pong game of adaptive inventions. In the closing years of the eighteenth century, two French brothers, Claude and Ignace Chappe, contrived to send signals that could be transformed into words through semaphore relaying stations placed ten to fifteen miles apart. In 1837 an English instrument maker, Charles Wheatstone, devised and patented an electric telegraphic system using five needles to point to letters of the alphabet. He conducted experiments in electricity, optics, and acoustics of sufficient excellence to earn him a professorship at King's College, London, despite his lack of formal education. Wheatstone had been drawn to telegraphy through his efforts to measure the velocity of light. Two years earlier Samuel Morse, building on the work of another American, demonstrated that signals could be transmitted by wire, using electric impulses from a sending apparatus connected by an electric circuit to a receiver that operated an electrical magnet that produced marks on paper. From this, Morse composed his famous code of dots and dashes representing letters of the alphabet.

Although Morse quickly gave a public demonstration of his telegraphy, its transition from model to mechanism took another five years and a subvention from Congress. Morse's telegraphy eventually became the one most widely used, but not before Germany's Ernst Werner von Siemens, founder of the great electrical engineering corporation, developed a telegraphic system based on Wheatstone's that Eastern European countries adopted. All these successes in telegraphy came amid dozens of failed efforts, sunk by the technical problems of transmitting messages through space.[29] Contemporaries found something magical about transmitting messages in seconds. Soon telegraphy became an integral part of running a railroad. Its signals speedily shuttled information about arrivals, departures, and breakdowns across continents; its poles lined the roadbeds, vivid evidence that the space dividing people was collapsing.

Siemens came to telegraphy through his military post in the artillery workshops of Berlin. In Germany, he oversaw the laying of the first submarine lines and received credit for saving the town of Kiel from an advancing fleet when the Germans were fighting the Danes. In 1845 his patented machine delivered the message that the German Assembly had voted in favor of a German emperor. Morse's first message was also political: The Whig Party had nominated Henry Clay for president. More famous was the biblical quotation that the young daughter of a friend had suggested for a message: "What Hath God Wrought!" Thirty-three years later, in 1877, God wrought something even more portentous, the telephone.

For both Germany and the United States, the railroad became the most effective nation builder and spur to economic growth. It also dramatized for all to see that speed modernized how people thought and behaved, effectively dividing premodern and modern epochs in human history. Train stations created new public spaces. They were frequently the largest buildings in towns; in cities architects designed them to be temples to progress. German conservatives bemoaned the fact that riding on railroad would breach the walls separating social classes. And of course they did. Manufacturers dispersed throughout Germany became railroads' first beneficiaries and their most powerful sponsors. They saw the enormous advantages in simultaneously reducing transportation costs and widening the market for their products. Laying track rapidly connected German manufacturers with the producers of food, timber, and iron ore. Germany's unification in 1871 only intensified the synergy of political and economic development. With Germany's incessant railroad building, its mileage surpassed first France, then Belgium and had drawn even with Great Britain by 1875.

Because of the very backwardness of Germany, railroad building jumpstarted the economy by joining hundreds of local markets to a universe of commerce. Railroads gave regional manufacturers a chance to reach the larger, more complex market of a united Germany and its international trading partners. Railroad building stimulated considerable demand for iron products as well. Railroads were the first big business in both countries and, for many years, its only big one. In the United States, railroads were seen as so essential to national unity that the federal government lent its army engineers to lay out the first routes. West Point was in fact the major engineering school in the country at the time. Once railroads were established, maintaining them called for continuous experimentation to improve road beds and rails. Unlike the secrecy surrounding the steam engine, information about railroad construction and operations flowed easily across national borders. Civil engineers shared their findings and visited one another's countries, sometimes on their own, sometimes sponsored by their governments.[30] They wrote reports; they published pamphlets.

The Role of Banks

Even more important in the history of capitalism were the size and permanence of the investment in railroads. A measure of the railroads' central importance to an economy can be gleaned from the fact that in 1865 the New York Central Railroad alone had assets equal to one-quarter of all American manufacturing wealth. The substantial capital that constructing railroads required changed the operating strategies of their owners because their assets were much greater than the cost of running the roads. The fixity of capital in railroad lines made retrenchment ineffective. Railroad investors had to devise strategies to stimulate uses to spread the fixed costs over more freight and passengers.[31] They strove to keep the volume of traffic as high as possible or to recoup capital costs through higher fares. The fixed capital in plants and the adjustments that it entailed represented the new constraints of industrial capitalism. The equation of time with profit became crystal clear; the expensive equipment had to be kept in productive use.

The impact of railroads upon the overall economy went from transportation to production to finance. Through the first half of the century Germany's fate had been closely tied to the prejudices and preferences of the landed aristocracy, which preferred to invest in mortgage bonds and government annuities rather than commit their considerable funds to industrial ventures. It took new institutions to meet the heavy capital demands of railroad construction. By mid-century investment banks had appeared in Cologne, Berlin, and Leipzig. They concentrated on industrial investment, giving German finance a different cast from that of either France or England.[32] Railroads also became integral to the business plans of others—not just manufacturers but farmers as well, all of whom were highly sensitive to rate schedules or any shenanigans that might be used to raise rates. Railroads quickly became a kind of public utility, making them vulnerable to government regulation.

The capital in capitalism needed its own institutions to entice savers to investment in new ventures and enable them to guard against the risk of losing their money, once invested. There was sufficient capital in Europe to finance industrialization if it could be mobilized. This is where banks came in. Banks played a critical role in funneling capital into industry by turning savers into investors. Expanding to mutual companies that accumulated the savings of ordinary people, they performed a great service by luring cash out from the mattress and into the hands of business borrowers, who then paid interest to the savers. Usually everyone benefited except when banks failed, as they sometimes did, taking these small accounts down with them. While rarely initiating ventures, banks acted as catalysts once development began. Of course channeling other people's money created opportunities for fraud and speculation, an inseparable, if less respectable, twin to enterprise.

Banks floated bonds that allowed governments to cover extraordinary expenses. Insurance companies sold policies to people to guard against future loss from death and accidents like fires and the sinking of a cargo ship plying the waters of the Pacific, Atlantic, or Indian Ocean. Modern statistics gathering came out of these risk management efforts. Industrial workers in England formed friendly societies to collect money to be paid out to their members or their families in the event of mishaps. When they sought information from the government about the frequency of industrial accidents, Parliament intervened, claiming its authority to be the sole institution to gather such information. Statistics got its start here in the early nineteenth century.

The importance of political and religious support of enterprise can't really be appreciated except in contrast with places where that support didn't exist. In the Muslim world Koranic injunctions hindered the formation of corporations and the inheritance of partnerships. Deaths could dissolve partnerships and pools of capital without the legal instrument of incorporation.[33] Being unable to bequeath a firm's shares often made it impossible to maintain businesses. Unlike Muslim countries, Europeans developed financial institutions especially for handling investment money.

German banks began as private institutions, becoming joint-stock companies later. As so-called universal banks they offered a range of financial services from extending short-term credit to taking deposits, discounting bills, selling insurance, and handling mortgages while underwriting and trading in securities.[34] Britain industrialized at the leisurely pace of a pathbreaker. Most of its financing came from personal savings and the shrewd reinvestment of profits. Both England and France had central banks, but the German regional banks proved to be just what was needed for them.

Napoleon had created the Bank of France in 1800. Established by merchant bankers outside the inner circle of financial officers, the Bank of France had a monopoly on issuing notes and refused until the 1860s to establish branches outside Paris.[35] After banking restrictions were lifted in 1848, financiers formed the Crédit Mobilier, but it didn't really help French industry much because French investors preferred to send their money overseas for more exotic investments than those near home.

Between 1871 and 1911, the British annual rate of savings was 12 to 15 percent; Germany had an even more impressive rate of 15 to 20 percent. Savings were important because they created a pool of capital that enabled businesses, in Thornstein Veblen's words, to expedite their "quest of profits," a wry observation that well captures the restlessness built into capitalism.[36] Those enjoying that momentum didn't appreciate efforts to slow it down that often put industrialists and bankers, especially in France and Germany, at odds. Nobody, it is said, loves his banker. Certainly many a business resented its bankers' insistence upon rationalizing procedures in accounting, borrowing, and personnel policies.[37]

Americans started two stock exchanges in Philadelphia and New York in the 1790s, two decades after British brokers had formally established "the Stock Exchange" to replace their informal gatherings in coffeehouses and on the streets. Although dealing primarily in government issues, the stock exchanges in London, Antwerp, Amsterdam, Paris, Lyon, and Marseille became cosmopolitan oases where men of many different nationalities, from Armenians and Jews to Swedes and Frenchmen, conducted business cheek by jowl. Thomas Paine wrote that commerce "cordializes men," introducing a neologism that never caught on. Voltaire caught the spirit of the exchange when he wrote that "there the Jew, the Mohammedan, and the Christian transact together as though they all profess the same religion, and give the name of infidel to none but bankrupts."[38] Railroads did usher in a more complex stock exchange in the United States when Wall Street began trading railroad stocks and bonds. Not until the end of the nineteenth century did trading in corporate stock become the main activity in stock exchanges around the world. Mindful of the rowdiness of brokers, governments kept a close eye out to ensure order.

In the 1850s the world economy got a phenomenal boost when James Marshall discovered gold at the site of a sawmill he was building in 1848. Nine days later the United States signed the treaty that ended the Mexican-American War and gave the nation California. The volatility of a gold find in an area not yet outfitted with the clothes of government produced a unique situation. Fortune hunters sped to California from the west coast of South America, Hawaii, Australia, Tahiti, and China. Those coming by water took one-third the time of Americans coming from the East Coast. Within 4 years California had attracted a quarter of a million immigrants from twenty-five countries. Most actual miners were Chinese. Both Great Britain and France dumped convicts into the boiling cauldron of San Francisco. At the same time, indigenous men and women died in great numbers at the hands of the lawless and racist newcomers.[39] More gold was dug up in the 1850s than all places put together in the previous 150 years. Lubricated by an influx of gold that increased the world's currency sixfold, world trade almost tripled. Gold surpassed silver as the standard currency. More countries adopted the gold standard as finds in Australia, Alaska, and South Africa bulked up the gold supply.

Every country has its own financial history. In America, the Bank of the United States, the country's only central bank, fell victim in 1836 to Andrew Jackson's determination to strangle "the monster bank." It could never be said that a central bank was necessary to economic development since the United States saw phenomenal growth without one. The vibrancy of the economy sustained this rickety monetary structure. Only the exigencies of paying for the American Civil War got Congress to support a network of federally chartered banks that could issue notes in 1863. The provision that the banks had to deposit their cash reserves in New York City consolidated that city as the country's financial center. Prior to the war, banks—hundreds of them—had supplied the nation's currency by issuing notes, giving counterfeiters a field day. The North issued greenbacks that depreciated almost as fast as had the continental notes that paid for the American Revolution. By war's end the greenbacks and war borrowing amounted to half the annual gross national product! Taxes had paid for only a fifth of the crushingly expensive war. The war's burden continued when widows' pensions became the largest expenditure in the national budget.[40]

From Thomas Jefferson at the beginning of the century to William Jennings Bryan at the end, many American leaders have articulated their fellow citizens' unease with the invisible part of the economy: the money that circulated, the savings that went into banks, the borrowed capital that financed enterprises. The greenbacks actually proved a blessing to those who wanted to stabilize the currency and have a federal bank. When the government offered to redeem them for gold in 1879, few took up the offer. The old American faith in credit extension and soft money reasserted itself. Any correction of the fiscal mess would bring hardship, and the majority of entrepreneurs wanted to avoid pain. Currency expansion was the promoters' slogan whether by adding silver to the country's legal specie or by issuing more bank notes. Quite reasonably most investors were counting on the country's sunny economic prospects. Mark Twain captured the spirit of the early 1870s in the character of Colonel Beriah Sellers. Moving from small-town America to New York City, Sellers bragged to friends that he had arrived in the city penniless and now owed half a million dollars. Like many actual Americans, Sellers expected his creditors to keep him afloat.[41]

Like most wars, the American Civil War accelerated the pace of change. For decades cotton exports had dominated the American economy, orienting northern agriculture and industry toward southern consumption. The Union army's demand for uniforms, tents, rifles, wagons, and foodstuffs soon took the place of cotton. This new market acted like a catalyst in the industrialization of the economy. After the war the party of Lincoln became the party of nascent industrialists. Economic opportunity burgeoned in the West as well. A 1913 law put in place the Federal Reserve Banks, which consolidated federal power over the currency.[42] These diverse experiences suggest that while mobilizing capital was important, how it was done was less so.

A narrative account of a subject like capitalism tends to focus on the key developments that advanced progress or unblocked obstacles halting forward motion. It needs to be stressed that much happened in capitalism's history that did neither. Falling from view are the millions of dollars, pounds, francs, and marks along with untold man- and woman-hours that went down the ratholes of ill-conceived projects. Their presence reminded investors that innovation was never risk-free, but success was frequent and conspicuous enough to keep the flow of investments coming. What capitalism needed above all was capital, not just the nest eggs of inventors and their friends and family but freshets of cash from those who didn't want to produce anything except a return on their money.

The Benefits of Incorporation

Nothing revolutionized industrial finance more than the legal form of incorporation that gave limited liability to the owners of enterprises. Incorporation had long existed as a means for giving cities or charities a specific and largely autonomous scope of power in perpetuity. We still have incorporated residential areas. Pooling capital through partnerships operated superbly when the right participants came together, and still does. Partners usually wrote contracts that enabled each to break up the enterprise in deference to the vicissitudes of life. This ease of dissolution acted as a significant drawback to the long-term growth of a company.[43] As the name suggests, incorporation created an artificial person who paid taxes, could sue to collect debts in the company's name, or could less happily be sued. The corporation could borrow money and sell shares in the company to members of the public to raise money. This meant that records were open to shareholders' scrutiny, though access became more restricted as companies grew in size. Management often had controlling shares of stock in the nineteenth century, but incorporation enabled a separation between investors and managers. It also had the advantage of locking in large sums of money. And because they are artificial, corporations could exist forever, removing the threat of inopportune dissolution that partnerships carried with them.

There was a downside. Corporations cost money in fees from lawyers and the government. Once gained, the privilege could be enjoyed free, a gift from the government and its people to private persons. The separation of shareholders from managers, celebrated in the lore about corporations, sometimes invited irresponsibility, if not outright corruption. High-flying corporate heads could fiddle with the books, contract with their own firms, or pay dividends out of capital instead of earnings. Worse they could sell new shares of stock to pay dividends, amounting to Ponzi schemes.[44] Still, corporations became popular among American and British entrepreneurs. General incorporation laws in the nineteenth century made it easier and cheaper to turn private companies into public incorporated entities than it had been. This was particularly the case in the United States, where the states chartered thousands of limited liability companies. They far outnumbered those in Great Britain until halfway through the nineteenth century.

A bad experience in the eighteenth century had led the British Parliament to pass the so-called Bubble Act, restricting incorporation. Limited liability companies became popular there after 1856, although family firms were common well into the twentieth century.[45] Even more encouraging to enterprise were the liberal bankruptcy laws, which favored business borrowers over their creditors—that is, making money over having money. When industrial incidents, such as a flying spark from a railroad engine, ignited a farmer's haystack, the farmer had a difficult time winning a tort case against the railroad company. Laws, and even more emphatically judges, were loath to punish employers when their workers were hurt on the job. American law, much as it differed from state to state, usually came down firmly on the side of enterprise.[46]

Since the whole world is not composed of investors and entrepreneurs, the concept of limited liability did not always charm those who weren't either. The principal complaint was avoidance of personal responsibility through the creation of an artificial entity. There was also a deep-seated suspicion of speculation and paper profits implicit in buying and selling something as seemingly unsubstantial as a share in a company expressed on a piece of paper. Lightly regulated until the end of the nineteenth century, corporations then became more subject to legislative and judicial restraint. Shareholders and managers insisted that corporate taxation represented double taxation since shareholders paid taxes on their dividend income.

The desideratum of investors was to protect their investments while receiving a regular and robust return. Easier said than done; the investor was at the mercy of his or her own ignorance about the business involved. On the other side of the investing equation, those who actually developed new applications of technology wanted investors who willingly took risks and left the operational details to them. The railroad builders' voracious appetite for funds put pressure on the normal pools of capital. Necessity became the mother of invention. Financiers came up with debentures, long-term fixed-rate loans that operated much like government bonds. Another stratagem was to issue vendor shares to the suppliers and contractors of mining or railroad companies in lieu of cash. And then there were preferential shares that gave their holders the first crack at returns before dividends were paid to the holders of common shares. One of the great scams of American economic history was another Crédit Mobilier, this time an American company organized in 1867 to extract profits from railroad construction by inflating costs, which were assumed by government subsidies, which in turn paid for bribing members of Congress, which held off investigations until the presidential campaign of 1872.

A great deal of attention has been given to the excellence of the English and American corporation as a vehicle for capitalist expansion, but for small and medium-size enterprises, the costs could be discouragingly high. So much so that at the end of the nineteenth century, German legislators introduced a new business form, the private limited liability company in which partners could write legally enforceable contracts that specified the terms of the partners' relationship. This eliminated the principal drawback of partnerships, the unexpected incapacity or irresponsible acts of a partner. The private limited liability company found a happier home in France and Germany with their civil code legal systems than in Great Britain and the United States, where the common law, favoring individual rights over state concerns, prevailed. So uncongenial was this type of partnership to common law countries that it was not available to entrepreneurs until 1907 in Great Britain or in the United States until the second half of the twentieth century.[47]

German industrialists and their bankers coalesced into a new class, not the gentry elite or the urban, professional middle class but one composed of industrial giants and their lucky associates who had been made millionaires. They were willing to raise the money for railroad projects; they supplied the cargoes to be shipped out as well as the new customers for the freight coming in. They mined coal and fabricated iron ore just as the European machine industry heated up. This global economy promoted specialization and an international division of labor. If the Junkers, who still dominated politics, sneered at these new men, they did so privately because most Germans saw these big industrialists as public-spirited men contributing to the great cause of strengthening the German Empire.[48] Where enterprise became a kind of national pastime in the United States, in Germany it was confined to a class still inclined to admire aristocratic tastes.

The Protracted Depression of 1873

The year 1873 proved to be a bad one in the history of capitalism. A depression began that lasted in some areas for another twenty-six years! One of the problems with the free enterprise system comes from its dispersed decision making. With individuals and private companies acting on what they calculate as their best interest, it's hard to know what's going on generally. No one, as it were, is in charge. Prices and rates deliver information, but the causes behind the decisions that produced those particular prices and rates have to be interpreted. When things are going well, there's little incentive to explore the meaning of market behavior. Only when things go sour do people clamor for explanations. In 1873 the challenge was greater.

Efficiencies in production outpaced effective demand. That is, there were more goods than people ready to buy them.[49] In what you might call the adolescence of capitalism, trouble spots could gather like black clouds before a summer storm. People called them slumps, the word itself conveying an image that things would soon right themselves. Not so this time. A stock market crash in Vienna and the failure of a major bank in New York marked the beginning of two decades of economic instability. Added to the manufacturers' inventory problems were bounteous harvests from America, Argentina, and Russia. Low grain prices wiped out thousands of those farmers throughout Europe who were still following traditional methods. Even French and English agriculture tanked.

The crisis of 1873 proved the integration of world markets when downturns in the United States and Europe plagued economies in South Africa, Australia, and the West Indies. The cumulative impact of long-term developments kicked in to prostrate most Western economies. America's output increased in the last decades of the nineteenth century, but prices stagnated. Most industrialists had worked hard to keep wages low, inadvertently impoverishing potential buyers of their goods. Conservative attitudes toward the importance of thrift contributed to the problem. Still dominated by an aristocratic ethic, upper-class Europeans looked down upon the spending of ordinary people, especially if the display of their purchases threatened to blur the lines between people of refined taste and their social inferiors. Today we would just say that a trade glut caused the excess of goods over purchasers, but we would be wrong. There was also a cultural lag.

When the price of silver began to fluctuate wildly in the 1870s, the awkwardness of using both silver and gold as currency became apparent. Great Britain had maintained a single source of value, gold, to settle accounts, and Germany, the Scandinavian countries, France, Belgium, the Netherlands, and the United States followed suit in the 1870s. Now each country's currency—mark, franc, pound, dollar—had a fixed exchange rate with gold. If a German investor sent two hundred marks to the United States, he or she could be sure exactly how many dollars it would be worth. The gold standard proved to be an invisible taskmaster, nanny, jailer, and seer. It influenced everything from imports and exports to the price of wages. If a country ran a trade deficit, gold left the country, causing a drop in the domestic purchasing power, which in turn hurt sales. Manufacturers had to lower costs to gain back customers. They generally did this by pushing down wages.[50]

The gold standard underwrote a new intensification of global trade, greatly aided by telegraphy, international business news, and improved oceanic transportation. People became more confident that their money would be fairly exchanged in other countries; they started investing abroad, especially in the United States, now the largest economy and also the land of the best opportunities for high returns on capital. Argentina and Egypt also benefited from the endless search for the best investment. The speculation that had buoyed Germans before the depression of 1873 began came to a halt. Still, the forward momentum of pent-up entrepreneurial energies proved stronger than the depression's brakes. By 1880 the German economy was again in ascendance. But the 1880s and 1890s were also decades of hardship.

Midwestern American farmers almost threw a spanner into the new regime when they began railing against the new specie tyrant. Suffering from low prices in the 1890s, they blamed the fixed exchange of the gold standard for their woes. They advertised a list of the people's enemies, starting with the British financial elite, followed by international bankers in general. They found a champion in the Democratic Party's standard-bearer William Jennings Bryan, who brought delegates to the party's convention in 1896 to their feet with his dramatic injunction to the money masters: "You shall not crucify mankind upon a cross of gold." Things were touch and go until the Republicans triumphed over these renegade populists in the fall presidential election.

Though we rarely think of it this way, the United States too was undergoing a process of unification in the 1870s.[51] The American Civil War—no eight-month romp like the Franco-Prussian War—had taken a terrible toll in lives, property, and peaceful pursuits during the four years between 1861 and 1865. By 1870 the last of the southern states had been readmitted into the union, and the North was ready to call it quits on reconstructing the states that had joined the Confederacy. Turning toward the West, in 1871 Congress passed the Indian Appropriation Act, which made Native Americans national wards and nullified all previous Indian treaties. The Civil War had interrupted the efforts to integrate California into the nation; four years after Appomattox, the Central Pacific tracks joined those of the Union Pacific from the east. A gold spike attached the two at Promontory Point, Utah. The transcontinental railroad connected the two coasts of the United States, pulling in all the sparsely settled places in between. The victorious North was ready to impose its national vision upon both the South and the West.

With the Civil War behind it, the United States could turn toward devel-

oping the vast tracks of unoccupied land acquired in 1803 in the Louisiana Purchase and through the treaty that ended the Mexican-American
War in 1848. Meanwhile its urban population had been exploding. Total
population grew twelvefold between 1800 and 1890 while those living
in cities increased an astonishing eighty-seven times. Gustavus Franklin
Swift helped forge economic ties across the continent with his invention
of refrigerated railroad cars. Now the cattle ranging over the grazing lands
west of the Mississippi River could be driven to Omaha, Kansas City, and
Chicago to be slaughtered and their dressed meat shipped to the densely
populated, urbanized East. In a society where almost everyone could
afford to eat meat, refrigeration furnished the missing link between supply and demand.

Prosperity in the second half of the century, if not steady, still brought
positive improvements in wages, public health, and food costs. The United
States has long been viewed as the paradigmatic capitalist country. Its persistent economic advance has been laid to the favorable ratio of people to
land, the absence of a feudal past, the rich endowment of just the right
mineral resources needed in industry, and the hardworking, disciplined
young men and women issuing from America's family-owned farms.

Washington Irving coined the phrase "the almighty dollar" in the
1820s. A century later President Calvin Coolidge famously announced:
"The chief business of the American people is business." The insight bur-
ied in that rather banal observation should not be dismissed. There were
very few competing values or career options in the nineteenth century.
The father of Henry and William James, who was independently wealthy,
bemoaned the fact that people in his country always asked him what he
did for a living, an inquisitiveness that sent him sailing back to Europe.

In capitalism, the cumulative private decisions of participants exercised coercive force throughout the economy. Denied the protection of
monopoly control, the most efficient operators forced the less efficient to
imitate them or retreat from the active management of their resources.
Capitalist activity was not dependent upon any particular person, region,
or family. If one passed up a moneymaking opportunity, another would
see the potential gain in it. This is an optimal assessment that has to be
balanced against the fact that capitalist wealth also created rich oppor-

tunities for graft such as the bribing of politicians by the builders of the American transcontinental railroads.

At the beginning of the century the United States had fewer than four million people, almost all of whom lived on the Atlantic shelf on the North American continent. They had shared a common history for a very brief period. Germany, like the United States, was composed of disparate parts in 1776, but those disparate parts shared a history going back to the time of Charlemagne in the ninth century. Americans loved novelty; Germans feared it. The American practiced religious toleration; Germans had fought bitter wars over differences within the Christian faith. Germans accepted authoritarian politics; Americans celebrated the weakness of their political institutions. Still, Germany almost equaled the American economic record without its "exceptional" advantages.

Nothing undermined the dominance of inherited wealth more than this capitalist principle of the interchangeability of participants. A son who depleted his family's fortune created opportunities for someone else more attuned to making than to spending money. Unlike an aristocracy, capitalism didn't depend upon the virtue, prudence, or boldness of anyone's progeny for growth. Americans accepted and admired these capitalist imperatives. Germans were less convinced of their virtue. Throughout the nineteenth century engineers and manufacturers struggled against the contempt of upper-class Germans toward parvenus, a word with hardly any meaning in the United States.[52] But it didn't really matter because impersonal forces would maintain capitalism's momentum once enough key players had jump-started the development process. Americans more easily took risks in keeping with the entrepreneurial spirit of capitalism, but Germans had a disciplined tenacity that contributed to their country's successful economic development.

Along with the obvious advantages of being a first mover in economic development like Great Britain, there came some distinct disadvantages that rivals might exploit. Britain had a heavy investment in its trailblazing textile industry, but success made its entrepreneurial class timid. English investors looked elsewhere for opportunities. The United States and Germany benefited from this. They could move into new industries and tap the pools of capital, looking for promising new investments.

Nation building, important to both countries throughout the nineteenth century, acted as a catalyst for economic development. America had a pervasive entrepreneurial spirit and a vast continent lying ready for cultivation. In Germany a rising class of industrialists was ready to integrate economically the nation that the aristocratic Junkers had brought into being. Both countries were rich in the natural resources vital to railroad building and heavy industry. Their citizens proved to be amazingly adept at copying and modifying English inventions. More important, they soon started innovating in chemistry, electricity, and automobile making. In retrospect, their surpassing Great Britain seems almost overdetermined. The British economy didn't decline; it simply lost its relative position while maintaining an impressive level of productivity, as the Dutch had earlier.[53] The mystery is why France did not step up to the mat.[54]

The relentless revolution of capitalism kept up a fast pace during the nineteenth century. The size and scope of enterprise had penetrated every continent. As the twentieth century began, the philosopher Max Weber called capitalism an "iron cage." If people really wished to live as their forebears had, they could find a way, but fewer and fewer wanted to live that way. Behind the bars of the iron cage, products and services expanded. Life expectancy increased; improvements in public health enhanced the quality of life. Quite naturally people would like to have it both ways: enjoy the fruits of the enormous wealth that capitalism created but without suffering the loss of old ways of life.

At the end of the nineteenth century scarcity in capitalist countries was just beginning to yield to abundance. With this cushion, the capitalist world was poised to demonstrate just how wasteful, rapacious, and indifferent to the long-run consequences of its habits could be. In the ratcheted-up use of fossil fuel, that essential element in economic development, capitalist aggressiveness would pass beyond the earth's surface to its life-sustaining atmosphere. We still might have it both ways if we could build in restraints without killing the goose that laid the golden egg of prosperity.

7

◆

THE INDUSTRIAL
LEVIATHANS AND
THEIR OPPONENTS

T HE PREEMINENT INDUSTRIAL powers of the nineteenth century
—Great Britain and its two rivals, Germany and the United States—
transformed the physical world. They laid iron tracks across thousands
and thousands of miles. They built enormous factories, to which they drew
millions of men and women, most of them recently off the farm. They collected capital in banks, consumed coal, finished steel, dug minerals from
the earth, leveled hills, diverted the water from rivers into canals, and
generally displayed the previously undetected strength and ingenuity of
human beings. Despite the impersonality of all these changes, particular
people brought them about: swashbuckling heroes of enterprise and the
workingmen and women whose lives industrialization had turned upside
down. A few men so completely grasped the dynamics of capitalism that
they established firms that are still among the world's largest. The initiative

200

lay with these industrialists, yet their workers found ways with courage and determination to organize vibrant oppositions to the new rulers of their universe. The success of these labor movements depended upon the political tactics, ideological assumptions, and historical precedents within the different capitalist countries. The story begins with the entrepreneurs.

Because capitalism created unparalleled freedom of action in the economy, its history is studded with stories of personal endeavors. Major accomplishments in science and engineering gave direction to nineteenth-century entrepreneurs who scoured these advances for their commercial potential. As the scope of enterprise grew larger and larger, a few individuals carved out large economic domains of their own. Cornelius Vanderbilt, Andrew Carnegie, and John D. Rockefeller in the United States and August Thyssen, Carl Zeiss, and Siemens in Germany were the giants who carried their nations to economic preeminence in the nineteenth century. They founded the companies of Carl Zeiss, Thyssen, Krupp, and Siemens in Germany and the New York Central Railroad, U.S. Steel, and Standard Oil in the United States. These leviathans of industry created powers as sweeping as those of monarchs, which ironically meant that these hyper-competitors shrank competition because of the size of the market share they commanded. Too large to be run by a single man or even a family, they formed giant corporations that came to characterize capitalism in the twentieth century.

These men didn't just make huge fortunes; they pioneered the industries that were to dominate their age: railroads, steel, oil, electrical-powered tools, scientific apparatuses, pharmaceuticals, and dyes. American entrepreneurs like Vanderbilt, Rockefeller, and the Scottish-born Carnegie were fierce competitors who beat down prices as they simultaneously drove rival companies out of business. German leaders like Zeiss and Siemens more typically relied on institutional support for research to advance and diversify Germany's economy. Thyssen was called the American, a sobriquet that doubled as criticism of his ferocious individualism more typical of American entrepreneurs than German ones.

Often these founders of megafirms came from prominent families. The German industrialist Alfred Krupp took over the management of his father's ironworks firm. Thyssen's was a family of successful entrepreneurs.

In our own time, Bill Gates got a boost from a wealthy father. Yet other industrial giants sprang de novo into the world of trade with little in their backgrounds to suggest a future fabulous success. The perfect example, Cornelius Vanderbilt, began his ascent from a modest waterside farm on Staten Island. Carnegie came from a poor immigrant family, and Rockefeller started at the bottom of the business hierarchy. Siemens got his start through service in the German Army, and Zeiss grew up in a family of toymakers.

Vanderbilt's talents unfolded with the country's revolution in transportation as he moved from running ferries to transatlantic steamships to railroads. The rivalry among early railroad operators produced near chaos in an area where coordination was essential. So Vanderbilt reorganized the untidy mess of diverse railroads coming into New York City, making Grand Central Station a permanent tribute to his organizational acumen.[1] Starting in the old way with personal savings and family loans, Vanderbilt moved smoothly in middle age to the new financial world of stock trades, mergers, and clearinghouse transactions. While old-fashioned in many of his habits, he had no trouble adapting, as many others could not, to corporate capitalism with its fluid commerce in stock shares with fluctuating values. Through his no-holds-barred style, Vanderbilt managed to give competition a bad name, something rather remarkable in a country so committed to individual effort and laissez-faire policies.

Unlike the tyros of New York City financial circles, Vanderbilt retained the feral energy of his youth, probably best captured in his adventures in Central America. When thousands of Americans rushed to get to California during the gold rush, Vanderbilt set up a route through Nicaragua, building roads there to expedite the passage to the Pacific. His competitors tried to get the government to withdraw Vanderbilt's operating permit, so he brought down the Nicaraguan government. Vanderbilt's exploits dazzled and dismayed his contemporaries, particularly those who crossed him. He could also astound as when at age eighty he responded to the panic of 1873 by buying up those companies on the ropes to broaden his railroad empire. And then there was the 260-foot-long yacht with its grand staircase and ten elegantly-furnished staterooms to give authentic glitter to the name "Gilded Era."[2]

Carnegie and Rockefeller were also self-made millionaires. The arrival of steam-powered looms had destroyed the livelihood of Carnegie's father and prompted his mother to scrape together enough savings from her shop to move her family from Scotland to the sooty shores of the Monongahela River. Carnegie's stunning proficiency as a telegraph operator smoothed an upward path in the Pennsylvania Railroad Company, whence he became a venture capitalist dealing in railroads, bridges, and oil derricks.

Carnegie could be a charmer, which came in handy when he was selling bonds—often of dubious value—in Europe. Returning with substantial profits, he invested in ironworks, steel mills, and iron ore fields around Lake Superior. The Civil War with its demand for armament turned Pittsburgh into a major industrial center. When Congress raised a steep wall of tariffs in the 1870s, it gave Pittsburgh and Carnegie the protection they needed for their growing pains. He was one of the first industrialists to integrate their operations upward from the extraction of raw materials to the finishing of steelworks, mainly rails. He was a relentless competitor, whose goal was always to "scoop the bottom," beating out his rivals with lower prices, often aided by the hard bargains he drove with the workers. In 1892 he merged his various investments into the Carnegie Steel Company.[3]

A decade later the banker J. P. Morgan bought out Carnegie to form U.S. Steel. Morgan pronounced Carnegie the country's wealthiest man. Had his $100 million estate been liquidated at his death in 1877 it would have contained one-twentieth of all American dollars! Unskilled workers then earned about $8.50 a week. (By comparison, Bill Gates's $53 billion represents $1 in every $130 when a minimum wage job in 2009 would bring in $290 a week.) Giving away money with the same zeal he brought to earning it, Carnegie quickly shrank his estate, estimated at his death at $23 million. Grateful for access to a private library when he was a boy, he established more than twenty-five hundred public libraries in the United States, Canada, and Scotland, his homeland.

Carnegie may be one of the most complex figures in the history of American capitalism. Denied a formal education, he studied literature and history throughout his life. His intellectual interests went beyond reading. He also wrote voluminously about political systems and his philosophy of enterprise. His business archive is stuffed with letters to American

presidents, annotated board minutes, advisory memos to himself, memo-
randums to subordinates, accounting sheets, and drafts of the numerous
articles that he had submitted for publication. One thing that had distinguished his Scottish relatives was their radicalism in support of labor, a
tradition Carnegie left behind when he came to America. Typical of the
self-made man, he believed that any boy in America could succeed, discounting the limited space at the top. Still, he considered the pursuit of
profits distasteful, writing, "No idol is more debasing than the worship of
money!"

Like Vanderbilt and Carnegie, Rockefeller came from a farm family,
though his father at least had one thousand dollars to lend his son when
he wanted to set himself up as a commission merchant to sell grain, hay,
meats, household goods, and farm implements. In 1853, a scion of a distinguished New England family, Benjamin Silliman, demonstrated that
the petroleum that produced a smelly, smoky light was actually a mixture
of hydrocarbons that could be purified through fractional distillation.
This enhanced the value of the oil widely found in Ohio and Pennsylvania
by perfecting its preparation as a lubricant and a source of cheap, clean
light. Rockefeller decided to pursue a career in refining oil. He called his
start-up company Standard Oil.

Sizing up the railroad companies' need for secure returns to offset their
fixed costs, Rockefeller promised a steady freight volume in exchange for
lower fares for the transport of crude oil to his Cleveland refineries and
the return trip of refined oil to New York. With this cost leverage, he began
his long career of gobbling up other oil refineries, often lowering his prices
below cost just to rid himself of a competitor. Rockefeller had unshakable
faith in the future of oil even before the internal-combustion engine had
been perfected. When overcapacity sank prices in 1870, he bought up all
the companies whose owners had lost heart.[4] Then he mounted an aggressive marketing campaign.

Fractional distillation involves heating oil. Because the components of
oil have different boiling points, the process produces in sequence gas,
naphtha, gasoline, kerosene, and lubricating oil. Only gasoline had no
practical use at the time. Thirty years later the arrival of the automobile
changed that. Standard Oil enjoyed monopoly control of the oil indus-

try. In 1882 Rockefeller created one of the first trusts out of some forty separate companies, a business form that consolidated decision making. When such business combinations stirred up controversy, he defended them as essential to commanding capital and delivering more products at lower prices. In fact they facilitated central management. By 1896 Rockefeller was worth some two hundred million dollars, twice the fortune of Vanderbilt at his death twenty years earlier.

Rockefeller's business tactics had not escaped critical notice. A devout Baptist, he recoiled at the hardhearted reputation he had acquired, especially the way Ida Tarbell depicted him in a popular muckraking magazine series. Following the advice of a public relations consultant, Rockefeller increased his giving to Baptist churches and began funding medical schools. Having embarked on a new career as a philanthropist at the age of fifty-seven, Rockefeller sponsored the idea of matching funds, where he would contribute to a project only if others did. He founded the University of Chicago through such a method and then in 1913 set up the Rockefeller Foundation to "promote the well-being of mankind throughout the world." After divesting himself of five hundred million dollars, Rockefeller died a popular man.

Retrospectively, the lives of successful entrepreneurs appear boringly similar, especially if they started out poor. As boys they excel at whatever jobs they take at fourteen or fifteen, thrive as precocious self-improvers, display a determination to set up their own businesses, persevere assiduously to some level of prosperity, attract the attention of sponsors, and then launch themselves into new industries, all along divining the direction of economic growth. What stands out is their single-mindedness and their inability to stop their upward climb until they've reached the top or even created a top higher than anyone had ever imagined. Vanderbilt in railroads, Carnegie in steel, and Rockefeller in oil rode the tiger of fixed capital costs into the new world of giant corporations and trusts. They and their peers changed the landscape of capitalism. Adam Smith had argued that the invisible hand of competition would work to deliver goods at lower prices as entrepreneurs strove for a larger share of the market. But this assumed easy entries for new competitors. Instead high fixed costs limited competition to those with ready funds.

German Entrepreneurs

When August Thyssen died, the *New York Times* obituary dubbed him "the Rockefeller of the Ruhr." This was a concession to the alliteration of *r*'s, for Thyssen was more like Andrew Carnegie. His fierce, competitive energy transformed the German steel industry. He came from a wealthy Rhineland banking family. His marriage at thirty brought even more money to his enterprises. Thyssen began buying up mills to meet the growing demand for the strip steel used in barrels, bales, crates, tubes, and pipes. He marketed his goods as far away as Russia, establishing foreign sales as a major component of his business. When the crisis of 1873 depressed prices, Thyssen boldly expanded production, diversified his enterprises, and turned to sales promotion. This of course is what Vanderbilt did, both men demonstrating the risk-taking and counterintuitive decisions that made them the stuff of legends.

By the end of the 1880s the operation of Thyssen & Company included coal mining, iron smelting, blast furnaces, steel mills, and machine engineering. The specialized, quality products that Thyssen offered in German, French, and English catalogs contrasted with the standardized high-volume production of American companies. He had a fine technical education, and he turned out to be a natural business organizer, developing a highly sophisticated structure of operations. He expected his department managers—often men in their twenties and thirties—to be as versatile as he was in handling both technical and marketing matters. The vertical integration he achieved in most of his production lines gave him enormous cost advantages. Yet despite the size of his operation, he maintained family control until the 1920s. Thyssen was a larger than life figure. He invested in new technologies that involved a constant addition of capital, a response that contrasted sharply with the now-cautious British entrepreneurs.[5]

Ernst Werner von Siemens was more a scientist, an engineer, and an inventor than a businessman, yet he founded one of the world's most successful corporations. The Prussian budget, when he grew up, devoted almost as much money to education as it did to the military. Not having enough money to study civil engineering, he entered the Prussian artillery corps in 1835. Six years of technical study brought young men exemptions from two years of military service and a commission in the army reserve, complete with a uniform! The army benefited as well from this program. Siemens's early inventions included a gold and silver electroplating process, a differential regulator, and several devices to improve the Wheatstone telegraphy machine. After leaving the army, Siemens concentrated on practical applications to gain money for his beloved experiments. He was the first to suggest using gutta-percha, a latex extracted from various tropical trees, to wrap electric cables for underground and underwater cable lines. He developed instruments for continuously testing cables like the one that linked Great Britain and India.

In 1847 Siemens's first company moved aggressively into the new field of electricity. Siemens discovered the dynamoelectric principle that enabled batteries to generate continuous current and high voltage. In the 1860s he patented inventions involving electricity. New products moved through his laboratory with the regularity of the solar system. Publishing papers on dynamos, heat resistance, and measuring instruments and various electric magnetic apparatuses, Siemens pointed German industry toward new processes and products. He left a company that has remained closest to his founding initiatives in energy, electrical engineering, and communications.

Carl Zeiss came out of the strong German handicraft tradition that gave to many cities and regions a specialty: the gold, silver, and copper wares of Augsburg, the woodcrafts and toys of Nuremberg, the knives and scissors of the Rhineland, steel tools from Remscheid and brass ones from Stolberg. To which we might add the beer of Bavaria. After a twelve-year apprenticeship, Zeiss benefited from the biologists' new interest in examining cells. He won a contract for making and repairing all of the scientific apparatuses of the University of Jena in 1846. Twenty years later his firm produced its thousandth microscope; forty years later, its ten thousandth. In 1866, Zeiss teamed up with Ernst Abbe to study the pressure that the latest microscopes put on glass. Their challenge was to modify glass to meet these demands. At the same time, they were experimenting with cameras, an invention of increasing importance to consumers, scientists, and manufacturers. Together Zeiss and Abbe discerned that rays from lenses focused on different places. Studying the mathematics of this phenomenon led to the new wave theory of light. In 1870 another glass chemist, Otto Schott, joined the Zeiss and Abbe enterprise.

At this point the firm moved beyond the horizons of most German artisans by emphasizing new product design. In Zeiss's insistent improvement of scientific apparatus to accommodate scientific advances, he, along with his contemporaries Siemens and the chemists Justus von Liebig and Fritz Haber, linked German capitalism to technological frontiers. After Zeiss's death in 1888, his firm achieved microscopes of magnification of 2000X that could identify good from bad bacteria. Today it produces binoculars, cameras, planetariums, microscopes, semiconductors, nanotechnology, spectrometers, and optronics.

Haber directed his research to agricultural searching for a way to replace the fertilizers German farmers needed during World War I, when the British blockade cut off their supply of nitrates from Chile and Peru. Haber's synthesis of ammonia made possible the nitrogen fertilizers that plumped up crop yields worldwide. His Nobel Prize citation said that he had wrested bread from air. Haber had also experimented with chemical gases, leading to the development of pesticides, among them Zyklon B. In a bitter coda to a successful life, the Nazis used Zyklon B in its concentration camps, where several of Haber's relatives died.[6] Less macabre but still worrying, we can appreciate today that many of these advances compromised the atmosphere's future with their accelerating use of fossil fuel and chemical fertilizers.

All through the century, people moved in a chain migration from farm work to rural industry and small-town shops to factories, mines, and railroad jobs. Without the protection that wealth confers, they had to accept changes whether they wanted them or not.[7] These men and women could be old-fashioned or up-to-date in their attitudes, loyal, insubordinate, diligent, slovenly, slow, or bright, as human beings are wont to be. But in capitalist calculations they counted as commodities, subject to the laws of supply and demand. Malthus had interpreted one of these laws applying to laboring men and women when he predicted that the growth in the supply of babies in response to young people's employment opportunities would sooner or later get caught in the scissors of declining harvests.

He had not counted on the improvements in farming that enhanced crop yields. Still, his point about the short-run effect of increasing births was on the mark.

In the first half of the century the working class did not do well in Europe. Living standards were dropping in both rural and urban areas. The patterns of birth and death that had continued for centuries were being disrupted by greater fertility and lower morality. Wages did not keep up with expenses, and women in particular suffered. Though life had never been easy for the rural poor, in the cities there was marked job discrimination. The persistent short supply of food led women to defer to their husbands' greater need for nutrition. In the English countryside when farmers, lured by new farm equipment, switched from raising livestock to growing grain, they pushed women out of paid farm work and into poor-paying work or homebound drudgery.[8] Women also suffered from their husbands' vulnerability to layoffs and industrial accidents.

Changing Options for the Poor

The mechanization of farm equipment, at first drawn by horses and later by steam and internal-combustion engines, had a worldwide impact. The bountiful harvests of American farms, thanks largely to Cyrus McCormick's reaper, ushered in a period of prosperity for America's family farms and drove down world commodity prices. Cheap American grains prompted calls as early as the 1870s within European countries for tariff protection. Easily transported across the Atlantic by the steam-powered shipping industry, America's abundant harvests slowly wiped out the peasant economies of eastern and southern Europe. There ensued a reordering of agricultural production as countries rushed to find a place in the global division of agricultural specialties. In this system, farmers planted one or two crops instead of the diversity that they had grown earlier. Agricultural corporations began to replace farming families, whose members crowded into nearby cities or emigrated.

An alternative to enduring bad living conditions in Europe was to look for a new home in the countries of North or South America or to go yet farther, to Australia or New Zealand. As early as 1818, officials in Westphalia reported "a wandering spirit" and "the craze to emigrate to America." By the 1840s one thousand Europeans were arriving in the United States each week. Two decades later most European countries had lifted all restrictions on travel for women and for those men who had completed their military service. Starting at the end of the nineteenth century, redundant rural workers in Poland, Russia, Hungary, Italy, Serbia, and Greece crossed the Atlantic to make a fresh start abroad. Others moved to their own industrializing cities. In 1892 a receiving center opened up on Ellis Island in the harbor of New York City. When immigration peaked in the first decade of the twentieth century, almost a million men, women, and children were arriving every year.

Everywhere people were on the move. In the Pacific, waves of Chinese left for Siam, Java, the Malay Peninsula, British Columbia, New South Wales, and California, which also attracted immigrants from Japan. An estimated three million Indians went to Nepal and East Africa as migratory workers.[9] In all, close to fifty million left southern China and India for Southeast Asia, and the same number of Russians and Chinese moved to Central Asia, Siberia, and Manchuria.[10] Spain sent more than a million people to Cuba and Latin America. Italians went to the United States, Argentina, and Tunisia; the French to Algeria. Despite its advanced economy, Great Britain sent twelve million of its men and women to the United States, New Zealand, Canada, and Australia while six million Germans emigrated to Brazil and North America. Once a beachhead of Bavarians or Irish or Swedes had been established abroad, it was easier for relatives and friends to make the journey. Clearly the new economic practices associated with capitalism were having profound and far-reaching effects.

While European populations grew, in the United States population exploded, going from five and a half million in 1800 to seventy-six million in 1900. A decade later there were ninety-two million Americans. White Latin Americans longed for European immigrants to whiten their population; manufacturers in the United States needed men and women to run their factories. In all, fifty-six million European men, women, and children made Atlantic crossings in what was the largest migration in history.[11] The slave trade had brought eleven million. Since most of the immigrants were young and male, the United States had a low dependency rate with its men and women working at full tilt. Relatively few people were too young or too old to work.

In the century and a half between 1750 and 1900, European population went from 140 to 430 million people. It had once represented 17 percent of the world's people; now it had a quarter of them. The immediate causes of this dramatic increase in population came first from a drop in the death rate. During the course of the nineteenth and early twentieth centuries, better health, sanitation, and medicine extended life while mortality from age-old killers like cholera, typhus, tuberculosis, smallpox, and typhoid also abated. Enhanced fertility rates explain the long-term gain in population. In 1870, these dropped rather precipitously, but population continues to grow with rising life expectancy.

Overpopulation without matching economic development exacerbated ethnic tensions. Pogroms in Russia, Poland, and other Eastern European countries sent a large number of Jews to swell the tidal wave of immigrants washing on American shores between 1880 and 1914. Motives for leaving home ran the gamut from avoiding military service, fleeing taxes, hungering for adventure, getting higher wages, wanting land, or seeking political and religious freedom.[12] Steamships sped up the trips while steerage rates remained low. This steady flow of cheap labor came at the right time for corporate America, which was de-skilling many jobs as it set up factory assembly lines.

Steel plants, oil refineries, sweat shops, and a myriad of factories beckoned from Pittsburgh, Buffalo, Youngstown, Toledo, and Newark to those who landed at Ellis Island. Most immigrants manned the factories, but some from Sweden and Norway went west to settle the newly opened land in Iowa, Wisconsin, and Minnesota. Women, depending upon the customs from their native Greece, Germany, or Ireland, took factory jobs, worked as servants, or stayed home making artificial flowers, hats, and clothes. For the latter group, the sewing machine was the key invention. Sometimes whole families toiled in their tenement apartments turned each morning after breakfast into miniworkshops.

These additional workers acted like an abundant supply of any element in production; it lowered prices—i.e., wages. In most American cities with populations of close to five hundred thousand, two-thirds of the people would be foreign born or had parents who were. Arriving in a country still run by WASPs, the white Anglo-Saxon Protestants of British and German descent, they became what were called hyphenated Americans, as in Polish-American or Italian-American, according to their country of origin.

Debating Capitalism's Origins

Industrialization reshaped the working class. Members of a new proletariat reacted differently to the economic changes that were remapping their country. Industrialization had come more swiftly to Germany, Belgium, and France in the middle decades of the nineteenth century than to Great Britain and the United States. Its arrival assaulted customs whereas in the Anglo-American world the mechanization of the workplace began in the eighteenth century and spread slowly. Stretching over generations, this leisurely pace made it credible to think of industrialization as part of an evolutionary unfolding of their society's natural potential for economic development, as Adam Smith had argued. Not so across the Channel. There critics saw industrialization as a rapacious transformation engineered by an upstart upper class eager to destroy both the aristocracy and the peasantry, which had once been protected from economic turbulence.

With a shared perspective on the disruption and exploitation of industrial capitalism, opponents multiplied rapidly. Differing more in what they recommended than in their understanding of the disaster that had hit Europe, they fell into large ideological groups. Syndicalists, especially strong in France, believed in organizing direct action like general strikes to wrest control of the workplace from owners. Because they wanted unions or syndicates of workers to be in charge, they got the name "syndicalists." Anarchists wanted to abolish all government, arguing that government worked hand in glove with the industrialists. As their principal theorist Pierre-Joseph Proudhon said, "Property is theft." Here Proudhon was emphasizing the potent idea that private property was not natural but rather a device for confiscating the benefits of the industrial wealth that workers were actually creating. More idealistic than the others, anarchists looked to a future in which a kind of volunteer mutuality guided social decisions. Karl Marx had a more complicated theory about history itself: He saw industrialization as a stage in an inevitable progression to the socializing of the great wealth industrialists had created. For him, communism represented the final development in which government would be confined to the administration of things, not the rule of people.

These theories became the organizing principles behind proselytizing efforts. Working days of ten or twelve hours in six-day weeks at factories hazardous to health made men and women receptive to organizers. Campaigning for the eight-hour day came first. In 1864 the radicals and their followers founded the International Workingmen's Association in London. Often called the First International, the IWA met annually in cities in Western Europe. It peaked with a membership of five million. Insurgencies in several European countries in 1848 had made governments particularly suspicious of labor agitation, so police and informers regularly attended labor gatherings.

Marx and Proudhon influenced each another, but they differed on the use of force. Proudhon believed that peaceful change was possible. The anarchists split from the Marxists in the First International, but later anarchists advocated violence in the service of social justice. With the array of radical explanations available, labor supporters differed on whether to form a political party to change government, join the Marxist wait for the overthrow of the capitalist system, or work within the system to spread the fruits of industrialization.

Labor Activists in Europe

The growth of radical groups alarmed leaders in the capitalized West. After two assaults on the life of Kaiser Wilhelm I in 1883, the German government outlawed all Social Democratic, Socialist, and Communist organizations. It renewed that law every three years. Unlike the United States, Germany had a tradition of social support, stemming from the paternalism of an earlier era. The draconian law about workers' organization passed in the midst of an outburst of welfare legislation. In the words of Chancellor Otto von Bismarck, the propertyless classes must recognize that "the state is not only an institution of necessity but also one of welfare

... serving their needs and interests." Within a decade he had secured laws to insure workers against sickness, industrial accidents, old age, and incapacity. With employers charged for these programs, the insurance policies operated universally and efficiently.

The fear of labor unrest pushed manufacturers closer to, if not exactly into the arms of, the aristocratic Junkers while the menace of socialism prompted the Junker-dominated German government to champion social legislation that also slowed emigration from Germany.[13] The German government spent generously on primary and secondary education. In a nourishing exchange of influences, industry profited from literate workers while industrial occupations animated workers to become politically active. Extending the suffrage was seen as a curb on radical effort to redistribute wealth. Despite the government's outlawing of radical groups, support for the Social Democratic Party of Marxist lineage continued to grow.

More than half a million Englishmen and -women turned the old pagan holiday of May 1st into an international workers' holiday when they marched to Hyde Park to demonstrate for the eight-hour day in 1890. In Latin America, labor unrest began in the second decade of the twentieth century. Syndicalists and anarchists in Argentina, Brazil, and Uruguay organized general strikes not just to secure gains for labor but to bring down the governments that colluded with bosses and landowners to maintain control over the working class. Even in the United States, the National Socialist Party, the Socialist Labor Party, the Farmer Labor Party, and the Communist Labor Party fielded candidates for elections in 1918 and 1920. Still, American workers did not take readily to radical ideas, preferring to work within the system to improve conditions and pay.

Germany and Great Britain saw powerful labor parties arise to compete with conservatives for political power. Following decades of struggle against the government and within the sprawling labor movement itself, English workers formed a labor party in 1900. Craft unions, representing the best-paid, best-educated part of the labor force, confined their activities to incremental improvements in wages and conditions. Unskilled workers who formed unions in the 1880s were much more aggressive, risking arrests and incarceration from their noisy public demonstrations for eight-hour workdays and safer conditions. They made the public look at the faces of women disfigured by the phosphorus they worked with in making matches. Not being able to restrict entry to their trade as the craft unions could, unskilled workers turned to strikes, picketing, and public marches to gain attention. Riots were not uncommon.

Buffeted by competition from Germany and the United States for their share in international markets, British industry fell on hard times. Job losses and stagnating wages became labor's best recruiters. Prominent British intellectuals formed the Fabian Society to persuade the public to endorse such socialist measures as nationalizing major industries. Those who favored building a political movement won out. Within two decades the British Labour Party had displaced the Liberal Party as the principal rival of the Conservatives.

The Unique Struggle of American Labor

Labor's situation differed strikingly in the United States. Without an aristocracy or even a recognized elite as in the colonial era, Americans felt themselves to be politically undifferentiated members of an embrasive democracy. Class distinctions, while evident, grated on Americans' self-image. Even men without property got the vote during the nineteenth century, the Fourteenth Amendment securing it for African American men as well. Industrialization after the Civil War brought new opportunities to native-born white workers.[14] As corporations took over from family owners and partnerships, business bureaucracies expanded. Native-born workers' literacy and familiarity with American ways gave them a leg up, enabling many to exchange their blue collars for white ones. As clerks or supervisors they were able to move off the shop floor and into offices, where work was cleaner, the workday shorter, and the wages better. Like all Americans, they benefited from the steady stream of immigrants who came to take jobs in American factories because cheap labor kept the price of goods low. Farming also remained an option through most of the nineteenth century, even if the best land was gone. The actual number of farms in the United States increased until 1950, though the percentage of agricultural laborers steadily declined.

The plight of industrial workers worsened. As in Great Britain, skilled workers belonged to craft unions that focused on ensuring their privileges. Foreigners expanded the great pool of unskilled laborers who had few rights at the work site. Employers could fire them "at will . . . for good cause, no cause or even for cause morally wrong, without thereby being guilty of legal wrong."[15] American common law, following that of Great Britain, dealt with labor complaints under centuries-old master-servant statutes that were skewed in the master's favor. The employer, for instance, was not responsible for an accident in the workplace if it had been caused by the negligence of a fellow worker. The law also construed labor unions as conspiratorial organizations, and foreign labor organizers were subject to deportation. Property rights trumped human rights consistently in court, despite measures favorable to workers passed into law. Unions did better during times of prosperity, when profit-happy employers were willing to make concessions.

Americans enthusiastically identified with the ideal of an egalitarianism citizenry and were generally indifferent to the great gaps in wealth among them. Foreign laborers strove to join the great middle group of their adopted country. Blacks constituted the most conspicuous exception to America's commitment to assimilation. Once southern whites put in place after the Civil War the regime for segregating blacks and whites in schools, buses, and restaurants, they became obsessed with keeping African Americans "in their place." An almost absolute social divide marked relations between the races, unlike anything in Europe. Of small comfort, this arrangement did provide opportunities for black entrepreneurs to bring goods and services to their communities.

The very distinctive ideology that dominated public discourse in the United States operated against organized labor. The public tended to view workers as individuals charged with taking care of themselves and their families. Thomas Jefferson made limited government a robust American value. As the champion of ordinary Americans Jefferson believed that curtailing federal power was the best way of shrinking the influence of a moneyed elite. The new concentration of power in industrial corporations undermined his assumptions, but it took a long time for the public to realize the need for a government equipped to monitor and curtail the great industrial enterprises. Populists, as the radicals were called, and the more cerebral Progressives, who followed in their reform path at the turn of the twentieth century, finally succeeded in alerting the public to the dangers of unchecked economic power.

Aroused, various disgruntled groups supplied the political muscle to get ameliorating legislation through Congress. They ranged from farmers dependent upon railroad companies to owners of small businesses threatened with being gobbled up by larger firms. Reform leaders among women exposed the wretched social environment in which immigrant families lived. Jane Addams and Florence Kelley, through their work in urban settlement houses, publicized the unsafe tenements and abusive employers that foreigners had to contend with. Drawing on the old anti-aristocratic rhetoric, turn-of-the-century reformers labeled the titans of industry "robber barons" and compared their highhanded ways with an aristocracy. It was a term with resonance in the United States because for so long the country had prided itself on not having a feudal past like Europe's. The sprawling native-born white middle class also associated the often violent strikes and protests of the closing decades of the nineteenth century with European inspiration. Only slowly did labor win the favor of the public watching on the sidelines.

People were concerned when corporate indifference threatened the food they ate. Upton Sinclair wrote *The Jungle* to awaken his fellow citizens to the terrible labor conditions in meat-packing plants. Almost incidentally he detailed how sausages were packed with various impurities like sawdust. Those vivid descriptions stuck in readers' minds. Congress passed the Meat Inspection Act and a Pure Food and Drug Act the same year as *The Jungle*'s publication in 1906. States also began to legislate to protect workingwomen and children. Civil service reform curbed the rampant municipal corruption of this so-called Gilded Age.

In 1902 Ida Tarbell enthralled the reading public month after month with a serialized history of Standard Oil, a tale every bit as fascinating as the adventures of Captain Kidd, with Rockefeller operating with the same moral compass as the pirate had. The public gained access to the shenanigans, shady deals, and sinister manipulation that went into Rockefeller's oil monopoly. Tarbell's book spoke to President Theodore Roosevelt, whose administration prosecuted Standard Oil under the Sherman Anti-trust Act.[16] Still, corporations continued to find sympathizers on the Supreme Court who ruled against laws that they thought would unduly restrain freedom of action in the marketplace. Workers' safety got short shrift from both employers and legislators. It was not until 1937 with the construction of the Golden Gate Bridge that a safety net was used on a construction site. It saved twenty lives.

The arrival of a million foreigners a year aroused the resentment of some native-born Americans toward these strangers who seemed to have taken over their cities. Not only were the newcomers darker in skin and hair color, but in the closing decades of the nineteenth century many of the newcomers were Catholics or Jews rather than Protestants like the overwhelming number of Americans. Such xenophobic sentiments had already led to the exclusion of the Chinese in 1882. Imbued with the sense of the United States as a refuge from bad conditions in Europe, some in the public considered the immigrants ungrateful if they agitated for better conditions, though most immigrant workers were too preoccupied with adjusting to a strange new country to respond to organizers unless they had already been radicalized in Europe. The flagrant poverty of immigrants packed into tenements in eastern cities, along with their strange habits, aroused suspicions and fueled campaigns to limit immigration. It was a challenge to turn a work force of such ethnic diversity into an effective labor movement.

Seven tailors formed the Noble and Holy Order of the Knights of Labor in the United States before the arrival of the so-called new immigrants. Starting in 1869, the Knights of Labor maintained strict secrecy to ward off government repression. It reached out to skilled and unskilled workers, blacks, and women as well as the mainstream white male laborer. The only groups officially excluded were doctors, bankers, lawyers, producers of liquor, and gamblers. Its agenda included an eight-hour workday, prohibition of child labor, a graduated income tax, nationalizing of public utilities and railroads, equal pay for equal work, and the establishment of cooperatives to offer an alternative to manufacturing with wage labor. Although it originally eschewed strikes, the Knights got involved in the Haymarket Square riot, which pretty much ended its upward trajectory.

This ugly incident began when someone among the Chicago marchers threw a bomb toward the police. Seven officers and dozens of civilians died. The public turned sharply against labor organizers, making it relatively easy to convict and execute four anarchists.

The Knights of Labor plummeted from a membership of close to a million to just a hundred thousand in the last fifteen years of the century. In the wake of this decline, Samuel Gompers, an English immigrant cigar maker, formed the American Federation of Labor in 1886. The most successful union organization in the United States, the AFL recognized the autonomy of its participating craft unions. Gompers, who remained at the head of the AFL until his death in 1924, actually saw the potential benefit for workers in capitalism. Stressing "pure and simple unionism," the AFL grew steadily as it worked for the immediate improvement of workers' wages and conditions. Its initial openness to unskilled laborers, blacks, and women closed over time, in part because of the prejudices of the member unions, which forced segregation on black unions. They viewed women at best as part of a pool of labor that, like illegal immigrants today, kept wages down. At worst, they were likely strikebreakers.

In keeping with its fierce loyalty to the federation's core membership of white men, the AFL urged Congress to renew the 1882 immigration restriction on Chinese in 1901. Still, the AFL never enlisted more than 5 percent of the work force. It had an uphill struggle because native-born Americans who were moving into the city from the countryside after the Civil War experienced real improvements in their standard of living, bolstered by steady factory work, accessible medical clinics, and free public education.

Gompers's "business unionism" offended radicals who wanted to bring down the capitalist system that they saw as unfairly monopolizing the profits from workers' productivity. The Industrial Workers of the World injected some radicalism into the American labor movement when it began in 1905. Among the crew of unionists, socialists, and anarchists who had had their fill of Gompers were Eugene V. Debs, Daniel De Leon, Joe Hill, Big Bill Haywood, and "Mother" Jones, all major figures in the American radical tradition. As if creating a contrasting mirror image of the AFL, the IWW strove for worker solidarity strong enough to overthrow the capitalist system. With the motto "An injury to one is an injury to all," the Wobblies, as they were called, insisted that employers had nothing in common with their workers. Displaying the fierce militancy of the miners who formed the initial core of their membership, the IWW recruited lumberjacks, the hoboes of migratory labor, silk makers, and textile workers, many of them in the Deep South and Pacific Northwest. Wobblies participated in 150 strikes in their first two decades. Despite a number of labor actions, the union movement in the United States remained weak, especially when compared with European countries.

Anarchists, many of them foreign, hoped that the violence would arouse America's workers to the evils of the industrial system. Two of them, Alexander Berkman and Emma Goldman, plotted in 1892 to kill Henry Clay Frick, manager of Andrew Carnegie's steelworks after he had crushed the steelworkers' union. Berkman failed to kill Frick and spent twenty-eight years in prison while Goldman went on to become one of the most effective speakers in radical circles. More successful at assassination was Leon Czolgosz, who shot the newly elected president William McKinley when he was attending the Pan-American Exposition in 1901. The IWW's aggressive stance toward American institutions elicited strong reactions from state and city governments as well as vigilante groups eager to mete out some rough justice to them.

After the successful Russian Revolution brought Communists to power in 1917, Americans became exceedingly frightened of the anarchists in their midst. Zealous prosecutors convicted Nicola Sacco and Bartolomeo Vanzetti for the murder of two pay clerks in Braintree, Massachusetts, largely on the basis of their being anarchists. Sacco and Vanzetti became martyrs after their executions, prompting yet one more anarchist bombing, this one on Wall Street, which left thirty dead, two hundred injured, and the office of J. P. Morgan destroyed. Mass deportations followed, including those of Berkman and Goldman. As they were departing, they received word that Frick had died. "Deported by God," Berkman commented dryly.

Critical of the AFL for resting on its laurels with 5 percent of the American work force, the Wobblies never gained more than fifty thousand members. Internal dissension along with public dislike halted their forward motion. Nor were the assassinations of the anarchists effective in stirring up American workers. Most radical groups opposed the First World War. One of their great disappointments was that war undermined the solidarity that they had been building for more than a half century among international workers. When the fighting began, each labor group repaired to the side of its own country. The AFL, with its more moderate policies and tolerance of differences among member groups, was better positioned to survive in the United States. Its comeuppance lay in the future, when the Congress of Industrial Organizations pulled together unskilled workers in 1938.

The public construed the strong foreign component in American labor unions as an explanation for union militancy. They found union strikes peculiarly menacing. Antipathy to the new immigrants' presence in the United States overrode the corporations' lust for labor when nativists succeeded in getting exclusionary immigration laws passed. The 1921 law set up a quota system that operated against the new immigrants of the 1880–1914 period. The law set a maximum of 357,000 immigrants annually, giving preference to those coming from northwestern Europe. Within another generation the hyphenated Americans had become thoroughly assimilated, but the national origins quota system lasted until 1965.

The Growing Importance of Consumers

Instead of the pyramid often used to describe a social structure with its great mass of people at the bottom tapering upward to a narrow elite at the top, American society was shaped more like a tomato with a rich slice at the top and a broad middle narrowing only gradually. With no aristocracy in its past and a working class that until recently had been composed mainly of farmers, the United States nurtured a sprawling middle class. Differences in taste, education, and local prominence persisted, but they lacked the backing of an influential upper class. No doubt refined tastes were cultivated in closed social circles. Snobs existed but, like garden snakes, with little venom. Most Americans liked being like one another.

The uniformity among the white population in the United States underpinned a new phenomenon of capitalism, the mass market in consumer goods. Rather than seek distinction, most Americans rather enjoyed buying things their neighbors had. "Keeping up with the Joneses" was not a search for distinction but rather for equality. Families took pride in being able to buy exactly the same things that their friends owned. Belonging to a homogenous middle group felt comfortable, an attitude perfect for mass production. Making the shift from an economy concentrating on toolmaking, railroads, and other elements of production in the opening decades of the twentieth century, corporations began churning out standardized home decorations, children's goods, entertainment items, and popular fashions.

Department stores sprang up in cities to gather all these consumer goodies under one roof. As if to gild the lily of the new retailing, department store owners hired famous architects to design handsome edifices to house their cornucopias of wares. Staircases, surrounding a grand foyer, gave a view of story upon story packed with ready-to-wear clothes, cookware, furniture, bedding, appliances, jewelry, cosmetics, and fabrics. Less glamorous than the department stores with their great ground-floor display cases were companies like Sears, Roebuck and Montgomery Ward that pioneered mail-order retailing. As early as 1900, their famous catalogs featured a thousand pages of illustrated items.[17] In the inexorable logic of market success, these modern emporiums began the long war of attrition against mom-and-pop stores, the little shops that had long serviced local neighborhoods. Capitalism's "creative destruction" had found a new battlefield.

Trains and trolley cars made it feasible to build houses in the suburbs of the cities where people worked. The same streetcars, interurban trolleys, and private automobiles that carried men "downtown," as the American city center became known, at the beginning and ending of the workday were also available for shoppers, most of them women, in the middle of the day. This became yet another homogenizing force for the great middling class of American consumers. Some families, being too poor to enjoy the goods lining store shelves and pictured in mail-order catalogs, were excluded from this great spending spree, but the goods acted as a mighty incentive for them to join the consuming crowd. Sidewalks, paved streets, and telephone lines announced the connection of outlying neighborhoods to one of the hubs of commerce that stretched across the country.

Much had happened to make possible the surge of consumer spending. In a certain sense, capitalism had created its own consumers. Workers' wages had grown. The organization of giant corporations called into being a battery of white-collar jobs—accountants, clerks, stenographers, salespersons, lawyers, and bankers. For reasons more pertinent to social prejudice than capitalist preferences, many firms resisted hiring married women for many of these positions. Instead unmarried women flooded into downtowns to fill the office buildings that rose up alongside the department stores. The national standard of living got better, life expectancy increased, and factories disgorged an endless stream of inventions to delight the senses and minimize drudgery in the kitchen, on the farm, and on the shop floor.

Women became a new and powerful force in the economy through their buying habits.[18] In Europe the emergence of what we now would call a consumer culture dealt the deathblow to aristocratic leadership in style and manners. Instead a wide band of middling consumers emerged to exert their preferences in the marketplace. The plethora of electrical equipment that eased domestic chores—mixers, stoves, refrigerators, washing machines, and mangles—left many women time to shop. They also were charged with preparing their children to choose well in this new world of multiple options. Those who didn't work had time to develop recreational outlets, pursue high culture, and support philanthropic outfits while the brigades of young female clerks and salespersons sharpened urban fashions, even among men. The wide range of consumer goods provided a rich palette for painting one's identity.

These new patterns of consuming behavior created their own challenges to producers. Up to this point capitalist enterprises had responded pretty much to a demand that was steady, what economists call inelastic. People spent the largest part of their household budgets on food, shelter, and clothing. Manufacturing and extractive industries bought machinery and equipment, predicated on calculable needs. All that changed when the important buyer became an ordinary man or, more likely, woman. With the fascinating new items getting cheaper, more people found the money to buy them—if they wanted to. There was the rub: the uncertainty in optional spending, spending out of desire rather than need. By the beginning of the twentieth century, consumers were spending considerable amounts of money on inessentials like fashion accessories, upholstered furniture, electrical conveniences, cars, and entertainment paraphernalia. Demand reflected not just purchasing power but what we might call preference power. Those firms catering to consumers had to deal with tastes or, worse, fads that came and went with dizzying speed.

Anything as important as the new consumption tastes had to develop its own experts. Soon they appeared in the form of advertising agencies devoted to spreading information and inciting desire. The need to advertise arrived simultaneously with popular magazines and radio shows that became the means for paying for both media. Print advertisements and radio commercials, since they involved grabbing the public's attention, put a premium on colorful pictures, persuasive voices, and psychological savvy. A popular magazine, *Good Housekeeping*, established an experimental station to test new household items in 1900. Soon it was giving a "seal of approval" to its advertised products. Electric outdoor signs had become visible in big cities by 1910. Promoting products and producing entertainment worked interactively to create a popular culture in which people were as likely to whistle a commercial jingle as a romantic ballad.

Marketing too became important as firms competed with one another to get their soap or shampoo, medicine or road maps, handbags or hosiery at "the point of sale" in department stores, pharmacies, and grocery stores. Brand names vied for buyers' loyalty. Some became so well-known that people turned them into common nouns like "hoover" and "kleenex." Ad campaigns lobbed new lines into public discourse like "I'd walk a mile for a Camel" or descriptions of soap as being "99&44/100th percent pure." Whole new industries emerged to give advice about what to buy. Catering to customers' tastes became imperative, as did extending credit through charge accounts and installment plans. Chain stores appeared at the beginning of the twentieth century, often enticing customers with extended credit. Schools even helped train children to become wise consumers with programs that encouraged savings for spending.[19] An inconclusive debate raged throughout the twentieth century on whether advertising manipulated buyers by implanting fake needs and false expectation or whether consumers used their purchasing power to get the market to give them what they wanted.

Despite the activism of a whole generation of labor organizers, the labor market in the United States remained pretty much unfettered by regulations, though a convergence of interests in the 1910s led states to pass workers' compensation laws. These took conflicts over on-the-job accidents or illnesses out of the courtroom and created prepaid insurance to take care of workers' losses.[20] Employees and employers shared costs and accepted limited liability. Even though unions picketed plants, went out on strike, and campaigned vigorously for the eight-hour workday and a decent wage, they rarely triumphed. Most companies had difficulty seeing their employees as citizens or prospective buyers of their goods. Much more to their liking were company union, towns, and company-run stores, where they could control their work force.

The United States moved into a consumer-dominated economy a decade or two before other capitalist countries.[21] Typical of his probusiness bias, AFL president Gompers was quick to see an opening for labor in industry's new capacity to turn out goods, especially when they produced more goods than demand registered in the market. Mass production, after all, was profitable just because it produced so many of the same things. Gompers saw that workingmen and women had an unexploited potential as buyers rather than as mere elements of production. The prevailing view about how wages were set, propounded in the early nineteenth century, argued that employers would always push wages down to the minimal amount a family needed for subsistence. This "iron law of wages" operated that way through much of the nineteenth century, but if wages rose, it was possible to see that this could stimulate the whole economy.

Marx had seen the downward pressure on wages as central to the industrial system and part of the reason why it could not sustain itself. Marxist labor leaders in Europe and the United States confidently believed that capitalism was doomed to extinction. Gompers, no theorist, took a different tack about the frequent layoffs and long workweeks endured by laborers. Working men and women, he said in 1887, needed "more": more money, more leisure, more freedom. He clearly had caught the spirit of capitalism when he emphasized, "We do want more, and when it becomes more, we shall still want more. And we shall never cease to demand more until we have received the result of our labor."[22]

Gompers's "more" campaign explained that treating laborers as the cultural and social creatures that they were would solve businesses' central conundrum of being able to make more goods than there were buyers for them. Younger economists agreed with Gompers as they deserted the labor theory of value for one that highlighted demand. Wages, if still sporadic, did in fact go up; the eight-hour workday was becoming common without a drop in the average wage rate. Gompers was not alone in recognizing that the economy had fundamentally shifted from a basis in scarcity to one driven by plenty. The American economist Simon Nelson Patten in his 1907 study *New Basis of Civilization* added intellectual firepower to the notion that the age of abundance had arrived.

This question brings to mind economic debates in late-seventeenth-century England, when the idea that popular spending might have an impact on the economy first surfaced. Then those in foreign trade actively stimulated new tastes with their imports of colorful calicoes. They waxed eloquent about the unlimited wants of human beings. It was not the inelastic demand of food and shelter that was going to drive the economy forward, they said, but the elastic demand for superfluous goods like a third or fourth blouse. Standing fiercely against this cheerful commentary were the manufacturers for whom ordinary people appeared as lazy, improvident, tardy, accident-prone, and surly laborers. Three centuries later the tension between these two groups of capitalists plays out in battles over protective tariffs, minimum wage laws, and expanded social benefits. Yet the ever-growing productive capacity of capitalist economies makes it even more imperative to choose between keeping wages down or enhancing the purchase power of workingmen and women.

Businessmen are not by nature reflective; they like to act. The leviathans of industrial capitalism had worked wonders in mills, plants, and mines across the world during the nineteenth century. Proud of their own accomplishments, they had contempt for employees who would use group power to coerce concessions from them. Yet there existed a puzzle at the heart of their economy that Gompers and Patten had hit upon. Workers were both employees—an element in determining prices—and customers, with the power to drive sales with their purchases. It takes time for ideas to catch up with events. Consumer capitalism came on quickly, pushed forward by the marvels of electricity and telegraphy. What it revealed was that men and women play many roles in the economy: breadwinner, full or part-time worker, saver, spender, consumer, register of tastes, and producer of future workers. Any adequate analysis of the developing economies of the West has to probe the meaning and efficacy in all these phases of a person's experience.

8

◆

RULERS AS

CAPITALISTS

D URING THE LAST QUARTER of the nineteenth century, European nations became venture capitalists with unhappy results for them and much of the rest of the world. For the previous two hundred years the free market economy had followed the path that private investors laid out. The informal communication of the market, spoken through the language of prices and rates, directed participants to the best deal. Information itself became a material good, orienting workers, producers, and investors toward their interests. During this long gestation period, governments played a supporting role. They sponsored industrial espionage, erected tariffs, and adjudicated contracts in their courts of law. In some countries they built railroads and established national banks. Still, kings, presidents, chancellors, and prime ministers gave the high politics of diplomacy and war making the lion's share of their attention.

European leaders were no longer willing to sit in the stands, watching their people steer this prodigy alone. They had acquired a lot of money from their wealthy subjects, and they began using it to invest in empire building, not to extract tribute as the Romans and Mongols had, but rather to command subjects' labor and resources to make things for the market. Kings and statesmen became entrepreneurs. Much attention has been given to the challenge of accumulating capital; much less thought has gone into studying how excess capital has affected economic choices. By the end of the nineteenth century most people in the West knew that money should be making money—all the time. The idea of idle money seemed abhorrent. Rulers in this regard were no different from others. With their enhanced revenues, the heads of state for Britain, France, Belgium, Germany, and Italy turned to reckless overseas adventures. Capitalism's unparalleled capacity to generate profits had reshaped the political landscape.

Bringing the peoples of Asia, Africa, and Latin America into capitalism's orbit promised both power and wealth to Europe's rulers. But, alas, capitalism hadn't modified the intense rivalries among European nations. Thomas Paine anticipated that commerce would "cordialize" mankind, but that was not to be. Instead countries now had more money for arming themselves. More arms spawned grander ambitions. Western European countries began competing for territories abroad while Spain, France, Great Britain, and Portugal had old empires to exploit. Generating new sources of income provided the means and the motives for Europe's rulers to engage in an international contest that ended in the disastrous First World War.

Neither the world nor capitalism would ever be the same after Western nations thrust themselves into the hinterlands of Africa in search of exotic raw materials. The difference between industrial and commercial expansion became crucial. Trade had touched only merchants, their servants, and those who lived near coasts, whereas producing goods in foreign lands involved whole populations put to work for their new masters. Typical of earlier foreign forays was the conduct of Great Britain toward China in the 1830s. Its East India Company was eager to establish a trade in opium grown in India. The Chinese government was loath to allow its people access to such an addictive drug. It prohibited the trade and expelled British merchants. Despite protests at home, the British forced their will upon China. After bombarding coastal cities, they succeeded in gaining commercial access to five Chinese ports and took control of Hong Kong. Though violent, the intrusion was limited.

Mobilizing labor abroad changed the character of capitalist enterprise, for it took more than economic incentives to ensnare the men and women found living near oil deposits and tropical forests. Harvesting tropical crops and extracting precious minerals created a need for workers close to these raw materials. Of course the factories in the fields of the seventeenth- and eighteenth-century Caribbean sugar plantations and the silver mines of Mexico and Peru offered something of a template for the new capitalist thrust to make colonies centers of production.

Governments had what companies lacked, the power to commandeer workers by extorting concessions from their compliant leaders or moving in with force where there was no recognized political order, as in much of sub-Saharan Africa. European colonies already existed on the coasts as supports to long-distance commerce. The untapped riches in the African interior stirred imperial designs. European countries began to scuffle over who would get what, with little thought of the people who lived there. Cupidity, curiosity, Christian proselytizing, and militant strong-arming came into play. Abuses, unacceptable at home, became common when capitalism moved outside its original borders. Long forgotten was how long it had taken before the forebears of the colonizers had adjusted to modern work rhythms. Their new colonial subjects just appeared to be backward, evoking little interest in their well-being from their new masters. Their resistance was met with violence.

European Missionaries to Africa

Considering the amazing reach of Western explorations, it's quite stunning how little was known about sub-Saharan Africa before the 1850s. Somehow it had never become a candidate for colonization as had North and South America, Australia, New Zealand, Indonesia, and India. Deadly diseases, especially malaria, made it a deathtrap for Europeans. Just as remarkable, a single person, David Livingstone, opened up the eastern half of the continent.

Livingstone has one of those life records that shame mere mortals.

From the age of ten until twenty-four he worked in the cotton mill of his Scottish hometown. Awakening to learning and Christianity in his late teens, he taught himself Latin, a requisite for a college education. He even contrived a way to read during his fourteen-hour shift by mounting his books on the spinning jenny. He saved enough money to go to medical schools in Glasgow and London. From there he went to South Africa as a medical missionary and soon married into a prominent missionary family. Livingstone found his twin vocations as Christian healer and intrepid explorer soon after he arrived in Cape Town in 1841. The two remained entwined for the next thirty years as he organized expeditions into "darkest Africa," a popular designation that suggests both a lack of knowledge and the skin color of the inhabitants.

Until his death Livingstone traveled by foot and oxen into the center of the continent, following the course of rivers, going up and down and around mountain ranges where no white man had ever been. Trekking through thousands of miles of pristine savannas, plateaus, deserts, lakes, streams, and rapids, he filled his journals with evocative descriptions of Africa's flora, fauna, and people, the whole interspersed with affirmations of his abiding Christian faith. Livingstone was the first European to cross the African continent from the Atlantic to the Indian Ocean. In these arduous trips he discovered the beauties of Africa and the fortitude of its people. Suffering bouts with both lions and malaria, he wrote copiously about the diseases he treated, among them malaria, against which he effectively used quinine. Subsequent explorers were less fortunate. Malaria remained a deadly disease, which, as late as 2006, killed a million African babies annually.

Unwittingly Livingstone stoked the avarice of his compatriots with concrete details about a land filled with resources in mint condition. Returning to England in 1857, he published *Missionary Travels and Researches in South Africa*, which excited readers much as *Raiders of the Lost Ark* does fans today. But Livingstone was no Indiana Jones. All agreed that he was the gentlest of men, a trait that explains how he always succeeded in winning over tribes hostile to his intrusion.

In the course of bringing his medical skill and Christian faith to those he met, Livingstone came face-to-face with a lively slave trade carried on in central Africa by Muslim and Swahili-speaking Africans. Powerful Arab leaders had penetrated Africa from both the west and east coasts during the nineteenth century, converting many tribes to their faith. They also enslaved Africans, sending them to buyers in Zanzibar, Persia, Madagascar, and plantations on the Arabian Peninsula. Livingstone devoted the last decade of his life to exposing the cruelties of the East African slave trade. When his *Zambesi and Its Tributaries* appeared in 1865, hundreds of Christians rallied to the cause of ending this nefarious trade, made even more odious to them by its Muslim imprint. Horror at this slave trade and European's insatiable demand for ivory for their pianos, billiards, jewelry, and furniture inlays proved mutually reinforcing. The universal respect accorded Livingstone sustained a new and vigorous campaign to bring civilization to the people of the "Dark Continent," a European conceit that covered a multitude of sins. Returning to Africa once more, Livingstone plunged into the interior, this time to find the source of the Nile. He lost all contact with European correspondents for five years, adding a fascinating mystery to his already great reputation as a humanitarian.

At this point in the story entered a Welsh immigrant from the United States, Henry Morton Stanley. A Civil War veteran, a foreign correspondent, and an amateur geographer, Stanley in 1871 accepted an assignment from the *New York Herald* to find the missing Livingstone. Knowing that Stanley had fought on both sides in the Civil War gives some idea of his versatility. His quest through central Africa took six months, but he had succeeded by the end of the year, when he did in fact greet the missing missionary with the famous salutation "Dr. Livingstone, I presume." Stanley and Livingstone became household names during the next few years. They stimulated the imagination, the curiosity, and the ambition of Europeans who had come to think of the entire globe as their domain.

During the next six years Stanley continued to explore Africa, circumnavigating Lake Victoria. He located the southern sources of the Nile, ending with an epoch-making journey down the Congo River. Unlike the trusting Livingstone, Stanley traveled with a well-armed band of 190 men and displayed more the attitude of a Western master than a humble Christian. He thought much like the English who went to North America in the seventeenth century, for he considered the African continent empty of people, or at least of people who counted. Feted as one of history's greatest discoverers when he returned to England, Stanley did his best to get the British government to claim the heart of Africa. But to no avail.[1]

The Imperial Ambitions of King Leopold of Belgium

Across the English Channel, there was a European of significance fired up by the promise of Africa that Stanley had advertised. He was Leopold II, king of the Belgians. Leopold had inherited a lot of money from his father, who had astutely promoted Belgium's industrial enterprises, among them the first European railway system. Intent upon gaining a colony to enhance the importance of his little country, Leopold actually scoured the Indies archive in Madrid to learn just how much Spain had benefited from its colonies.[2] He kept up with news of Africa by reading his favorite newspaper, the *Times* of London, which came to him early each morning by special messenger. Here he read an English explorer declaring that Africa's "unspeakable richness" was awaiting an "enterprising capitalist." At the time Livingstone's posthumous journals were horrifying readers with the graphic accounts of how unscrupulous slave traders seized African men and women, even children and sold them into slavery. Enthusiasm for stamping out a slave trade that had been pretty much unknown previously played into Leopold's plans to create a colony in Africa. He engaged missionaries, geographers, and antislavery advocates to organize on behalf of Christianity, science, and humanitarianism. Privately he laid plans to get what he called "a slice of this magnificent African cake."[3]

Nothing will give you a greater sense of how the nineteenth-century world differs from ours than following Leopold as he managed with megalomaniacal determination to acquire for his country an African colony seventy-six times the size of Belgium. But that isn't quite correct. For the Free State of Congo that Leopold created with such hubris was a personal possession that he ran as a company with the approval and financial assistance of the Belgian Parliament. Because Britain's leaders showed no interest in acquiring a colony in the interior of Africa, Leopold was able to snag Stanley, the intrepid survivor of years of explorations. He put him under a five-year contract and forthwith sent him back to central Africa with the cash to build roads, establish stations through the Congo River network, buy land, and sign treaties. This Stanley did over the course of five years with great panache, persuading 450 chiefs of the Congo basin to accept his gifts in exchange for territorial rights.

Meanwhile in Europe, Leopold carried on a brilliant diplomatic campaign under the guise of furthering science and philanthropy. His International Association of the Congo was nothing but a front behind which he manipulated the United States, Great Britain, Germany, and France into accepting his acquisition of a vast territory in central Africa with no restrictions on his personal sovereignty.[4] Leopold didn't want to push the native inhabitants out of the land he coveted, for he had in mind using their skilled arms and strong backs to labor for him. What followed was as cruel a travesty as the world has ever seen, traceable to the West's outsized appetite for the riches of Africa.

The Congo Free State, as Leopold styled it, was anything but free, for he established a vicious regime, exploiting the men and women as thoroughly as the slavery he had vowed to eradicate. All uncultivated land became his property, leaving most of the people landless. Backed by white soldiers and black mercenaries and working with compliant tribal chiefs, Leopold used threats of murder, backed up by the wholesale destruction of villages, to force the Congolese to collect latex from wild rubber trees, dig for diamonds, and hunt elephants for their ivory. Rubber alone made the Congo a commercial success. More like a modern CEO than a crowned head, Leopold followed market indicators closely. With astonishing ruthlessness, he sent regular shipments of rifles to his minions in the Congo. A similar melancholy tale unfolded in the Amazon basin, where professional rubber tappers brought their diseases and weapons to the indigenous population.[5]

By the end of the century Leopold's treatment of the Congolese had aroused critics who could not be ignored. A company employee became suspicious of what was going on. Swedish and American missionaries who were eyewitnesses to the abuse launched a crusade against Leopold's Congo venture. People as capable of expressing themselves as Sir Arthur Conan Doyle, Joseph Conrad, and Mark Twain began writing about Leopold's mendacious brutality. The riches he monopolized stirred as well the indignation of British free traders. To add insult to injury, Leopold sustained the fiction of his benevolence by building the Tervuren Museum filled with displays of African art to celebrate the Congolese people's liberation from paganism and slavery![6] Nearing his death in 1908, Leopold ceded his fiefdom to the Belgian nation, at which point it received the name Belgian Congo.

Other European Nations in Africa

Leopold's is the most extreme record of European rapacity, but his European neighbors lost no time joining in the plunder of Africa and its people. France, having lost New France and its holdings in India at the end of the eighteenth century, started a new empire by invading Algeria in 1830. Smarting from defeat in the Franco-Prussian War a generation later, it next sent expeditions up the Senegal River. From there France eventually succeeded in seizing the northwest quarter of Africa, four million of the continent's some twelve million square miles, including Tunisia and Morocco.[7] In addition to its holdings in Africa and Indochina, France held Tahiti, where Paul Gauguin set up his studio in 1890.

Starting de novo like King Leopold, the Germans had to cast about for a colony because they had not participated in the sixteenth-century adventures in the New World. Before pushing into Africa, Germany found a place in the South Seas sun. The drastic shortage of raw cotton occasioned by the American Civil War had hit hard the Rhine Valley textile mills and the ports that depended upon cotton exports. A prominent and imaginative entrepreneur from Hamburg sent agents to the Pacific to seek spots along the equator where cotton might be grown. He managed to get a toehold in Samoa. The German government followed up by convincing Spain to sell it the majority of the islands among the Solomons, Carolines, Marianas, and Pelews. Neither France nor Great Britain was ready to cede these luxuriant South Pacific islands to Germany, so they parceled out among themselves the remaining islands in eight different groups. Farther west, Great Britain in 1898 signed a ninety-nine-year treaty with China to hold on to Hong Kong. Meanwhile back in Africa, the Germans laid claim to Togoland, Cameroon, Namibia, and Tanganyika, located on both sides of the African continent.

Italy entered this African land rush last. It acquired Libya, Eritrea, and part of Somaliland but sustained an embarrassing defeat at the hands of the Ethiopians. Only Ethiopia and Liberia, the colony that Americans established for freed slaves, held on to their independence during this European free-for-all for territory. For France and Britain, the toeholds established earlier became launching pads for further global appropriations, though with markedly different styles.

More attentive to commerce than to territorial acquisition when Leopold was finalizing his plans in 1875, Great Britain tightened its control over Egypt. Britain had acquired an interest in there after the defeat of Napoleon, who had invaded the country in 1798. Formally an Egyptian dynasty ruled the country under a loose connection to the Ottoman Empire, but practically it remained within the European sphere of influence. This humiliating arrangement became a bone of contention for Egyptian nationalists, whose agitation introduced social turmoil that threatened Great Britain's huge investment in Egypt. On top of this, more and more of the British commercial fleets began using the Suez Canal after its opening in 1869. This hundred-mile waterway joined the Red Sea to the Mediterranean. Its vulnerability to violence was unacceptable to British investors. The British government ordered an invasion of Egypt in 1882, demonstrating the fusion of public and private economic interests that became increasingly conspicuous.

At the other end of the continent, Great Britain was having trouble in South Africa, which it had seized from the Dutch East India Company during the Napoleonic Wars. Cape Town played a crucial role in British overseas commerce, servicing commercial and royal fleets going to and from the Orient. Britain acquired as well a population of Dutch farmers who grew restive under British rule after Britain mounted a campaign against slavery in 1833. Some six thousand of these Afrikaners, or Boers, as they called themselves, decided to move north to establish their own settlements, taking with them some six thousand slaves and the herds of sheep and cattle that sustained them. The British were unwilling to yield sovereignty to either the Transvaal or the Orange Free State, especially after an African discovered a diamond there one day in 1867. Only a bloody conflict in the closing years of the century settled the matter in Britain's favor, by which time Europeans had assumed control of most of the continent's habitable land.

A great aid to the Europeans in their appropriation of African territory turned out to be the machine gun that the American Hiram Maxim had developed with them in mind! Someone had suggested to Maxim that if he wished to make money, he should "invent something that will enable these Europeans to cut each other's throats with greater facility." Instead they used their new Maxims against the Africans. This portable automatic machine gun fired five hundred rounds per minute, delivering the firing power of a hundred rifles, as it ingeniously used the energy of each bullet's recoil to eject the spent cartridge case and insert the next round. In one engagement in what is now Zimbabwe, fifty British soldiers prevailed over some five thousand warriors with four Maxim guns. The repeating rifle and various improvements on the Maxim served Europe well whether in the hands of soldiers or of entrepreneurs who wished to speed up the pace of Africa's occupation.

Like any frontier, Africa attracted freebooters who sometimes acted as the point men for their country's acquisitions. Such a man was Cecil Rhodes. Rhodes followed his brother to South Africa in 1870. Within a decade he put together the De Beers Mining Company, which extracted the bulk of the diamonds taken from Africa over the course of the next century. Rhodes was inspired by a vision of planting the British flag "from Cape Town to Cairo." This alarmed the Portuguese in Mozambique and the Germans busy settling into East Africa. With the effrontery that sometimes builds great empires, Rhodes took over a territory that bore his name for half a century. Slow to respond to his high-handed ways, the British government finally asserted its sovereign power. Thanks to the disgraced Rhodes, that power now extended over a substantial hunk of southern Africa.

During its long history, capitalism often acted like a talent scout finding new uses for plants and products that had been around for ages. Rubber was one such. Grown wild in the rain forests of the Congo and in equatorial lands from Brazil through Malaysia and India, rubber had waterproofing qualities as well as elasticity, which had been appreciated. The

American Charles Goodyear discovered how to take the stickiness out of the product, but it was not until the Englishman John Dunlop successfully made pneumatic tires for his son's tricycle in 1887 that its capacity to give wheeled vehicles a smooth ride found a major commercial use. A bicycle craze ensued. Just around the next corner in technology's forward movement was the automobile with prototypes of the modern car being developed in half a dozen countries. The demand for rubber for automobiles promised to integrate the previously neglected equatorial and Middle Eastern areas into the world economy.

It was not just rubber that found new uses; oil, nitrates, even cactus leaves acquired commercial value. The mechanical reaper was transforming American agriculture. Its widespread use occasioned another farm mechanism, a knotting device that bound wheat shafts with twine. Landholders in the poor and dry Yucatán Peninsula somehow learned of this and saw the possibility of making twine from cactus. A group of entrepreneurs emerged ready to enslave the peasants, if necessary, to get them to use their machetes to cut off the cactus leaves. As so often happens in the history of capitalism, as one group suffered from a development, another prospered. This was the case here: While Mexican workers hacked at cactus leaves with little reward, farming families on the American plains prospered from the mechanization of their labor.[8] The long reach of capitalist innovation in our time found coltan, a very special metallic ore from the Congo, which helps shrink the size of cell phones.

The leading European industrial powers sometimes treated their less advanced neighbors with the same arrogant sense of entitlement that they displayed in Africa. In 1873 a consortium of German and British companies bought the Spanish mines in the Andalucian coastline along the Río Tinto that legend said were none other than those of King Solomon. Probably the oldest copper mines in the world, they date back to the time of the Phoenicians. The new Rio Tinto Company brought in modern equipment and set up a residential community for its British employees. This may have been one of the world's first "gated communities," designed principally to keep out the Spanish. Any Englishman who married a Spaniard lost the right to live in Bellavista. The company quickly turned the area into a moonscape and caused an environmental disaster by regularly burning pyramids of copper sulfides. More than twelve thousand outraged local sufferers, tired of breathing sulfur, in 1888 launched a protest that Spanish authorities put down with unstinting violence.[9] The Rio Tinto Company made news again in 2008, when the Aluminum Corporation of America joined forces with the Aluminum Corporation of China to buy 12 percent of Rio Tinto's shares.

During most of the nineteenth century the United States had expanded by pushing aside the Indians living beyond the Appalachian Mountains. Armed settlers backed by the U.S. Army helped the country fulfill what it considered its "manifest destiny" to occupy the North American continent. With the states of California, Oregon, and Washington filling up rapidly, the country's leaders began to see the United States as a Pacific as well as an Atlantic power. The rage for empire infected many Americans. An opportunity arose just ninety miles off the coast of Florida. While other European powers were racing to acquire new colonies, Spain was having trouble hanging on to Cuba, Puerto Rico, and the Philippines, the last three possessions of its once-great empire. In 1898 the Cuban struggle for independence captured the sympathy of Americans, whose new tabloid newspapers sensationalized the rebellion going on there.

Blaming Spain for the explosion on an American battleship, the U.S. Congress gave the president authority to use force against Spain and, incidentally, declared Cuba independent. Once at war, the United States sank the Spanish fleet in Manila Bay, more than ten thousand miles from Cuba. The United States forthwith annexed Guam, Midway, and Wake. The Hawaiian Islands had already been formed into an American protectorate in 1893. Meanwhile back in the Caribbean, after a few skirmishes, Spain granted Cuba its independence and ceded the Philippines to the United States. Furious at being handed over to another country, independence-minded Filipinos struggled against their new masters for sixteen years. The fight was brutal. Even American soldiers were horrified at the atrocities committed by their army. Despite a vigorous anti-imperialism movement at home, the United States joined the imperial club. The Filipinos had to wait another forty-eight years to achieve their autonomy. American imperialists, like those in Europe, touted the expansion in manufacturing, trade, and employment their new conquests would nurture.[10]

The Awakening Conscience of the West

In the years following the great divvying up of Africa, David Livingstone and Henry Morton Stanley became emblematic of the two impulses that had brought Europeans to Africa. Stanley stood for arrogant exploitation while Livingstone represented dedication to the well-being of others, both physical and spiritual. Private ventures like Stanley's upended the cultural integrity of countries strong in many things except the capacity to repel the might of the West. Christian missionaries cared about the African people but were just as intent on changing them. Despite the moral chasm that lay between Stanley and Livingstone, both men displayed traits remarkably congruent with venture capital: their insatiable curiosity, their endurance of short-run discomfort to achieve long-run goals, and their overriding tenacity.

Commercial avarice, heightened by the rivalries within Europe, had changed the world. When the burst of acquisitions ended, half the earth was under the control of nine nations. If you were to assign colors to Spain, Portugal, Britain, France, the Netherlands, Germany, the United States, and Belgium to designate their areas of domination—even Denmark would need one for Greenland—the map of the world would look like a colorful fabric design. These national carriers of Western capitalism had to coin new words for their possessions, conjuring up "mandates," "spheres of influence," "protectorates," and "annexations" to specify the particular nature of their domination around the world. At a conference in Berlin in 1884–1885 they put their seal of approval on the African holdings of all nations present.

Westerners continued their march across the globe, considering it part of the grand plan of human progress. The urge to exploit resources everywhere was rarely seen as part of the capitalist dynamic. More often it got folded into the assumption that Europeans were agents of historical development. They did accomplish many good things abroad, and they witnessed firsthand the great cruelty of local potentates and the rigidity of social hierarchies that guaranteed the oppression of the many by the few. Still, their wounding arrogance blinded them to the harm that they were doing among people whom they little understood or cared about.

Whatever advances can be associated with Western domination outside Europe, they came at the high price of giving their foreign subjects a lingering and debilitating sense of inferiority.

In the twentieth century, Hannah Arendt put her finger on the problem: Outside their own boundaries, Europeans were willing to engage in practices intolerable at home.[11] Europeans weren't more violent than their contemporaries around the world, but they could, as others could not, inflict death and destruction on a grander scale. The capitalist motor, acquiring more horsepower with every decade, drove Europeans to easy conquests. Contempt for those with different faces immured in strange customs eased the consciences of these carriers of civilization, as it had slavery among white Americans. One might say in retrospect that capitalism acquired a sinister patina when governments took the initiative away from the private investors who had been running the capitalist show.

Defenders of capitalism are wont to tout their positive features while drowning accounts of their abuses in a pool of references to the human capacity to do wrong. That capacity for violence is certainly pervasive. Jared Diamond gives us a particularly shocking example of it in the case of an isolated South Sea island whose inhabitants had long fostered gentle habits. Hearing about their lack of any weapons, an expedition of Maoris, distant relatives who had been separated for centuries, sailed to the island and wiped out the community, slaughtering all the men and carrying off the women and children.[12] Europeans got hoisted on their own petard by insisting on their superior virtue while pursuing ugly ends.

During the eighteenth century, a revolution in sensibilities had taken place, one that was initially directed to the evils within European societies. A new humanitarianism, based on personal empathy for other human beings, however different, had taken root. Vividly expressed in European literature, philosophy, and the arts, this humanitarianism offered Europeans a new and more benign identity.[13] The father of E. I. du Pont named his son Eleuthère Irénée, which means "happiness and peace," in celebration of the goals of the Enlightenment. Captured in the French Revolutionary slogan of "Liberty, equality, and fraternity," this new spirit lost some of its appeal in Napoleon's campaign to dominate Europe. Then scientific investigations in the nineteenth century, without disavowing humanitarianism, led to studies describing how and why racial differences existed. This discourse gave European empire builders some cover for their aggressive conduct.

At the popular level, two justifications were offered for European transgressions: The men and women affected were too ignorant, lazy, and superstitious to know what was happening to them, or Europeans were carriers of great gifts from their superior culture, manifested in its religion, its tools, and its wealth. As civilized nations they would bring public education, higher standards of cleanliness, better transportation, and more respectful attitudes toward women to their benighted new subjects. When reformers publicized the wide gap between projected benefits and actual accomplishments, empire building lost its luster, even though its forward moment was strong enough to cause a war that stretched like Europe's possessions across the globe.

A New Rival in the East

Under the radar, during this period of European expansion, Japan had been undergoing a remarkable transformation, culminating when the feudal Tokugawa regime gave way to the Meiji Restoration in 1867. For reasons that remain obscure, in 1637 the third shogun of the ruling Tokugawa line in Japan had issued a "closing of the country" decree.[14] He was probably reacting defensively to the presence of Spain, Portugal, the Netherlands, France, and England in the Indian and Pacific oceans. This self-denying ordinance certainly accords well with the xenophobic attitude in the Japanese national spirit, but it rankled Westerners, who were used to going where they wanted. Western impatience with countries that preferred not to join a trading system stacked against them became marked as imperialism swept up European leaders. A British fleet bombarded Kagoshima in 1863 in order to gain access to the southern Japanese area of Satsuma. The bombardment destroyed one-third of the city.

Two dramatic events led Japan to reverse course: the arrival of an American fleet demanding that Japan join the informal world trade system and a more or less peaceful coup d'etat, the first in 1853; the second in 1869. The American appetite for trade throughout the Pacific had been whetted by the acquisition of California ports in the Mexican-American War, which ended in 1848. Japan appeared to Americans as an oyster that just needed a little pressure to reveal its pearls. They sent Commodore Matthew Perry with a fleet across the Pacific to pry it open. Perry was the right man for the job. He studied his subject well and arrived with an impressive combination of modern weaponry and the elaborate trappings of ceremony. His heavily armored steamboats were meant to impress the Japanese with Western technology, as the imposing black line in the harbor of Toyko most certainly did.

Perry would deal only with the highest authority and demonstrated his readiness to fight by repelling any Japanese who attempted to board one of his ships. He also had patience, giving the Japanese half a year to make up their minds. It proved enough time for them to realize that the only way they could create the strength to repel outside influence would be to tap into the modern power of foreigners. After fifteen months of tense negotiations, underlined with threats to use force, Perry succeeded in gaining a treaty and wounding Japanese pride.

While these so-called openings were battering Japan, a reforming wing of the samurai, the traditional aristocracy, which composed about 7 percent of the Japanese population, orchestrated a reshuffling of noble and imperial power. The leaders of the Meiji Restoration, named after the young emperor, were opportunistic enough to borrow every Western idea that might turn Japan into a modern nation. Unhappy with the commercial treaties that had been foisted upon their country, they strengthened distinctive Japanese institutions like the Shinto belief in the emperor's divinity. A shared religion became important as a unifying force. Schools and the army also helped instill loyalty and a strong sense of civic duty among the Japanese. Perhaps even more important, Meiji reformers replaced the old classical, moral, and Confucian education with a more scientific and technical one. In an interesting paradox, if not contradiction, Meiji leaders wanted both to preserve what made Japan unique and to prepare their people to enter a multinational, modern world.

Longer-term changes were already converting the country's network of self-sufficient villages into an integrated, commercial economy. With a vibrant agriculture, Japan's standard of living was probably as much as a third higher than that of its neighbors. A nascent middle class made up of wealthy farmers, small traders, and urban professionals provided critical support to the restoration effort. Over the next few decades, the central and centralizing authorities went on a crash course to modernize Japan while using industrial power to build up its military. The goal became achieving "Great Power Status."[15]

Merchants and artisans in the rural area favored the restoration, hoping for a larger ambit for enterprise along with opportunities to participate in politics. In 1889 a constitution was promulgated, setting up a bicameral legislature, composed of a lower house—the Diet—and a House of Peers. The constitution reserved most powers for the emperor, but these were exercised by his advisers. Political parties existed, but a dominant concern with harmony and a new aristocracy to interpret what that harmony consisted of severely limited their effectiveness. The constitution itself represented the acme of achievement for those Meiji critics hoping for a more liberal order than they got.[16]

Meiji administrators turned out to be experimental and pragmatic without yielding on their goal of catching up with the West. "Catching up," as it turned out, meant jettisoning the country's feudal arrangements, its addiction to traditions, its costly samurai, and a tax system that favored the feudal overlords over farmers. They turned samurai stipends into bonds that could be used as bank capital and unified the multiple currencies into one. The old and new sectors of the economy grew concurrently and were often mutually enhancing. In fact the capital for modernizing came from accelerating growth in venerable craft and textile trades.

Japanese farmers had a long tradition of using family labor in both agriculture and cottage industry. They continued to make textiles at home long after modern factories had been established in the cities. This labor-intensive work went a long way to compensate for Japan's lack of capital. Japan exported cotton yarn and cotton cloth, silk spun yarn and cloth, and an array of inexpensive parasols, European-style umbrellas, paper products, pottery, glass bottles, lamps, ropes, mats, and soap.[17] Foreign trade brought fertilizers to farmers and cotton dyes to textile makers. Export demand for Japanese silk doubled in five years.[18]

The new government developed a national banking system. It reordered the nation's finances by reducing the stipends to the samurai. It replaced the old agricultural tax with a set land tax, turning land into a capital asset and giving the new farmer-landlords, rather than overlords, the benefits of improvement. It recapitulated swiftly the agricultural changes in sixteenth- and seventeenth-century England that had released workers and capital for commercial and industrial enterprises. The government invested heavily in railroads, highways, and a merchant marine. Under the slogan "Rich country, strong army," the new leadership changed the laws, the schools, and the priorities of the country. It abandoned the lunar calendar derived from China in favor of the Gregorian calendar, which England had adopted in 1752, necessitating a loss of eleven days as September 3 of the old Julian calendar became September 14 of the new. Soon smokestacks, telephone poles, railroad tracks, shipyards, and coal mines dotted the picture-perfect Japanese landscape.[19]

The dislike of foreigners that had kept the country isolated found expression in a domestic ideology of emperor worship. Japanese xenophobia actually got stood on its head as copying Western dress, aesthetics, and technology became identified with patriotism. The forced concessions wrested by Great Britain and the United States continued to abrade Japanese pride and provide the emotional fuel for an expansive foreign policy. More menacingly, Russia was moving east toward Manchuria, Sakhalin, and Korea, as the Trans-Siberian Railway took shape during the 1890s. China too was angling for more control over Korea, something intolerable to the Japanese government, which was willing to spend one-third of the national budget on soldiers and weapon systems.

Integral to Japan's drive for autonomy was the determination to repel Western powers that intruded too far into East Asia. They'd all already arrived—the British in Hong Kong, the Dutch in Macao and Timor, the Spanish in the Philippines, the French on the Pacific island of Tahiti— and then, in 1867, the United States bought Alaska and the Aleutian Islands from Russia and acquired Midway Island. The new Meiji government was able to dispatch a challenge from China in the successful prosecutions of the Sino-Japanese War of 1894–1895. When Russia extended into Manchuria, more action was called for. Negotiations over mutually exclusive spheres of influence broke down, leading to a Japanese attack on Port Arthur in Manchuria in early 1904. A very swift war ensued, with Japan again emerging victorious. Peace negotiations in New Hampshire brought an end to hostilities and a Nobel Peace Prize to President Theodore Roosevelt in 1906.

While the English were learning of these victories, they were also enjoying Gilbert and Sullivan's popular spoof of imperial Japan in their 1885 operetta *The Mikado* with little thought of the wounds to Japanese pride. Japan added the colony of Korea in 1910 to that of Taiwan, acquired in 1895, and annexed Korea in 1910. With little regard for the neighbors that they would "save" from the West, Japan moved into China next. Like its European imperialist mentors, Japan saw its mission as civilizing its backward neighbors. At the same time, American and European artists and architects discovered the Japanese aesthetic and began incorporating Japanese designs into their work. Western consumers, attuned to novelty, responded with great enthusiasm to these objects and styles.[20]

The well-known slogan of the Meiji Restoration about "enriching the country and strengthening the armed forces" describes what happened as Japan replaced backward methods with the latest Western technology, but what it doesn't reveal is even more important. Japan yielded to demands to come out of its isolation at the same time that its leaders worked diligently to achieve the autonomy that had eluded so many of the non-Western countries brought into the Western orbit. This meant to them maintaining government direction of economic development in order to build a strong military presence. Skilled administrators, not business leaders, oversaw industrialization, though the latter were always ready to take advantage of any economic opportunities that opened up. Japan became famous for its borrowings. Even its constitution reflected a respect for English political institutions, but its leaders eschewed the West's faith in the free market to allocate resources. You might say that Japan copied every arrow in the Western economic quiver except its theories about free enterprise.[21]

While Japan had startled the West by handily sinking the Russian Baltic fleet in Tsushima Strait, the impact of this display of its prowess astounded Asians. It thrilled them, for Europe's long dominance of their homelands had left a legacy of anger, bitterly larded with a sense of inferiority. One of their own defeated the mighty Europeans, even if it was the backward czarist Russia.[22] Never had Europeans sustained such a resounding defeat at the hands of an Asian nation. The novelist Pramoedya Ananta Toer in his *Buru Quartet* gives lyrical expression to the exhilaration felt as far away as Malaysia at this stunning, unexpected triumph over the arrogant Europeans.

Imperial Japan actually acted as midwife for two revolutions, both precursors of world-shaking ones. The humiliating defeat of Russia spurred the leaders of the premature Russian Revolution of 1905. More directly, Japanese leaders encouraged Chinese revolutionaries, reasoning that it would facilitate their plans to control Manchuria. The five hundred Chinese students who came to Japan to study in 1902 had grown to thirteen thousand by 1906. Many of these political radicals returned home to support Sun Yat-sen. The Japanese government had subsidized the successful creation of a Chinese Republic in 1912, figuring that it would open up a power vacuum in Manchuria.

Since the Meiji Restoration, Japan had come to control considerable territory outside its island borders. These acquisitions strengthened the military as well as financial and industrial leaders, who began to participate in the political parties previously dominated by the landlord class.[23] When the United States invaded the Philippines in 1898 during the Spanish-American War, it announced the policy of the open door. Although it sounded benign in its invitation to all to participate, the Japanese saw it as a threat to their maturing plans for dominance in China. The Japanese military, which had grown stronger with every decade, joined Japan's big industrialists in backing the government's view of Manchuria as a prime colonial area. The stage was set for protracted conflict.

Restructuring of Corporations

At the turn of the twentieth century, that chameleon capitalism changed pace and structure once more. In sharp contrast with the imperialists' pell-mell approach to acquiring new territory, business firms, now the key players, were becoming more rational and efficient, and much better organized. The earlier development of railroads and telegraphy had made complex business structures both possible and necessary. Trains and telegrams broke down the isolation of villages and towns and linked cities far apart. Their lines and rails kept up a constant movement of people, goods, and information. When the new firms were organized well, their size made possible cutting costs while buying materials, organizing production, and attracting customers. Bigness promoted organizational restructuring and paid for it.

By the opening of the twentieth century capitalism was no longer an obnoxious intruder disturbing settled ways. It was the ascendant economic system in Europe, the United States, and Japan. The previous century had demonstrated the potent connection between an ever-evolving technology and risk-taking entrepreneurs. The experience of Germany and the United States in surpassing Great Britain offered many lessons, though rarely were they studied. For starters, risk taking was an essential, but disruptive, part of the capitalist dynamic. Innovation sustained economic development, and cultivating consumption was as important as enlarging production. Panics and recessions reminded people that no one was explicitly in charge of an entrepreneurial economy, even if some participants had a great deal more power than others. Coming to terms with that fact alone has proved difficult for people and governments. The accumulation of market choices expressed in private decisions to produce, save, spend, hire, work, lend, and borrow could, can, and will continue to deliver surprises, not all of them pleasant.

In the closing decades of the nineteenth century, fierce competition was eating up profits throughout the capitalist world, and it happened while technological innovations soaked up more money. At first, trade associations held out the hope of moderating price wars; creating a holding company of many outfits was an even more effective solution. The "firm"—a shorthand term to refer to private companies—took over at the closing of the Vanderbilt-Carnegie-Rockefeller era. In fact, Rockefeller made a novel move when his Standard Oil Company of Ohio achieved a near monopoly of oil fields, pipelines, and refineries. Under his Ohio charter, he could not legally own stock outside Ohio, so he came up with a new strategy. He created a board of trustees to hold stock in his various enterprises, creating the Oil Trust in 1881. Not only was competition suppressed, but the new firm became big enough to both need and pay for a managerial make-over.

Surprising as it sounds, bureaucracy is what distinguished the firm from earlier business arrangements, bureaucracy and the separation of ownership from management. Long before the U.S. government set up its landmark bureaucracies with their alphabet soup acronyms like ICC and SEC, the Pennsylvania Railroad, DuPont, Standard Oil, and International Telephone and Telegraph put together sophisticated organizations whose very complexity brought into being a new profession, management. Managers acquired prestige as they learned new skills. Concurrent developments merged to create more complex organizations. Compulsory education upgraded the work force while trained managers learned how to use statistics, financial reports, procurement strategies, and technical papers.

You can grasp the principle behind the new business structures if you imagine the typical organizational chart with its stacks of boxes, descending from the top layer. The boxes looked at vertically denote authority; the board of directors with final authority sits atop the chart, but the presidents were in charge 24/7. Salaried executives, who later were called chief executive officers, instead of owners, now ran the companies. Each organizational unit in the firm had a specific task in the operation along with its own hierarchy of managers, their staffs, accountants, engineers, technicians, salespersons, and, for production units, workers and foremen. These unit managers reported to those above them through an established chain of command and connected to one another through a flow of information pulsating back and forth.

Though the new organization was slightly military in its rigid structure, its essence was fluidity, the ability to respond quickly to subtle changes in all the markets the firm had to deal with. There was an incentive for firms that relied more upon capital than labor to adopt the new organizational structure because they benefited most from following the drumbeat of regular upgrading.[24] No one heard the whistle of competition more loudly than the CEO and his team of middle managers. Like good generals, professional managers kept their teams attuned to ways for widening their market, staying abreast of innovation, riding hard on competitors, and cutting costs.[25] Research and development had to be constant. Many of the new firms were big enough to dominate their line of business. The concept of market share now joined steady profits in the lexicon of success. Alfred P. Sloan, Jr., the legendary organizer of General Motors, for example, raised GM's market share from 12 to 52 percent over the course of his career from 1920 to 1956.

In 1893 another downturn in the economy coupled with price wars among capital-intensive industries created incentives to dampen competition through amalgamation. New Jersey gave American companies a break with an incorporation statute that let corporations hold stock shares of other corporations, regardless of where the corporations had been chartered. Merging companies then became a favorite strategy for reducing competition in the United States. Mergers, following the time-honored principle of the economy of scale enabled three or four large companies to enjoy the cost savings of size, but bigness is beneficial only if it leads to savings.[26]

Cooperating businesses had the choice of forming a trust or getting a state charter for a new company that pooled the shares of existing firms. The return of prosperity set off the largest merger movement yet seen. More than 157 giant corporations swallowed up 1,800 separate businesses between 1895 and 1904. Close to 100 of these new corporations had a commanding share—from 40 to 70 percent—of their markets. Large companies in oil, tobacco, steel, and automobile making obviously flourished, but literally hundreds of other attempts to follow this model failed because they couldn't benefit from either size or scope.[27]

For many firms, the most treacherous passage was the one from family company to impersonal corporation. Families, like the Swifts, Deeres, Eastmans, Schwabs, Firestones, Dows, Watsons, McCormicks, Westinghouses, and Armours maintained control over their firms longest because they grew through internal developments rather than acquisitions. Still, while personal attachment counted for much, the challenges to grow and diversify intensified. Not all heirs were equally able, steering expansion required a breadth of knowledge, and most family firms did not have the deep pockets to meet the considerable costs of vertical integration and managerial reorganization. For instance, only the Vanderbilts had the money to modernize their railroad system.

The gifts of Pierre du Pont make this point better. Responsible for restructuring the DuPont Company after 1904 and General Motors after 1920, du Pont was both wealthy and astute enough in financial affairs not to have to repair to Wall Street for expansion. He had an intuitive sense of which managers would succeed and the good sense to get out of their way as they tackled the daunting task of modernizing operations while maintaining profits. At General Motors, du Pont's promotion of Alfred Sloan was enough to secure the company's prosperity.[28] But his rare success raises another point. If unusual talent is needed to carry complex organizations like a corporation across the bridge of critical change, which plays the more important part in success: the unique individual or the optimal structure?[29]

A list of the two hundred largest firms in 1917 gives us a picture of what had replaced the local meat-packer, farmer-retailer, seamstress, and wheelwright. Think American Tobacco, United States Rubber, Quaker Oats, Standard Oil, and Pittsburgh Plate Glass. With assets in the millions and employees in the thousands, these corporations produced food, tobacco, textiles, apparel, lumber, furniture, paper, printed items, chemicals, petroleum, rubber, leather, glass, metals, machinery, transportation equipment, and instruments.[30] Sometimes referred to as managerial capitalism, this consolidation into behemoths depended on the legal foundation of the corporation for perpetuity, limited liability, and a protected scope of action. Given incorporation generously by state governments, stockholders rarely recognized it as the gift that it was.[31]

Private banks like that of J. P. Morgan created a market in shares of industrial securities. These sales financed the many mergers that were consolidating whole industries. Banks bought sufficiently large blocks of equity to be able to have their weight felt in dividend and investment policies at shareholders' meetings. This arrangement worked until the bankers' influence appeared as a threat to the interests of the public, whose advocates demanded laws curtailing this financial capitalism. Over time banks lost some of the power they had exercised at the end of the nineteenth century. Not only was there more federal regulation, there were new sources of capital available to big companies, like their savings or stock issues. New or expanding smaller companies became the Wall Street banks best customers.[32] As the separation of management and ownership widened, shareholders' capacity to monitor management weakened.

Just as new machinery made it possible to break up the production process into individual steps, so the complex arrangements of offices and departments facilitated the paper work of ordering, billing, bookkeeping, letter writing, and preparing marketing material to be assigned and accounted for in separate units, each with its own managerial team. The goal was to coordinate the diverse activities that stretched from buying raw materials, building plants, and training a work force through to the manufacturing, marketing, and delivering of goods to cutting checks, accounting for costs, and carrying on relevant research. Employing workers, which used to be done by the shop foremen, got professionalized with the addition of personnel offices and efficiency experts. With this elaboration of business bureaucracies came the new language of bureaucratese we're so familiar with, captured in phrases like "functional specialization."

The deep pockets of corporations paid for the expensive transformation of innovative design into sellable commodities. In the United States, where government remained relatively small, these business enterprises became the country's largest, most intricate social organizations. Government at the state level offered few obstacles and some important incentives to corporate reorganizations. As the New Jersey statute suggests, the federal system with shared power between the state and national governments served business interests well. States competed for resources; chartering corporations brought in tax revenues; incentives were strong to give corporate boards what they wanted. New Jersey attracted the majority of incorporations with its accommodating law. Despite the trend toward building giant corporations, more efforts failed than succeeded. National Novelty, National Salt, National Starch, National Wallpaper, and National Cordage all bit the dust. Even today most people work for small businesses. Of the Fortune 500 firms established before 1910, only twenty-nine exist today.[33]

The competition that promoted the formation of large, market-commanding corporations in the United States had a different result in Germany. There the depression of 1873–1896 encouraged manufacturers to form cartels, organization of producers within a single sector directed to achieving collective goals. By 1911 there were more than five hundred cartels; by 1923, fifteen hundred. The common law of England and the United States construed the price regulations of a cartel as a restraint of trade. When Franklin Delano Roosevelt in the midst of the Great Depression of the 1930s shepherded through Congress the National Recovery Act, which imposed cooperative rules upon manufacturing companies, the Supreme Court declared it unconstitutional. No such obstacle operated under Europe's civil law. This meant that in Britain or the United States cartels could be formed, but their rules could not be enforced in a court of law. The scrappy competition that marked enterprises in the eighteenth and early nineteenth centuries had given way to the imperative to moderate the destructive aspects of competition.

Cartels reflected a cautious, defensive strategy. Aimed at conserving earnings rather than exploiting opportunities, cartels promoted slow, orderly advances in their particular industry, usually setting prices at the level of the least efficient producer. When it became obvious that stability required more than price setting, cartels became even more intrusive by allocating shares of the market, or quotas, to individual firms. Like most institutions that prevail for a long time, cartels had both advantages and disadvantages.[34] They tended to reduce obsolete practices through the spread of information, and they prevented erratic swings in returns by setting prices. They encumbered individual decision making and sometimes the innovations that came along with it.

As a collaborative endeavor, a cartel relied upon direction from professional administrators working at cartel headquarters to make industrywide decisions that would smooth out the ups and downs of trade. They also protected individual companies from being swallowed up by larger outfits. Whereas Carnegie Steel and Federal Steel each produced 35 percent of steel ingots and 45 percent of rails in the United States, no steelmaker in the Ruhr Valley produced as much as 10 percent of either product.[35]

With its own highly bureaucratized regime in place, the German imperial government was in a position to channel economic developments, but in fact both the federal and state governments pretty much left the industrialists alone. What the Prussian government had done since the beginning of the nineteenth century was to initiate technical and scientific research that was diffused through a network of engineering schools.[36] This became the source of Germany's competitive edge in chemicals, metals, and electrical and heavy machinery. Having put in place tariffs to protect the German steel and iron industries from English and Belgian competition, the government left it to its industrialists to run their companies. The United States followed other European countries in raising tariff walls to protect their "home" industries. By the 1890s German and American economic preeminence was pronounced and accelerating.

The English, the pioneer of free trade policies, along with the Netherlands and Belgium, declined to erect tariff barriers, and they suffered from that decision. Not that they got much credit for it. A typically jaundiced view was expressed by a diplomat who compared Great Britain's free trade policy with someone climbing a tree full of fruit and kicking away the ladder to it.[37] But in fact everyone benefited. Britain's willingness to hold to free trade during downturns in the world economy meant that countries suffering from gluts had some outlet for their goods, a not inconsiderable service that stabilized the market for the long run, despite short-run costs to itself.[38] Everyone came to appreciate this service after it ended when adverse circumstances forced Great Britain to abandon its leadership in 1931. In another "peculiarity of the British," they had a penchant for keeping control of businesses in the hands of family owners and so did not undertake the corporate restructuring that the Americans and Germans had done. The failure to do so was painful as these firms watched the biggest shares in the international markets in steel products, electrical equipment, and dyestuffs pass to their competitors. Small may have been beautiful, but it was not as effective at the end of the nineteenth century.

One might expect cartels and tariffs to breed a complacent business environment, but German producers performed well, competing for shares of the domestic market. The momentum created at mid-century by railroad building was strong enough for an almost seamless transition to the new technologies in electricity, chemistry, and precision engineering.[39] The Germans became the world's trailblazers with these new winners of capitalism. The German electrical engineering industry was moving toward global dominance. By the early twentieth century it was marketing half the electrical products in the international market. At the same time Germany achieved almost a monopoly of European commerce in fine chemicals, dyestuffs, and optics.

The Scope of Industries

Germans devoted substantial resources to scientific education even while they shared the high premium Europeans put on classical studies. German researchers during the nineteenth century only later found practical applications for their discoveries. And those applications were astounding! Germans gained more knowledge of energy, electricity, and optics than their peers in France and Great Britain combined. Academic researchers and business leaders worked hand in glove in what contemporaries sometimes called a secret marriage. By 1890 there were twice as many chemists in Germany as in Great Britain. They gave their country a virtual monopoly of dyestuffs before 1914. Their laboratories led the way in synthesizing natural materials, like fertilizer and dyes. After Germany's humiliating defeat by Napoleon some concluded that their country would do better concentrating on science and the economy.[40] From Waterloo to Verdun, Germany industrial production grew an amazing forty-fivefold while agricultural output increased by three and a half times with population more than doubling. Malthus had been proven wrong; agricultural productivity had kept up with population growth.

Again the technological trajectory of the United States differed from that of Germany. Individual American inventors, like Thomas Alva Edison and Alexander Graham Bell, built major companies from their own workshops. Both men set up laboratories from the early returns of their inventions. They succeeded in establishing landmark corporations to capitalize on what electricity had wrought. They had been born in the same year, 1847, but it would be hard to find two more different men. Bell was the son and grandson of distinguished Scottish educators and came to the telephone by way of a career devoted to helping the deaf. Edison was an autodidact. When he quit school, he left behind teachers convinced that he was a slow learner. He educated himself in chemistry while working as a telegraph operator.

Remembered most for the incandescent light bulb, which banished the darkness of night without smoke, soot, heat, or the danger of fire, Edison had a genius that was as prolific as it was profitable. With 1,093 patents, he still holds the world's record. He also nurtured the talent of others. From Edison's lab came Nikola Tesla, a Hungarian immigrant whose patent for the radio the Supreme Court upheld. Simultaneously, a slew of talented men from many countries had been working on the radio, including James Clerk Maxwell, a Scotsman; Mahlon Loomis, an American dentist; and the Italian Guglielmo Marconi. Many of Edison's ideas emanated from telegraphy. Bell too began with telegraphy, and his great contribution was making electricity do the work of transmitting sound. Others working with both electricity and telegraphy developed phonographs, telephones, and motion pictures. The commercialization of these inventions fostered popular modes of entertainment that became the cultural signature of the twentieth century.

Electricity did more than inspire new inventions; it provided a new form of power. Switching from steam to electrical power in manufacturing proved complicated and costly. It was not just a question of turning on a switch, but of converting the entire equipment of a plant. Sources for electrical power had to be secured. Both water—hydropower—and steam-driven turbines produced electricity for manufacturers who could either purchase their electricity from a new utility company or generate it at their sites. George Westinghouse played a major role in popularizing electricity by developing the transformer, which could deliver electricity over long distances. He tapped the power of Niagara Falls through generating stations that lit up Buffalo twenty miles away. He was also the champion of alternating current when Edison championed direct current. Direct current had the disadvantage of fading after traveling a mile while Westinghouse's alternating current went hundreds of power-filled miles. This contest took a bizarre twist when publicists claimed that the danger of AC was proved by its efficient use in New York's electric chair.

The transfer from steam to electricity was uneven and took more than half a century. Apparel and printing firms led the way, with fabricated metals and transportation equipment following closely behind.[41] Unforeseen ramifications unfolded. Elevators, for instance, made possible the skyscrapers that characterized modern architecture. Electricity changed one of the most conservative occupations, that of the building trade. The circular saw, lathe, router, and drill sped up the work of construction, but the rhythms remained human. The man (and sometimes woman) walking the beams on a building site still control the tool in his or her hand. The same could be said about the wonderful gadgets that began filling kitchens and home laundries.

In almost every Western country a mechanical wizard was working on a model of an "automobile." As early as 1771, the Frenchman Nicholas Joseph Cugnot had designed a steam-powered vehicle. The Germans Gottlieb Daimler and Wilhelm Maybach succeeded with a two-cylinder internal-combustion engine. Their competitor Karl Benz put a car into production. He celebrated his three-wheeler's success by taking his wife on a motor tour in 1888. The American Ransom Olds enthralled the American public in 1901 with his "merry Oldsmobile," the first car produced in any quantity. At the turn of the century there were fifty start-up companies attracting millions of venture dollars, marks, francs, and pounds, each trying to exploit the potential of placing a machine inside a carriage and letting it rip. The group backing the new Ford Motor Company wanted to produce cars for the rich. Their inventor, Henry Ford, had a different idea. He wanted to figure out how to cut costs, speed up production, make partners out of his salesmen, and supply cars for Mr. Everyman.[42]

His 161 patents demonstrated Ford's technical prowess, but his real genius turned out to be in the classic capitalist activities of production, competition, labor management, and marketing. In all these aspects of running a successful company, everything Ford did was original, totally original. His investors were not. When they failed to get on board his program, he bought them out. Most critical to Ford's phenomenal success was his vision that the car could be a popular acquisition if he could cut costs and enhance efficiency on the shop floor. This was his lodestar.

When Ford began, cars were made by craftsmen, one at a time. He revolutionized production by taking unskilled laborers, assigning them simple tasks in a thorough division of the labor, and assembling the cars

in a line. He invented mass production. His mass producers at one factory spoke fifty different languages, but it didn't matter, because they
needed to know how to do only one task.[43] Ford's success can be measured by the fact that his famous assembly line, when perfected, could
turn out a car in ninety-eight minutes! The Model T made its appearance in 1908; it was elegant in design and engineering and available in
any color, Ford announced, "as long as it was black." More important,
most middle-class Americans could afford one, including Ford's workers, whom he started paying five dollars a day in 1914. His goal was for
his men to earn wages high enough for them to buy what they produced.
And buy they did.

The scientific management of labor had already attracted the attention
of Frederick Winslow Taylor, who carefully observed men working in the
steel industry in the 1880s and 1890s. Taylor brought to his research the
conviction that scientific management could blend the interests of bosses
and workers. This was probably too much to be expected, but Taylor did
describe how to make time and motion at the work site more precise and
management more attuned to workers' rhythms. He introduced the idea
of rest breaks in the work schedule. Production rates rose. Taylor had the
distinction of being admired by both Adolf Hitler and V. I. Lenin. Taylor-
ism became the perfect complement to the rationalization of corporation
management and what came to be known as Fordism, a melding of mass
production and mass consumption.

By 1929 the River Rouge plant in Michigan was turning out a car
every ten seconds. In the previous two decades the cost of a Model T
had dropped from $850 to $260—or fifty-two daily paychecks for someone working the Ford assembly line. The 122 million Americans then,
half of them under the age of twenty-six, were enjoying the pleasure of
driving seventeen million cars, a good percentage of them Fords.[44] At
the same time, France, Germany, and Great Britain, with an aggregate
population comparable to that of the United States, had fewer than two
million cars. Amazingly, America led the world in both agricultural and
industrial output.

Ford pioneered another marketing innovation. He established dealerships where his Model Ts, or tin lizzies, as they were called, might

be bought and serviced. By 1912 seven thousand Ford dealerships had opened with fancy showrooms to lure in consumers from Harrisburg to Houston, Portsmouth to Portland. Still, he had to compete with 273 other companies manufacturing cars in 1909![45] The automobile had taken the place of the railroad as the first gear of the economy by 1920. When Henry Ford closed down his River Rouge plant for six months in 1927 in order to switch to the Model A, America's industrial production index dropped 11 percent.[46]

William Durant proved that there was room for more than one genius in the automobile industry. Beginning with the Buick, Durant next acquired Oldsmobile and seized the chance during the stock market panic of 1907 to buy up lots of other automobile companies along with firms that made automobile accessories. By 1908 he had created General Motors, which was to give Ford more than a run for its money. Like a cat with more than one life, Durant went under in 1911, only to bounce back with a fierce competitor to the Model T that he called Chevrolet. Seeing an opening in Ford's insistence upon making black cars that looked like boxes, Durant offered buyers attractive colors, softer seats, and the chance to buy one of GM's five cars—Cadillac, Buick, Oldsmoble, Pontiac, and Chevrolet—on credit.[47] As a later president of General Motors, Alfred Sloan, said, a "car for every purse and every purpose." Soon Ford had to follow suit; a pattern had been set for Detroit automakers.

Moving through the ranks of the automobile industry was Alfred P. Sloan, Jr., who became GM's president in 1923. An electrical engineer and graduate of the Massachusetts Institute of Technology, Sloan turned General Motors into the largest automotive corporation in the world— a leader in both sales and profits. In the 1930s he made the Chevy, not the Ford, the car of choice for most American buyers. Taking advantage of Ford's fetish about standardization, Sloan introduced style changes for each year's models, much to the delight of American consumers.

While the kinks were being worked out of automobile production during the first decade of the twentieth century, Wilbur and Orville Wright had been experimenting with kites, gliders, and biplanes in anticipation of their highly publicized fifteen-second airplane flight from Kitty Hawk, North Carolina, in 1908.

Imperatives of Automobile Driving

Retrospectively, the conversion to private transportation seems to have unfolded smoothly, but consider what a demanding novelty the car was. Instead of sitting in a bus or train, ordinary people had to learn to operate a complicated machine. Driving any distance depended upon the construction of roads as well as the availability of fuel. Formerly bought in grocery stores, the oil needed by the car promoted a new retailing business, drive-in gas stations along the roads between cities. People even had to acquire new mores to accommodate the automobile. The limited distance covered by a walker or horseback rider had now extended far beyond the watchful eyes of parents, bosses, and policemen. Greater mobility and an enclosed space allowed for greater sexual freedom—or at least parents feared this was so.

Initially cars used the rutted roads of carriages, carts, and wagons, but the rattling of passengers' teeth drove home the point that a smoother ride would be desirable. Macadam roads made of pressurized broken stone had been around for a half century; with cars, various additives were tried to give the macadamized roads more stability. Tar with crushed rocks did yeoman service for a while until cars triggered their own solution to the paving challenge. The steady demand for petroleum produced more and more by-products, like asphalt, that proved excellent in surfacing road-beds. Urbanites preferred cement, which was smoother and better suited for making curbs, a new addition to the modern city. It's staggering to think of the thousands of construction teams sent out across the country to level, grade, and lay mile upon mile of paved roads, all summoned by the automobile and its rough cousin the truck.

Cars also had the capability of hurting people and damaging property, so they gave the insurance industry a big boost. And then there was the need for trained mechanics to tune these complicated machines lodged in the garages of millions of people for whom a look under the hood was an invitation to vertigo. That did change, and many an American lad spent his Saturdays lying underneath the family car tinkering with its engine. Tires frequently went flat; changing them became an imperative skill in the male repertoire until radial tires, introduced in the 1970s, made flats a thing of the past. Microprocessors now operating in cars have taken their repair out of the hands of amateurs.

Probably no other invention matched the automobile in its global reach or its power to accelerate the commercialization of raw materials like rubber and oil. Ford may have turned out his Model Ts in ninety-eight minutes, but it took a lot more time to get the needed supplies to the assembly line. Rubber, growing wild in King Leopold's Free State of Congo, Brazil's Amazon basin, and Malaysian jungles acquired a new value. With profits beckoning, these "tappers" were virtually enslaved. Even with control, their habits appeared too chaotic for the increasingly rationalized economic system capitalism was becoming. When a British botanist, Henry Alexander Wickham, hybridized seeds sent from Brazil, Great Britain established rubber plantations in Malaysia that in time wiped out the harvesting of wild rubber in Brazil, Africa, and elsewhere. The next step was to make a synthetic rubber, but that development awaited the stimulus of acute rubber shortages during the Second World War.[48]

And of course there was the automobile's voracious appetite for fuel. Bubbling up to surfaces all over the globe, oil had been a source of heat, though kerosene had been used in lamps. Gasoline had been an unimportant by-product. When Ford, Olds, Buick, Benz, Daimler, Austin, Morris, and the Peugeot brothers began rolling out their new automobiles, the demand for gasoline soared. Internal-combustion engines soon drove buses, trucks, and military vehicles. They made Rockefeller the wealthiest man in America. As the demand for oil and its many by-products expanded, oil entrepreneurs fanned out across the globe in search of the fossil fuel hidden for millennia beneath the earth's surface. Enriching foreign investors and local potentates, the "black gold" craze for oil put a premium on local labor. In Europe in the 1880s both the Rothschilds of the banking family and the Nobels of the explosives family became involved in producing oil in the Baku region of Russia.

A Nobel scion had gone to the Caucasus with twenty-five thousand rubles to buy walnut rifle stocks for his brother's company. Arriving in the midst of an oil boom, he bought a refinery instead and plunged his family into the international oil business. Competition from the likes of

Rothschilds and Nobels forced Rockefeller to turn Standard Oil into an international corporation.[49] Finding oil in Sumatra, a Dutch visitor started drilling in this jungle site, even gaining permission from William III of the Netherlands to call his company Royal Shell. When oil was found in Curaçao in 1914, the island again became a part of world capitalism. On the site of the old slave market rose a complex of oil refining equipment built by the Royal Shell Company and the Dutch government. Discarded kerosene cans, either blue for Standard Oil or red for Shell, got converted into stoves all over Asia.

British, Dutch, and American firms made a fateful decision when they sought out oil in the Arabian Peninsula and adjacent lands. They found it in great abundance, but not without planting seeds of hatred. As Abdel-rahman Munif's brilliant novel *Cities of Salt* poignantly demonstrates, many Middle Easterners' first contact with Westerners came from the arrogant company managers and roustabouts on oil rigs that were built in the 1930s. As in Africa, so in the Middle East, the Europeans and Americans involved in foreign enterprises had little respect for the people or the cultures they encountered. They exploited the resources of distant lands as though there were no tomorrow and relied on compliant local leaders to give them access to laborers and the resources they wanted.

Because of the spectacular speed with which the United States outpaced all other countries in the opening decades of the twentieth century, its mass production and managerial organization have taken on the aura of an inexorable and optimal development generated from within the very logic of capitalist enterprise. This orthodox interpretation is misleading. By no means inevitable or sealed off from larger trends, the mergers and reorganization of American corporations were very much the product of political circumstances and social values. To name three: the weakness of government, an abundance of cheap labor, and a large public receptive to standardized products. Americans readily took up the role of consumer, snapping up cheap goods, even if they all looked and tasted alike. This receptivity to standardized items meant that companies could benefit from the cost savings of mass production, a reaction businesses could not always count on in Europe, where buyers still appreciated handcrafted goods.

American Federal Power

The first serious curtailment of corporate power came in 1887, when Congress created the Interstate Commerce Commission, which could regulate transportation lines that extended beyond state lines. Three years later, the Sherman Antitrust Act made a first stab at regulating large corporations whose size could be interpreted as restraining trade. But the horses had already left the stable. Corporations made their moves toward consolidation before the era of big government began. Within twenty years, fewer than six hundred corporations controlled half the assets of the country's four hundred thousand corporations. Only when the Supreme Court ruled that trusts came under the Antitrust Act did mergers taper off a bit.

Forced to dissolve his trust, Rockefeller created a cluster of smaller Standard Oils. And therein lies a capitalist morality play. When in 1909 a federal court ordered the dissolution of Standard Oil, managers who had chafed under the centralization of authority in the company's New York City headquarters had the chance to try new techniques. There's almost a law hidden here, a corollary to Joseph Schumpeter's famous remark that capitalism involved creative destruction. Capitalism benefits from periodic liberation from established authorities, freeing those who yearn to experiment, innovate, and learn from fresh ideas.[50]

Corporate power in the United States waxed strong as the nineteenth century came to an end. The imperialist forays of Western governments into Africa and Asia made them more accommodating of their domestic capitalists. It took ratification of the Sixteenth Amendment to the Constitution in 1913 before the federal government had an effective way to raise revenue, but the difficulty of passing an income tax gives a sense of the unusual limits on government power when confronting business interests in the United States.[51] On racial and sexual matters, on the other hand, states drastically restricted the movement of African Americans and dictated the norms of intimate behavior.

When the twentieth century began, Western nations, most of them monarchies, had embarked on their own capitalist adventures, carrying modern objects, attitudes, and institutions to Asia and Africa along with attitudes of cultural superiority. They exercised overwhelming, not to mention overweening, power over those they considered backward, and they congratulated themselves on their civilizing mission. Within the private sector, there had been a weeding out of small firms as giant corporations consolidated their markets. With a more populous planet and more mechanized production the use of natural resources, particularly fossil fuel, increased at an alarming rate. Small countries outside the West and advocates for the public realm within the West struggled to come to terms with the fact that imperial states and expanding corporations were in the driver's seat and likely to run roughshod over them.

9

◆

WAR AND

DEPRESSION

I N 1914 WAR CAME to Europe through the measured minuet of mobilizing
armies. It was a slow dance. When discretion suggested to some countries to start early to get their forces ready, prudence dictated to others that
they must not be left behind. Many nations had sought safety in numbers
as international tensions tightened. These alliances only multiplied the
occasions for triggering hostilities. Germany and the Austro-Hungarian
Empire, later joined by the Ottoman Empire, faced Great Britain, Russia,
and France. The wealth that capitalism had generated in the preceding
half century enabled all these prospective belligerents to build big armies
and trade in their wooden naval vessels for steel-plated battleships. The
military scoured industrial plants for promising improvements. Corporations like England's Vickers poured its profits into the development of
armament, as did its competitor Krupp, the German manufacturer of iron
and steel. The heady feeling that came from their worldwide resources
created feelings of invincibility among Europe's leaders.

The race for industrial superiority that had fueled Germany's impressive development in the nineteenth century entered a second lap in the competition for colonies with Great Britain at the end of the nineteenth century. Both stoked the fires of national militancy. The jingoism that had justified the imperial ambitions of each country soon justified an arms race. Propaganda, a word that got a new meaning in this period, spread aggressive messages about national superiority. The eagerness with which the combatants in World War I cultivated the means and motives for going to war still astounds. It is hard not to see its outbreak in 1914 as overdetermined, even though there weren't really any causes for it, if you except widespread imprudence and massive miscalculations.

Contemporaries' skill at solving international disputes did not match their demonstrated capacity to create wealth. The expectation that any war would be a short one like the Franco-Prussian War of 1870–1871 contributed to the rampant bellicosity. Few bothered to remember the bloodbath of the American Civil War in 1861–1865.

Europe had not seen a total war since the sixteenth century. Perhaps Americans' vivid memories of their civil war explains why the United States didn't enter the European conflict until 1917, after it had been raging for three years. By that time everyone had been disabused of the notion that the fighting wouldn't last long. Instead grinding, stupid, indefensible trench warfare took on a kind of permanence along what came to be known as the western front. Just how bad things were going to be became apparent in the first three months of the war, when a million and a half soldiers died in battle.

Such casualties only increased the two sides' determination to prevail. Making sense of such horrendous losses to the public meant ratcheting up descriptions of the villainy of one's enemy. At least sixty-four million Europeans were mobilized in addition to three million outside Europe. Russia alone had an army of twelve million. Of the total sixty-four million soldiers and sailors, eight and one-half million died, twenty-one million were wounded, and another seven million were declared missing in action. Total war meant that industrial production at home went at full tilt. Many women joined the work force, especially on the assembly lines turning out munitions. (The Germans fired a million shells on the French fortress of Verdun in one day.)

Every participating country, except the United States and Japan, survived this war of attrition tired, disillusioned, and deeply in debt. These statistics pale only when they are compared with the casualties of World War II, which broke out twenty-one years later. The grimmest reaper of all remained disease. The great flu epidemic of 1918 and 1919 killed twenty million men, women, and children, worldwide. As in the Thirty Years' War of the sixteenth century, civilians suffered even more than did the combatants.

The most spectacular event in the war came before its end when a sequence of revolutions dispatched the Russian monarchy and installed the world's first Communist regime. The Union of Soviet Socialist Republics startled the world with its rejection of both the monarchy and its parliamentary successor. During the next seventy-two years of its existence, the USSR repeatedly affronted the Western world with its flaunting of its indifference to property rights and free enterprise. Central planners began immediately running the Soviet economy. Any domestic resistance to Soviet initiatives met severe repression. The USSR signaled its intention to break with conventional political forms when it released confidential czarist state papers that embarrassed European diplomats. Few could doubt that a new era had dawned.

Karl Marx had imagined a country with an advanced economy like Great Britain or Germany becoming Communist, not a backward one like Russia that needed to catch up even to maintain its autonomy. After withdrawing from the war, Soviet leaders devoted Russia's resources and man and womanpower to modernizing the country, an effort that ranged from promoting women's rights and literacy to imposing new standards in hygiene. Collective farms took over from private farming, despite tenacious resistance from the peasantry. Soviet leadership announced a five-year plan that put before the world the agenda of a command economy. It signaled its disdain for conventions like the gold standard and withdrew as much as possible from international trade. A deep suspicion of communism took root in the homelands of capitalism as the gravity of the Soviet challenge sank in.

After such a bloodbath as World War I, wisdom was in short supply. Europeans and Americans proved more adept at producing heavy artillery, chlorine gas, machine guns, submarines, tanks, war planes, and artificial limbs than at getting along with their neighbors. Wartime propaganda had depicted both sides as ravenous monsters. Victory gave the Allies the smug conviction that they had been correct. Their ally Russia, having dropped out of the war, lost any hold on the victor's moral triumph. Revenge animated the French and English when they sat down at the various peace tables to work on the complex problems left at the end of hostilities. As textbooks frequently note, the drafters of the treaties redrew the map of Europe. Knowing that they would be creating new nations out of old empires, the Library of Congress assembled a superb collection of maps and placed them at the disposal of delegates to the peace talks in a chic Paris hotel. No one ever visited the collection. The diplomats preferred working on scraps of paper.

Global Reactions to World War I

The war spelled the end to the Austro-Hungarian and Ottoman empires as well as the German monarchy. President Woodrow Wilson, who represented the United States at the peace negotiations, thrilled suppressed people around the world with his stirring call for self-determination for all peoples. To fight a world war, the European nations had mobilized all their resources, which included their vast colonial holdings. Participation made the colonial people themselves aware of a larger world in which they might take an independent place. Though in retrospect, Wilson seems to have been thinking only of Europe, his summons to build nations around the ethnic identities of the people made him a hero to nationalists in Egypt, China, India, and French Indochina. They too read his speeches. A young Vietnamese named Ho Chi Minh actually scraped together enough money to go to Paris in the vain hope of talking to Wilson.

Having entered into secret agreements about how to split up the territory of the Middle East, the leaders of France, the Netherlands, and Britain clearly thought imperialism had a second life. Since they had won, they were not to be deterred in enjoying the full fruits of war. The colonial powers brutally suppressed any moves toward independence. They now had access to German holdings in Africa too. After the war, the countries of Asia, the Middle East, and Latin America were even more tightly integrated into the Europe-centered commercial world. The moment of independence from European domination had not arrived, but the crushing disappointment that nationalists throughout Asia and the Middle East experienced when Wilson acquiesced to the punitive terms of the peace treaties laid the foundation for enduring anti-American feelings. Remembering is selective. Those wronged hold on to their memories longer than do their suppressors.

There was one brilliant exception to this dismal pattern of squelching national self-determination. Mustafa Kemal Atatürk turned the center of the Ottoman Empire into the secular nation of Turkey. Atatürk and his "young Turks," as his followers were known, abolished the Muslim caliphate and embarked on a crash course in modernization. Atatürk appealed to the young to participate in raising a republic. He turned out to be a brilliant nation builder with a legacy very much alive today, In Atatürk's Turkey even women could become judges. With a toehold on the European continent, Turkey could be considered Europe's single Muslim country.

At war's end, Germany was a devastated country, on the verge of starvation. Kaiser Wilhelm II had fled to the Netherlands. The successor government, the Weimar Republic, was established in early 1919, if "established" is the right word. It had to struggle for stability against paramilitary socialist groups and the defeated military leaders who longed for the return of the monarchy. Perhaps what happened is best captured in the Theodor Plivier book title *The King Goes, the Generals Remain*. The Versailles Peace Treaty very much complicated Germany's recovery by taking away 13 percent of its territory and assigning 10 percent of its population to other countries. The industrially rich Alsace-Lorraine was given back to France, and the Allies occupied the Rhineland for fifteen years. Behind these simple statements lies the reality of hundreds of thousands of lives turned upside down and bitter memories sown that were not likely to be forgotten.

Crushingly high reparation payments were exacted from Germany as well. This was payback from the French who had been forced to pay reparations to Germany after the Franco-Prussian War thirty-eight years earlier. The victorious leaders set up the League of Nations in hopes of settling future disputes openly with guarantees of collective security to replace the treaty system that had led to war in 1914. The U.S. Congress declined to join the League, but it did participate in a number of conferences that the League sponsored. More significant, it played a major role in the postwar financial arrangements as the principal creditor nation. It actually contributed to the financial turmoil by demanding the repayment of the large debts that France and Great Britain had run up to pay the staggering costs of waging war.

Signals in the 1920s of impending economic trouble were decidedly mixed. No one predicted the major downturn that ensued. There had been the challenge of repairing the great losses of the war, a project undertaken by people utterly exhausted by the war itself. Still, the former belligerents had recovered their agricultural and industrial capacities within five or six years. What lasted longer were the distortions that the war caused. Feeding sixty-seven million men under arms had greatly challenged the world's farmers. They met the wartime demands, heavily cropping and bringing new land into cultivation. The cessation of hostilities left these farmers with gluts of foodstuffs and raw materials. For many countries, especially in Eastern Europe, agriculture remained their economic backbone. When an agricultural depression ensued, whole economies teetered on the edge of collapse.

The new nations of Hungary, Austria, Bulgaria, Romania, Yugoslavia, and Czechoslovakia made recovery of international trade more difficult by abandoning the free trade that those in the Danube basin had enjoyed as members of the Austro-Hungarian Empire. Seeking the impossible goal of economic self-sufficiency, these new nations raised high tariffs against one another's imports. Even transportation from one country to another was made difficult.[1] And then there were the money problems. Reparations, war debts, and paper money substitutes for gold triggered inflation almost everywhere. Germany suffered from hyperinflation. In May 1922 it took 275 marks to buy one U.S. dollar; by November it required 7,000. Those who lived off pensions and returns from bonds, rents, or savings were almost wiped out, but creditors and German companies like Thyssen and Stinnes were able to pay off their debts with cheap money.[2] The costliest legacy of the war was the popular preference for revenge over help in nursing a wounded world back to normal. This made the scarcity of enlightened leadership conspicuous.

The so-called Roaring Twenties typically roared for people coming of age in the 1920s. Their older brothers and sisters were more likely to be dispirited, if not cynical and wounded. People in the United States suffered many fewer casualties from the country's brief twenty months in the conflict. It soon became evident that the war had killed more than people; it had finished off many traditional values, especially those affecting the relations of men and women. Women's bobbed hair and short skirts announced a freer social spirit. Fertility had been declining throughout the Western world since the 1870s, with families in the United States half the size—fewer than four children—at the end of the nineteenth century as at its beginning.[3] Such a shift affected women more than men. If one thinks of women's liberation as having a long gestation period, this decrease in fertility can stand as a beginning. More timesaving appliances, the proliferation of white-collar jobs, and the experience of wartime employment outside the home also need to be included as liberating forces. By 1925 most economies were moving into prosperous times. And with them came a social style in full revolt against the straitlaced mores of the Victorian age.

The famous logo for the phonograph, a popular component of the new cultural style, featured a dog listening to "his master's voice." More likely the phonographs blared out the jazz music coming from the American black community. That community too was on the move, sending its young people up north. Movies with sound tracks replaced the silent films. The United States got its first commercial radio station in 1920. Within a decade more than half the American homes boasted a radio.[4] Even in Germany and Great Britain, almost three million families had radios by 1929. Rural isolation was vanishing. In the midst of this rather raucous public space of the 1920s, the New York Stock Exchange began its "great bull market." As stock prices rose, moneyed people began to pull out of their European investments and buy American securities. In typical bubble fashion, prices went up, up, up, drawing in more eager investors with every record set.

The First World War jumbled things up in the Pacific as well as in the rest of the world. Japan had won inclusion in the group of leading European imperialist powers that divvied up Africa in the Berlin Conference of 1885.[5] Its decision to go to war for dominance in East Asia fitted in well with the spirit of the times. Although aligned with the Allied powers, Japan did little fighting and a lot of producing. Its economy benefited from Allied orders for munitions and other war materials. The removal of Western competition in both its domestic and mainland Asian markets could also be considered another dividend from the war.

The inevitable slump after World War I extended through the 1920s in Japan. Early in its push for modernization, the government had favored large firms that could be depended upon for capital and conformity to national goals. During the 1920s every Japanese industry formed cartels to ward off undue competition in difficult times. More giant firms emerged like Nissan in the 1930s with its ambitious plans to turn out fifteen thousand automobiles a year. Various holding companies moved into mining, chemicals, fisheries, marine transport, and civil engineering. When Nissan produced its first passenger cars, the company's motto was "The Rising Sun as the flag and the Datsun as the car of choice."[6]

In Europe, the aftereffects of the war were as much emotional and intellectual as material. Being on the winning side didn't save Italy from a parlous postwar situation that opened up Italians to radical political ideas. A socialist journalist named Benito Mussolini built a career and a new party by advertising the defects in the West's liberal system of electoral politics and self-correcting markets. The Fascist movement Mussolini launched carried him to power in 1922. Having moved sharply to the right, he worked quickly to silence opposition, steamroller Parliament, and suppress workers' unions along with any other kind of independent political activity. Mussolini organized employers and workers into confederations whose relations the government mediated. He used tariffs, quotas, and subsidies to shield the Italian economy as much as possible from world trade. What fascism offered was a lively nationalism to take the place of personal satisfactions. It knitted the country into a giant corporation in which individuals yielded to the good of the whole, as defined by Il Duce.

By 1935 Mussolini was ready to show what his Italy could do outside its borders. He invaded Ethiopia, which had successfully repelled the Italians forty years earlier. For this act of sheer aggression, the League of Nations imposed sanctions, but its member countries proved unwilling to sustain any sacrifice, especially a loss of oil sales to Italy. Mussolini called the League's bluff, and it fell along with Ethiopia. A virile masculinity, suggestive of violence, came to represent strength in contrast with the weakness of the rest of Europe with its faith in civil liberties and individual decision making. Mussolini's corporatism and economic self-sufficiency, laced by investments in a military buildup, brought Italy out of the depression looming on the American and European horizon.

A Spreading World Depression

Two slow, inexorable movements help explain the increasing severity of economic downturns, exemplified by the depression that began in the early 1930s. Men and women—usually young—moved from rural jobs in farming and services to the urban industrial centers, and national firms became more and more connected to a world market. Both developments signaled progress, but they also exposed more and more people and firms to disruptions from faraway places. Nations had less and less control over their economies. Another feature of capitalism kicked in to make these downturns painful in their suddenness. This can be traced directly to the optimism that is integral to free enterprise. Participants have to imagine attractive earnings to keep investing their time and resources in future outcomes. One way to keep hope alive is to ignore distant clouds and focus on the sun that is still shining. It's hard to balance optimism with caution. Underneath the many particularities of the stalled years of the 1930s were the general trends of greater global integration and an insistent go-ahead spirit.

The big question about the Great Depression is not why it occurred—such downward slides in economic activity had become regular features of the market economy—but rather why the normal rebound didn't take place. Why, as one contemporary commented, did the world economy pass from a cycle to a crisis to a chute as businesses went bust and some national unemployment rates rose as high as 30 percent. Unsold inventories stacked up in warehouses and barns; the price of cotton, wheat, sugar, wool, coffee, silk, rubber, butter, rice, tobacco, and corn stagnated from one harvest to the next. The consequent discouragement, fear, and pessimism encouraged saving instead of spending, one of the perversities that make bad times worse. Despite all the efforts to remedy these adverse conditions, the recoveries that did occur didn't last. One day people would agree with relief that things had bottomed out only to watch sales and prices plunge downward anew. To explain all this, there was a stunning variety of opinions from monetarists, market stabilizers, interventionists, planners, corporatists, and advocates of laissez-faire, the philosophy of letting things alone.[7]

Today, almost eighty years after the Great Depression, there is still no consensus among experts about its causes. Most people agree on the relevant factors: gluts of farm commodities and raw materials, insufficient purchasing power for the amount of factory goods being produced, an unstable financial system, high tariffs, the one, two punch of a speculative stock mania followed by near-zero investments, and, of course, the powerful aftershocks from the First World War. And yet with all these dangers, few foresaw that their economies were going to swoon. In fact international trade and industrial production rose almost 20 percent higher in 1929 than they had been in 1925.

One thing that the experts do agree upon is that the precipitous drop in American stock prices on Black Tuesday, October 24, 1929, didn't trigger the Depression, largely because the causes had kicked in earlier and been ignored in the general euphoria of a rising stock market. The crash led to a lot of financial distress and heartbreak as the index of stock market prices skittered from a high of 381 to 199 in three weeks on its way down to 79 two years later. Of more immediate influence on the Depression was the loss of confidence in banks—big-city banks, country town banks, central banks. Banks had proved very convenient in serving the needs of savers and borrowers. They held people's money safely, paid interest, and gave them instant access to it. They lent money for new ventures, usually more money than they had on hand at any given time. This made banks peculiarly vulnerable to a run of depositors wanting their money at the same time that they feared for the safety of their savings. Such runs were exactly what happened throughout the capitalist world, especially in the United States when nine thousand banks closed their doors between 1930 and 1933. In Germany the entire banking system collapsed.

Progress had seemed unstoppable until the Great Depression. It was particularly hard on the United States because its economy depended more upon consumers, whose reactions were harder to read, than it had earlier. The stock market crash of 1929 produced headlines about investors jumping to their deaths from the tops of high buildings, but the people who really hurt from the ensuing depression were already at the bottom—or near there. Layoffs that had been seasonable now became permanent, as people lost confidence and stopped buying. Savings and retirement plans disappeared into foreclosures, evictions, and bankruptcies. Whole families found themselves unemployed. The charitable network of ethnic mutual aid societies and church welfare was strained to the breaking point. Unlike European countries, the United States had relied upon private relief when the economy turned sour. The Great Depression revealed its inadequacy.

Single men tramped the country, looking for work, often "riding the rails" from city to city where "hobo towns" formed on their fringes.[8] These were often called Hoovervilles in reference to President Herbert Hoover, who was blamed for letting the good times slip away on his watch. Manufacturers were thrust into a catch-22. As they lowered prices to compete for new customers, they suppressed the wages of their workers. With little to spend outside of bare necessities, these men and women became a drag on the consumer side of the economic equation. The ignored plight of workers during these years fostered the formation of brigades of capitalist critics who marched under the banners of socialism, unionism, regulation, economic justice, or nostalgic calls to return to the farm.

The world economy was very much a ship adrift without a captain. Great Britain, the capitalist trailblazer since the eighteenth century, had long exerted leadership, especially in monetary exchanges and international bank loans. Other national currencies were measured against the British pound sterling, in part because the Bank of England gave a fixed amount of gold for the pound. By 1931 Britain could no longer sustain this commitment and went off the gold standard, as did the United States.

Twenty-six other countries joined them a year later, meaning that they no longer backed their currencies by gold. A crazy quilt of currencies now appeared, the free-floating British pound and the American dollar among all the wildly fluctuating others. The gold standard, which most capitalist countries had adopted in the 1880s, no longer existed to facilitate the settling of international accounts. All this might not have hurt so much had most economies not depended upon international trade to keep their economies humming. A depression of epic proportions had arrived.

The United States had the most powerful economy; its industrial production represented more than 40 percent of the world's output and twice as much as that of Germany and Great Britain combined.[9] It could have stepped in as the new guardian of stability but didn't, preferring to act as the Lone Ranger. It protected its domestic markets by raising tariffs to an all-time high and refused to use its wealth to steady currency fluctuations. High American tariffs made it hard for France, Britain, and Germany to pay their war debts because they couldn't sell their goods. At the same time, American banks wouldn't lend more to these countries either.

For many nations, including Chile, Mexico, Spain, India, Brazil, and Japan, the collapse of their export markets proved to be the proverbial "blessing in disguise." But not before their purchasing power had fallen more than 50 percent below the levels of 1929. With no foreign exchange reserves to pay for manufactured goods, these countries began making the things that they had earlier imported. In this widespread "import substitution," dozens of small industrial enterprises sprang up. India expanded its output of cement and other processed goods. The Brazilian government bought and destroyed coffee to relieve the glut it was suffering. More important, the government poured money into industry. By the end of the decade Brazilian manufacturers were making 90 percent of the country's cloth, clothing, leather goods, and furniture. Japan became nearly self-sufficient in textiles, railroad equipment, and electrical machinery, all of which it had previously paid for with profits from silk exports.[10]

On top of all these structural and transient problems, most political leaders, including socialists, held to their belief in balanced budgets with a tenacity that matched their conviction that the earth circled the sun.

Extending unemployment benefits might actually have stimulated the economy and certainly would have helped those out of work, but instead governments cut benefits to balance their budgets. Jobs were so scarce that many families moved back to the country, even though farmers were laden down with redundant wheat, corn, and cotton harvests. In statements that bring knowing smiles to our lips, lots of experts expressed the fear that the age of invention and expansion had come to an end. Some critics hailed the Depression as a reproof to a materialistic age. It posed, they said, an opportunity to return to the simple way of life that had prevailed before the invention of the steam engine.

The severity, universality, and duration of the Great Depression disproved the contention that the economy had its own means for righting itself. The unwillingness of the United States to demonstrate the enlightened self-interest of a leader willing to take a few hits for the benefit of long-term recovery disappointed. The Depression also exposed the need for mechanisms to stabilize currencies, credit, and the flow of goods. The major players—Great Britain, France, Belgium, the Netherlands, Sweden, the United States, and for a while Germany and Italy—began to recognize the importance of political action to improve the market mechanisms in which their economies were now tightly entangled. They signaled this new awareness with studies, commissions, and conferences, many of them, like the World Economic Congress, ending without concrete results. The wish to cooperate existed, but it wasn't strong enough to overcome the dominance of national priorities.

Theories about the workings of the economy enter the history of capitalism by way of policy makers. They offer analyses that can be used to predict outcomes, which then become critical in deciding how to achieve desired effects. Policy makers are very much like stage managers. They don't write the plays, make the props, or act the parts, but like stage managers, they can determine how smoothly the show goes on. Waiting in the wings as the Depression reached tragic dimensions was a novel economic script. Reexamining the fundamentals of economic reasoning, Britain's John Maynard Keynes recommended that the governments stop balancing budgets and begin spending money, going into debt, if necessary, to "prime the pump" of their economies.

Not only did Keynes challenge the assumption that national budgets needed to be balanced, but he also took aim at the postulate of economics that said that buying and spending in the market would maintain a positive equilibrium with optimal employment. Not so, Keynes explained. A new equilibrium had not taken place as predicted when unemployment drove down wages. Manufacturers had not been lured to start producing again. Nor would they invest, Keynes insisted, because if times were sufficiently bad, people had a "liquidity preference." That is, they preferred to save, so money wasn't invested, goods and services weren't produced, and laborers were thrown out of work. This of course is exactly what was happening in the 1930s when he was writing his grand theoretical tome.[11] To counter this development, Keynes recommended that government provide jobs through new programs. This would make good the deficit in private employment and help restore confidence in the economy, the most precious commodity of all.

The New Deal in the United States started to follow this prescription. Welfare legislation had been much more common in Europe than in the United States with its traditional partiality to individual liberty and self-help. In his famous "first hundred days," President Franklin Delano Roosevelt shepherded through Congress laws giving direct relief to the jobless. Next came funding for work projects, later incorporated into the Works Progress Administration and the Public Works Administration, which built everything from aircraft carriers to schools, bridges, and roads. Millions entered the government's payroll, constructing post offices, public art, and conservation projects.

The major effort to coordinate industrial policies, the National Recovery Act, ran afoul of one of the strongest and most distinctive American values, the commitment to freedom over social planning, to individual rights over the general welfare. Two kosher butchers had been fined and jailed for so-called destructive price cutting. Fighting this verdict all the way to the Supreme Court, the Schechter brothers won a unanimous decision that the industrial code embedded in the NRA legislation was unconstitutional. Blocked by this decision, Roosevelt tried to increase the size of the Supreme Court, enabling him to make congenial appointments. Americans didn't like tampering with their Supreme Court either, and he backed down. After the Court declared parts of the National Recovery Act unconstitutional, Congress extracted the sections dealing with labor and put them in the Wagner Labor Act of 1937, which greatly enhanced opportunities for successful union negotiations with employers. Quickly unionized nonagricultural labor accounted for 36 percent of the work force, its highest level ever.

Probably the most successful New Deal program was the Civilian Conservation Corps, which gave jobs for six months to two years to young men between the ages of eighteen and twenty-three who promised to give most of their pay to their families. Working principally on federal land, the CCC helped the Bureau of Reclamation fight soil erosion with seeding and terracing, the National Park Service build campgrounds and picnic sites, and the U.S. Forest Service protect timber from fire, disease, and insects. The government had to borrow to fund these programs, thus upsetting the goal of balancing the federal budget, but the classical economists' conviction that the market would balance itself no longer convinced the public, which rewarded Roosevelt with four elected terms as president. Still, as is frequently the case with new ideas, leaders hedged their bets. The old budget-balancing orthodoxy reasserted itself. After his landslide victory in 1936, Roosevelt raised taxes and cut spending, and as Keynes had predicted, unemployment went up again. An international crisis then took over. When war broke out in Europe, the United States girded its loins to help Great Britain. Government spending reached levels high enough to bring the nation out of the Depression.[12]

If the causes of the Great Depression elude experts, it's because there are too many of them interacting in hidden ways. This underlines the point that in a free market economy, though some people have much more power than others, no one is in charge. All the material aspects of the economy—available capital, plant capacity, fiscal instruments, transportation, and communication systems—rely on personal and institutional choices. More perplexing, not only do the individuals making decisions have different cultural values, but their attitudes will vary according to whether they were old enough to have lived through the last depression at the end of the nineteenth century or have just entered the world of commerce. The economy is not so impenetrable that governments can't pass measures to prevent a rerun of the latest downturn, but an unforeseen development is usually in the offing.

Lingering Grievances from World War I

As it sadly turned out, the worst consequence of the First World War was not economic but political. The day after the inauguration of Roosevelt in March 1933, Adolf Hitler received full power to govern Germany by decree. The experiences of the 1930s tarnished the reputation of liberal democracies with their representative legislatures and civil rights, free markets and personal political freedoms. Hitler's success, as did Mussolini's, fed on the discontent that accompanied the tanking economies of the postwar period. Ambitious in his plans for Germany, which after all had been the second-largest economy before World War I, Hitler spent massively to provide jobs as he rearmed Germany in defiance of the Versailles Peace Treaty. Like Mussolini, whom he admired, he used the minions in his Nazi Party to suppress unions and all independent political institutions like newspapers. Hitler too had uniformed followers whose enthusiasm he sustained with military parades and giant convocations, where he harangued them for hours on end. He stoked his countrymen's rage at their treatment after the First World War and played on their anti-Semitic prejudices with a horrendous campaign to rid the world of Jews and their culture.

Hitler had unilaterally abrogated many of the terms of the treaty that ended World War I. He seized Austria and Czechoslovakia, but it was not until he invaded Poland in September 1939 that Britain and France woke up to the threat that he posed and declared war. They now faced Hitler's strategy of lightning war, which exploited all of the technologies of mobility—airplanes, tanks, and motorized infantry. He succeeded famously in the first year, polishing off Poland in concert with his new ally the Soviet Union, and then invaded Denmark, Norway, Belgium, the Netherlands, and France. By the end of 1940 Britain was confronting Germany alone, saved from invasion by the Royal Air Force working with the new radar and antiaircraft defenses. After Germany forced the evacuation of all English forces from the Continent in June 1940, most of

Europe was his. The British turned to defending the Suez Canal and India while the United States began tooling up to send them material support. This decision gave Britain something of a breather.

Fresh from victory over France, Germany invaded Russia a year later. Hitler's expectation of another quick victory got ground down by the unexpected ferocity of the Russian defenders of their homeland. They successfully blunted the German offensive and threw the invaders on the defensive. Both Russia and Germany suffered horrific losses. While Russia didn't definitively defeat Germany, it delivered the crippling blow that tilted the war in the Allies' favor. Britain and the United States pounded German factories and the civilian population from the air, cutting their productivity and diverting precious German resources to defending against these attacks. With improved navigational aids the Royal Air Force could switch to bombing at night. After a steady stream of aviation improvements, the United States turned out the first intercontinental bomber, the Boeing B-29, nicknamed the Superfortress. By the summer of 1944, when the Allies were ready to take the war back to France, the Americans had mobilized all the D-day units for a fully mechanized invasion, the largest in world history.[13]

When Japan entered World War II, as an ally of Hitler's Germany and Mussolini's Italy, it had already been pursuing for almost a decade an aggressive campaign under the rubric of the Greater East Asia Co-Prosperity Sphere. The "Co" in the title was illusory; this was a program to bring its neighbors under the control of imperial Japan. One wag turned Rudyard Kipling's famous line about the white man's burden upside down when he said that Japan would now relieve the white man of his burden. Japanese opinion makers cultivated the idea that as descendants of the sun goddess the Japanese had the moral purity and cultural superiority to lead Asia out of the quagmire Western powers had made. While some Japanese intellectuals responded to the promise of replacing Western imperialists with a pan-Asian community of nations, the government's goals were more concrete and exploitative, focusing upon garnering the raw materials that Japan lacked and monopolizing Asian markets.

The brutality of the Japanese Army squelched any possibility for genuine cooperation. After achieving a protectorate of Manchuria in 1933,

Japan moved into Inner Mongolia and China proper. There Japanese forces met those of Chiang Kai-shek, who, despite cooperation from the country's Communists and help from the United States, failed to halt their advance. While pacifying China, Japan moved into Indochina and points west and south. American opposition to these acts took the form of an embargo of scrap steel and oil, providing a motive for Japan's attack on Pearl Harbor four years later. Western snubs, like its unwillingness to include a racial equality clause in the League of Nations Covenant and the immigration exclusions in the United States and Australia, kept alive the anger that fueled much of Japan's expansion. The outbreak of full-scale war had the effect of stifling a nascent domestic opposition movement against the Japanese military's dominance in foreign policy.[14]

The attack on America's Pacific fleet at Pearl Harbor at the end of 1941 was enormously successful, destroying eight battleships and damaging seven others. The Japanese followed up this feat with devastating strikes on the Philippines and Hong Kong. At Singapore, they surprised British naval officers by invading overland. They immobilized America's military presence in the Pacific for more than a year. The United States now faced enemies in both the Atlantic and the Pacific, but enjoyed the advantage of being the world's greatest industrial power. In battles depending upon mobility on the sea, in the skies above Europe, and on the ground everywhere, this proved decisive. Once Japan's military campaigns were folded into World War II, the "Co-prosperity Sphere" became a front behind which the Japanese manipulated local puppet governments with slogans like "Asia for Asians." The unintended consequence of this rhetoric was to promote fierce national identities in Japan's occupied territory.[15]

A successful Japanese offensive in 1944 linked Japan to its empire, stretching from Korea to Malaya. Now the way to the Indies was opened just in time for prosecuting an all-out war, made more urgent by Japan's need for oil, bauxite (for aluminum), and rubber from the islands of the Dutch East Indies and Burma, all of which it eventually occupied. At last Japan had the raw materials required for prolonged hostilities, but alas, the new possessions were far away, leaving its merchant and naval fleets vulnerable to attack.

Japan executed its air strikes brilliantly, but it had already made a fatal mistake in not developing a full antisubmarine program. The German U-boat successes of World War I had convinced American and British strategists that both submarines and defenses against these new underwater vessels would play a crucial role in future wars. The United States had several companies producing the electric diesel motors used in submarines, so it was well positioned to speed up production of submarines when war broke out. It also had in place a well-thought-out antisubmarine doctrine, which included training its naval crews to fight fires ignited by enemy submarines. After the United States broke the Japanese code used to track its ship movements, the American submarine fleet wreaked havoc on the Japanese merchant marine plying the waters between Japan and the East Indies. It destroyed a third of Japan's naval vessels and, by the summer of 1945, three-quarters of its commercial fleet.[16]

Impressive Wartime Production

The critical need for producing war material put maximum pressure on the economies of all the belligerents. Great Britain, Germany, the United States, and the Soviet Union mobilized in ways congruent with their differing industrial strengths and war goals. They initially met wartime demands by providing employment to those left unemployed by the Depression rather than having to preempt domestic production. This government spending brought the Great Depression to a close. A year into the conflict, one-half to two-thirds of the industrial work force had been drawn into war production. War aims interacted with the character of the political system of each belligerent to fine-tune its conversion to a wartime economy.

As the aggressor Germany devised the strategy of lightning war, which, as its title suggests, emphasized speed and mobility. German production was geared to replacing the weaponry its blitzkrieg forces would need for the next campaign, whereas England and the United States did not know where or how Germany would attack, so they had to plan for diverse scenarios in a more protracted struggle.[17] Air and sea power became integral to their strategy, in large part because they didn't have the manpower or material available to return to France. The Russians copied the superior features of the German tank divisions entering their country. The Soviets showed an impressive capacity to improve its models throughout the war. Up-to-date weaponry was scarce in the Far East, so most belligerents there fought with rifles and light artillery when not actually using knives and swords.[18]

The Germans clung to their tradition of fine craftsmanship and performance-enhancing detail while the Americans relied on their mass production expertise.[19] Karl Benz met Henry Ford. The Germans also pursued many designs for tanks while the Americans churned out nothing but Sherman tanks until the Pershing tank replaced them. Most large American firms became defense contractors, but none got the publicity of Ford Motors, which built the world's largest factory at Willow Run, Michigan. By late 1943 three hundred B-24 bombers were rolling off the Willow Run assembly line each month though General Motors actually surpassed Ford in its war production. In another example of productive wizardry, in Richmond, California, Henry Kaiser built more ships than any other manufacturer and even managed to pioneer a company health plan at the same time. When the war in the Pacific drained the Japanese and American navies in 1942–1943, Japan built seven new aircraft carriers. American shipyards turned out ninety.[20]

In wartime, all economies become command economies, so in this sense war production in Communist Russia did not differ so much from that of its free market Allies. Confronted with a fight for national existence and with a considerable part of its land occupied by Germany, Russia carried out the most intense war effort. More important and surprisingly, Soviet mobilization was far more effective than that of Nazi Germany. Even the United States, with the least experience in state planning, did a much better job of prioritizing war production. By 1944 American factories were sending a mighty stream of tanks, trucks, armored cars, even canned food for the defense of Russia. With an industrial plant much larger than any of the other combatants, the United States still outdid itself, supplying through lend-lease agreements up to a third of Great Britain's material needs and a quarter of those of the Soviet Union.

Wars have always acted as a catalyst for technology, but in World War II science made spectacular contributions with the development of radar, computers for charting ballistics, rocketry, jet-propelled aircraft, and a slew of synthetic products developed to substitute for the natural resources no longer available to the belligerents through trade. Small advances sometimes had large impacts. America's two-way radios enabled the Russians to improve their tank tactics. Another technological breakthrough, the atomic bomb, brought the Pacific war to an end two months after Germany surrendered in May 1945.

With millions of lives hanging in the balance, the warring nations made exertions of heroic proportions, a tragic reminder that human beings perform at their highest pitch when threatened with annihilation. World War II exacted a terrible cost from its belligerents, civilians suffering even more than combatants. As might be expected with the perfecting of new weaponry, the casualties of World War II topped those of World War I. A total of seventeen million combatants died, with civilian deaths reaching thirty-three million, the preponderance of them Russian and German, with six million Jews of many nationalities eliminated in Nazi concentration camps. Millions more were displaced by the war, wounded, or left to die from starvation. Heavy aerial bombardments leveled houses, ships, bridges, railway lines, factories, airfields, docks, and sometimes whole cities. Only the Western Hemisphere escaped war's awful fury.

World War II put the far-flung empires of Great Britain, France, Belgium, Italy, Portugal, and the Netherlands on life support if not actually writing finis to them. During the war Japan had seized the American Philippines, the Dutch East Indies, French Indochina, and British Burma and Malaysia. In defeat, the Japanese played the spoiler and encouraged agitators for independence as they were departing from what was to become Indonesia. A new federation of Malaysia emerged from which Singapore became a separate republic in 1965. Great Britain accepted the creation of two nation-states, India and Pakistan, in 1947. Bangladesh broke away from Pakistan, and the island of Ceylon formed Sri Lanka. The United States granted independence to the Philippines in 1946, almost fifty years after promising it.

France waged protracted war with Algeria until 1962, but the other North African Arab states escaped European domination more easily. The French fought in Indochina as well. Laos and Cambodia gained independence, but the United States took over France's war against Vietnam as part of its Cold War effort to halt the spread of communism. It suffered defeat there in 1973. Portugal fought off national liberation movements in Angola and Mozambique. Only with the toppling of the Portuguese dictatorship did its colonies gain freedom in 1975. The British, after a decade of brutal fighting, finally yielded in 1963 to the Mau Mau to make Kenya the thirty-fourth independent African nation. The British Empire came to an official end when in 1997 the Union Jack was lowered over Hong Kong, a city it had leased from China for a century. The wars of national liberation came to an end just as thirty-five nations gathered in Helsinki to sign accords on the right to self-determination in 1978.

People sometimes refer to a great power as a juggernaut. They perhaps are not aware that a juggernaut, according to Hindu myth, is one of the eight avatars of Vishnu, whose devotees throw themselves under the wheels of the vehicle carrying a statue of the god in annual processions. By the end of World War II capitalism could be compared to a juggernaut. Its direction was uncertain, its power was conspicuous, and its devotees were capable of great self-destruction. In 1945 the capitalist juggernaut faced a radical challenge coming from its wartime ally the Soviet Union. They had truly been strange bedfellows, the one with an economy run on venture capital eager to get other countries to adopt its ways, the other a command economy with the mission of spreading its Communist institutions globally. Of the fifty million military and civilian deaths, Russia sustained twenty million. Despite these truly horrific losses, the Soviet Union came out of the war stronger than ever once it established control over the countries of Eastern Europe, including a third of Germany. Now capitalism with its prejudice against the centralization of power confronted a block of countries determined to expose, intensify, and exploit its flaws.

Those persons born in 1880 who watched the construction of roads for the automobile, the proliferation of electrical tools and appliances, and the refashioning of city centers with skyscraping office buildings and opulent department stores would have lived long enough to suffer from a world war, a decade of depression, and the resumption of hostilities in an even more catastrophic world war. In old age they could have contemplated an utterly new kind of rivalry between the United States and the Soviet Union in what seemed at the time to be a gigantic struggle about fundamental truths rising above opposing economic systems. And while the United States and Western Europe confronted the Soviet Union and the countries of Eastern Europe, the peoples colonized by Europeans demanded the self-determination that was denied them in 1918. No longer could places on world maps be designated with a few European imperial colors. Two world wars and a worldwide depression had demonstrated capitalism's capacity for destruction. The time had arrived to prove its beneficent qualities.

10

◆

A NEW LEVEL

OF PROSPERITY

U NDER THE EXTREME pressures of World War II, the men and women
of the belligerent countries performed near miracles of effort and
endurance. In this they were helped by the heavy industry that now dominated capitalist economies, making possible a level of production that
broke all records. Necessity again proved to be the mother of invention
with all the contenders innovating in synthetics, medicine, communication, aviation, and, of course, weaponry. When hostilities ended, the
destructive power that had been unleashed sobered everyone, vanquished
and victorious alike. It had been a dreadful thirty-one years, but most had
survived.

For a second time in a quarter of a century, Europe had been devastated. For a second time the United States flexed its remarkable industrial muscles. For the first time a country implacably hostile to capitalism
appeared on the world scene. Spurred by two world wars with a depression in between, governments learned to play a larger role in economic
matters. Both Keynesian economics and socialist prescriptions provided

rationales for maintaining a permanent role in economic matters, if only to prime the economic pump during persistent downturns.

In World War II the belligerents set rules for producers and laborers, freezing prices and wages. They even took over some private companies and commandeered whatever resources were deemed necessary for the war effort. By 1945 there were many bureaucrats experienced in telling investors, entrepreneurs, managers, and laborers what to do. Quite naturally they looked upon their recommendations as constructive. Many advised continuing government oversight of the economy. Prominent socialists in Great Britain, Italy, and France called for the abandonment of laissez-faire policies. It was an open question whether capitalism would move back into a modern version of the political orbit that it had escaped in the eighteenth century.

Three paths opened up for postwar leaders as they confronted the task of reestablishing their physical plants, transportation systems, financial institutions, and the trade arrangements that had structured their global economy. We might call these paths the indicative, imperative, and informative. In the first, the road forward is indicated; in the second one, it is ordered; and in the third, the coded language of markets informs participants about their choices. The government too responds to information rather than acts out of ideological imperatives. The most powerful commercial players after the war were corporations, many of them international, but the catch basin of capitalism contained hundreds of smaller outfits and even more people detailing projects on the backs of envelopes.

France, Sweden, and Great Britain chose the indicative option. In a four-year plan, the French government set the direction for economic planning, using subsidies and loans as guide dogs. The British Labour government came into office in 1945 under the banner of eradicating the five giant evils of want, squalor, disease, ignorance, and unemployment. Quickly the government nationalized the railroads, utilities, the Bank of England, coal mines, and steel factories. A national health plan gave "cradle to grave" coverage, and the government invested heavily in public housing. Sweden was the most generous of all industrialized nations, providing universal pensions, health and disability insurance, child and family allowances, poor relief, and subsidized low-income housing. These governments established priorities and pointed out the direction for private enterprise.

The Soviets had a command economy in which almost all enterprises were owned by the state. Central planners set production goals with little attention paid to market signals. Because Europeans had come to prize the private property rights they had wrested from monarchs long ago, many Russians resisted the appropriation of their property, so political repression had accompanied the Soviets' economic restructuring. After the war, Soviet planners announced new economic goals that made control even tighter. The Soviet government was determined never again to be exposed to a horrendous invasion like that of Hitler's, so they created a buffer zone comprising the countries of Poland, Hungary, Yugoslavia, Romania, Czechoslovakia, Albania, and Bulgaria. Buffering, as it turned out, involved imposing upon these nations command economies, one-party rule, and subordination to the Soviet Union. Only Yugoslavia avoided the embrace of the Soviet leader Joseph Stalin.

Russian industry had performed magnificently during the war. Its economy recovered prewar production levels within five years. Without the imperatives of war, government planners became less surefooted. Little was actually known about the poor outcome of the Soviets' successive five-year plans until much later. This left Marxists in Italy, Germany, Britain, France, and even the United States free to agitate for communism in their countries.

American leaders chose the informative option. Not having experienced war at home and without a very strong labor tradition, Americans had little interest in radical programs that allowed the government to direct economic initiatives. Those members of Roosevelt's New Deal who had favored more political control had been replaced during the war by businessmen, the so-called dollar-a-year men, who won back public confidence by meeting war production goals. Lost during the Depression, this renewed confidence bolstered their arguments against allowing the government's wartime intervention to become a prelude to more central planning.

The Depression had exposed the two great weaknesses of capitalism: its wayward oscillations between good times and bad and the vastly unequal distribution of the wealth it produced. While American leaders rejected both central planning and central guidance, they recognized the need to moderate these tendencies. There would be no returning to the business mentality of the early twentieth century even if Americans remained loyal to free enterprise. The term itself became freighted with ideological meaning as the differences between the Soviet Union and the United States passed from principles to form the matrix for foreign policies.

American diplomats involved in reviving the prostrate countries of Europe favored letting market forces do the job. America's great wealth and wealth-making capacity gave its preference preponderant influence, and these were to let loose the efficient operation of markets rather than follow political dictates. But the Depression had left leaders aware of the need to restrain some nationalist impulses for international free trade to operate optimally. The failure of Congress to go along with the League of Nations after the First World War remained a vivid memory. Roosevelt and his advisers began planning for peace while the war raged on. They had learned from experience and secured agreements before their allies could start fiddling with their currencies and protecting domestic industrial and agricultural producers.[1]

Always alert to the need of bringing the public along with him in formulating policies, Roosevelt gave priority to a conference on food and agriculture, knowing that Americans would feel keenly the need to feed a starving people after the war. Held in 1943, the conference provoked the acerbic British economist John Maynard Keynes to ruminate that Roosevelt "with his great political insight has decided that the best strategy for post-war reconstruction is start with vitamins and then by a circuitous route work round to the international balance of payments!"

When victory seemed certain in 1944, Keynes got his meeting on fiscal matters when 730 delegates with their staffs, representing forty-four countries, arrived on special trains at the newly refurbished Mount Washington Hotel at Bretton Woods, in New Hampshire's White Mountains and hammered out an impressive agreement to end the nationalistic practices that had scuttled recovery from the Great Depression.[2]

Two catastrophic wars had crushed the spirit of vengeance. The pervasive influence of the United States carried the day. Hopes for an international trade organization faded, but at least countries were willing to buy into the General Agreement on Tariffs and Trade. GATT negotiations have been functioning ever since, now under the World Trade Organization. At Bretton Woods, the participants established the World Bank and the International Monetary Fund, the first to make the long-term investments in developments that private entrepreneurs balked at and the second to manage loans and monitor currencies. The magnetic center of world trade moved permanently from London to New York. It actually had passed after World War I, just as London had taken over from Amsterdam in the eighteenth century and Amsterdam from Genoa in the seventeenth century. By 1958 the monetary system established at Bretton Woods worked so well that all major European currencies could be converted into dollars.[3]

Europeans did not experience the immediate prosperity that Americans enjoyed. War had plunged some people back into a primitive past. The winter of 1946–1947, the second since peace returned, was unusually severe, so severe that it ruined the potato crop. In Germany, even when farmers had potatoes to sell, they wouldn't do so because the value of the currency was too unpredictable. Germany, once at the pinnacle of capitalist development, witnessed scenes of city people going into the countryside with a lamp, chair, or picture frame to sell, returning home with sacks of precious potatoes. The next year brought a record-setting drought. The harvest of 1947 was the worst of the twentieth century. Millions in Germany and elsewhere were homeless, left to wander through the rubble that everywhere marked the destructive power the war had unleashed. Refugee became a common status for men, women, and their children, who had been dislodged or expelled or rescued from prison at war's end. Several million Jews survived Hitler's fiendish plans to eliminate them. Now free to move about, refugees took to the road or clustered in new displaced persons camps.

The extraordinary dimensions of need actually prompted an ambitious program for recovery. It started very much as a trial and error operation with a low budget. What the many people battered by war needed at first were the basics—food, clothing, and shelter. Then they faced the challenge of repairing the widespread destruction, and finally they required infusions of money to resuscitate their peacetime economies. Uncle Sam had the money and the will and began dispensing funds through the United Nations or directly from Washington. Canada too mounted a major relief effort. People do learn from experience. American leaders finally recognized the absolute necessity for the United States to accept the responsibilities of world leadership that it had eschewed after the First World War.

General Marshall's Plan

Despite American and Canadian aid, getting the war-battered nations back on their feet was slow enough to raise doubts about capitalism and even stir sympathy for the Communist alternative to a market economy. In 1947, worried about this, Secretary of State General George Marshall announced a new program. Approved by Congress, the Marshall Plan appropriated dollars in loans and grants for food, seed, and fertilizer to feed the people, followed by money for capital goods, raw materials, and fuel to stimulate productivity. Though invited to participate, the Soviet Union declined for itself as well as its Eastern satellites. Sixteen Western European countries met in Paris to discuss the American offer. They ended their meetings by forming the Committee of European Economic Cooperation. Only Francisco Franco's Spain failed to receive an invitation to join the group, though five years later right-wing dictatorships were accepted as allies in the fight against communism. Then the United States extended aid to Spain and received permission to establish air force bases there.

Overall, the United States invested eighteen billion dollars in the European Recovery Program between 1948 and 1952, at a time when the typical American clerical job garnered twenty-four hundred dollars a year. The quickness with which the Marshall Plan beneficiaries rebounded made the plan seem like a general panacea for economic backwardness. In 1948 the principles embodied in the Marshall Plan were applied outside Europe in President Harry Truman's Point Four program for India. The uneven success of this costly effort clearly suggested that economic

development required more than money, but this was not a popular conclusion. Many experts spoke, and continue to speak, of market success as
a consequence of autonomous laws of nature when history teaches that
capitalism functions like other social systems through indeterminate, personal interactions.

Europe in the postwar period is interesting to the history of capitalism
because its different trajectory reminds us that there are many ways that
enterprise can thrive. After the war it took devastated Western Europe
about five years to recover its full industrial power. In 1950 its gross
domestic product equaled that of the United States in 1905! That was the
last time for such a disparity. The next two decades registered the largest
sustained period of economic development ever recorded until that time.
In the four years between 1948 and 1952, Western European economies
grew an amazing 10 percent each year.

The Allies' occupation of Germany, vexed by the conflict between the
Soviet Union and the United States, resolved itself by splitting the nation
into the Russian-occupied East and the western area, which the United
States, Great Britain, and France supervised. The Western powers quickly
realized that a recovered economy in West Germany, formally recognized
as a separate country in 1949, was essential to their well-being. Just replacing the despised Nazi currency with deutsche marks had an impact. West
Germans responded with alacrity to a sound currency. Hoarding stopped;
shops became well stocked. It was a dramatic entrance for a currency that
has maintained its strength for sixty years. So quickly did it happen that
people called it an economic miracle, a term soon applied to the rapid
recovery of all of Western Europe.[4]

Catching up put Western European economies into high gear as they
moved beyond restoring their industrial plants to incorporating the technological developments of the past two decades. Capital from the United
States greased the wheels of the new locomotive of recovery and supplied
a model of economic advance. Western European countries already had
the skilled labor force, savvy investors, sophisticated banking systems, and
world-class educational institutions needed to revive their leading sectors
of steel, automobile making, pharmaceuticals, and electric products. Perhaps the most elusive benefits of the Marshall Plan came from the confi-

dence it conveyed and the easing of national rivalries. In the years between 1948 and 1964 the productivity from capital doubled, pretty much closing the gap between Western Europe and the United States.[5] In this environment, even Ireland, Spain, Portugal, and Greece prospered.

Continental Western European countries adopted a corporatist economic form. Governments guided growth with fiscal and monetary policies, central banks virtually monopolized venture capital, and unions secured worker representation on corporate boards. Development with stability became the collective goal. This was especially true in Germany, where the Nazi regime had soured just about everyone on a powerful state, including socialists and the grand industrialists. Instead they sought mechanisms to contain the inevitable jostling for advantage among market participants. This system legitimated interest groups and created new institutions to determine the direction of the economy.[6]

There were obvious trade-offs in the corporatist and free market economies. Few vulnerable members of society fell through the European safety nets, as they did in the United States. While large corporations sponsored excellent research, especially in pharmaceuticals, innovation took a backseat to security in Europe. Groups making decisions for banks, management, labor, and government proved more risk-averse than individual entrepreneurs. Private persons in the United States found it easier to get backing for new ideas, and they were left to succeed or fail on their own. The economy, as a whole, benefited from the entire lot of efforts to build the proverbial better mousetrap.[7] But turbulence remained a prominent feature of the American economy.

The immediate postwar agreements led to sustained international cooperation among the world's industrial leaders, animated by the sense of mutual concerns that had been missing in the interwar period. Most people realized that economic growth was not a zero-sum pie. Nations got richer if their neighbors were rich, as Adam Smith had pointed out years ago. While protective tariffs didn't disappear, they were moderated considerably from their mid-nineteenth-century highs. Still, all countries backed away from tackling the contentious issue of taking away domestic support from their farmers, a powerful political group everywhere.

The Committee of European Economic Cooperation metamorphosed into the Organization for Economic Cooperation and Development, which extended membership to the United States and Canada and later to Japan and Australia. With its European Payment Union working effectively, world trade grew at an average annual rate of 8 percent. World manufacturing output grew threefold between 1950 and 1973.[8] Not only had productivity taken a huge jump, but governments took advantage of increased revenue to provide extensive public services.

New Initiatives in International Cooperation

It is said that it's an ill wind that doesn't blow some good. The eruption of two devastating world wars within twenty years of each other would certainly test that proposition. The shortness of the interval of peace explains one good wind. The adult years of men like Jean Monet and Robert Schuman covered both wars. By the end of the second catastrophic conflict, these leaders were determined to do things differently this time around. Monet had learned about British, American, and European commerce representing his family's brandy firm before becoming a diplomat serving in the League of Nations. Schuman, who had gone from being a German to a French citizen when Alsace-Lorraine was returned to France after World War I, made a career in French politics.

The two men proposed a dramatic plan: link the steel and iron industries of Western Europe under a single authority. This was definitely an idea whose time had come. In 1951, France, Germany, Italy, the Netherlands, Belgium, and Luxembourg formed the European Coal and Steel Community. With one market for coal and steel products, the members hoped to assure a steady supply. They encouraged profit making in order to pay for the constant pace of modernization. What a difference a second bloodbath made! How unlike the vengeful spirit of Georges Clemenceau at the Versailles treaty negotiations was that of Monet and Schuman and the others who helped them succeed.

While the actual results were more inspirational than practical, the ECSC succeeded in bringing Germany back into the European fold.[9] This accomplishment kept the powerful concept of transnational union alive. Six years later the Treaty of Rome created the Common Market, formally known as the European Economic Community. The Maastricht Treaty of 1992 went one step further with the establishment of the European Union and a European citizenship for the people of the initial dozen member states. During the thirty-one years it took to be ratified, Maastricht's original economic and monetary union expanded to include policies for justice, foreign relations, and security. Capitalism triumphed over nationalism.

There's a crucial point about capitalism to be made here. The economic integration of Europe, while no panacea for all market woes, has been fundamental to the peace and prosperity of its participants. Yet nothing in the behavior patterns promoted by free enterprise points to such a cooperative effort. The replacement of competition with cooperation and a nationalist spirit with an international one came from individuals like Monet and Schuman, not from any economic laws. These men and others imagined a different world from the one whose horrors they had witnessed. And here is where the critical importance of the Marshall Plan came in. The United States used its gifts to leverage the war-wracked countries to move toward free market institutions. At the same time, the shower of money mitigated the sacrifices demanded by such breathtaking acts of conciliation.[10] The shape and direction of capitalism are always set by its participants and never by any inexorable laws. Experts' generalizations contain the unstated premise of ceteris paribus—this will happen if all else remains the same—but all else rarely stays the same with human beings, especially when successive generations imbibe different lessons.

Unlike American efforts to level the playing field through antitrust litigation, European countries tended to foster a front-runner in its industrial sectors, thinking more in terms of national growth than internal competition. The role of government in the economy was far larger than it had been before the war, but its investment never exceeded one-third of a nation's total. There was in fact a nice division of responsibility: The government offered help to its citizens who needed it and relied on the private sector to produce goods and services.[11] In Europe, many business leaders believed that the social democratic welfare state mitigated public unhappiness during economic downturns and tempered labor agitation for higher wages. With access to the technology generated in the United

States and without its military expenditures, it might be said that Western Europe had a good deal.

European countries did exceedingly well in steel production, automobile manufacturing, pharmaceuticals, and electronics. Germany also played a big part in the development of automaking in the postwar era. Karl Benz and Nikolaus Otto had pioneered commercial cars. It took the slowdown in the 1920s for American automakers to get a foothold there. General Motors took over Opel, and Ford established a successful subsidiary. The Depression reduced Germany's 150 auto companies to a dozen, including Opel and Ford, but the ones that remained were strong.

Automobile Makers and the War

With the coming to power of the Nazis in 1933, car manufacturing had acquired a political cast. Hitler wanted to imitate Ford with a mass-produced car.[12] At this point the Austrian automotive wizard Ferdinand Porsche entered the picture. Daimler Motors brought him to Germany but, after its merger with Benz, Porsche failed to please with his ideas for a Mercedes-Benz. He fared better with Hitler, who chose his design for his Strength through Joy automobile. Hitler planned a new factory, a kind of German River Rouge. Its work force was composed of German military prisoners, concentration camp inmates, captured Poles, and Russian POWs; the town that grew up around the plant resembled concentration camps with their accompanying abuses.[13]

The people's car never got beyond the prototype. The plant turned out a kind of German jeep during the war until the British army took possession of it in 1945. Renaming the car Volkswagen, the army ordered ten thousand of them. Then it offered the factory to British automakers, who laughed at the VW's ridiculous shape. Ford wasn't interested either, nor were French automakers. The plant reverted to the German government.

Meanwhile Ferdinand Porsche was detained for twenty months as a war criminal. The French government arrested another leading auto manufacturer, Louis Renault, for collaborating with the Nazi Vichy government. He died in prison. The complicity of these automobile makers was too egregious to be ignored by Germany or its conquerors. Porsche's son

Ferry was apolitical but, like Ferdinand, a superb designer. Eager to get the money to secure his father's release, Ferry made a sports car. The Porsche 356 became the first car to carry the Porsche name, soon to be associated with a succession of upscale models.

The government invited the Porsche firm to work on the VW design and gave it a royalty on all future sales of what now was called the Beetle in recognition of the VW's unique profile. In the ensuing years, Porsche produced close to one hundred thousand 356s while twenty million VW Beetles rolled off the production line and onto the streets of every country. In the 1990s yet another Porsche, Ferdinand's grandson Ferdinand Piech, brought Volkswagen out of the financial doldrums, making it one of the world's top four automobile companies. Germany's postwar rebound owes much to these successes, for one out of every seven jobs in the country depended on automaking with VW, Daimler-Benz, and BMW dominating the market.

The rate of growth in Western Europe after 1950 could not have been sustained without an influx of immigrants, even though European agriculture continued to shed workers as European farmers mechanized. Political instability and economic hardship produced freshets of refugees who were lured to Western European countries by their abundant jobs. Labor shortage became so acute in the 1960s that Germany, France, Switzerland, and Belgium invited in "guest workers" from Portugal, Spain, Italy, Greece, Yugoslavia, Turkey, and North Africa.[14] England received immigrants from the Caribbean Commonwealth countries while in a reverse migration some English and Scots moved to New Zealand and Australia. Jewish survivors of Hitler's concentration camps found new homes in Western Europe, the United States, and the new state of Israel, created from former Palestinian lands in 1948. Emigration to the United States continued strong after World War II, but more people came from the countries of Asia and Central America than from Europe.

With economic growth so strong, immigrants in Western Europe found employment, but not a comfortable place in their chosen society. Not considering themselves "lands of immigrants," as the United States did, European countries resisted incorporating the newcomers into their fabric. The guest workers tended to be residentially segregated as Latinos and African Americans were in the United States. When growth slowed, as it did in the late 1970s, calls came for sending the "guests" back to their homes.[15] Their presence strengthened xenophobic political parties. Still, long-term labor shortages loomed as the baby boom of 1946–1960 passed into retirement and the decline of European birthrates accelerated. By the 1960s countries throughout Europe had passed below the 2.1 replacement rate. Prosperity and a widening ambit of possible careers for women changed the mores of millennia. The individual decision making at the center of capitalism has infected whole societies.[16]

The American Economy in High Gear

The first two years after the war in the United States saw the swiftest peacetime conversion on record. Government control boards disappeared as fast as the military demobilized its soldiers, sailors, nurses, and merchant mariners. The more than 12 million men and women in uniform dropped to 1.5 million. (In 1939, at the start of European hostilities, the U.S. Army numbered 120,000 officers and soldiers!) Just as quickly as the military shed personnel, the labyrinth of prohibitions, priorities, quotas, limitations, set asides, price controls, subsidies, rationing, and interest rate pegging that had characterized war production disappeared.[17] While taking a backseat in economic decisions, Congress greased the wheels of the transition. The top income tax rates remained at 87 percent until 1981, but corporate tax rates came down. Withholding income taxes from wages and salaries had begun during the war and continued. By 1959 the Internal Revenue Service had the world's largest collection of personal data.

As an expression of gratitude to its veterans, the government dispensed favors that had a salubrious effect on the economic climate. Almost a million veterans took advantage of the GI Bill, which paid the costs of a college or technical education along with a stipend to live on. At the peak year of 1947, nearly half of America's college students were vets, the majority of them the first in their families to go to college. Quite incidentally this investment in education yielded a talent dividend for years as skilled labor became more and more important in the work force. (So important was it that economists added "human capital" to their discussions of the labor-land-capital component of production.)

Another nine hundred thousand unemployed veterans, almost half of those in the work force without jobs, drew upon the fifty-two weeks of unemployment benefits that Congress voted them. Several programs enabled veterans to get cheap mortgages. This promoted a construction boom. A developer named William Levitt built seventeen thousand houses within a stone's throw of a large U.S. Steel Company plant on Long Island, New York. Levittown was the first of a number of instant communities. Developers across the land began building tracts of houses on level land within commuting distance of America's cities. They mass-produced houses from similar blueprints with many items like cabinets trucked in. True to the prejudices of the day, blacks were usually excluded.

Investing as though good times were going to last forever, American firms expanded. They financed conversions and improvements with earnings, wartime savings, and new issues of company stocks and bonds. When unemployment rose above 5 percent, President Dwight D. Eisenhower pushed Congress to pass the Federal Highway Acts of 1954, 1956, and 1958. In Keynesian fashion, government funds poured into building an interstate highway system with ribbons of four-lane roads tying the country together as it generated hundreds of thousands of jobs. As a young lieutenant colonel Eisenhower had participated a generation earlier in the caravan of army vehicles sent across the country to see how easily troops could be moved from the East to the West Coast. "Not very easy" was the answer. The trip took sixty-two days and sometimes required oxen to pull the trucks out of the mud. The new interstate highway system followed the same route, the old Lincoln Highway, as the army convoy of 1919.[18]

Organized labor became a force in the American economy after passage of the Wagner Act, formally known as the National Labor Relations Act of 1935. This Magna Carta for labor gave statutory protection to organizing workers. Public opinion, as well as court decisions, had begun to turn in labor's favor, first in the twenties for the right to assemble and then during the Depression for the right to organize. Congress restricted the use of injunctions to stop labor meetings; in successive decisions in 1938 and 1939 the Supreme Court interpreted the First Amendment as making streets and parks a "public forum" that protected peaceful picketing.

A bitter rivalry marred labor's coming into its own when eight unions in the AFL withdrew to protest its indifference to organizing unskilled workers in mass production industries. Their exploratory committee turned into the Congress of Industrial Organizations in 1938. The CIO was much more welcoming to immigrants as well as to African Americans. Under the banner of "Negro and White: Unite and Fight," the CIO added half a million black workers during World War II. Racism among American unions was just as strong as it was among white-collar workers, but the CIO, led by the fiery mining workers' leader John L. Lewis, was pushing hard against those destructive attitudes. The CIO also successfully recruited immigrants and their second-generation progeny. Here it acted as a democratic force, showing these outsiders how to claim power at the work site and take up their place in a culturally diverse citizenry.[19]

With the increase in war production, many companies settled with their laborers in order to win military contracts, swelling the ranks of union members. When after the war those companies tried to scale back wages, unions fought successfully to hold on to or increase their gains. During the decade and a half of citizen solidarity, forged through the shared pain of the Depression and war, labor succeeded in convincing most Americans that wages should not be set by the impersonal workings of some "law" of supply and demand. Rather they put forward the twin goals of achieving a living wage and fully incorporating blue-collar workers into the prosperity beckoning when peace finally came. Disputes continued; big labor, big industry, and big government found a balance they could work with.

It was a magical combination for the American economy. Where war made most of Europe and part of Asia destitute, the American economy had actually grown 50 percent between 1939 and 1945! Canada and Argentina had grown even faster. People who'd lived in apartments all their lives bought houses; returning service personnel got married and began having those children destined to compose the baby boom of 1946 to 1960. Small businesses flourished, many of them serving families in the proliferating suburbs with bicycle shops, cleaners, and the like. The American peacetime economy, stalled since 1930, moved into high gear, where it stayed for a quarter of a century.

If one of the signs of a healthy economy is its capacity to recover from disruption, the speedy return to peacetime production indicated a strong constitution. The resiliency of the American economy astounds. Between 1945 and 1947, it found work for the nine million veterans who did not take up the GI Bill and it absorbed the twenty-two million employees formerly holding military-related jobs. Pent-up demand and all those savings in war bonds helped, but not as much as the restoration of confidence in a free market.[20] Before the war the United States economy had been half the size of the combined economies of Europe, Japan, and the Soviet Union. Seven years later it surpassed all of them together.

A Chilly New Peace

Americans interpreted the Soviet Union's suppression of its neighbors as part of a plan for world domination. In 1947 President Harry Truman announced his intention to contain communism by sending military and economic support to Greece and Turkey, both fighting Communist insurgencies. The Truman Doctrine advanced the notion that Soviet pressure through surrogate rebel groups, if successful, would produce a domino effect, with one country lost to communism bringing down its neighbors. The increasing mutual hostility between Russia and America inspired a full-scale propaganda battle, backed up by aid like that which Truman sent to Turkey and Greece. Winston Churchill coined a memorable metaphor when he announced in a speech in the United States that an "iron curtain" had dropped down between Eastern and Western Europe. A cold war between the former Allies took over from the hot one that they had fought together. Capitalism became the signature economic system for the West, its wealth-producing capacity carrying new moral overtones.

Russian paranoia and the near hysteria about socialism in the United States worked effectively to build mutual distrust and animosity. Every event became grist for propaganda; every foreign country's allegiance became a trophy to be won by one side or the other. A realist might add that the two systems of belief and governance were too divergent to make any other outcome likely. Free enterprise, free elections, and the personal freedoms of movement, speech, religion, and political participation came to epitomize the West's cherished values; the Soviets extolled their full employment, public ownership of the nation's goods, and equality of treatment for its people. Anticommunism united the nations of Western Europe and the New World. It also limited the range of acceptable political thought in the United States, which threatened to stifle the robust public debates that an economy based on innovation and initiative needed.

The East-West rivalry became more intense than those preceding the First and Second World Wars, but there was a crucial difference that prevented the Cold War from heating up. As World War II ended, the atomic age began. In 1949, after a crash program, Soviet scientists produced an atomic bomb like the ones that the United States had dropped on Japan. Closely following the U.S. program, the Russians then followed up with development of the more powerful hydrogen bomb and an intercontinental ballistic missile system for delivering the bombs. Now both countries, appropriately called superpowers, were capable of obliterating each other. Mutual annihilation became a clear and present danger. In the years that followed, seven other countries acquired the secrets of the Manhattan Project through a handoff from their allies. Perhaps four more are moving in that direction today.

Countries that had just come out of World War II now faced the aggressive policies of the Soviet Union. No one had a very good idea of how well the Soviet economy was doing, but everyone did know that the Red Army was a formidable fighting force. During an August night in 1961, when the East German government erected a wall in East Berlin to stop the flow of defectors to the West, Churchill's iron curtain no longer seemed like a metaphor. Western Europe remained dependent upon the military strength of the United States, which began ringing the Soviet bloc with army bases and missile sites.

Despite several very scary episodes in the 1950s and 1960s, the United States and the USSR managed to curb their extremists and avoid mutual destruction. In this they were helped by the United Nations, formed in San Francisco by fifty participating countries in 1945. Given powers denied the defunct League of Nations, the UN Security Council and

General Assembly kept alive the forms of deliberation, if not always their spirit. It remained more under the control of the United States than the Soviet Union, but Russia's veto power in the Security Council acted as a balancing, if annoying, mechanism.

New Institutions for International Trade

Some farsighted people after the war saw the chance to achieve a relatively free world market, a goal that had eluded the best of intentions earlier. One of the seventeenth-century developments that had given England an economic boost had been the dismantling of local obstacles to trade within the kingdom. In France at the same time you couldn't drive a car twenty-five miles without having to pay someone to cross a bridge or pass through a shortcut. The privilege of collecting such fees were highly prized and protected. In England goods and people moved within a single unified market, instead of the local and regional ones that dominated elsewhere. This had been a widely recognized stimulant to development, but national rivalries had nixed any effort to apply it to international trade. Instead countries erected tariffs or filled trade treaties with picayune demands for special treatment for a favored product or interest group.

World War II provided a new opening for international cooperation. The United States supplied its European allies with armament before its entrance into the war, through lend-lease treaties. In these, the American government demanded that after the war, recipients pitch in and help create a multilateral trade world that would speed recovery and promote growth, much as England's internal market had done three centuries earlier. Despite its history of protecting so-called infant industry, the United States became the strongest advocate of free trade. Particularly offensive to American producers were the favored terms of trade within the British Commonwealth. Like the British powerhouse of the nineteenth century, the United States promoted free trade as a virtue rather than as the advantageous policy of the strong. The United States sometimes acted like a wealthy, but grouchy, uncle as in the final settling of the lend-lease agreements.[21] Such behavior is not surprising. Rising above obnoxious national postures was the novelty.

The institutions established after the war created a propitious environment for economic development among the countries that participated. The dollar anchored international trade. By 1956 all Western European currencies could be converted easily, helped along by the European Payment Union. Beginning with a grant from the United States, the union promoted multilateral commerce by easing the means of payment. The dollars each country received from the Marshall Plan not only bought necessary goods but enabled it to buy from one another. Accounts for every country were settled at the end of each month, with only large debits or credits settled in gold or dollars.

Already geared toward consumption, the American economy boomed when millions of families bought big-ticket items like cars, refrigerators, washing machines, and dryers. A change in lending and borrowing made this great spending spree possible. Earlier, department stores and upscale groceries had created charge accounts. One of the conspicuous features of department store interiors was the pneumatic tubing that carried charge slips from every department up to the credit office, where they were sorted for monthly bills. So credit was not new to Americans, but it had never before been crafted into one of the pillars of prosperity. After the war, banks, retailers, manufacturers, lenders, collection agencies, and state and federal officials took the haphazard local lending industry of America and turned it into a coherent national system.

Americans now had enough purchasing power to pull the incredible flow of goods coming out of the postwar factories right into their houses and garages. From the borrowers' point of view, buying cars, houses, and major appliances on an installment plan made lots of sense in a period of inflation. With steady and well-paying jobs as abundant as goods, the default rate was minimal. Buying on credit no longer seemed like an indulgence, but rather like prudent spending. By the 1960s national credit cards had begun to take over from individual charge accounts. That same decade saw the beginning of the malling of America as developers began creating entirely new shopping areas, often enclosed within walls with air conditioning against inclement weather. Usually anchored by a major department store, the malls that mushroomed across the country signaled the early obsolescence of downtown retailing. Even in this era of conspicuous consumption, though, creditors continued to discriminate against blacks and women.[22] Assumptions based on the separation of a man's world of work and a woman's world at home dissolved slowly. Still, female employment began hitting new highs in the 1950s, despite the return to the home of women who had been wartime workers.

Technology's Social Impact

Into the American living room in the 1950s came the biggest novelty of all, television. The inventor of television, Philo Farnsworth, proves the randomness of mechanical genius. Growing up in Beaver County, Utah, Farnsworth tinkered with electricity from the time he was twelve. The first person to transmit a television picture, as he did in 1927, Farnsworth appropriately chose the dollar sign to send in an image with sixty horizontal lines. Although he lost a patent battle to the Radio Corporation of America, Farnsworth went on to invent 165 other devices, including vacuum tubes, electrical scanners, and the cathode ray. Farnsworth beautifully exemplifies one of the strengths of capitalism's dependence upon innovation: It can't ignore outsiders.

World War II gave a tremendous boost to the electronics industry with its developments in radar, sonar, radio navigation systems, and proximity fuses.[23] Large orders for these radio-related products left American firms like RCA with expensive laboratories that at last could be devoted to long-delayed television projects. Far from representing a luxury for the very rich, television struck people of modest means as a lifetime entertainment investment, and besides, it could be paid for in installments. RCA, which represented a merger of U.S. and German companies, took the lead in commercializing television. It introduced color TV in the 1950s. By 1960 forty-five million homes had TV sets. Movie attendance took a dive, and radios found their best audiences in cars.

Widespread ownership of TV sets promoted one of the most intrusive novelties of the 1950s, the television commercial. A natural extension of newspaper, magazine, and radio advertising, the TV commercial seemed particularly impertinent. Television stations timed them for maximum viewing, interrupting plays, football games, and the news. The picture that is worth a thousand words became the thirty-second sequence of pictures that informed, persuaded, and irritated. Roundly criticized, TV commercials succeeded in selling everything from deodorants to life insurance. Soon political candidates saw the promise of television commercials for generating support. More effective than door-to-door canvassing, commercials soon took the lion's share of campaign budgets. Fund raising acquired a new importance in American politics. Once again, commerce showed its power to shape institutions in unexpected ways.

Another newcomer to postwar American consumers was air travel. The U.S. government had promoted aeronautic research after the Wright brothers' successful flight in 1903 but ceased to do so after World War I. The original airlines like American and United emerged from aircraft companies. Charles Lindbergh drew world attention in 1927, when he flew from New York to Paris in a single-engine monoplane. Lindbergh then became a pilot for Pan American, which, like the other pioneering, commercial airlines, relied on income from carrying the mail, especially to the countries of Latin America. During the 1930s fear and expense curbed commercial flying. One marketing effort to confront these obstacles boomeranged. An airlines company discovered that wives worried enough about their husbands' safety to keep them from flying. To address this problem, the company extended free tickets to women who accompanied their husbands on business trips. Following up with questionnaires to the participating spouses, the advertisers discovered—from the angry replies they received—that not all the husbands had taken their wives!

World War II again involved the government in plane design and production. Like much else, air travel took off after the war. Jets took over from propeller planes in the 1960s, replacing such planes as the four-engine Constellation and the DC-3, which had carried cargo or twenty-one passengers for six decades. Jets could carry more passengers and get them where they were going faster. Greeting the new planes at Dulles Airport was a magnificent building designed by Eero Saarinen that looked as though it might take flight itself. At first jets were such a novelty that people went out to their local airport to see them land and take off.[24] The Federal Aviation Administration took over safety issues and air traffic control in 1958.

Novelties didn't end with television and flying. In the 1967 hit movie *The Graduate*, a family friend assails the hero at his graduation party with "I just want to say one word to you: plastics." And he was right; there was a great future in plastics. Developed originally as a substitute for ivory in billiard balls, cellulose had intrigued chemists in England, the United States, Switzerland, and France for almost a century. Plastics took off after World War II.[25] Then nylon stockings replaced silk ones, Bakelite dinnerware filled kitchen cabinets, and vinyl found its way onto sofas and lounge chairs. Manufacturers used polyethylene, the number one selling plastic, for soda bottles, milk jugs, storage containers, and dry-cleaning bags. Soon plastic Silly Putty hit the toy stores; Velcro came along later to replace buttons, snaps, and shoelaces. Very much a triumph of chemistry, plastics carried synthetics to a new commercial high.

The Push in American Higher Education

The most profound scientific influence on American thinking came not from the United States but from the Soviet Union. In 1957 the Soviets launched a 184-pound satellite into outer space. A month later a heavier Russian spaceship went into orbit with the dog Laika on board. Both transmitted a beep, beep, beep that was heard around the world. Americans were stunned; they had been beaten to the punch. Within four months the United States joined the Soviet in space with *Explorer 1*, but *Sputnik* had already done its public relations work, dispelling the notion that the Soviets were backward. The American reaction to this spectacular milestone in technology is what makes *Sputnik* so important to the history of capitalism. Pundits and politicians agreed that the United States had to make a gargantuan effort to excel in science and engineering; they agreed as well that American universities, not government research facilities, held the key.

Within a decade, public and private universities embarked on expansion programs that had the effect of changing the nature of higher education here and elsewhere. Because sending *Sputnik* into space represented the acme of achievement, there was no question of watering down college offerings, even with hundreds of thousands of new students. Besides, the

GI Bill had shown how students from modest or even poor backgrounds had thrived in college. Women too entered universities in larger numbers in the postwar decades and often moved into nontraditional fields. The push for the inclusion of minority students came a bit later, but the post-*Sputnik* expansion provided the template for that effort. Enlarging higher education put special pressure on graduate programs to prepare more scientists and scholars for faculties all across the country.

The president of the University of California Clark Kerr played a major role in shaping public opinion. In a famous Harvard lecture of 1964, Kerr laid out a vision of a college education as a general right, not as something reserved for the privileged few. When he was born in 1911, only 5 percent of America's eighteen-year-olds went beyond high school. Now Kerr insisted that the country must make room for every able student. He also called on universities to turn themselves into multiuniversities, offering a broad range of knowledge, theoretical and practical, ancient and current.[26] *Sputnik* acted as a catalyst, but it had also become increasingly obvious that capitalism's growth was dependent upon engineers, physicists, business experts, and skilled mechanics.

Responding to this challenge, the California legislature passed the 1960 Master Plan for Higher Education, which developed a three-tiered avenue for students: The top eighth of California's high school graduates could enter the University of California, the top third of graduates had a guaranteed place in one of the campuses in the state university system, and others could go to community colleges to prepare for later entrance into four-year institutions. Many states followed this model with multiple campuses radiating out from the original state university. In the East, where private education dominated, Massachusetts and New York started their first public university systems.

Expanding American universities rather than institutes of technology like those in California and Massachusetts, the U.S. government became a patron of the liberal arts as well as of the sciences. This is because in the United States, the first two years of college are dedicated to what is called general education, unlike other national systems, which have students specializing in secondary schools. So along with all the newly minted scientists who found good jobs in higher education there were thousands in literature, philosophy, history, political science, and sociology who did so as well. With tenured positions within the academy, much of the country's intelligentsia lost the acerbic tone of skeptical outsiders, common in Europe. The economist Joseph Schumpeter feared that capitalism would fail because of its cultural opponents. The American public has resoundingly supported capitalism and its demands on society in part because they have not been exposed to the withering commentary of critics.

State legislatures and private philanthropists got behind the monumental effort to build university systems by opening up their purses. For that, they expected gratitude from the students. Instead campuses throughout the country and Europe became hotbeds of hotheads. Under the law of unintended consequences, the larger intake of students shaped by a liberal education in a conformist society, as that of the United States was at the height of the Cold War, produced protests and demonstrations over free speech, civil rights, and the war that the United States was fighting in Vietnam. The regents of the University of California removed Kerr in 1967 because of their unhappiness with student activism. By that time he had presided over the expansion of the university to nine campuses. Kerr, who then became head of the Carnegie Commission on Higher Education, commented that he had entered and left office "fired with enthusiasm."

The Contribution of German Scientists to American Technology

Sputnik did more than promote higher education. It turned the exploration of space into a Cold War competition for which Congress obligingly spent billions of dollars. The United States may have demobilized its armed forces quickly, but it retained a major research and development program for new weaponry, as did the Russians. *Sputnik*, like America's *Explorer*, drew upon German wartime developments. These in turn built on the work of America's Robert Goddard, Russia's Konstantin Tsiolkovsky, and Germany's Hermann Oberth. Goddard had succeeded in firing a rocket using liquid fuel in 1926, but this aroused little interest in the United States. Quite the contrary in Germany. A young Wernher von Braun became fascinated by the possibility of space travel through the writings of Jules Verne and H. G. Wells. He joined a rocket society when he was seventeen in 1929 and learned about the work of Goddard, Tsiolkovsky, and, of course, Oberth. Three years later, von Braun entered the army. With a doctorate at age twenty-two he headed up the so-called rocket team that developed ballistic missiles. Nazi propaganda minister Joseph Goebbels named the first model "Vengeance Weapon No. 2." Von Braun's V-2 could deliver a two-thousand-pound warhead five hundred miles at a speed of thirty-five hundred miles per hour. Fortunately, it did not become operational until late in 1944.

But this is where the story of rockets gets really interesting. Although the Germans had relied upon many American patented devices such as gyroscopic controls, they alone possessed the knowledge of how to make liquid-propelled rockets. This pushed the American and Soviet military into a race to locate and bring back home as many scientists as possible once they entered Germany. Von Braun had seen the end of the war coming and was determined to place his work in the hands of the Western powers. He had actually arranged for the surrender of some five hundred German scientists along with lab papers and testing apparatus. Simultaneously in the summer and fall of 1945, the occupying armies were hunting down former Nazis to bring them to trial for war crimes. And here was the rub. The sought-after scientists were Nazis; no one could have worked on such sensitive programs without joining the party or one of its affiliates. Worse, some of them could also be charged as war criminals since they used slave labor in the Baltic factory that produced rockets.

The American State Department considered most of the German scientists unsavory applicants for admittance into the United States. A fight with the War Department ensued. The two departments agreed to a compromise to bring a select group of German scientists to the United States for debriefing. This revealed how extensive and profound German science had been during the war, ranging from work on rocketry to studies of the effects of radiation on the human body. The American military wanted these scientists to continue working in the United States, safe from any prospective enemy. "Ardent" became the relevant adjective to disqualify someone from entrance to the United States. Had he been an ardent Nazi? Another compromise was worked out. Only the scientists whose work appeared vital to U.S. interests would be allowed to emigrate. More than a hundred German physicists and engineers passed this screening. They were labeled "paperclip scientists" because the military reviewers had put paper clips on their papers to signify their importance. Lasting into the 1970s, the Paperclip program brought a total of seventeen hundred German scientists to America, where they laid the foundation for the American space program at White Sands, New Mexico, and Huntsville, Alabama.

This educational push greatly influenced the economy because it represented a huge investment of money and provided the intellectual infrastructure for the new wave of innovations in computers, pharmaceuticals, and aeronautics. Americans got a wonderful system of higher education, but they also took on the burden of paying for an accelerating program of research and development for military hardware from hydrogen bombs and atomic submarines to a full-fledged space program. The goal of security seamlessly succeeded that of winning the war, but wartime attitudes lingered. Secrecy sometimes cloaked inefficiencies in procurement, and members of Congress proved overly accommodating, especially if an item was made in their state. Aware of this, the Defense Department in the 1980s managed to parcel out the parts of the B-2 stealth bomber to every state in the Union.

During the war the army and navy, working on different tracks, developed the machine with the greatest future, the computer. Engineers and mathematicians had been struggling to design a device that could quickly do the complex calculations of modern mathematics. After Pearl Harbor, such an invention became even more imperative to compute firing and bombing tables. By June 1943 the first electronic, digital computer had emerged from the labs of the University of Pennsylvania, working on an army contract. The navy followed with a computer designed at the Massachusetts Institute of Technology. This one had a greater memory. The navy was about to abandon the project because of its prohibitive expense when the Soviet Union set off its atomic bomb in 1949. Now there was no turning back. The army's pioneering ENIAC was a behemoth weighing in at thirty tons! Could anyone then have imagined that in another sixty years, people would be able to buy inexpensive handheld computers with vastly more power, speed, and versatility?

Spending on military research only increased during the long Cold War of 1947–1991. Institutionalizing this new security concern, Congress in 1947 combined the old War, Navy, and Air Force departments into a new Department of Defense. The computer introduced a revolutionary concept with widespread applicability, digital transmission. Here information or voices are converted into streams of binary digits (the bits we hear about). Analog transmission sends information as a continuous modulated wave form. During the Second World War the U.S. government funded the research that converted analog voice signals to a digital bit stream and in the 1970s installed the first fiber-optic cable system for digital data transmission.[27]

Contracting with universities, the government invested heavily in the research and development that corporations had already found to be the key to economic success. It took the lead in research in electronics, communications, aerospace design, and materials testing done by physicists, chemists, and ceramicists. The government did the heavy lifting, and in time companies like International Business Machines found commercial uses for much of this research. The American Telephone and Telegraph Company ran its own Bell Laboratories, and pharmaceutical companies also maintained first-rate research facilities of their own.[28]

Three days before he left office, President Dwight Eisenhower warned about the dangers of something he dubbed a military-industrial complex. Calling attention to the permanent war footing of the country and the vastly more complicated weaponry involved, he asked Americans to be alert to "the equal and opposite danger that public policy could itself become the captive of a scientific, technological elite." After noting that the United States annually spent more on military security than the net income of all U.S. corporations, Eisenhower urged "the proper meshing of the huge industrial and military machinery of defense with our peaceful methods and goals, so that security and liberty might prosper together.[29] Only the catchphrase "military-industrial complex" caught on; the warning went pretty much unnoticed. Those corporations that benefited from the government's largess formed themselves into a powerful lobby to ward off any cuts in the Defense Department budget. Eventually American military spending surpassed the total military expenditures of all other nations.

Unhappily this glory period in the history of capitalism brought more environmental damage than all the horrendous destruction of the First and Second World Wars. A new term, "ecology," the study of the relations of living organisms to their surroundings, began to penetrate public consciousness. What were we doing to our ecology? From an ecological perspective, economic progress had entailed a concerted assault on all facets of the environment. World population had grown from 1.6 billion in 1900 to more than 6 billion in 2007. These new people—burning fossil fuel, disposing of their waste, diverting rivers, dredging, earth moving, and plowing the earth's surface—polluted, contaminated, and despoiled their habitat. Reversing this appalling process would not be easy.

Constructing magnificent dams in fact became the cherished achievement of nation builders. Their words capture the spirit of economic advance with no hint of the consequences. Winston Churchill, visiting Lake Victoria, saw the waters of Owen Falls rush into the Nile River below and rhapsodized not about the spectacular beauty but about the failure to tap into its force: "So much power running to waste . . . such a lever to control the natural forces of Africa ungripped, cannot but vex and stimulate the imagination. And what fun to make the immemorial Nile begin its journey by diving into a turbine." Colonel Gamal Abdel Nasser, who came to power in Egypt in 1952, agreed. With unabated zeal he planned and funded the Aswan Dam, remarking: "In antiquity we built pyramids for the dead. Now we build pyramids for the living." More briefly, Prime Minister Jawaharlal Nehru called his country's new dams "temples of modern India." These dams delivered cheap electricity and regular irrigation water, but at the high cost of interrupting the deposit of river silt on depleted soil, destroying fisheries, and causing salination.[30] Environmentalists, a new phenomenon in themselves, delivered a wake-up call about this complex pattern of environmental degradation.

German scientists in the United States continued their research on radiobiology, ophthalmology, and the new field of medicine for those in outer space. All were subject to inquiry about the German use of prisoners in medical experiments without any very satisfactory resolution of the issue. The war created imperatives for combating infections, treating malaria, and healing the wounds of soldiers. This acted as a hothouse for medical research. The British scientist Alexander Fleming, had first isolated penicillin when he grew a mold that could dissolve disease-causing bacteria. British scientists came to the United States to continue this research during the war. The Pfizer Company took a heroic risk on a new way to produce penicillin that worked. By D-day, when Allied troops landed in France in June 1944, penicillin was available to treat the wounded. In three years the cost of a dose dropped from twenty dollars to fifty-five cents.

Working off Fleming's penicillin, biochemists discovered a new class of drugs that proved particularly effective in combating pneumonia, meningitis, and other bacterial diseases. Fleming published his research results in 1929. His sulfanilamides, or sulfas, as people quickly shortened the name, became available in the treatment of the war wounded on both sides. Produced in powder form, soldiers carried their own rations into battle. When the Japanese cut off the Allies' access to the quinine used to treat malaria, research produced a synthetic drug. Called atabrine, it saved the lives of thousands of Americans fighting in the South Pacific. The American Charles Drew discovered that blood plasma could replace whole blood that deteriorated rapidly. Soon the Red Cross began operating blood banks. By war's end it had collected and sent to the battlefronts more than thirteen million units of blood. The pharmaceutical company Squibb pioneered a hypodermic syringe of morphine that medics could easily use on the battlefield.

The deployment of these new drugs and treatments to the civilian population laid the foundation for the postwar expansion of the pharmaceuticals industry. By 1952 Pfizer's Lloyd Conover had taken a naturally produced drug and modified it to produce the antibiotic tetracycline. From this research a succession of antibiotics directed to specific infections became available throughout the United States and Western Europe. In Europe, governments provided universal health care while the United States stuck to a private system, extending help with the mounting costs of the myriad ways of staying well only to the old and the very poor.

The money the government spent advancing the science and technology behind computers, medical care, and aeronautics had a tremendous impact on the postwar economy, contributing significantly to the innovations that reached the market in the 1970s and 1980s. Not only did government pay for research hard to justify with future profits, but its contracts enhanced the size of each industry's leaders, leaving them with enough revenues to continue costly research and development programs. The extended period of government support for research demonstrated the critical importance of maintaining a learning base not only for defense but for economic growth as well. Between 1941 and 1960 the government's share of R&D funding increased thirteenfold until it represented 64 percent of the national total.

Another new element in the postwar economy was the rapidity of technological change. Corporate leaders had constantly to be on the lookout for the next significant racehorse. Yet they always risked betting on the wrong animal or moving their prospect too early or too late. On top of these problems, any new product inevitably destroyed its predecessor, which usually had been bringing in steady revenue and was familiar to both the fabricating and sales staffs.

The Entrance of Computers

One of the great success stories of the postwar era was IBM, which benefited from government research and an inspiring chief executive officer. Starting in 1911 with a line of scales, coffee grinders, time clocks, and adding machines, IBM found its Alfred Sloan when Thomas Watson joined the firm three years later. Like the great entrepreneurs of the nineteenth century, Watson infused his ideas and values into every facet of his firm, creating a loyal group of employees. A generous employer, he paid well and provided good benefits. He even built a country club accessible to all for a dollar a year and saw that regular dinners served there would spare wives some cooking. His obsession with teaching his staff how to please customers prompted him to create a company song and publish a monthly magazine filled with pep talks and product information. His employees responded fervently, imitating their boss in dress and behavior, often hanging Watson's photograph on their office walls.[31]

The career of International Business Machines captures all the drama of staying out in front. IBM benefited more than other firms from government's spending; various federal contracts paid half its research costs. Major contracts with the Defense Department gave IBM engineers access to the most advanced technology in magnetic core memories and circuit boards. IBM's key product before the war had been the punch card, a little rectangle that conveyed data through punched holes. IBM steadily refined these cards, going from mechanical to electric to electronic processing. Watson's idea was to confine all the elaborate collecting of information to one punch, which then could be stored, correlated, or printed. Hating to fire anyone, Watson continued making punch card machines when sales began to fall during the Depression. Happily for him, federal programs like the National Recovery Act and Social Security Administration required the manipulation of enormous amounts of data. When calls came for more IBM processing, there they were, stored in warehouses! The Nazis used IBM cards to code and manipulate the German census, with grim results.

Because of the complexity of the giant corporations that now dominated the economy, handling data became very important. All the statistics garnered to separate fixed from variable costs, returns on investments, and inventory ratios could be fed into an IBM machine to sort out. "Number crunching" entered the lexicon of management. Postwar insurance companies and banks relied on IBM punch card machines or, more exactly, relied upon IBM, for the company offered leasing contracts that included maintenance services. These were highly desirable because the apparatus became increasingly complex.

Relying heavily upon well-trained sales personnel, IBM spent considerable sums on their training. The company's emphasis upon customer relations kept it in first place. Costly as it was to maintain sales staffs of thousands of men and women knowledgeable about IBM's products, the firm prospered. Computers were too new and complicated for most customers to understand, but they did have confidence that IBM knew what it was doing. Watson kept IBM focused first on punch card machines and then on computers, eschewing the opportunity to become a conglomerate like Remington Rand or RCA. He even turned down the chance to buy the patent for the Xerox machine. Where people once wrote words, they now "processed" them! And all the while the amount of data that could be stored was doubling and tripling while the price of computers dropped. It was a rare technological trajectory, which subsequently became more familiar. In the first three decades after the war, the use of computers spread from the government to businesses to private persons.

IBM teetered on the edge of the computer revolution, uncertain about abandoning its punch card machines. Not until 1950 did it move from electrical to electronic data processing and then mainly because of the influence of Tom Watson, Jr., who became president in 1952. The critical shift was going from cards to magnetic tape. It proved the right move; IBM became the world's largest producer of computers. In the late 1950s IBM added as many as twenty thousand new employees in some years. The data needing to be filed and manipulated in these marvelous new machines grew exponentially too. IBM also operated a separate branch, World Trade, where computers were made and sold abroad. Watson Senior was not an engineer, but he had an engineer's cast of mind. Like Ford, he also thought like a salesman, educating his sales force and encouraging close relations with the firm's customers, whose opinions were carefully weighed in management decisions. Despite all this, Watson remained old-fashioned. When his son decided that it was high time to make an organizational chart, he discovered that forty-seven units had been reporting directly to his father![32]

Laws and litigation in the United States promoted and protected competition. After the war, European countries began to follow this American lead. Backed by the authority of the Sherman Antitrust Act, the Justice Department kept pretty close watch on America's giant corporations. Its lawyers viewed IBM's leasing policy as a restraint of trade because its comprehensiveness closed out companies that sold peripherals like monitors, printers, synchronous motors, gearboxes, keyboards, and scanners. They also challenged the Radio Corporation of America and American Telephone and Telegraph for their unwillingness to license patents.[33]

A 1956 consent decree stopped monopoly practices, opening up opportunities in data processing, consumer electronics, and telecommunications. Now both American and foreign companies could obtain precious licenses and develop their own lines in the growing field of electronics. A second antitrust suit in 1969, lodged against IBM's bundling of services, enlarged competition in the field of plug compatibles.[34] Soon the telecommunications industry would feel the sting of antitrust investigations.

Meanwhile IBM designed a computer system that could be disassembled for delivery and reassembled quickly. Over time customers had begun to complain about the fact that IBM's seven different computers could be used only with their specific peripheries. At this juncture, developing something more adaptable would be risky, but so too would be not doing so. In 1961 IBM committed itself and five billion dollars, the equal of three years' revenue, to designing a swifter, smaller all-purpose computer to replace all its special use ones. Its architecture was totally different. Its reception rewarded the risk taken. The impact on the computer industry of the System/360 was revolutionary, but alas, in the postwar environment of constant technological advance, even revolutionary systems hold the day for only a decade or two. Since any innovation kills its predecessors, stakes were high.[35]

The New Social Force of Labor

In the seventeenth and eighteenth centuries and in much of the nineteenth century, labor in the United States had been scarce. Farmer owners had represented a large proportion of the working class. With abundant land, American colonies had reversed the European ratio between abundant population and scarce land. This had a long-lasting effect on attitudes toward workers. European travelers were always astounded by the independence of servants in America. They also remarked on the intelligence and knowledge of men and women in rural areas. The flood of foreign labor into American factories at the end of the nineteenth century changed the character of the working class and created a large social gap between laborers and managers. After World War I, millions of black men and women moved into northern and southern cities to become part of the new proletariat.

It had been a stiff challenge organizing a work force riven by racial, ethnic, and religious differences. Unions, when successful, replaced the paternalism operating in most factories with explicit processes for hiring, firing, promoting, and evaluating workers. Elected stewards became the most important persons on the shop floor.[36] For black workers the benefits were enormous, for within segregated plants—and most of them were—bargaining required that they cultivate their own leaders. Union halls offered sociability, entertainment, and education. Organizing had also provoked demonstrations, protests, walkouts, and the famous sit-down strikes in the automobile industry in 1936 and 1937.

Labor representatives won more than higher wages and complaint procedures when they sat down with management at the bargaining table. They gained respect that many managers had long been loath to extend to them. Beneficent employers from Wedgwood to Watson treated their employees as fellow human beings, but it took unions to secure recognition that manual laborers had legitimate interests of their own in the workplace, even if someone else owned it. Labor and management settled most conflicts peacefully, but strikes continued. President Truman ordered the U.S. Army to take over the railroads to end a 1950 strike. He tried to do the same thing with steelworkers in 1952, but these flare-ups did not halt the spread of union shops across America. Still, prosperity offered the best road to higher wages. The percentage of people living below the poverty level went from one-third in 1950 to 10 percent in 1973.[37]

What Americans didn't get was a social safety net like those that were being put in place, or perfected, in Europe. Walter Reuther, head of the United Auto Workers, had taken a world tour for thirty-two months before the war, working around the globe. When he became head of the UAW after the war, he threw himself into lobbying Congress for full pensions, health care, and workers' wage protection during bad times. His efforts coincided with Americans' growing hostility to the Soviet Union, making his ideas sound like socialism—or worse, communism. They were rejected so Reuther, who had started out campaigning for all American workers, changed course and won these benefits for UAW members at the bargaining table. Those workers without unions had to catch as catch can.[38]

In retrospect, business leaders like General Motors' Alfred Sloan made the wrong decision when they opposed public financing of pensions. They saddled their companies with costs that kept growing when the burden might have been spread through public funding, as was the New Deal's

Aid to Families with Dependent Children. Aside from the expansion of higher education, the engine of social reform had an uphill push in the 1960s. Progressive income tax rates and rising wages shrank the gap between rich and poor for twenty years while the economy moved ahead at full tilt. President Lyndon Johnson declared war on poverty, but the real war in Vietnam undercut many of his domestic goals.

The quest for acknowledgment of labor has been made more difficult by the language of economic analysis that depersonalizes workers. Labor is bundled with land and capital as the principal components of enterprise. In a subtle way, this has a dehumanizing effect, for it obscures the enormous difference between the human and material elements in production. We might consider the capitalist perspective that dominates public discourse as another perk for business. A recent *New York Times* headline announced, LABOR COSTS SOAR IN CHINA.[39] Why not say, WORKERS' WAGES HAVE RISEN IN CHINA? Even liberal institutions like universities act like hard-nosed employers when it comes to their own labor relations. In economic analysis, gains to labor can still be labeled "expropriation of profits by trade unions" and linked analytically to "extortion by organized crime."[40] From an ideological perspective, organized labor started with a deficit, relying, as it must, on collective action in a nation that celebrates the individual, even though it was the giant corporations that did most of the employing.

When companies changed owners, contracts won were lost. Union activity created strong incentives for management to mechanize as many tasks as possible. Far more significant for labor, business interests began a long campaign to push back on the Wagner Act's support for unions. They succeeded with the Taft-Hartley Act of 1947 in limiting some union activity. From its heyday in the twenty years after World War II, union membership has steadily declined. In 1970, it peaked with 27 percent of all workers; in 1980 one in five workers belonged to a union; in 2007 one in eight, most of them working in the public sector. Legislative efforts to gain a Wagner Act–like protection for state and local government workers foundered in the 1970s.

The ease with which business interests passed the Taft-Hartley Act just a dozen years after the Wagner Act signaled the loss of momentum for organized labor. To avoid unionization, carpet and furniture-making firms began moving their plants to the South. Once there the manufacturers in the North formed a coalition with southern members of Congress to check labor's demands for supportive legislation.[41] Employers who wanted to keep out all unions kept up a steady eroding pressure on the power of organized labor. Representing a small minority, the business interests in the United States obscured in public discussions the interests of the great majority of wage earners. What management lacked in the number of its voters, it compensated for in superb organization.

There were other forces working against labor in the United States. The union's reliance on mandatory dues and closed shops offended a sense of fairness to many in the public. Scandals over union bosses and their misuse of funds eroded respect. And then there was the fact that jobs were moving out of the industrial sector to workplaces harder to organize, like restaurants and hospitals. A renewed flow of immigrants, both legal and illegal, gave employers access to a compliant labor force, particularly after a change in the law in 1965 that eliminated the preference for European immigrants.[42] Labor even lost out rhetorically as less and less was said about the "working class" and more about the "middle class," a term that obfuscated the profound differences between well-paid professionals and those who worked but still lived in poverty.

Corporations employ not only laborers but salaried clerical and managerial employees. Their relations have not been as confrontational as those with wage earners, but they were often just as harsh. Top executives could be fired with brutal swiftness. Probably unique was the dismissal of a National Cash Register executive by CEO John Henry Patterson, who dragged the man's desk outside, doused it with kerosene, and set it on fire. Still others have returned from lunch to discover workers scraping their names off their office doors.[43] The stress of middle management—those who mediate between upper management and the work force—has spawned its own extensive literature.

Clerical workers rarely got paid what their skill and responsibilities would merit in other work, but the largely female work force accepted this disparity. When Sandra Day O'Connor, the first female member of the Supreme Court, left Stanford Law School, the only job offered her was as secretary in a law firm. She had graduated second in her class. (Supreme Court Chief Justice William Rehnquist was the first.) Once women moved into the professions in large numbers in the 1960s, clerical salaries went up. Soon there was a full-blown movement to secure "equal pay for equal work," a term that originated in the labor movement in the 1930s but came to refer exclusively to pay discrimination against women. In 1963 President John Kennedy signed into law the Equal Pay Act, and the venerable gap between male and female salaries began to close. Since then it has narrowed from fifty-nine cents to every dollar earned by men to seventy-seven cents.

Disparities among all employed Americans shrank all through the postwar era until 1973. The rising tide, extolled in business literature, buoyed by strong unions, *did* lift all boats. Business gained conspicuous public support in the stock market. The American Telephone & Telegraph Company announced proudly that it had 1 million shareholders. By 1952 there were 6.5 million stockholders, 76 percent of them earning less than ten thousand dollars, the salary of salesmen and entry-level university instructors.

In the liberal postwar environment, government interference with business decisions came from a new origin, the Bill of Rights. In 1955 the Interstate Commerce Commission banned segregation on interstate trains and buses. This proved to be the launching pad for a national movement to disband the segregation of the races in southern public places. Peaceful protesters for a full range of causes won when courts defined malls as public space where the expression of opinion could not be squelched. State and municipal fair housing legislation prohibited landlords from discriminating against prospective tenants, though the implementing machinery was rarely sufficient to police these common practices. In the same spirit, more recently, pharmacists have been denied the power to refuse to fill prescriptions, like birth control pills, that might violate their conscience. Private enterprise because of its intimate interface with the public could no longer make arbitrary decisions affecting that public.

"Follow the money" was the advice "Deep Throat" gave the investigative reporters in the Watergate scandal, but that's not always easy. What happened to the money generated by the golden period of postwar prosperity in the United States, Western Europe, Japan, and parts of Latin America? Certainly we can see that workers in Germany, France, Great Britain, and Scandinavia took a large hunk of it out in leisure with a predictable drop in productivity. Western European countries increased their investment in underdeveloped countries of the Third World and beefed up support for the World Bank. They paid more for public services. Their guest workers sent home remittances in the billions. At its peak in 2006, immigrants in the United States sent twenty-four billion dollars back to Mexico; remittances represented 29 percent of the Nicaraguan gross domestic product. Similar figures can be found for Turks in Germany, and those from Curaçao in the Netherlands and British Commonwealth islands in the Caribbean.

The End of the Postwar Boom

While most people old enough to have been alive remember where they were in 1963 when John Kennedy was assassinated, few recall their activities in 1973 with any clarity. Only in retrospect does that year emerge as the marker of more peaks and troughs than a roller coaster. The value of the dollar plunged, and the price of oil quadrupled. Union membership in the United States topped out, and the European birthrate began its long slide. Unemployment in the 1970s reached heights not seen since the Great Depression. Even increases in foreign trade, often described as an export boom, came to a rather abrupt stop in 1973 after having brought sustained prosperity to Western Europe and the United States. On average the rate of growth in the capitalist world halved in the next fourteen years.[44]

American military expenditures for the Vietnam War had greatly increased the number of dollars in circulation. Rather than raise taxes, President Lyndon Johnson preferred to have the Federal Reserve print money. This move exacerbated the ongoing weakening of the world's major currency. The resulting glut made it difficult for the U.S. Treasury to continue to convert dollars into gold as it had promised to do in the Bretton Woods agreement. Johnson's successor, Richard Nixon, pulled the dollar off the gold standard, in 1971. Now all currencies were free to float.

In fact, agitated by worldwide inflation, they splashed around furiously for two years.[45]

Eroding even faster was American oil production. The United States had supplied almost 90 percent of the oil that the Allies used during World War II. At that time, the Middle Eastern countries, including all of the Arabian Peninsula, produced less than 5 percent. The voracious appetite for petroleum products during the boom period of the 1950s and 1960s changed all that. The Persian Gulf became the center of the oil world. Oil fields in Texas, Oklahoma, and California pumped around the clock, but it wasn't enough. The United States had lost all its spare capacity at a time when world oil consumption was growing 7.5 percent a year. American production hit its high in 1955, and after that the United States turned increasingly to Mexico, Canada, and Venezuela for its oil. By 1955 two-thirds of the oil going to Europe was passing through the Suez Canal, which had regained the strategic importance lost when Britain left India a decade earlier. By 1973 the days of plentiful, and therefore cheap, oil were a thing of the past. Middle Eastern oil reserves were vast, but the actual production capacity of Arab states met 99 percent of demand, leaving a margin of 1 percent! Policy makers started talking about an oil crisis.

While the economic climate was losing some of its sunshine, far away a perfect storm was brewing. The hostility of the Arab countries to the presence of Israel in their neck of the globe led to the shock that made 1973 a year for capitalist countries to remember. It started on an October afternoon, when 250 Egyptian jets took off for the eastern bank of the Suez Canal to bomb Israeli positions in the Sinai Peninsula. The day was the holiest of the Jewish calendar. The Yom Kippur War might have remained a regional conflict had not other Muslim countries decided to use the "oil weapon." They raised the price of oil 70 percent and cut production 5 percent for several months running. The price of gas at pumps in Europe and the United States rose twelvefold. In the next two decades the gross national product of the advanced capitalist countries fell from an average of 4.6 to 2.6 percent. Inflation found a new partner in unemployment.[46]

These decisions taken by the Arab members of the Organization of Petroleum Exporting Countries were an announcement of sovereignty; previously they had pretty much taken orders from Western producing companies like Exxon and Shell.[47] Panic, shock, and disbelief coursed through the world, intensifying in those prosperous countries that depended most heavily upon petroleum products. The swiftness and unpredictability of the war and the subsequent embargo added more turbulence to the rising prices. It also caused episodic, local shortages. A whole way of life, a whole way of thinking about the future cracked, if they didn't actually shatter. A bit of good wind in this storm of ill winds blew the way of local farmers and craftsmen who recovered old customers lost to larger cities earlier. Higher gas prices raised significantly the transportation component of costs. Flower growers in the upper Connecticut Valley, for instance, got back the trade that had gone to "the flower state" of New Jersey, an example of the old adage that one man's disappointment is another's opportunity.

Cassandra was a Trojan princess to whom the god Apollo had given the power of prophecy linked to the fate of never being believed. A U.S. Foreign Service officer named James Akins became a modern-day Cassandra. Undertaking a secret oil study for President Nixon's State Department, he laid out in great detail the consequences of a rapidly expanding use of oil in the face of America's declining control over its production. His recommendations sound familiar because they have been posted so many times since: development of synthetic fuels, greater conservation efforts, a hefty gas tax, and research on alternative ways to run industry's machines.[48] Akins's proposals were summarily dismissed as exaggerated, possibly mendacious, and certainly un-American.

E. F. Schumacher, a German economist working in London, faired a bit better with *Small Is Beautiful*, a lovely book that appeared in 1973. Schumacher presented the oil crisis as a challenge to the West to mend its profligate ways. His critique of incessant consumption unfolded alongside his poetry, wit, and Buddhist wisdom. Admiral Hyman Rickover, developer of the atomic submarine, had sounded this alarm even earlier, in 1957. Schumacher's and Rickover's prescience reveals yet once again how self-interest can sharpen the mind. Schumacher worked for the British Coal Council, and Rickover was a prominent advocate of atomic energy.

For many observers the multiple setbacks of 1973 were just a bump in the road. In one sense they were right, but only if we ignore the shift in perceptions and attitudes. Artists and intellectuals were the first to get bored with the miracle years of prosperity. They began competing with one another to determine whether we had entered a postindustrial age or a postcapitalist or a postmodern one. Whatever it was, it was definitely "post." In truth many had become sated with the market's unending succession of new conveniences, new recreations, and new distractions. Several books published in the United States in the early sixties raised major issues that grew more insistent after the 1973 crisis.

Rachel Carson's *Silent Spring* caught the nation's attention in 1962 with its description of the environmental poison of pesticides and herbicides. A zoologist working for the U.S. Bureau of Fisheries, Carson detonated a fire storm with *Silent Spring*. Waiting in the wings were hundreds of experts who had been studying just how destructive the twentieth century had been to the planet that we inhabit. Environmentalists mounted one of the most successful political movements in history. In 1962 Michael Harrington in his *The Other America: Poverty in the United States* reminded the public that not everyone was prospering. Three years later Ralph Nader's *Unsafe at Any Speed* took on America's automakers; its subtitle delivers the message: *The Designed-in Dangers of the American Automobile*. Their words seemed even more prophetic with the multiple blows of an oil crisis, rising unemployment, and an inflation rate spiraling upward.

A younger generation took up the causes of the degrading environment, product safety, and the persisting plight of the poor and made them their own. Drawing upon the Enlightenment tradition of faith in reason with a commitment to social progress, the environmental movement took off in the 1970s. Dedicated to reestablishing a balance between human beings and nature, it also helped ease the tension generated in Western societies by the angry confrontations of the 1960s over civil rights, women's status, sexual mores, and the war in Vietnam. For decades Westerners had been busy polluting their air, their soil, their waterways, and the habitats of themselves and the animal world without caring much about it.

At the same time, other experts were predicting the inexorable spread of industry. In 1953 W. W. Rostow, who served as special assistant for national security affairs to President Johnson, published the book that popularized the idea of inexorable modernization. What the general reader took away from *The Stages of Economic Growth: A Non-Communist Manifesto* was the ease with which a few good Western programs were going to transform the rest of the world in their image. Flush from the success of the Marshall Plan in Western Europe, Westerners had every reason and many incentives to believe this to be true. Traditional societies had built-in resistances to profound changes, much like Europe before the seventeenth century, but outside forces could bring them along with the introduction of technology and, above all, capital. A critical contribution of this theory was the idea that countries were not destined to be backward, poor, and dominated by atavistic cultures; all could aspire to capturing "the magic of modernity." Today, having been immersed so long in the hopes and disappointments of modernization, we can easily miss how pathbreaking an idea this was.[49]

Readers could assume after reading Rostow that the quality of labor was a negligible factor in industrialization, as turned out not to be the case.[50] Capital was much easier to introduce into underdeveloped countries than were production skills and entrepreneurial energy. America's Alliance for Progress with Latin American countries had been a failure, as were other efforts to bring the Third World into the First, like the U.S. Point Four program in India. Evidently, it took more than the West's insistence and World Bank loans to deflect the course of traditional societies. The categorization of traditional and modern began to appear too crude, too truncated to do justice to the variety of social settings in which the world's people lived and drew meaning.[51] As it turned out, the West was merely impatient and had to wait longer to see the sprouts from its investment seeds.

Probably the most striking feature of capitalism has been its inextricable connection with change—relentless disturbances of once-stable material and cultural forms. More than promote change, it offered proof that the common longings of human beings for improvement could be achieved. It opened up to a significant proportion of men and women in the West the possibility of organizing their energy, attention, and talents to follow through on market projects like forging a new trade link or meeting an old need with a commercial product. And one could do it on one's own. One didn't have to be tall, good-looking, young, rich, well connected, or even very smart to form a plan, though all those qualities were helpful. Capitalism sustained popular support by commanding this imaginative field. Newcomers found it hard to attract venture capital, and there were more failures than successes. Even when individual ventures were successful, few foresaw the unintended consequences of all this manipulation of nature and society. Turbulence was written into the system, but capitalism had already become self-sustaining before anyone could clearly see this.

It took a bit of time to realize that the shocks of 1973 marked the end of the "golden age" of capitalist prosperity in its homelands. Rising prices usually accompanied periods of growth, but, this time around, they came in with stagnating production. This introduced a new condition and term, "stagflation," which in turn promoted an interest in monetary theory. In another disturbing trend, the gap between low and high incomes began its long stretch of stretching in 1969, though concern with this phenomenon rarely moved beyond rhetoric. With mounting studies documenting the neglect of the environment and the safety of workers and consumers in the most advanced societies, we could say that the greatest chapter in the history of capitalism ended with more of a whimper than a bang.

Meanwhile, back in the laboratories of Intel in Palo Alto, California, and Sony in Shinagawa, Tokyo, engineers were mapping out uses for something called a transistor. The transistor—short for "transfer resistor"—is a device that amplifies or switches the flow of electricity. It had been around for a couple of decades but now was being upgraded. Attached to an electronic circuit board, the transistor could do wondrous things because of its smallness and adaptability. Ingenuous people had found a new way to exploit the electromagnetism of our planet. This technological newcomer "creatively destroyed" the vacuum tube that had started off wireless technology. The relentless revolution continued without the benefit of a forward-looking name for the dawning era, though the United States acquired a new place-name, Silicon Valley, where things called start-ups and initial public offerings were creating a new crop of millionaires.

11

CAPITALISM IN

NEW SETTINGS

I N THE EARLY 1970S the unexpected rise in oil prices forced people to give some attention to other negative indicators in the industrial world: the slowing growth rate, intractable inflation, rising unemployment, the plunging dollar, and fluctuating exchange rates. The comfortable understanding among big business, big labor, and big government was coming apart. The unwelcome appearance of stagflation also signaled that national policy makers could no longer depend upon the economic prescriptions of John Maynard Keynes. He had given a central role to government to spend when private investments could no longer achieve full or near-full employment, as in the Great Depression. Most countries in the postwar West followed Keynesian policies to ward off recessions. Alas, few had had the courage to cut off popular spending programs when they no longer were needed to boost the economy. This negligence contributed to inflation, exacerbated by the 1973 spike in oil prices. But now inflation was accompanied by high unemployment. The facts no longer supported the original Keynesian proposition. Government spending, which he had recommended in times of falling demand, had created the "flation" in stagflation, and stagnating sales the "stag." What had seemed a stable, comprehensible, and predictable economic environment became fluid and puzzling.

When the smooth performance of the advanced industrial countries came to an abrupt end in the early 1970s, it was time to look for help in a new theory. This gave an opening to Milton Friedman, who had some insights appropriate to the time, or so they seemed. A University of Chicago economist, Friedman wrote extensively on consumer behavior and public policy, often in partnership with his wife, Rose. Friedman analyzed the new data and explained why a volatile inflation rate actually contributed to unemployment because it increased uncertainty. Its harm to creditors and those on fixed incomes also put pressure on governments to do something—wise or not. Friedman advised cutting back on government activity in the economy so that the market could do what it does best: communicate simple, unadulterated information through its prices to market participants, who could then make the soundest decisions with their resources.

As an influential writer on monetary theory Friedman recommended that government confine itself to a small increase in the money supply. As a public figure he wrote tirelessly to bring the public back to an appreciation of "economic man," that rational chooser upon whom Keynes had cast doubt. Friedman reaffirmed economists' early conviction that the market helped people choose what was in their interest. Competition, he said, worked best for consumers and producers alike. He won a Nobel Prize in economics in 1976. His ideas soon percolated into public policy first in Great Britain with Prime Minister Margaret Thatcher and then in the United States. As President Ronald Reagan announced in 1981, "It is time to check and reverse the growth of government," though he recognized that the imperative was to make government work better.[1] While Thatcher and Reagan were in power, Friedman was showered with awards, prizes, and appointments. In actual practice, monetarism enjoyed Federal Reserve support only for the years between 1979 and 1982. It failed to keep the country from sliding into recession.

Not all government intrusion into the economy had been inspired by

Keynesian theory. Much of it was in pursuit of a social goal. In the 1960s legislatures began controlling how factories affected the environment or endangered species. Other laws dealt with worker safety, discrimination in hiring and housing, and the protection of consumers. Without debating their social and moral benefits, Friedman pointed out their adverse effect upon competition.[2] His work became the basis of the deregulation movement that liberated credit institutions, telecommunication corporations, and the energy sector. His faith in self-interest's capacity to trump prejudice led him to predict that employers would not discriminate because it hurt them not to offer jobs to the best applicants, a position contested by many field studies. Perhaps the most interesting of these was the blind auditioning for orchestras that gave a considerable boost to female candidates. The recession in Japan in the 1990s and the meltdown of the Argentine economy in 2000 offered a reprise of the Keynes-Friedman debate over the relative merits of government spending and government restraint. Keynes came out the better in the contest of ideas while the countries themselves suffered from following Friedman's prescriptions.

Still, Friedman's ideas exercised a great influence on corporate heads and policy makers alike. Supported by both Democratic and Republican administrations, the first wave of deregulation came in the late 1970s. Laws freed the airlines and trucking companies for competitive pricing. Regulation had been especially heavy in the transportation industry because it was seen as a public service in need of stability and protection. More slowly a broad band of civic-minded men and women worked to deregulate investment banking. This came at the same time that traditional long-term relationships between banks and their corporate customers were breaking up under pressure from newly minted MBAs moving into the banks' executive suites with new ideas about improving banking profits.[3] Two laws in 1980 and 1981 eased accounting rules on savings and loan institutions and reduced minimum down payments on their mortgages. Sailing faster with less ballast, they floated many more loans, and American personal indebtedness began its three-decade climb. Within the next decade over seven hundred S&Ls went under at a cost of over one hundred billion dollars to their insurers, the American taxpayers, but without slowing the movement for deregulation.

The 1980s also brought wrenching changes to manufacturing in the homelands of capitalism. The worldwide circulation of people, investment, and goods took an unexpected turn when multinational corporations sought out countries with cheap labor to build new plants. The enhancement of global communication made this easier to do. The United States, in particular, lost high-paying factory jobs that had boosted millions of families into a prospering middle class. Soon the steel centers that stretched from Buffalo, New York, to Gary, Indiana, lost out to Mexico, China, South Korea, and Brazil. Cheap imported steel entered the country from Japan and Europe. The land of smokestacks became a Rust Belt. Millions of jobs were opening up in finance, computers, and the service sectors, but Americans were used to their manufacturing might. And the new areas promoted an income split: minimum wage work in fast-food outlets and nursing care facilities and higher wages for the denizens of Wall Street and Silicon Valley.

The novelist Tom Wolfe commented recently that we were witnessing "the end of capitalism as we know it."[4] That's a statement that could have been made many times in the past two centuries, for capitalism is a system constantly reinventing itself, a set of prescriptions peculiarly open to disruption, a work in progress. It looks the same only if you examine the categories instead of the participants and practices. For instance, people have long insisted that market economies flourish only in open, secular societies where property rights are enforced and individual ambition is cultivated at the knees of mothers. Seven success stories in the second half of the twentieth century suggest that capitalism can take hold in diverse social contexts under government supervision and within communitarian cultures—that it is, in fact, always adapting.

The Formidable Economic Power of Japan

First among the countervailing examples is Japan, which started its economic transformation more than a century ago. Next, the Four Little Tigers—Singapore, Hong Kong, Taiwan, and South Korea—charged out of their traditional cages in the 1960s and 1970s. Sometimes called the East Asian NICs (newly industrialized countries), their takeoffs diverged from that of Japan's as Japan's had diverged from those of Western Europe and the United States. India and China, coming along more slowly, portend even greater influence in the global economy, as befits the first and second most populous nations, with 37 percent of the world's people.

Japan appeared an unlikely candidate for industrialization, much less for rapid industrialization. An East Asian island of thirty million people in the mid-nineteenth century, deliberately cut off from the world, it burst into prominence as a military and economic power at the end of that century. In a report card for worldwide economic development between 1820 and 1970, Japan placed first. Its GDP grew twenty-fivefold, a growth spurt unique in human history.[5] Starting at the most advanced level in 1820, Great Britain multiplied per capita income ten times, Germany fifteen, and the United States eighteen. The Western sequence of industrialization went from textile making and mining to metallurgical industries, railroad building, and heavy industry generally, its source of energy from waterpower to steam created with coal fires to electricity powered by generators. Consumer goods slowly diverted investments from the production of capital goods, the whole accomplished in a more or less trial and error fashion, through the decisions of entrepreneurs and investors.

Japan did not reverse the process, but its deviations from the pattern set in the West shows the diverse paths that capitalism can follow. Japan lacked the raw materials that mattered in heavy industry, meaning that it would have to import its iron and coal. The government outlined a program of exporting textiles, shoes, and trinkets that could pay for these essential imports. Hastened by its ability to borrow foreign technology and guided by a very determined elite, it did everything fast. Its traditional industries like cottage silk reeling, food processing, and various handicrafts used waterpower well into the twentieth century, but electrical motors replaced steam engines so quickly in the first decade of the twentieth century that you could almost say that Japan skipped the steam age. It also followed its own traditional path in placing the modernization of production and finance in the hands of a very few families like the Mitsuis, Mitsubishis, and Sumitomos, who in turn launched joint-stock trading companies in different sectors of the economy like steel and automobile-making. These family concerns formed pyramids from the top down, unlike the United States, where managers usually came up from the bottom rungs of business. The great industrial families exercised tight control from the center and cultivated a privileged group of insiders. They also blocked investment opportunities for foreigners.[6]

Even with military expenditures, government spending in Japan represented only 7 to 11 percent of the total annual investment in the economy, compared with 28 percent in the United States. It played a much larger role in capital formation—probably 30 to 40 percent—until private investments took off during World War I. As would be expected, Japan had its Wedgwoods, Watts, Carnegies, Rockefellers, Thyssens, and Siemenses, who laid the corporate foundation for Japan's successful industrialization. Sakichi Toyoda, like Thomas Edison, was a natural inventor and an even better business organizer. Born in 1867 into a family of carpenters, he set out single-mindedly to design a better power loom and devoted his life to this goal. In his province almost every farmer had a loom in his cottage for the family to earn extra income weaving cloth, so he was familiar with its construction and operation.

After decades of work Toyoda caught the attention of the British firm Platt Brothers, which dominated the world market in textile machinery. In 1929 he sold it the right to manufacture his G-type automatic loom. The contract rewarded his genius and tenacity and signaled the progress of Japanese technology. For cotton cloth makers his loom looked like a good investment. It cost three times the price of a conventional loom and increased tenfold the output of one operator, but it failed to catch on. The failure of Toyoda's loom for Platt Brothers uncovered a central weakness in the British textile industry: the strength of organized labor. Few manufacturers bought the Platt-made Toyoda loom because their workers objected to being displaced. By acceding to them for short-run peace, the British industry lost its preeminence in the world market. Between the 1880s and 1930s, Britain's market share dropped from 82 to 27 percent while Japan's climbed to 39 percent. The ability of Japan's association of textile makers to buy cheap raw cotton contributed to this rise in market share. Eventually Japan lost out to countries with cheaper labor but retained the lucrative business of making the textile machinery.[7]

You probably already realize that the Toyoda Automatic Loom Works would not be getting this attention were it not for its parentage of the Toyota Motor Company. Sakichi Toyoda, on his deathbed in 1930, advised his son Kiichiro, another inventing genius, to find his own passion. Having been astounded by the mass production of Model T Fords when he visited the United States, Toyoda pushed his son in the direction of automobile making with a pot of cash to get started. At that time Ford and General Motors dominated the Japanese automobile market. Kiichiro Toyoda built his early automobiles on the technology developed for the family's automatic looms. He changed the name of his car from Toyoda to Toyota for reasons pertaining to Japanese calligraphy.

In 1936 the Japanese government, already well advanced in an aggressive colonial policy, used a new licensing law to throw most of the automobile business to Toyota and Nissan. Both became giant holding companies in the 1930s. Their executives were military men who based their market strategies on advanced technology. They used state funds rather than banks for their capital, though Toyoda did extract working money from Toyoda Loom's accumulated earnings.[8] The decision of the Japanese government to go to war in 1894 and 1904 and a generation later in 1937 and 1941 put Japanese industry on a war footing. The country's industrialists had been the most ardent supporters of the doomed Greater East Asia Co-Prosperity Sphere and Japan's aggressive prewar foreign policy. American bombing raids during 1945 destroyed Japan's war machine, but not the know-how that had built it.

From the point of view of the history of capitalism, Japan's capitulation to the United States in 1945 was more portentous than its earlier, but short-lived, imperial successes. Having accepted "unconditional" surrender with the one condition of maintaining the emperor, the United States was free to rebuild Japan in its own image. General Douglas MacArthur, the supreme commander for Allied powers in the area, took charge of the occupation. His thoroughness and the absence of atrocities from American troops stunned the Japanese. The country was demilitarized; jails were cleared of dissident liberals, socialists, and Communists; and political parties and labor unions encouraged to participate in the hoped-for establishment of a postwar democracy.

When the Japanese were slow to produce a constitution, General Mac-

Arthur's staff did it for them, investing power in a legislature like that of Great Britain and giving women equal political rights with men. Land reform placed more than two million acres in the hands of nearly five million tenant farmers. The rural economy began to blossom. Turning their attention to the manufacturing sector, the occupiers became intent on breaking up the giant holding companies of the prewar period.[9] World politics then intervened.

When Soviet-backed North Korea invaded South Korea, the United States led a United Nations action against the invaders. American attention went from reforming the Japanese state to strengthening its power to resist communism. The intensification of the Cold War in the East with the emergence of a Communist regime in China deflected American advisers from their initial push for democracy.[10] Becoming a frontier in the Cold War had major consequences for Japan. It sped up the end of the American occupation with a formal treaty ratified in 1952. At the same time, Japan signed an agreement to provide bases for American troops, ships, and aircraft, an act that aligned it with the West to the exclusion of Russia, China, and neutral countries in Asia. The Korean War jump-started industries, light and heavy, as Japan extended hospitality to American forces and supplied munitions and equipment to the war effort.

A remarkable American, William Edwards Deming, came to Japan in 1950 as an assistant to the supreme Allied commander and stayed long enough to impress an obsession with quality on the country's leading industrialists. Trained in physics, mathematics, and statistics, Deming was a natural teacher, churning out such student-friendly aids as fourteen points for transforming business effectiveness, seven deadly diseases, and four obstacles to progress. The gist of his message was that manufacturing is a system that can be improved by exquisite attention to detail and made cost-efficient by constant improvements in every phase of production. He originated the famous Japanese team system, in which personnel in research, design, sales, and production worked closely together, often achieving an esprit de corps that banished tensions from the work site. Japanese leaders consider Deming, awarded the emperor's Order of the Sacred Treasure, practically the father of Japan's postwar industrial rebirth.

American advisers threw their considerable weight behind Japan's conservative politicians once the Korean War erupted. Throughout the second half of the twentieth century, the Liberal Democratic Party enjoyed an almost unbroken run of dominance in Japanese politics, though in 1993 there was a temporary pause in the party's hegemony. Bringing the occupation to an end, the Japanese government began its own program of economic reform, what it called rationalization. The goal was to make Japanese producers competitive on the world market, beginning with steel. The most modern integrated steel plant on the globe rose from land reclaimed in Tokyo Bay in 1953. It took raw materials in a continuous series of processes through to the finished products.[11] Soon other Japanese steel firms copied it, demonstrating the perverse advantages of the wartime destruction of Japan's industrial base. Obsolescence was swept away with the rubble. In defeat, its industrialists discovered the virtues of flexibility.

That flexibility did not extend to the government. Japan's continued attachment to the American dollar has extended its dependence upon its World War II conqueror. Collusion among the bureaucracy, leaders of big business, and members of the Liberal Democratic Party have frozen out their opponents from making and implementing policies. The Socialist and Democratic parties have regularly elected members to the lower and upper houses of the Parliament but rarely exercised any real power. The big exception came in the 1970s, when the leftist parties, with a national consensus behind them, pushed the LDP to address the deterioration of the environment that industry had brought about. In this sense, they act as something of a safety valve on an otherwise closed system. This pattern of course is consistent with Japan's prewar institutions. It is also the case that Japanese leaders have been hampered from making policy changes or responding to unfolding events because of the intransigence of a very independent governmental bureaucracy.

While Europe and the United States were enjoying those two decades of strong prosperity between 1953 and 1973, the Japanese record was even more impressive with an annual growth rate of 10 percent, then unique in the history of capitalism, but now matched by China.[12] After the war, Toyota, Nissan, and Honda benefited from the growing domestic market, which the government protected from European and American competition. Under this umbrella Toyota and Nissan built new plants in the early 1960s. They pioneered so-called lean production with the "just-in-time productive system." This program of using one machine to do several tasks was born of wartime necessity, as was the inability to produce a large backup of items. Factory managers did not have the luxury of assigning one machine to turn out, say, left fenders. They also didn't have the space for a long assembly line. Hence they didn't stockpile parts, and they put together their vehicles in tight quarters.

Outsiders after the war analyzed just-in-time processes and declared them superior. They dubbed it lean production to contrast it with America's mass production. More than merely reduce the inventories for parts, lean production emphasizes precision assemblage with defect-free components put together by skilled teams of workers who show little tolerance for any imperfections along the line. An echo of "small is beautiful," lean production uses less space, fewer backups, and an appreciation of the importance of each move, each piece of material going into the vehicle. Parts are ready just in time.[13] General Motors, Ford, and Chrysler have seen their market shares melt like a piece of ice at a July picnic, but they've resisted copying some successful Japanese techniques. Here is another reminder that innovation keeps capitalism moving forward, but entrenched managerial elites can avoid responding to its promise.

Japan secured a very important quid pro quo from the United States. In return for basing troops and aircraft in Japan after the Korean War, the U.S. government promised the Japanese access to the American market. Detroit probably didn't pay much attention to the United States–Japan Mutual Security Treaty signed in 1960, though it would soon enough feel the competition from Japanese automobile exports.[14] During the ratcheting up of oil prices in the 1970s, Japanese automakers moved into the huge American market with their small, snappy fuel-efficient models. Rather than buy into foreign companies to get a share of their markets, both Toyota and Nissan set up their own dealerships and put a lot of money at risk by doing so. Soon they were building their own manufacturing sites in the United States. Almost fifty million new vehicles roll out of auto plants worldwide every year, making it the number one industry.[15] The Japanese were astute marketers of their cars, which helps explain how Toyota was able in 2008 to pass up General Motors after its seventy-seven-year run as the world's largest automaker.

The structure of European economies is corporate with the interests of labor and management worked on together through public and private organizations. That of the United States is more competitive than corporate, and we can characterize the Japanese economy as paternalistic. Its most prominent firms appear like an extended family with joint-stock companies running specific enterprises under the benevolent guidance of its holding company. This arrangement offered protection from hostile takeovers. Paternalism shouldn't be confused with patriarchal, for unlike America's hierarchical decision making, in Japanese companies, ideas percolate up from the bottom. Middle and local managers make many of the operational moves; all focus on cultivating skills and talent from within with eyes on long-term growth.[16]

Rather than members of a cartel for a single industry, Japanese firms belong to holding companies, but the competition among the parts of such a company can be fierce. While in recent years, family ties—both real and metaphorical—have loosened, loyalty to one's own group has retained an importance not found in the West. And like stable families and their friends, Japanese firms develop and keep long-term relationships. Even relations with labor have been marked by mutual trust after some long, bitter strikes. In exchange for firing 25 percent of its work force during a slump in the late 1940s, Toyota worked out a bargain with its unions promising lifetime employment, pay increases for seniority, and bonuses tied to profits.[17] Lifetime employment policies for firms with more than one hundred workers served to stabilize Japanese labor relations, even as it put in place a rigidity that was to hurt farther down the road.

Japan benefited from another event in the United States. The 1958 Supreme Court consent decree in the antitrust case against RCA, IBM, and AT&T forced these companies to give patent licenses to domestic applicants for free and to sell them to foreign firms. This lucrative possibility entranced RCA, which moved quickly to maximize short-term profits from its patent licenses while ignoring the research and design that had made it a leader in television and radio equipment.[18] The race for color TV resembled a NASCAR event. The lead car was RCA flying the colors of its founders, General Electric, Westinghouse, and Telefunken. Way out in the lead for many rounds, it made a fatal mistake. Sony, the hungry upstart in the field, saw its advantage and rushed to the lead. Having invested heavily in design and maintenance, the Sony entrant maintained its lead. RCA's policy of selling its patents sped up the transfer of color TV technology to Japan's leading consumer electronics firms.

RCA finally dropped out of the race altogether, pulling with it every other consumer electronics company in the United States. The race went to the Japanese firms of Sony, Sanyo, and Matsushita, which began buying up failing American companies. Then Sony, just twenty-six years old in 1972, moved to construct its own color TV plant in California, producing 450,000 sets a year. Toshiba, Mitsubishi, and Hitachi followed suit during the rest of the decade. So grateful were the Japanese that when RCA's CEO David Sarnoff visited Tokyo in 1960, the emperor awarded him the Order of the Rising Sun! (Sarnoff, as a young telegraph operator, had had the distinction of receiving the distress message from the sinking *Titanic*.) The size and scope of the Japanese corporate giants made possible these aggressive moves.[19]

The transistor stirred more military than commercial interest in the United States when it made its appearance in 1947, but physicists and engineers working for Sony quickly turned out a very popular commercial product, the transistor radio. Sony specialized in miniaturization. Having very deep pockets, it invested in the research that yielded audiotape recorders, stereo equipment, videocassette recorders, digital videodiscs, video games, and camcorders. In 1996 the Korean firm LG bought the major share of stock in Zenith, the last American firm to make TV sets. It looked like a fitting epitaph to the America's consumer electronics until Apple took away Sony's lead in digital music a decade later with its iPod.

Arrival of the Personal Computer

America maintained the lead with one of the market stars of the 1980s, the personal computer. Before PCs appeared on the scene and stole the show, data processing with computers had spread through manufacturing, retailing, and financial firms. This created a market for peripherals, software, and something called a chip, which is a small crystal of a silicon semiconductor that when put on an integrated circuit can do a lot of electronic tricks. A semiconductor, by the way, is not a part-time railroad employee, but an element like silicon that is halfway between a conductor and an insulator.

As the price of computer components came down, hobbyists around the country began putting together their own small computers. The cover of *Popular Mechanics* of January 1975, featuring one of these amateur efforts, caught the attention of Paul Allen and Bill Gates, ages twenty-two and twenty respectively. They joined the lists of computer tyros. Around the same time, Steven Wozniac and Steven Jobs started their Apple company in a garage when they too were in their twenties. Michael Dell went one better, assembling custom-built IBM compatible computers in his University of Texas dorm room! From these early efforts emerged three commercial PCs, those of Apple, Commodore, and Atari.

Observing these start-up companies, IBM set up a task force to consider the future of minicomputers. PCs were possible because of the great advances with silicon chips. The size of a postage stamp, they could hold millions of transistors. IBM's task force reported back in 1980 that IBM could enter this field quickly if it set up an autonomous unit within the company and designed an open machine that operated more like a system than an appliance. More crucially, it recommended that IBM buy the component parts for its microcomputers from those available on the market rather than create and patent its own.[20] Management gave the green light to the project. IBM chose Intel's micro chips. From Microsoft it ordered a language for its PCs and then an operating system.

These decisions assured the fame and fortune of Intel's Robert Noyce and Gordon Moore and Microsoft's Gates and Allen. Noyce, who came into computers by way of transistor inventor William Shockley, had put together an integrated circuit that could be combined with transistors on a single silicon wafer. Gates and Allen finally settled down near Seattle, where they produced an array of computer languages along with a disk operating system, MS-DOS. IBM's powerful marketing system redounded to the benefit of these two principal suppliers. When IBM further agreed to let Microsoft license its system to others, Intel and Microsoft gained the most lucrative franchises in industrial history. Bill Gates was on his way to becoming the wealthiest man on the planet, for unlike Intel, which counted on venture capital, he and Allen had borrowed for their start-up and plowed earnings back into it.[21] The early competition among PCs had produced a variety of incompatible systems. People wanted compatibility so that they could share files. Gates exploited this potential market with his IBM-compatible MS-DOS system that worked with the same generic hardware components that IBM used. With its closed system, Apple made itself a marginal player.

IBM executed its plan with dispatch. Within two years it was producing a PC every forty-five seconds and still couldn't keep up with demand. PCs flew into people's homes. Writers and teachers moved their sleek IBM Selectric typewriters to the garage or gave them to a charity as they began a journey of amazement and frustration with their new desktop computers. Like television sales in the 1950s, the popularity of PCs astounded everyone. Why would thousands of people, with no real need for a computer and far from conversant with its peculiar ways, plunk down upwards of thirty-five hundred dollars for a crude version of today's personal computers? Businesses soon discovered that they could use PCs at every workstation and construct a network among them. By the mid-1990s PCs accounted for 80 percent of every dollar spent on information technology.[22] "Interfacing" went from a term in dressmaking to one for attaching an electronic device like a memory chip on a computer or a peripheral like a printer. A *Time* magazine cover named the personal computer "Machine of the Year," and typists became word processors.

IBM's success put an end to the British, French, Italian, and German computer companies that had sprung up to contest the American near monopoly in the field. In 1997, more than a third of American homes had at least one PC, with sales mounting each year.[23] That same year IBM was shipping more than three million microcomputers to businesses. The opportunity to build PC clones spawned dozens of start-up companies that took advantage of the absence of patents for PCs. The popularity of desktop computers created a market as well for software designed for specific applications. The computer industry continued to be ferociously competitive, more Darwinian than anything IBM had faced before. By the end of the 1980s there was a tight race among Apple, IBM, Dell, and Compaq for PC customers. IBM's market share had slid from 50 to 22.3 percent by 1999.[24]

Automobile making was not the only major industry the Japanse took on. They moved into computers and consumer electronics like television, VCRs, and DVDs with alarming speed. They made a critical move in the 1970s, when British, French, Italian, and German companies failed to keep up with IBM's mainframes and plug-in compatibles, an ugly term for those items like printers or modems that can be connected to a computer. Japanese companies decided to continue making mainframe computers for its domestic market. Two unpredictable developments rewarded this decision: IBM moved into PCs, and the Internet created a new demand for large systems. In addition, large corporations began creating their own private networking systems, which produced a new demand for the mainframe computers that had been abandoned in the rage of PCs during the 1990s. Japan regained its European market for big systems and stayed current with electronic advances while the Europeans fell back on their excellent software.[25]

Another Technological Advance for PCs

Soon PC users got to connect with one another and then to a cornucopia of knowledge, information, data, and a personal message system. Networks joining people using the same mainframe computer within a company or organization gave several researchers the idea to create the technology for similarly joining individual PCs through telephone or cable lines. The actual origins of the Internet lay with the U.S. Department of Defense, which in 1969 linked together minicomputers in government and university laboratories. From this network, called ARPANET, came other networks, initially involving universities. Slowly ARPANET lost its military starch and became more like the wrinkled academic. What started out under government sponsorship became the twenty-first century's biggest, commercial success story.

The telecommunications network Telnet went into operation in 1969 with a commercial component in 1975. The desire to connect with other computers grew exponentially as people acquired PCs. A little more technological tweaking perfected the Internet.[26] Meanwhile in the late 1980s, Tim Berners-Lee and Robert Cailliau at the European Organization for Nuclear Research in Geneva came up with a system to go beyond connecting computers and arrange for transferring information over the Internet by using hypertext. Their World Wide Web did indeed go worldwide as computer users discovered the wonders of the Web. Commercial possibilities emerged immediately. Soon hundreds of newspapers from many countries were available on the Web. Banks and airlines encouraged their customers to do business through their Web sites. Then actually locating this plethora of informative stuff became a problem. The University of Illinois developed the first graphical Web browser in 1993. Mosaic became more familiar to the public as Netscape. Next, Microsoft's Internet Explorer began eating away at Netscape's market share, followed by Mozilla Firefox, in a seemingly endless race among improving services.

Like the PC, the Web browser's popularity was not predictable, though retrospectively its delivery of online instruction, encyclopedias, and downloaded movies and music make it hard to imagine the world without a telecommunications network and its Girl Friday, the browser. With capitalism's insistent search for new ways to make a profit, the Internet became a vehicle for retail shopping. Free access to the Internet drew viewers, who in turn formed the basis for a booming advertising industry. The moving graphics enticed as the instant information satisfied. In 2005 startup companies began putting lenders and borrowers together through the Internet to make loans without those middlemen called banks. Today Internet access is approaching a billion users just ahead of the six hundred million mobile phones.[27] Alas, the flexibility that so delights consumers also opens up avenues of fraud. Both the music and publishing industries have encountered serious problems protecting their products from illegal sharing through the Internet.

Jeff Bezos started Amazon.com in his Bellevue, Washington, garage in 1994. A pioneer in Internet retailing, he popularized ".com" as part of a firm name. Soon the request from stores and services to their customers to go to "www [fill in the blank].com" became ubiquitous. Branching out from its initial stock of books, Amazon grew rapidly, had a rough patch, but then recovered by opening up its site to other retailers. Today the Web has largely replaced the yellow pages of the telephone book as the place to go for information for everything from pleated lamp shades to Spanish anchovies. With all these retailing novelties, the cost of serving customers has sharply declined, contributing to American prosperity in the closing decade of the twentieth century, when most other economies were slowing. Competition in these ventures has acted as a goad to better performance, but the Internet's vast catch basin of customers has also intensified success, making for superbig winners and lots of failures.

Alongside these developments sneaked in something called e-mail. Begun with messages sent by those using the same computer system, e-mail became accessible to a larger audience through the Internet. E-mail's popularly soared in the 1980s; today more than six hundred million people e-mail, making it the most widely used facility of the Internet. While e-mail has not eliminated telephones, fax machines, and postal services, it has cut into their spheres of influence. The U.S. Postal Service acquired a new nickname, snail mail.

By 1996 a new Internet problem had emerged: how to retrieve easily the mass of information floating freely on the Web. Again two men in their twenties—Stanford grad students Larry Page and Russian-born Sergey Brin—came up with an answer in a new "search engine" that they called Google. Another phenomenal success, Google has been turned into a verb, as in "I googled Google to learn about its history." Winning a protracted competition with Yahoo, another popular search engine, Google saw its market value soar about two hundred billion dollars in 2005. By dint of constant improvising from ongoing research, it has developed an e-mail service with video chat capabilities. Google also bought YouTube, a video source where people can share news clips, entertainment, and amateur humor. Now the largest ad seller in the world, Google continues with seeming effortlessness to improve its proliferating features.[28]

One of Intel's founders, Gordon Moore, announced—with remarkable accuracy—that the number of transistors that could be placed on an integrated circuit would double every two years, greatly expanding computer and phone capabilities. Cell phones became smart phones; functions of PCs squeezed into Palm Pilots and iPods. Though no one predicted it, but equally impressive, the price of computers decreased annually by 20 percent.[29] Yet nothing quite compares with the price history of cell phones. In 1987 a Motorola cell phone was a luxury that cost $3,996; today cell phones are given away for two-year contracts with telecommunications companies.

Although Gates and Allen planted Microsoft near Seattle, William Shockley, who won a Nobel Prize for his work on the transistor, returned to his home in Palo Alto when he decided to begin his own firm, Shockley Semiconductor. Others followed him, collecting outside Palo Alto in what became known as Silicon Valley. Moving from Massachusetts to California proved propitious for start-ups because Massachusetts law favored established companies with strong "noncompete" clauses. Such laws limited the opportunities of former employees to set up businesses of their own with ideas learned on their previous jobs. Nearly invisible, these institutional arrangements can be crucial in nurturing innovation.

In the stylish world of high capitalism on Wall Street, the start-up millionaires in California were startling: youthful, informal, egalitarian in style, and decidedly brainy. Accepting the designation of "geeks," these soft and hardware engineers were anything but cool like the denizens of lower Manhattan. Initial successes enabled dozens of men (and some women) with an ingenious scheme to find backing from venture capitalists. The dot-coms of Silicon Valley flourished until they got their comeuppance. The NASDAQ stock market exchange attracted thousands of new buyers. With investors, large and small, rushing to get in on the action in information technology, initial public offerings became oversold. The hot air from speculation burst the dot-com bubble in the late 1990s, but the avidity of Silicon Valley engineers for finding new applications did not abate. After a decade of shakeouts, Silicon Valley rebooted, as those in the computer world say. It attracted $10 billion worth of venture capital in 2007 compared with $7.2 billion for all of Europe.[30] That same year American inventors filed for eighty thousand patents, a total larger than the rest of the world's combined.

Information technology exploited the American openness to novelty.

Consumers, by responding quickly to the chance to have personal computers, laid the foundation for IT's phenomenal growth. When IBM raced to catch up with the new product, it brought the resources, learning base, and marketing know-how necessary to sustain the young industry. When IBM's major suppliers Intel and Microsoft became billion-dollar companies, they poured much of their profit into advancing technology. At the same time, the PC craze undermined IBM's dominance. Without patented components, it became easy for newcomers to enter the field. The simplicity of PCs freed owners from reliance on IBM's legendary service. American success with computers, peripherals, the Internet, the Web, and e-mail boosted American capitalism, both materially and psychologically. But staying on top is never easy in a market of fierce competitors. After dominating the technological market, America in 2002 began importing more high-tech products than it exported. The trade gap in 2008 was more than fifty billion dollars.[31] Worry about this might be mitigated by awareness that when Apple imports iPods from China, it adds the valuable component to the product the Chinese make.

Unlike European computer companies, Japan's giant firms—Fujitsu, NEC, Toshiba, and Hitachi—were able to weather the American storm of success because of their size and experience in electronic equipment and telecommunications. Supported by the government, Fujitsu, NEC, and Hitachi became the world's largest producers of semiconductors.[32] The resurgence of demand for large computer systems in Europe, occasioned by networking, enabled Japan to compete with IBM in that market. When IBM opened itself up to cloning with its nonproprietary components, Japanese firms entered the PC market in a big way in the late 1980s. By 1996 only IBM, Dell, and Compaq had sold more PCs worldwide than Fujitsu, Toshiba, and NEC. The versatility of PCs had a cascading effect. New applications, peripherals, and improvements abounded. Sony entered the computer market with its CD-ROM (compact disc read-only memory) that transformed computers from data processing equipment to multimedia devices. Much of the sophistication and elegance of Japanese technology in consumer electronics and computers can be attributed to the circulation of ideas permitted by the close proximity of Japan's giant firms concentrated in Toyko and Osaka.[33]

Still, old contenders never seem to surrender. The makers of American semiconductors and PCs carried their competitive spirit back to the Japanese market itself. IBM and Microsoft made a major dent in the home market because they have solved two problems of incompatibility, that of the West's alphabet and the Japanese system of pictograms, or kanji, and the other of the diverse Japanese computers and peripherals that cannot be shared. Conjuring up that old generic magic, the new Japanese-language version of Windows, 31.J, became a great success. It can be run on any of Japan's high-end computers as well as on all PCs.[34] With this, the bouncing ball of technological innovation in computers bounced back to the United States.

Asia's Four Little Tigers

The world market for everything connected to microprocessing gave a boost to four Asian countries, the Four Little Tigers of Singapore, Taiwan, South Korea, and Hong Kong. Their successful trajectory challenged the widespread belief that countries outside the circle of the economic giants would not be able to vault themselves into sustained growth. In the warm glow of sustained prosperity in the 1960s, when the economies of Western Europe rose like phoenixes from the ashes of war, analysts turned modernization into an end stage that all countries would reach given enough investment capital. It was an extremely optimistic prediction, the first to put prosperity into every country's future.[35] When countries in Latin America, Asia, and Africa failed to respond to mere infusions of Western capital and know-how, modernization theory slipped into deserved oblivion.

With the Cold War's divvying up countries among capitalist, Communist, and nonaligned ones, a French demographer introduced the idea of First, Second, and Third Worlds to distinguish the First World of the West and the Second of the Soviet sphere of influence from the rest of the world, the unaligned. The first two categories never really caught on, but "Third World" served a real lexical need. A more sensitive public discourse exchanged the old term "backward" for "underdeveloped." The Third World, according to thinking in the First, was not so much poor as underdeveloped. No longer colonial dependencies, countries outside the West could be induced to modernize on their own, a conviction suggesting that development was just a few steps away.

In the late 1940s and early 1950s, Western advisers suggested to Third World countries, particularly in Latin America, that they could best accumulate the capital necessary for development if they specialized in exporting their raw materials—beef, sugar, or soybeans—and imported manufactured goods from the West because the terms of trade were going to shift in their favor. This never happened because the demand for manufactured goods pushed up prices more than the demand for raw materials. So the core of industrialized nations prospered while the peripheral nations stagnated. Tackling the question of why countries didn't or couldn't modernize, Raul Prebisch, Immanuel Wallerstein, and Andrew Gunder Frank developed dependency theory, which argued that Third World backwardness emanated from decisions made in the First World. Underdevelopment was not a stage but a permanent condition, the deliberate result of policies adopted by the economic winners. Far from being inevitable, modernization was a chimera. By encouraging Third World countries to find their niche in the world economy, the advanced industrial powers were consigning them to a permanent periphery, a state of dependency from which they could never escape unless they pulled out of a game where the cards were stacked against them.[36]

Dependency theorists recommended that the countries in the periphery do an about-face. They should make their raw materials more expensive to outsiders and start to produce for themselves the manufactured goods they had been importing. This import substitution program would thwart the West's exploitation and save precious exchange funds. They also hinted strongly that it was impossible for any undeveloped country to generate enough capital for a takeoff into economic development. Adding a conspiratorial note, some Latin American experts traced the region's problems to exploitation by the United States operating through the CIA and multinational corporations.[37] Further evidence of American malevolence accrued when Milton Friedman's monetary policies boomeranged when applied in Argentina in 2000. The International Monetary Fund became implicated after encouraging the countries to borrow heavily. The idea that peripheral countries could enter the world market on advantageous terms looked almost dead, until nations in East Asia showed how it could be done.

Hong Kong, Singapore, Taiwan, and South Korea proved dependency theory wrong. Their economies managed their own takeoffs into self-sustained growth, doing in thirty years what it had taken Japan a hundred to do. Successful development in Taiwan and South Korea started with land reform, a step strongly backed by the United States, which exercised a powerful influence on the leaders of Korea and Taiwan through its aid programs. Just moving landownership from the hands of a leisured elite to those of the working farmers had many profound and lasting consequences. Crop yields went up, lowering food prices and giving everyone more purchasing power. Tax revenues from the new landowners went into the purchase of fertilizer, equipment, and farmer education programs in a mutually enhancing spiral upward.[38] As in England in the seventeenth century, agricultural improvement required fewer workers, releasing men and women for other occupations, like manufacturing. The more egalitarian distribution of wealth created by land reform made rural radicalism less likely while it undercut opposition to modernizing reforms that entrenched landed elites usually mount. Less tangibly, the relative income equality in Singapore, Taiwan, South Korea, and Hong Kong consolidated the support from a prospering working class. One can only wonder what would have happened to the economies of Argentina and Mexico if they had undertaken similar land reforms.

More important, the Korean War of 1950–1953 had introduced a big spender into the Pacific basin trade universe. The founder of Hyundai, Chung Ju-yung, for instance, found good customers in the American armed forces for his two lines of business, construction and car repair. Born into a poor peasant family in North Korea, Chung had already demonstrated his intrepid character and knack for business during the Japanese occupation. In the years that followed, Hyundai manufactured cars from Japanese components and moved onto the world construction stage, building expressways, ports, nuclear power plants, and shipyards.

At first the United States had supported democracy in these countries as well as Japan, but the invasion of South Korea led American policy makers to take a sharp turn to the right. They tolerated repressive regimes in Singapore, South Korea, and Taiwan in exchange for a firm anti-Communist stance. Still economic benefits followed. In 1960 Singapore became the principal host for the Seventh Fleet of the United States, providing a place of repair, rest, and recreation, rather than a base for its ships. More relevant, the United States never wavered in its support of economic development, sending money and experts to South Korea and Taiwan.[39] The Four Little Tigers all had political cores made up of technocrats and market advocates who were able through pressure or repression to insulate their policy preferences from domestic critics. They also developed alongside hostile Communist neighbors, helping their leaders stifle dissent. Legislatures, where they operated, were kept weak, leaving the field of political action open to strong executives. Still, over time South Korea and Taiwan became more democratic.[40]

In their economic ascent, the Four Little Tigers rejected the policy of import substitution and decided to promote exports instead. "Decided" is the correct word because their political leaders did the thinking and planning. In no case was the domestic market of the NICs big enough to support the economies of size that would make them competitive in world markets. So, after some initial failures, they established free ports and became "superexporters," starting with traditional clothes, textiles, and footwear, then moving to consumer electronics like calculators and color television sets. Korea even manufactured iron and steel items. In the 1960s the United States opened its market to such imports, as did Australia and New Zealand. By 1980 their exports represented more than 50 percent of their GNP, compared with 8 percent for the United States and 16 percent for Japan.[41] This of course took money and workers. Here the population density of the NICs became an asset, as did their people's commitment to acquiring the skills and learning for labor-intensive, complex production processes. All four countries maintained high levels of domestic savings—above 20 percent—so reliance upon foreign aid investment tapered off once they got started.[42] Their particular mix of advantages is not easily duplicated, but the blueprint is pretty clear: export, educate, innovate, and find niches in the world economy.

Because Hong Kong, Taiwan, Singapore, and South Korea succeeded in the same area at the same time—Hong Kong and Taiwan in the 1950s, Singapore and South Korea in the 1960s—their similarities seem more important than their differences. Still, the differences are worth noting. Hong Kong was a British crown colony until 1997, when it was reincorporated into China. Singapore was a poor city when it was expelled from Malaysia in 1965. Commenting on its spectacular success, its founder, Lee Kua Yew, now calls it "a first world oasis in a 3rd world region." The same could be said for Hong Kong. Korea shared the distinction with Vietnam and Germany of being divided between Communist and non-Communist parts, but unlike Germany, it is still so divided. Taiwan too has a perilous existence as a breakaway island province from China, run for a long time by the Chinese Nationalist Party which fled China when the Communists took power in 1949. Singapore, steadfastly authoritarian, has had to integrate the most diverse population, composed of Chinese, Malay, and Indians with a strong representation of Christians, Hindus, and Sikhs. The other three are more homogenous.

Timing, location, and luck played their parts in the phenomenal success of Hong Kong, Singapore, Taiwan, and Korea. Two industrial giants, Japan and the United States, had a positive impact on their growth, which averaged 7 to 9 percent in GNP annually during the 1960s and 1970s. Both "sugar daddies" offered a big market for the NICs' products along with an infusion of investment capital. The Four Tigers caught the wave of explosive growth in consumer electronics and computers in part because Japan was challenging American dominance. The American firm Texas Instruments set up overseas assembly plants for semiconductors in Taiwan. Soon American firms were buying smaller peripherals and components from Taiwan. Taiwan also produced motherboards, monitors, keyboards, scanners, and mice leading to a major production of notebook computers. Hong Kong and South Korea got into these productive lines as well, especially semiconductors in Korea. Singapore too developed a strong manufacturing preference in the American-led PC industry, becoming the source of most American PC disk drives. Korea and Taiwan could shift their exports toward more skill-intensive products, such as consumer electronics, in the 1960s and 1970s because it already had a proficient work force.[43]

They made long-range plans and were lucky enough, despite some turmoil, to enjoy the order and peace that ripened their plans into mature performance. Their governments invested enough in utilities and communications systems to prevent the bottlenecks that have plagued other developing countries where poor transportation has delayed the flow of goods between production and shipping sites. The courts have worked well and fairly, though the draconian laws of Singapore still appall. In a unique mix of government direction and free market dynamics, these countries have confounded many an economic prediction, none more hallowed than the idea that inequality accompanies economic development.[44] They have benefited enormously from fitting themselves into the niches created by each new technological breakthrough. Korea, with a current population of forty-eight million, has a GDP ranking of eleventh in the world. Even their neighbors Malaysia, Thailand, and Indonesia are developing in promising ways.

Economic development transformed women's lives in these traditionally patriarchal societies. A measure of the preference of Asian families for boys can be demonstrated by their skewed sex ratio. Once ultrasound permitted a pregnant woman to learn the sex of her fetus, abortions of females began to climb. The normal ratio of the births of boys to girls is 105:100. In recent years it has reached the high of 120:100 in China, with other Asian countries close behind. Officials in most countries have soundly condemned the practice. In India a doctor or nurse telling a woman the sex of the child she is carrying violates the law that was passed to stem this practice. Yet it is widely violated. Estimates put the number of female fetuses aborted annually in India at ten million.[45] This hardly sounds like a benefit to women, but something is happening today in South Korea that suggests a turnaround as its sex ratio has dropped from 116 to 107.

A new appreciation for girls has emerged in this once deeply traditional society.[46] Good schooling has brought more and more women into jobs in business and the professions. At a practical level, parents no longer depend upon their sons to support them in retirement, for they are retiring with benefits. Their daughters, working outside the home, are no longer near servants to their husbands' families. They earn their own support and maintain the family's emotional ties better than their brothers do.

During the 1970s experts considered everything Japan did as optimal. But even the best of times must come to an end, as the saying goes, or maybe "what goes up must come down" is more apropos. After astounding the world by becoming its second-largest economy, Japan slid into a prolonged recession in the 1990s. The quality of its cars and stereo equipment continued to impress; its lean production put to shame American and European factory management, but these strengths couldn't prevent a downward spiral of prices. Stock market and real estate values dropped, leading to an accumulation of bad debts. To boost the economy, the government finally poured trillions of yen into public spending that pushed up the value of the yen and an unintended but consequent fall in exports. Nature kicked in with a major earthquake.

These problems proved intractable, and they exposed some of the structural weaknesses in the Japanese economy, the most prominent being the cozy relationship between its leadings banks and corporations and the government. This revelation garnered some important support around the world for America's strong antitrust policies. The Japanese had had antimonopoly legislation since 1945, but these laws were weakly enforced. When the economy took a dive in the 1990s, the government put some teeth into their enforcement. Japan broke up its telecommunications monopoly, as the United States had done in 1982.[47]

Although there was a modest recovery in Japan in 1997, prices declined again, and nothing seemed to relieve this deflationary pressure. When Thailand, Indonesia, Korea, and Singapore experienced a financial crisis that year, Japanese firms and households became more anxious, further deflating the economy.

The Asian crisis highlighted the need for more transparency in government programs, less rigid exchange ratios, and stronger, better-regulated financial systems. The International Monetary Fund shored up Japanese markets with large infusions of cash, much of which went to buy food, fuel, and medicine for those most distressed by the unexpected downturn. Other problems, like the absence of bankruptcy in Korea, came to light. As one expert noted, "capitalism without bankruptcy is like Christianity without hell. There is no systematic means of controlling sinful excesses."[48]

Walmart Retailing Wizardry

Microprocessing was by no means the only engine of capitalism in the last decades of the twentieth century, though it was integral to one of the most astounding successes of the century, Walmart. Sam Walton started a chain of discount stores in Arkansas, Missouri, and Oklahoma in 1962. He began an astounding ascent to the position of the world's number one retailer by figuring out how he could buy directly from manufacturers and bypass the wholesalers, who added 4 to 5 percent to prices. Walton turned his Bentonville headquarters in Arkansas into a distribution center that could receive bulk orders from suppliers and send them to particular stores through a fleet of Walmart trucks. Being able to buy big-city items at low prices made a big hit with customers in the small towns where Walton placed the stores in his expanding empire. Reminiscent of Tom Watson, Sr., at IBM, Walton became a bigger than life figure for his employees. His style was simple, direct, and a bit intrusive. Everyone was on a first-name basis; he drove around his vast empire in a pickup truck. He hired young men, often the sons of farmers, and instilled them with a spirit of company loyalty that merged into a shared evangelical piety.

Like Ford and Carnegie, Walton didn't know how to think small. When he wanted to start a new store, he'd fly over the chosen area, mark the spot most easily reached by a cluster of towns, land his plane, and buy up a piece of farm property.[49] And then another and another until some seven thousand Walmart stores sprang up, many outside the United States. Even though Walton was born in 1918, he became the retailing maven of the information technology revolution. First he networked his stores with computer connections. He installed the most advanced inventory control. Whenever a cash register rings up a Walmart sale, a message goes to company purchasing agents, the manager of the store, and the vendor saying that another Hewlett-Packard printer or Disney DVD should be sent to Bentonville.

This just-in-time restocking systems helped both Walmart and its suppliers. It also enabled Walmart executives to analyze what its customers wanted in winter or summer, flush times or lean ones, when celebrating an anniversary or anticipating bad weather. Walmart truck drivers keep in constant radio or satellite contact with headquarters to learn where to pick up items so that they can return from making deliveries with full loads. Expanding size and scope made this system more and more efficient. Computers track the pallets moving endlessly through the vast Walmart loading area. When its managers discovered that bar codes on items could be mutilated or unreadable, they switched to radio frequency identification tags that convey all the necessary inventory information through antennas and radio waves into computers.[50]

Everyone who works for Walmart is kept on a tight electronic leash. Critics say Walmart became the behemoth of world retailing by driving down wages and scaling back benefits for its own employees and those of their suppliers. Its vendors claim that its ruthless bargaining has reduced everyone's profit margin, sometimes to the point of vanishing. Admirers point to the boon of low prices for low-income families. Less entranced observers focus on Walmart's arrogance in insisting that all business with it be done in Bentonville, Arkansas. Sam Walton liked flying around rural America, but he didn't want to do business in Chicago, Los Angeles, or New York. Vendors have to travel to Walmart headquarters, and many keep offices there. A Disney executive wryly noted that when his company, not known as a pushover, had disputes with Walmart, it always lost and had to go to Bentonville to do so.

The Walt Disney Company has been selling its DVDs, toys, interactive games, and apparel in Walmart's seven thousand–plus stores. With Disney parks in Japan, France, and Hong Kong, in addition to the United States, the company has developed a large customer base for the consumer products that Walmart distributes. Of course maintaining a record of high-quality entertainment, especially for children, since 1929, Disney was already doing well. It had long been the largest publisher of children's books and magazines that go into the homes of one hundred million customers in seventy-five countries. Mickey Mouse, who turned eighty in 2008, is the most recognizable icon in the world. More Americans (95 percent) recognize him than they do Santa Claus. Movies made in the 1930s and reissued regularly have introduced Disney characters around the world. When rivals to Spain's president José Luis Rodríguez Zapatero wanted to blast his gentleness, they called him Bambi.

Competitors took notice of Walmart's success and emulated its system. Otherwise three other American discount retailers—Home Depot, Costco, and Target—would not be among the top thirty-five of the Fortune 500 companies. A retailer as extensive as Walmart has greatly enhanced the commercial reach of many American companies like Disney, not to mention introducing a host of foreign goods into American homes. Walmart imports one-third of all consumer durables produced in China.[51] Like a great oak that suppresses all growth around it, Walmart stores have made ghost towns of countless small cities by drawing customers to their exurban locations. Walmart has also steadfastly fought off unionization of its 1.4 million employees, an effort that has provoked a vigorous anti-Walmart campaign. Some of those employees took the company to court for violation of wage and hour laws, winning a fifty-two-million-dollar settlement. A substantial number of other Walmart employees share Sam Walton's linkage of evangelical fundamentalism with free market competition.

The conspicuous difference between America's number one employer at the end of the twentieth century and the automakers forty years earlier is that Walmart has not pushed its employees into the middle class. Instead it has been a cause and an emblem of a seismic shift in the fortunes of American workers. After World War II, powerful labor unions, buoyed by decades of prosperity, successfully bargained for high wages, worker safety, and generous benefits. Jobs in American industry that had been unsafe and unremunerative became the basis for a generous standard of life. People now regret the loss of all those great jobs in the steel mills, but they have put the horse before the cart. They were lousy jobs before their work force was unionized.[52] Over the succeeding decades, a variety of factors battered organized labor: vigorous political opposition from management, a shift of jobs away from industry to the more difficult to organize service sector, failures in union leadership, the intense competition of the world market, and the new technologies that made it easier for producers to move abroad, where there were pools of cheap labor. Most devastating, the American public lost its sympathetic connection to organized labor, no longer viewing a strong labor movement as good for the economy and essential for a vigorous democracy.[53] Once this was gone, an endeavor like

Walmart could switch public attention away from securing good paying jobs to having access to cheap goods.

Had wages not been driven down in recent decades, low prices would not figure so prominently in people's calculation of their interest. Globalization, that combination of marketing and messaging, has played its part in the shift of American labor from a coordinated, stable, securely earning group to an aggregation of individuals perpetually uncertain about the next paycheck. Moving in tandem, information technology and globalization have opened up markets and made them more out of the reach of any government's control. Even profits have been rendered less secure. Dependency upon unseen forces and unexpected shifts in supply and demand have introduced a stratum of worry that undermines the efforts of labor to win back its public voice and bargaining power. In the last decade, union leaders have raised the call for international standards for labor, revisiting the old issues of gaining living wages, safe working environments, and the eight-hour day for a global economy. The rapidity with which cheap labor centers have moved from countries like Mexico to China and then on to Vietnam suggests that this campaign may gather force in the next decade.

Globalization has thrust Western culture into all the communities of the world, evoking a powerful reaction to the intrusive images coming out of American movies and television shows. Criticism often comes from members of the educated elite who seem unable to appreciate that the commercialization of entertainment has delivered a powerful antidote to boredom. With more disposable income, millions around the world are patronizing the products of Hollywood and Bollywood and hundreds of other sites that produce drama and documentaries. Although an important economic force in itself, the American entertainment industry has influenced people's material aspirations in a way that's probably been more significant for economic development than its revenues. An alternative way of life comes in with its CDs, DVDs, videos, TV shows, and movies.

More Personal Choices with Capitalism

Capitalism has encouraged countless new drugs and medical procedures. Perhaps the most revolutionary of all for women has been effective birth control. This means that while busy generating wealth, the market has also increased the number of options in people's lives, setting off what might be called a rebellion of the womb. Birthrates are dropping precipitously, as women in the West and Japan are having fewer children, and many having none at all. This has shocked those who thought that they understood women's natures. In many countries, there are not enough births to replace the existing population. At the same time, in much of the West the sexual freedom of the 1970s has altered attitudes and practices about pregnancy and marriage. Now half the babies born in France and the United States, for instance, are born "out of wedlock." While the plight of the single mother is real, it is also the case that in the past illegitimacy carried the onus of a disgrace and one that fell on women more than upon men.

What capitalism has uncovered is what many people really want. The value systems of the past grew out of scarcity and restraint. Traditions prioritized ways to behave and ennobled values compatible with the scarcity of food and other goods. The international press, which capitalism has promoted, has also carried to the most remote places on the globe the spirit of the Helskini Accord on human rights, if not the actual text. In the first decade of the twenty-first century, an eighteen-year-old woman living among the Stone Age inhabitants of New Guinea fled to Papua to assert her right to choose her husband, and a ten-year-old girl in Yemen found a court where she could seek a divorce in 2008.

Pharmaceutical companies in the United States and Europe came into their own with a cornucopia of new drugs in the 1980s and 1990s. Many of them targeted the aging populations around the globe; new antidepressants also became hugely successful among men and women no longer willing to accept melancholy as a fact of life. In addition to the research done in corporation laboratories, European and American universities have devoted billions to finding new cures for old maladies, in some cases eliminating old diseases altogether. The U.S. National Institutes of Health and the Department of Energy launched in 1990 the Human Genome Project, which became an international effort to identify the genes in human DNA. An astoundingly ambitious effort, the project determined the sequencing of the three billion chemical base pairs that make up human DNA. Slated to take fifteen years, it finished early in 2003, when a private geneticist, Craig Venter, turned the project into a race between competitive sequencing efforts. Still undeveloped, genenomics is pushing genetics in new directions, many with commercial possibilities. This has aroused fears about interfering with natural processes. There is also concern that disinterested science will become a thing of the past with pharmaceutical companies lavishing gifts upon researchers. Of the top twenty pharmaceutical companies, twelve are American, two Swiss, and two German. Britain, Sweden, Japan, and France have one each.

Capitalism had proven its adaptability and its capacity to nurture technology and commercialize its findings. Firms, universities, and whole countries have built impressive learning centers, most of them open to outsiders. Curiosity about how the world works has been sustained; talent has often trumped wealth, as the computer revolution demonstrated. Since World War II, institutions to promote development and cooperation among Western nations have gained in influence, but not without generating discontent. The industrialized nations have often played their strong cards with indifference to the other players in the world market, ignoring calls for eliminating domestic subsidies, for instance. Not exactly a tradeoff but relevant has been the decline of violence—both public and private—since 1975. Even with the war stories that clog our newspapers and nightly news shows, casualties on various battlefields are minuscule compared with the first three-quarters of the twentieth century. Forget the carnage on a single day in a World War I battle, and just compare the forty-seven thousand American battle deaths in five years of fighting in Vietnam with the four thousand plus in six years in Iraq.

And then there is the ambiguous link between capitalism and democracy. The United States has been a vocal booster of both. The connection was actually forged much earlier when the market economy in late-seventeenth-century England revealed that quite ordinary people could take care of themselves and make reasonable decisions about their welfare. Over time these observations replaced earlier assumptions that men and women were woefully fickle creatures, derailed by their emotions and cursed with a tendency toward wickedness. With an improved view of human nature, sober thinkers could entertain the idea that rule of the people—democracy—might be a good form of government. The United States put these ideas into practice after its Revolution. A few years later it ratified a constitutional order that sharply curtailed the will of the majority and guaranteed a panoply of civil rights. The joining of capitalism and democracy in popular thinking caused a Russian woman, looking at her empty cupboard, shortly after the collapse of the USSR in 1991, to announce that there would be no democracy in her country until that cupboard was full. To her, evidently, majority rule meant abundance, presumably because both were found in the United States.

The disintegration of the post–World War II synergy after 1973 introduced a period of fluidity and fluctuations in the fiscal and commercial stability of Japan, the United States, and Europe.[54] Critics look for structural changes that will undermine capitalism as a system. They often underestimate the two enduring strengths of capitalism, encouragement of innovation and a capacity to create new wealth along with the real satisfactions that wealth brings to a growing population of recipients.

The shame in the flourishing of capitalism is the stark inequality between nations and regions of the world. Measures of well-being like life expectancy, family purchasing power, and children's nutrition reveal greater inequalities than fifty years ago.[55] A statistician might point out that this spread is as much a function of the improvement of billions of people as the want of others. It's very much of matter where one directs a spotlight, but when you illuminate America's Rust Belt or Zimbabwe's child mortality rate, capitalism looks like a failure. Cities like New York, Geneva, Seoul, and Tokyo tell a different story.

The race we know goes to the swift, but we should also be wise enough to realize that the analogy between a footrace and life is imperfect. Lots of evidence indicates that competitive international trade brings wrenching social and moral pain. When the creative destruction of competitive enterprise hits, the losers suffer. We have vigorous preservationist movements because we often learn too late that not all improvements improve. The second millennium went out with widespread anxiety that the computers we had come to depend upon might not be able to make the change from the dates 1999 to 2000. It turned out that they could, and so could we. A year later an attack on one of the symbols of capitalism, the World Trade Towers of New York City, made it obvious that we all were moving into an unknown and disturbing future. Still, the arrows don't point in the same direction. New threats, new opportunities, new problems, new solutions, new perplexities, and new possibilities abound.

12

INTO THE TWENTY-

FIRST CENTURY

S EVERAL BILLION PEOPLE sat dazzled before their television sets on August 8, 2008, when a blaze of fireworks lit up the Beijing sky while 2,000 drummers announced the opening of the XXIX Olympiad. What followed was a feast of color, choreography, sound, rhythm, syncopation, and precision movement. It was thrilling to watch China remind the world of its four great inventions: gunpowder, papermaking, movable type printing, and the compass. State-of-the-art entertainment displayed pottery, bronzes, and cliff paintings dissolving into ink-and-wash paintings with black figures moving across a giant scroll. Another 3,000 singers chanted Confucian sayings while 897 more performers, dressed as Chinese characters, formed the words "peace" and "harmony." The Communist Party pulled out all the stops to introduce itself to its twenty-first-century neighbors, rivals, and customers. Zhang Yimou, China's top moviemaker, directed the 15,000 participants in the opening ceremony that cost over one hundred million dollars. The world was impressed. Four months later the Chinese celebrated the thirtieth anniversary of the economic reforms that made this great exhibition of cultural riches possible.

India did not have an occasion to demonstrate with such spectacular showmanship its entrance into the world's leading economies or the same need to flex its material prowess rather than its muscles. Yet India's economic growth merits a big celebration too. The dynamism of China and India has shattered major Western assumptions about economic growth. Governments can, it seems, transform fundamental institutions and promote the individual initiatives critical to a market economy. Just as the success of the Four Little Tigers in creating their own capital independent of the West threw a spanner in dependency theory, so the carefully calibrated introduction of private capital, individual decision making, and market-determined prices in totalitarian China has undermined assumptions about the linkage of democracy and free enterprise. The relentless revolution has now swept up the two largest countries in the world, and they may well change the character of Western capitalism.

The trajectory of China and India has thus far developed in more compelling ways than that of Russia and the countries in the old Eastern bloc that have also deserted command economies. The vigorous multiparty democracy of India was in its sixth decade when the people elected a leader to revive its sluggish economy. The Chinese Communist Party kept a firm hand on the rudder of the ship of state as it sailed into the choppy waters of free enterprise in the 1980s. The United States is the major customer for both countries. Were American consumers not willing to run up large debts, India and China would have developed much more slowly. Building free market economies on a socialist base, both India and China insist that they will not tolerate for long America's large income gap or its lack of universal health care and cheap education. This will be a tall order for them to fulfill considering that they have levels of poverty unknown in the West and that economic development has brought them both a much wider disparity between rich and poor than exists in the United States.

Moving into its second decade, the twenty-first century has already been packed with stunning changes. In the 1980s the center of world trade shifted from the Atlantic to the Pacific Ocean, just as it had moved from the Mediterranean Sea to the Atlantic Ocean in the seventeenth century. With half the world's population accessible through the Pacific and that half endowed with growing purchasing power, the move was sure to come as the two sleeping giants, China and India, made their economic power felt worldwide. In a way they are coming back to a former position. In 1820 China and India together contributed nearly half of the world's income; by 1950 its proportion had dropped to one-tenth. This slide has decisively stopped. Expectations are that by 2025 their share will be one-third in a vastly richer world. Both China and India are societies of ancient lineage with impressive achievements in science, religion, and the arts. As their potential for economic growth has burgeoned in the last two decades, their voices have grown louder in international meetings.

The World Trade Organization and Its Critics

China and India refused to accept the 2008 round of trade negotiations conducted at Doha, capital city of Qatar, under the umbrella of the World Trade Organization. The breakdown in the Doha round looked a lot like Yogi Berra's "déjà vu all over again." The sight of nations jockeying for special privileges to the neglect of shared concerns brought back scenes from the 1920s. The depths of the Great Depression and the horrors of World War II had convinced Western nations to give up protective tariffs and accept restraints imposed by the Bretton Woods agreement. Fast-forward sixty-one years, and the snake of national interests has reappeared in the global Garden of Eden.

A lot has happened since 1947, when twenty-three nations agreed to meet regularly to facilitate multilateral trade agreements and promote international economic development under the General Agreement on Tariffs and Trade, the WTO's predecessor. Probably the most portentous of that "lot" are the waning hegemony of the United States and the waxing power of China and India. The WTO's persistent and intrusive summons to reform has made many countries restive. WTO members outside the advanced capitalist nations are balking at the West's distressing tendency to talk up free trade while protecting interest groups at home. Their leaders resent Congress's doling out billions of dollars to growers of corn, cotton, sugar, soybeans, and wheat to shield them from Third World competition. Some point with incredulity to the fact that the European Union subsidizes every cow grazing in its members' fields by more than nine hundred dollars.[1] Even more censurable were the measures the International Monetary Fund took to force developing countries to accept foreign investment and short-term flows of foreign capital without restriction even though such policies increased the volatility of their already fragile economies.

In the Cancún round of negotiations of 2003, India and China had joined Brazil in turning the tables on the European Union and the United States when they demanded the removal of agricultural subsidies and other barriers to trade. Then, in 2008, India and China broke with Brazil and other developing nations by rejecting the new Doha agreements. China, eager to get its textiles into the United States, had initially favored free trade, but since 2001 a new problem has appeared on the horizon for both India and China. Oil shortages and high food prices have pushed to the fore concerns about nurturing an already pretty destitute group of subsistence farmers. Both countries wanted permission to throw up a wall of protective tariffs should there be a surge of farm exports. For the post–World War II free traders this sounded very much like moving backward. For other developing countries it seemed like a fracturing of their solidarity. Resistance to this request will be strong because most analysts realize that behind the walls of legislative protection flourish inefficiencies and corruption.

India was one of the original nations in the World Trade Organization. Since 1947 another 126 countries have joined the first 27, with an additional couple of dozen negotiating to enter. China did not belong to the WTO until 2001. It wanted to join so badly it agreed to eliminate most of its trade barriers, a deal that forced other countries to follow suit by cutting tariffs on Chinese exports. When China entered this global club, it signed on to allowing foreign banks to enter its economy by 2006, but with lots of conditions. Still simmering is the contentious issue of intellectual property rights. China gets enormous heat for its infringements of them, a sore point with the music industry of the United States and Europe. Just how difficult protecting them can be gleaned from the fact that pirated copies represent 30 percent of all DVD and CD sales in Spain, a WTO member in good standing. Perhaps history can give us some perspective. When Charles Dickens visited America in 1842, he found to his dismay unauthorized copies of his works spilling off the shelves of American bookstores.[2]

Sadly the big losers from the failure to ratify the Doha round were those nations at the bottom of the world trade universe, poor, smaller countries desperate for the Western nations to stop subsidizing the crops that they want to export to them. Proponents of a new agreement had hoped that high food prices might entice protected farm blocs in the West to back off. Even America's Democratic Party, now in power, has embraced the rhetoric of protection. Progress won't come to a halt with the failure of the Doha round. Bilateral trade agreements will replace this multilateral one, and a new round of talks will surely begin. When it does, it will become obvious that it is no longer a joust between the West and the rest, but rather a game with at least three contending groups: the developed West and Japan; the Four Little Tigers, China and India now enjoying enough economic progress to make their own demands heard; and other developing countries like Brazil and Chile threatened by their former friends India and China, whose enormous markets and accelerating exports are changing the playing field once again.

The World Trade Organization is a favorite target for protesters who sometimes ignore the fact that its 153 members and 28 observers (Russia among them) represent almost all the countries on the globe from China to Liechtenstein. Though dismissed as a tool of the United States, the WTO has taken in members like Cuba that the United States opposed. Still, as a trade organization working through a capitalist world, it often conforms to the law of the jungle, where lions get to throw around the most weight. With the lion's share of wealth, experts, and hubris, the movers and shakers of the WTO have tried hard to ignore the demands and needs of those down the food chain. Some criticize the outsized clout in the WTO of the multinational corporations in agribusiness, pharmaceuticals, and financial services.[3] The WTO exercises too much caution, others say, in its enforcement of quarantines designed to protect humans, animals, and plants. Caution seems to abound; many of the WTO's accords for cutting tariffs won't go into effect for another twenty years.

Within the European Union and the United States there are plenty of critics of the World Trade Organization as well. Organized labor resists heartily having to compete with low-wage labor around the world. The race to the bottom by international corporations has prompted a vigorous campaign to include labor standards in future WTO accords. Opponents to this campaign say that the WTO can't take up every good cause supported by Westerners. Considering that labor is central to all production, its concerns hardly seem peripheral. Libertarians resent the active role given to a highly bureaucratized international organization (France alone has 147 people working at the WTO).

As corporations have become international and now multinational in the lexicon of globalization, so supranationalism is replacing internationalism, with more and more agencies, commissions, and international treaties dictating terms of behavior to nations. Activists in the West want international organizations to combat labor exploitation and protect the environment while national leaders and business interests in developing nations tend to view these as sham concerns meant to restrict trade in their goods. The WTO refuses to act against tuna nets that might trap dolphins or to place restrictions on hormone-fed beef, but it has worked to suppress protective tariffs and subsidies.[4] The universal benefit of global access to goods and information may well triumph over protective impulses. All the more so now that the world's countries, including India and China, realize that they are in the same boat whether it sinks or floats.

Dramatic Change for Each Generation in China

Generations, important everywhere, are particularly so in China. When a cohort of men and women comes of age, its members will share the common growing-up experiences. This has become apparent in modern times, when mores, practices, and technology change rapidly enough to separate parents' worlds from those of their children. Historians don't pay a lot of attention to generations because the continuous birth of babies makes it hard to tell when a particular generation arrives on the scene. They tend to treat differences in a thirty-year time period without thinking much about the specific perspective of young adults making their way. In China each new cohort has been marked by a violent eruption beginning in 1949, when Mao Zedong and his Communist forces successfully pushed the Chinese Nationalists across the Strait of Taiwan, then called Formosa. This brought to an end years of civil war that included the disruptions from the Japanese invasion and occupation of Manchuria in the 1930s and early 1940s.

Within seven years, Mao had launched the Great Leap Forward, his program to modernize the Chinese economy. He organized the countryside into communes of roughly five thousand families. Within two years seven hundred million people were living in more than twenty-six thousand communes. Eschewing Stalin's push for a large, heavy industrial sector, Mao wanted to start with small units like his communes. His principal goal was a sound one: to provide incentives to keep farmers in place and to improve their output so they could feed more industrial workers. Mao championed rural manufacturing with large electrification projects to fuel rural factories.[5] As the government slogan went, "Leave the farm, but not the countryside." Most innovative in Mao's grand scheme (and the most mocked) were the backyard furnaces to which people brought their metal cooking utensils and tools to be turned into steel. Through a mix of bad luck, bad weather, and bad planning, the Great Leap Forward ended in disastrous famines, possibly killing as many as twenty million people. This clearly marked the generation coming of age in the mid-1950s.

In quick succession came the Cultural Revolution of 1966, which turned upside down the lives of China's youth. The Communist Party mobilized students as Red Guards to work alongside the People's Liberation Army to root out reactionary elements found among teachers, former officials, and intellectuals generally (possibly their own parents). Youngsters tramped across the country, denouncing people and staging mock trials, which led to thousands of suicides. At the same time, former businessmen were sent to labor reform camps. By mid-1970 Mao had turned on his Red Guards. He renamed them "educated youths" and dispatched them to the countryside to live with peasant families for reeducation. This was a lexical switch that turned millions of young enthusiasts for Mao into pariahs of the state. Many young men and women stayed in the country for five or six years. It's hard to measure the psychological impact of such experiences, but it is certain that very few people living on this planet have ever been so closely watched and capriciously manipulated as the Chinese under Mao.

China's Economic Reformer

Mao died in 1976, leaving a society dispirited, poor, and entangled in layers of party control. He had subjected the economy to politics in two senses, oversight and a push for industrialization to the exclusion of consumption to keep out foreign influence. He also presided over great leaps in life expectancy and literacy, which were going to stand the country in good stead later.[6] Two years after Mao's death, Deng Xiaoping came to power and soon put in place a program to breathe life into the stagnating economy. In 1971, President Richard Nixon had traveled to China after an unusual diplomatic rapprochement conducted across the Ping-Pong table. By 1978 the United States had formally recognized its Cold War enemy. The State Department now maintains that it never wants to see bilateral relations with any nation become so sour that it must appeal to Ping-Pong players to carry an olive branch. Deng also presided over a popular confrontation that affected the generation coming of age in 1989, a standoff between protesting students and Communist Party officials that took place in Beijing's Tiananmen Square.

Thousands of young people had poured into Beijing. Perhaps a million camped in the square, erecting barricades, while another two or three million workers milled around outside, railing at the government. This prodemocracy agitation is known in China as the June Fourth Incident because that day army tanks moved in to clear the square. The best estimate of the deaths from this sweep is seven hundred, but thousands more were arrested, and many of the student organizers imprisoned. The United States granted at least forty thousand residency permits after the crackdown, most of them given to Chinese students already studying here. Since a harsh wave of government repression never materialized, Tiananmen probably taught a different lesson to its young occupiers: The party could be frightened especially by the prospect of its "best and brightest" connecting with the discontented among the working class.

Yet the greatest shaper of the lives of the young in the 1980s was actually not Tiananmen Square but what had been going on in the economy, where the party had improvised an intricate dance. It released enough control on economic decisions to stimulate enterprise while retaining sufficient oversight to assure that its billion and a third people didn't starve or rebel. First let the foot up, next down, and then start over again by releasing a bit more pressure. A step to the side would allow for an examination of the progress. Above all, the party has to keep the patterned dance from breaking into a dangerous free style.

"Miracle" is a religious term, part of Christian dogma. A miracle gives evidence of divine power and grace. The Catholic Church does not canonize anyone who is not considered to have performed a miracle. Secular society has appropriated the word. And surprisingly—considering its provenance—miracle is a favorite way to describe economic success. When the French saw the amazing prosperity across the Channel in the early eighteenth century, they called it the English miracle. The strong resurgence of Western European economies after World War II was called a miracle as were the rapid transitions to capitalism of Japan and then the Four Little Tigers. Now it's China's turn to have a miracle. And it's a spectacular one.

The obstacles in the path of China's rapid economic development covered the gamut. The first cultural one came from getting enough Chinese to accept the prospect that some Chinese would get rich while others stayed pretty much the same. Equality was a bedrock Communist value, a fact of life confirmed in housing arrangements and food allotments. Yet it is stunning how rapidly China has gone from a relatively egalitarian country to one of the world's most unequal ones, more so than Sweden, Japan, Germany, India, Indonesia, Korea, and the United States, but still less than Mexico and other Latin American countries.[7] Another obstacle to economic progress has been the enormous risk ordinary Chinese must run if they move from government posts or running government stores or restaurants to starting enterprises of their own. They forgo a guaranteed wage, however small, described in street parlance as "breaking the iron rice bowl." That hundreds of thousands have done so to their benefit of course encourages others, mainly the young, to follow suit.

By this point in my narrative the story of how another country vaulted itself into the forefront of the world economy may seem a bit predictable. Yet China succeeded against the odds and the experts. Chinese development almost seems like a mystery story. Only instead of a dead body you have data, which admittedly can be a little deadening. Party leaders yielded parts of the economy to market imperatives as they gradually integrated them into international economic institutions. The market slowly took over from the command economy and performed its usual wizardry. Since 1979 the Chinese economy overall has grown 10 percent annually. There are other ways to express this unparalleled economic growth. The GDP of China expanded sevenfold in twenty-five years, and its world purchasing power rose, in the fifteen years between 1989 and 2004, from 5.4 percent to more than 12 percent. It moved from a low-income to a middle-income country like Turkey or Brazil within twenty years, and it did it while keeping tabs on more than a billion men and women.[8]

The party's first move toward the market was to sell off its small and medium-sized state-owned enterprises. It kept the large ones but changed operating principles. Maintaining the benefits of owners' equity, the party turned the running of these large enterprises over to managers who in time were rewarded for their performance. The state-owned outfits in heavy industry largely served military needs. In 1984 the government allowed even some of the quasi-state-owned enterprises to sell excess output at negotiated prices. As these state firms became more autonomous, returns actually went down because they used what we would call profits to raise wages and enhance benefits. These firms were at a distinct disadvantage, for they were saddled with redundant workers and retirement pensions.[9] Nor did they serve the country's much greater need for light industry and service enterprises. Automaking remained a state enterprise or became a joint venture with foreign firms, an arrangement that became popular for hotels as well.

China's Economic Zones

Deng established four special economic zones on the south coast that could trade freely and accept foreign investments. These proved so successful that fourteen other coastal cities soon got the same privileges. Values changed with practices. Before the creation of these zones, the party had considered the prosperous southern province of Guangzhou tainted by Western barbarian businessmen because of its proximity to booming Hong Kong. After the British returned Hong Kong to China in 1997, it became a model of modernization for China.

Opening up on many fronts, the party sent a group of young leaders on tours of Western Europe, the United States, Japan, South Korea, and Singapore. They came back convinced that China should emulate the crash program of Japan's Meiji Restoration a century earlier. The collapse of the Soviet Union enabled Deng to overrule party leaders who still favored central planning. He also possessed the necessary managerial skills for the chairman of a party that ruled such a vast area, for he knew how to delegate authority and mediate differences.[10] He continued Mao's policy of decentralizing decision making, which was aided by the deeply entrenched party officials in rural areas whom Mao had entrusted with much responsibility. Overcoming the opposition of conservatives, reformers performed a bit of lexical sleight of hand, calling their move one toward a "socialist market economy," treating their former central planning as a method needing retooling.

To accommodate its mix of private and state-owned firms, the party introduced a dual-track system of prices and exchange rates that applied at both retail and wholesale levels. Since they diverged quite a bit, people scrambled to buy things at the state rate unless there was a marked difference in quality. The dual track encouraged graft as well. People used their party connections to buy things at the lower state price or to resell industrial material to private enterprises at much higher prices. This form of corruption exposed the party to criticism and hastened the move toward private production. By 1993 a floating system of exchange rates had replaced the special rate for the Bank of China, and the dual track was eliminated. Bribery and graft constituted an intractable obstacle to China's otherwise straightforward progress. Bribery is by no means confined to the East. The great Germany company Siemens paid the largest fine in corporate history, $1.6 billion, in 2008 for illegal payments made around the world over the course of sixty years.[11]

China had begun its reform program in 1978 with a peasant agrarian economy. Rural population was 71 percent, down from 89 percent when the Communist Party came to power, but still disproportionately large. Two very old problems dogged the Chinese economy: not growing enough food yet having more people in the rural areas than jobs for them.[12] Just before Deng's reforms in late 1978, one collective farm secretly leased out its land to individual households and divvied up the obligatory procurement quotas. The success of this clandestine reform demonstrated the gains to be had from privatizing farming, for despite a drought, this collective in Anhui Province increased its output by 30 percent. So the party caved in and gave up on collective farming, at least for the poor and mountainous areas. Then when the government became aware that local officials might strip the assets of the old collectives, it sped up the privatization of farming so that local officials could not sell collective property to their cronies at bargain basement prices. The new system became known as that of household responsibility.

In 1984 China's Township and Village Enterprise brought industry to the rural areas that partially solved the old problem of providing jobs for the surplus population there. Rural industrialization generated more than two-thirds of the thirty million new jobs originating in the countryside. Keeping the people in place saved on infrastructural costs and absorbed cheap off-season farm labor. The program began with the stipulation that after fifteen years the private enterprises would be returned to collective ownership, but this provision was extended to thirty years and probably will be dropped altogether. The number of people living in rural areas didn't begin to decline until 1998. Deng's reforms raised the economic growth rate to 7.4 percent even in the remote western hinterlands, compared with a startling 12.8 percent growth rate along the coast.[13]

Rural households, wishing to avoid discrimination against private enterprise, often registered as having collective ownership. Villagers called this dodge wearing the red cap. The original household registration system tied peasants to the land, but discrimination against private ownership tapered off after 1992. An article in the China Daily in 1994 noted that private firms no longer bothered to feign having a red cap.[14] These local enterprises became more competitive with an expanded market within the country. Their contribution to China's export sector can be gauged by the fact that one municipality turns out some 35 percent of the socks sold throughout the world! China's abundant labor still plays an enormous role in its economic development.[15]

The lagging wages in the countryside have prompted fourteen million Chinese women and men to head off for richer parts, with the number rising as the effects of the 2009 recession spread. This continuing trend presents a serious challenge to social stability, despite there being benefits for both receiving and sending areas. Migrants can double their incomes, even though they make less than regular city dwellers. Like America's undocumented workers, migratory Chinese workers get marginal jobs with long hours, bad conditions, and low pay. While China has managed to avoid the creation of slums around its big cities, migrants must live in dormitories, in shelters, or on work sites. In Shanghai, for instance, the living space for a family in 1999 averaged 17.27 square yards (roughly 15 by 10 feet); migrants, leaving their families behind, have only half that space.[16]

On the thirtieth anniversary of Deng's Open and Reform policy in late 2008, party leaders moved even further away from collective farming with a provision that allowed farmers to sell their thirty-year land use rights to other farmers or to companies. As Chinese annual growth drops from 10 to 8 percent, reviving the rural economy has become paramount. With this reform, the families of some eight hundred million peasants would be able to borrow money on their farm collateral or sell their stake in land and join in the surge of consumption that China's urban population has enjoyed. This would lift domestic sales as exports slackened in the world recession. While some sold farmland might be taken out of cultivation for other uses, plots could also be consolidated for efficiencies of size. With fewer farmers and more investment in agricultural improvements, leaders hope productivity will rise.[17] Chinese peasants are also savers, so the government is hoping that with greater earnings they might start consuming and make up for the deficit in exports.

China is close to the physical size of the United States, but much more mountainous. Its hilly interior remains far poorer than the plains of the coastline. Compared with the American population of two hundred million at the end of the 1970s, the Chinese was almost one billion. Drastic measures had been taken to slow further population growth. In the 1970s came the "later, longer, fewer" campaign, which urged couples to marry later, wait longer between conceptions, and have fewer babies in all. In 1979, Deng introduced the one-child policy. The government plans to continue the one-child limit until 2010 at least. It applies only to the Han Chinese living in the populous coastal area. Still, even with its many exceptions, the Chinese reproduction rate has dropped to 1.7, higher than Western Europe's 1.4 rate, but lower than that 2.1 replacement rate in the United States. The success of the policy can be gauged by the fact that in the 1950s China had 30 percent of the world's population, and it now has 20 percent.[18] One unintended consequence has been a skewed male to female ratio caused by many couples' aborting female fetuses to guarantee that their one child is a boy.

Before the effects of the one-child policy were felt, infant mortality dropped in the 1960s, producing a bulge of work-ready young people. With productive jobs awaiting them, this generation coming of age in the 1980s added to China's prosperity. The longer-range improvement in health and life expectancy has also had a positive impact on economic development. In recent decades, China's dependency rate (the number of children and elderly depending upon workers to pay for their care) has increased. By now two generations have grown up without sisters, brothers, aunts, uncles, and cousins. The number of job seekers entering the labor force is declining as the number of people retiring skyrockets. By 2010, 332 million Chinese men and women will be over fifty. A sobering thought for Americans: The government may have to cash in some of its $1.4 trillion in U.S. Treasury notes that China holds to pay for the retirement of its aging population.[19]

While often divided on how to proceed forward, the Communist leadership has agreed that it is essential to maintain the party's control over the daily lives of the people. Yet moving toward a market economy, even a "socialist market economy," meant encouraging men and women to act on their own. Private initiative and state control exist in an awkward tandem. Reform leaders subscribed to the bird cage economy doctrine, in which the central plan is the cage, and the bird the economy. The moral: Without the cage, the bird will fly away, but the bird has to have the feeling of space, so the cage must be swung to create the illusion of greater space to keep the bird happy.[20] But Westerners might say that the party now has the tiger by the tail. It can't slow down or reverse course because the gains have been too conspicuous and widely shared. A phrase in a *Los Angeles Times* article caught something of the world-turned-upside-down aspect of Chinese development: "former Red Guards-turned-millionaires."[21]

The June Fourth Incident was a wake-up call for the party. It would take strong material progress to hold the demands for more freedom at bay. In 1992 Deng Xiaoping went on a speaking tour in the south of China. Invariably referred to as his "famous trip," it prepared the country for a round of new reforms that would be instituted in subsequent congresses of the China Communist Party. The law and the party looked more favorably upon private property. A 1999 constitutional amendment gave private ownership the same status as state ownership. Trading in company stock was regularized; employers were allowed to fire unneeded workers. This latter advance recalls the clothiers in sixteenth-century England who convinced the Privy Council that it was wiser to let them save their capital for the return of demand than to spend it keeping weavers employed. Capitalists were allowed to become members of the Communist Party. Party membership grew by 10 percent in the five years before 2007, when it hit seventy-four million.

Importing technology and enhancing technological education continue apace, though China's investment in education is half that of Brazil and considerably less than that of India. China sends its brightest young people to foreign universities to learn the best engineering and science firsthand. This has been a policy sword with a double edge. Of the some thirty-five thousand students sent abroad in the late 1990s, only nine thousand came back to China.[22] But the return rate is improving, and in 2006 the United States sent more than 11,000 students to China. It's hard to understand why the Chinese government doesn't spend some of its vast savings developing a system of education commensurate with the third-largest economy in the world.

After fifteen years of letting up on party control in the economy, the Communist Party began in 1994 to rebuild itself by giving party members incentives to participate in economic development. So far the result has been more concentrated power but with a new efficiency in the state-controlled enterprises in energy, steel, transport, communications, electricity, and health. A new coalition of elites is in charge, rewarding itself for successful initiatives all the way down to the local level. Despite the increasing gap between rich and poor, the party has spent a great deal on social services with special attention to the backward areas in western and central China.

China's Mixture of Investment Capital

China's banking system is a mixture of four giant state-owned banks, derivative of the socialist economy; joint-stock commercial banks founded for development purposes in 1994; and city banks. The government owns a majority interest in almost all state banks. Direct foreign investment is large and comprised mainly of long-term commitments. Termed "patient capital," these commitments allowed China to survive the Asian financial crisis of 1997–1998 much better than most countries in the region. The Chinese are great savers, so interest rates have continued to be low. Private and public savings in China have formed America's great piggy bank in its twenty-first century spending spree. Corporations in China still have far to go in creating sound organizations. State banks are plagued with insider favoritism. The security of Chinese investments is going to depend upon putting in place financial accountability, better laws, and transparency. As a step in that direction Chinese bank regulators in 2008, partly in response to the worldwide recession, increased the number of qualifying examinations candidates for positions in finance must take as well as widened the range of employees who must take them.[23]

New laws permit foreigners to invest directly instead of through joint ventures. Unlike most developing nations, China enjoyed the patronage of lots of rich Chinese living outside the country. They were either expats, many of whom had fled to Hong Kong in the 1950s and 1960s, or descendants of emigrants from earlier Chinese diasporas. Now that China has embraced the market, these ethnic Chinese have been eager to invest in the country and found ways to do so formally as well as informally through money clubs and shops. And they have very deep pockets. In the

Philippines ethnic Chinese represent 1 percent of the population and own close to 60 percent of the wealth. In Indonesia their wealth is greater with 1 percent of the population controlling some 70 percent of the country's private economy, including its largest conglomerates. The Burmese economy is even more dominated by ethnic Chinese.[24] Backed by this wealth, foreign capital and foreign companies flooded into China. A new profit tax replaced the system of profit retention.

China has found its best customers in Japan and the United States, but it is now embarking on a program to make its Tibetan cities nexuses of commerce with India. China's premier Wen Jiabao visited India in 2005. His trip served as a catalyst in the process of building overland trade routes between the People's Republic of China and India through Tibet. As with so many developments in China, this one is directed not so much to get the biggest bang from the yuan as to serve social and political needs. The Red Army of the People's Republic of China invaded Tibet in 1951. Eight years later the Dalai Lama fled Tibet and began a global campaign to achieve more autonomy for his former country. China has encouraged its people to move to the region and would like now to accelerate the integration of Tibet into the nation proper, a move vigorously contested by native Tibetans.

Pouring resources into its poor western region serves other social and economic goals. The completion of a new railway from the Tibetan border makes it much easier to access Calcutta, which is 750 miles from the southwestern border of China. At the same time, China has built a blue water navy to patrol the Arabian Sea and Indian Ocean sea-lanes used to carry its oil. Border disputes have kept India and the PRC at arm's length for half a century, but with both countries ready to exploit new economic opportunities, they may well want to bury the hatchet. The threat of declining sales in Europe and the United States makes this policy more attractive. Trader fervor has even extended to the violence-pocked frontier of Kashmir with trucks of apples and walnuts going from India and returning with rice and raisins.[25]

China's exports exploded in the last decade of the twentieth century, those going to the United States alone doubling from $100 billion to $197 billion in the first four years of the twenty-first century. The wrenching contraction of demand for China's exports during the economic down-turn, off by 18 percent in the closing months of 2008, is testing the flex-ibility of its economic policy makers. At the same time, the sophistication of its exports increased with computer peripherals and consumer elec-tronics joining footwear and toys. Exports include auto parts, as befits China's robust automobile manufacturing sector.[26] In 2004 China passed the United States as the world's leading exporter of information and com-munications technology, a strong sign of its success in preparing a skilled labor force. Domestic spending absorbs little more than one-third of Chi-na's annual production, compared with two-thirds in the United States.

Like its people, the government is cautious with its great wealth, stash-ing most of it away in U.S. Treasury notes. This is a boon for the Ameri-can economy, but not necessarily good for the Chinese one. It leaves a great scope for continued economic growth in China if the party can find the means to turn its many savers into spenders. The economic downturn of 2008 makes such a campaign more imperative, but it won't be simple. The Chinese save because they don't have Social Security, so the govern-ment would have to expand pension programs. Manufacturing priorities would have to change. Chinese consumers would want a different range of items from the mini hi-fi systems and high-priced footwear Western-ers cherish. Still, the effort is being made. The government is encouraging its banks to lend more and to lower down payments for house mortgages from the current 20 to 30 percent. Turning the Chinese into mall rats would have an impact on the entire global economy, for presumably there would follow more imports from abroad.

Economic development in China is coming along nicely, but social changes are proceeding more slowly. Chinese men and women must cross the Rubicon of privatization with the party sitting on their shoulders. Or to use a Chinese expression, they are crossing "the river by groping the stones." Because the Communist Party maintains comprehensive con-trol, it influences a range of what would be private, individual decisions elsewhere. A residents' committee is responsible for everything that hap-pens outside people's work units, which have their own party committees monitoring behavior. The residents' committee looks after housing but also arranges weekly political studies, operates day care centers, and dis-

tributes ration coupons.[27] On top of this structure rides the party discipline committee, founded in the early 1980s to prevent and punish party
members' abuses of power. It is staffed by retired party members, as are
various street patrols. This control mixes poorly with the free and easy
communication introduced by information technology. The American
search engines Google and Yahoo have repeatedly had to struggle against
bouts of censorship imposed by the Chinese government, no friend to
free speech.

The interconnectedness of the global economy and the world press that
covers it guarantees that no bad deed will go unpublished, if not unpun-
ished. Press coverage like that of the tainted milk scandal of 2008 could
have been suppressed when Chinese leaders ran an autarkic economy.
Those leaders who succeeded Deng have been willing to accept this tradeoff, recognizing that there is no development without closer and closer
linkage to the world even though the global connectedness means that it
cannot squash studies like the one the World Bank did in 1997, when it
estimated that air pollution costs China 8 percent of its GDP.[28] The world's
news media exhaustively covered the earthquake in May 2008 in Sichuan
Province, where eighty-eight thousand died or were missing, and five million were made homeless. This natural disaster quickly became a political
one when it became apparent that shoddily built schools accounted for an
exaggerated death rate among children.

These contacts will change China's people and their relation to the
world, even if we can't predict exactly how. Foreign reporters now publish
stories on the extent of corruption in China. Estimated to absorb between
3 and 15 percent of China's seven-trillion-dollar economy, corruption
takes many forms from inside trading and crony deals among local officials to shakedowns and counterfeit money in paychecks. The government
punished more than five thousand local officials for corrupt practices in
2008, but party members form the backbone of its governance. Bribery
to ensure a successful operation, entrance into a school, or to get a driver's license is common. With more money sloshing through the society,
opportunities for graft have escalated. Victims can and do post protests on
the Internet, but they risk violent retribution.[29]

As the 2008 Summer Olympics in Beijing demonstrated, China is not only ready to be a world player but willing to spend billions to put on a global show of its talent, discipline, and creativity.[30] Just how far China has come can be measured in little as well as big ways. In 1987, one flight arrived in Beijing every twenty-four hours from Tokyo's Narita Airport, one daily flight between a city with some ten million people and another with twenty-nine million! Think how many flights crisscross the space between Los Angeles and San Francisco or New York City and Philadelphia or Boston. But that was then. Now there are many airlines and dozens of flights. Shanghai, for instance, has a 240 mph train taking passengers to its airport. From Hong Kong ships carrying those boxes that revolutionized cargo shipping leave at the rate of one per second, year round, the equivalent of forty million standard containers. Confronted with worldwide recession in 2009, China slowed down, but the pace before had been hectic.

Shock without Therapy in Eastern Europe

China's reforms, though profound, were gradual, unlike those in Eastern Europe, where as one commentator said of Poland, we underwent "shock without therapy."[31] Simultaneously Russians embarked on perestroika, economic restructuring, and glasnost, creating transparency in the exercise of political power, in the 1980s. The peaceful collapse of the Soviet Union in 1991 came in the midst of this double effort to convert a party-dominated political order into a democracy and a command economy into a market-oriented one. In the early 1990s, exuding a bit of the triumphalism occasioned by "the fall of the Wall," Western experts advised the former Communist nations to enter the market with a big bang. Speaking through the World Bank and the International Monetary Fund, these advisers recommended an immediate freeing of prices from all controls and a selling off of state-owned properties to private parties. They expected that the economies would tank for a short while, then quickly recover. Instead production took a long slide, and prices rose to inflationary rates.

Russia saw its so-called Soviet nomenklatura grab everything of value they could lay their hands on in a hasty privatization of state property. Criminal organizations formed faster than government's capacity to control them. There was too quick a selloff of state properties, too large a gap yawning between the newly rich and the remaining poor, too tense a relationship between civil society with its pesky organizations and the nation's testy authoritarian leaders, not to mention the rivalry with upstart billionaires. It's always difficult to analyze what didn't happen, but the comparison with China and India suggests that Russia lacked leaders knowledgeable about modern economics and a people capable of slipping into the rhythm of working in order to spend. Nor was its legal system up to the task of reining in the Russian mobs and criminals that took advantage of the weakened state of the transition government. Another problem plagues Russia. Unlike the most populous countries of China, India, and the United States, it is losing population at the staggering clip of half a million persons each year. In fifteen years it will drop from the ninth-largest country in the world to fifteenth or sixteenth, close to Turkey in size.[32]

At this point it remains a question whether Russia's development will add an arrow to capitalism's quiver. The resumption of sovereignty among the old Eastern European bloc nations, which are also experiencing population declines, led to similar dual efforts to democratize the political order and dismantle the old command economy simultaneously. Poland, Hungary, and the Czech Republic have done this with a bit more success, though their neighbor Bulgaria was named the most corrupt nation in 2008. Russia enjoys the clout of being an oil-exporting country, a fact that stays the hand of the European Union when faced with Russian intransigence on certain issues. But natural resources work in many places to embarrass development. Their revenues relieve leaders from gaining popular support; their "quick riches" fix encourages the postponement of the more strenuous tasks of building a strong economy.

Britain's Complex Legacy in India

India has developed even more slowly than China, but much more promisingly than the Eastern European economies. Its vibrant political and intellectual life may yet prove more of an asset than China's authoritarian system. For three hundred years before it achieved independence,

India had been a colonial possession of Great Britain, the trailblazer for capitalism—and not just any colony but a uniquely important one given its culture, population, size, textile manufacturing, and strategic location. In the late seventeenth century, the English East India Company began bringing home printed calicoes and striped ginghams from India. These colorful cottons caused an instant sensation with the English, who could now adorn their bodies, their windows, or divans with light and bright fabrics. At the height of the calico craze, the company carried the designs for favorite English patterns like paisleys to Indian weavers to copy. Pretty quickly, English clothiers summoned their political clout and got laws passed to reduce these imports to a trickle. Thus began Britain's deindustrialization of India, whose fabrics had been famous since the time of Heroditus. The East India Company stopped buying finished cloth and instead imported raw materials for English clothiers to work up. Indian cloth manufacturers confined themselves to nearby markets that didn't interest the English.

This story bears heavily on the colonial history of India. Attached to the British economic behemoth, India became the recipient of millions of English pounds sterling in public works, but they were directed to benefiting the empire, not India per se. After 1830, British officials began promoting production over trade. In mid-century they started to build offices and residences for their many officials, along with canals, roads, lighthouses, postal services, telegraph lines, and irrigation projects. Laying railroads across India became crucial to the consolidation of British political and military domination. For the sixty years between 1860 and 1920, British engineers constructed nearly six hundred miles year in and year out. By 1900 India had the fourth-largest railroad system in the world.[33]

Great Britain looked upon this investment as a great civilizing effort for which the Indians should be thankful. As Queen Victoria memorably said when announcing her kingdom's desire to stimulate the peaceful industry of India, "their contentment [will be] our security, their gratitude our best reward." But the wretched poverty of the Indian people and the sight of the fruits of their labor stacked on the decks of home-bound British freighters animated a core of critics and activists. One of them, Dadabhai Naoroji, became the first Indian to win a seat in the British

Parliament, from which he attempted to educate the English about their oppressive regime. The British raj, he said, was bleeding India for "a cannibalistic imperial economy." A gifted mathematician, Naoroji developed statistics to prove his case, estimating that England was taking 200 million pounds sterling from India, where per capita income, measured in rupees, was 20, compared with 450 in Great Britain. The British reaction was to form a commission to study the issue, a classic delaying tactic. In 1885 Naoroji participated in the formation of the Indian National Congress. He also became the mentor of a young admirer named Mahatma Gandhi. At first working within the British system for reforms, the INC later led the anticolonial movement that achieved independence in 1947.[34]

From the perspective of capitalism's history, India's critics are significant for two reasons. They astutely perceived that British officials treated economics as though it were a natural system like physics instead of a social system created by human beings for their purposes. Maintaining that economics is natural is politically useful. It reduces railing against the workings of the economy to cursing the rain clouds. If instead the market were seen as a set of social practices and institutions, patriotic Indian reformers could reasonably agitate for change. Exposing the ideological basis of the convenient fiction that natural laws govern economic relations became essential for the Indians if they were to get outside the mind-set of their British rulers. They needed to understand why India's integration as a producer of raw materials within the global economy led to their impoverishment.

Even more important, the Indian critique of capitalism predisposed Indian leaders, after independence, to pull away as much as possible from the global commerce centered in Western Europe and the United States. Instead they promoted cottage industries, handicrafts, cooperative banks, and credit societies that would ground their economy in the traditions of the rural communities where most Indians lived. Even now corporations with global connections employ only 7 percent of India's workers.[35] In the late 1940s, when the Western world was on the cusp of its greatest period of economic expansion, the leaders of both India and China crafted self-sufficient economies to match their new political autonomy. The Indian one was socialist and democratic; the Chinese, Communist and authoritarian. Perhaps as important, India maintained intellectual contact with the Western world while China became as isolated from Western influences as possible. Most educated Indians continued to speak English; Chinese English speakers got older with every year as the prerevolutionary elite aged.

The fact that in 1820 China and India contributed nearly half of the world's output is a good reminder that they had been prosperous countries earlier. Unlike many emerging markets in the contemporary scene, they had historical roots much deeper than those in the West, giving their people a strong sense of identity as Indians or Chinese. Their cultural traditions were not weathercocks but deep-harbor anchors. They also carried with them a heavy burden from the past. One of the most distinctive features of Indian society is its castes, those inherited statuses that have long defined privileges and prescribed behavior and occupations.

Literally hundreds of castes exist in India, arranged in a hierarchy with the untouchables, who make up 16 percent of the Indian population, at the bottom. The highest caste, the Brahmins, gave its name to an English word for "a highly cultured or intellectual person," as in "the Brahmins of Boston." In 1973, a bus carrying eighty-six persons was trapped in floodwaters southwest of New Delhi. A passerby waded out to the bus with a rope that he had tied to a truck, asking the passengers to haul themselves to safety. But since the passengers belonged to two different castes, they refused to share the same rope, preferring to stay in the bus as it was swept away.[36] A little-recognized feature of capitalism is its impatience with such distinctions. For example, the economic stagnation of the American South after the Civil War persisted in part because of the legal system of segregating African Americans in public places.

The Indian Constitution outlaws caste-based discrimination, and it has largely disappeared in the cities. Yet as late as 2008 the relatives of a girl who received a love letter from a fifteen-year-old boy of a different caste threw the teenager in front of a train after giving him a public humiliation. Oddly enough, lasting traces of caste remain in politics, where castes act as interest groups. In 2008, Uttar Pradesh, the largest state in India, stunned the nation when it elected an untouchable woman as its head. Kumari Mayawati has put together a coalition that has attracted voters from all ranks of the Hindu caste system.[37] A convenient organizing principle, caste-based politics promote patronage practices that undermine merit as a basis for promotion in both politics and economics.

Despite its democratic beginnings, in 1947 newly independent India went through a blood-soaked separation of its Hindu and Muslim populations. Great violence attended the exodus of the Muslim population from India to Pakistan and later to Bangladesh. Nor was the separation complete. India today has the third-largest Muslim population in the world, a frequent source of violent conflict, as the 2008 terrorist attack in Mumbai sadly showed. Because of China's impressive economic development, some experts are jumping to the conclusion that authoritarianism and capitalism can live well together. They say that the firm hand of the Communist Party may have been essential for a stable transition from a command to a market economy, something unnecessary in India, where partisan politics disturb without destabilizing. Others rush to point out the superior environment democracies offer, though India's politics are far from admirable. Of the 522 members of Parliament in 2008, 120 were facing criminal charges.

The powerful Congress Party, which has ruled India since independence, must now put together fragile coalitions to rule at all. Biting the bullet to execute urgently needed reforms gets harder and harder, for Indian legislative sessions are raucous, unruly affairs.[38] A more interesting question perhaps is whether there are elements in capitalism, such as private decision making, easy communication through the market, promotion of innovation, and the indulging of consumer tastes, that create a tide pulling developing countries toward more participatory politics. Both Taiwan and South Korea went from authoritarian politics to democratic ones. Singapore is an excellent test of this proposition since its laws are severe and its economic progress is remarkable.

India's Modernizer

The architect of India's new prosperity is Manmohan Singh, who started steering the Indian economy in a new direction when he became finance minister in 1991. A Sikh, Singh took advantage of an acute financial crisis to dismantle the socialist elements in India's economy. He privatized public companies, invited in foreign investments, and stimulated both imports and exports. Most significant, he got rid of the License Raj, an elaborate system of regulations whose red tape had been choking enterprise for decades. Put in place by Pandit Nehru in 1947, the License Raj instituted the Planning Commission that administered the economy through Soviet-style five-year plans. Singh became prime minister in 2004. Although an intellectual and moderate, he has built a power base in the working class, as distinguished from the jobless impoverished who still predominate in the countryside.

Most Americans became aware of India in the global market when they telephoned their computer companies for technical support and found themselves talking to someone with an English-accented, Indian-lilting voice. In the 1990s American companies seized the opportunity to outsource their customer services to India, where there was a huge, fairly well-educated, English-speaking, low-wage work force. American and British banks are outsourcing clerical work as well. Service out-sourcing, as distinguished from moving factories to cheap-labor sites, started two decades ago, when New York City banks airmailed their daily transactions records to Ireland, where another group of well-educated, English-speaking, low-wage workers processed them for a quick return flight. As American firms send their "back office" work to India, so European companies are turning to Eastern European countries for their number crunching and bookkeeping. In a new development, India's off-shore specialists have begun hiring thousands of Americans to help them compete for higher-end work in technological services. Indians want to move up the white-collar ladder.

The importance of these call centers to India can be gleaned from the predominance of work in the service sector of the economy. While the actual number of farmers has declined steadily to 24 percent of the population, the percentage of those in service work has grown to 50 percent. By comparison, China has become the world's factory with almost 50 percent of its workers in industry. Each country has found its comparative advantage in the world market. And their investment in higher education reflects this difference. Fewer than 1 percent of Chinese men and women have had any college education, compared with 3 percent of Indians, both extremely low numbers for countries that want to be world leaders.[39] Both countries have suffered from a brain drain as some of their most talented young people seek better jobs abroad. India has produced legions of software engineers, many of whom have emigrated to the United States. With prosperity and progress evident back home, some of these people have returned to participate in the great national effort to build economies equal to their country's distinguished histories. And they often bring new skills and fresh capital with them.

Two-thirds of India's 1.1 billion people live in the countryside, though some of them, as in China, work in rural factories. A quarter of this population, some 215 million people, live in degrading poverty despite the enormous changes in Asian agriculture made in the 1970s and 1980s. Looked at a bit differently, 65 percent of Indians live on agriculture, representing less than 18 percent of the GDP. With independence, the rate of Indian population growth accelerated, along with that of much of the Third World. The British had invested little in agricultural improvements in India, even though their own agricultural sector performed marvelously. The disappearance of cholera, smallpox, and malaria in the 1960s extended lives in India before fertility rates began to drop, wiping out any economic gains of the 1950s. To meet this new Malthusian crisis of too many mouths for too few bowls of rice or loaves of bread, Western aid groups embarked on a crash course to avert famines.

Former New Deal Agricultural Secretary Henry Wallace persuaded the Rockefeller and Ford foundations to come to the rescue of hungry people, starting in Latin America. Once on board, the Rockefeller Foundation established the International Center for Maize and Wheat Improvement in Mexico and the International Rice Research Institute in the Philippines. There they drew upon the skill of geneticists to develop new strains of rice, wheat, and maize that would respond to new fertilizers and grow short, stout stalks to hold up heavier heads of grain. Norman Borlaug, like Wallace an Iowa farm boy, who knew a thing or two about raising wheat and corn, won a Nobel Prize for his modified strains of wheat and rice. Starting in 1963, Ford, Rockefeller, and the United States Agency for International Development carried these seeds to the southwestern wheat belt that extends from India's Punjab district through to Turkey. Soon honored as a Green Revolution, these high-yield varieties doubled 1995 cereal production in Asia. Real per capita rural income doubled even though land under cultivation increased by only 4 percent. Diet improved, adding significantly to the extension of life expectancy.[40]

These advances in Third World agriculture were not without cost. Many farmers overused both water and fertilizers, adding to the degradation of the environment. Inequality in rural areas increased because many of the poorest farmers ignored the new seed and techniques for applying fertilizers. Larger harvests from the improvers sent food prices tumbling, so the poorest got poorer, as had happened during the Agricultural Revolution in England three centuries earlier. After a promising start, the advances of the Green Revolution began to stall in the 1990s. The governments quit financing new irrigation projects, failed to lend farmers money, and didn't build the transportation links necessary to get harvests to city markets. It also pulled back on research.

Half the children in India today suffer from malnutrition, despite an economic growth rate moving into double digits. The need for public health and sanitation programs is crucial. Still in the much-touted state of Kerala on the southwestern tip of India, life expectancy and literacy match American rates. As a model Kerala is mixed. The leftist state government invests heavily in health and education—and it shows—but the scarcity of jobs sends almost two million of its young men and women abroad each year. From their adopted homes, these workers in Dubai and surrounding areas send back remittances that account for a quarter of Keraleans' annual income. All remittances from Dubai returned to Pakistan, Uzbekistan, and Bangladesh in addition to India total sixty-five billion dollars a year!

Next to the United States, India has the world's most acres under cultivation. Given its wide variation in soils and climates, India could well be a cornucopia of fruits and vegetables for its people and for the world.[41] Yet much of this land is in semiarid areas, where water shortages hamper the introduction of high-yield seed and improved fertilizers. Others get too much water from seasonal flooding. Both India and China face future water shortages. India has been forced to import rice and grain, putting more pressure on world food prices. These imports stirred the government to raise the prices of the grains it bought from farmers as a way to encourage them to expand production. Even grimmer signs of distress in the countryside have been the hundred thousand desperate farmers who committed suicide in the last two decades. Prime Minister Singh has promised that the government will act to relieve rural misery.

Though it would seem that there are enough acres in India to accommodate both manufacturing and farming, in fact farmers and manufacturers clash bitterly and repeatedly over land usage. India's automaker Tata drew up plans for a plant on the delta plains of the Ganges River, where the soil is so fertile that farmers get two rice crops a year along with growing garden vegetables, all easily transported to New Delhi by a new national highway. Such a location was ideal for Tata, but protesters succeeded in stopping the construction. The conflict highlighted the militancy of India's farmers; it also signaled a fresh and strong move to develop manufacturing. India has differed from its Asian rivals and neighbors by concentrating first on its domestic market rather than going for exports, as had China, Taiwan, and South Korea. Now that is changing.

John Deere, LG Electronics, the Essar Group, Honda, Toyota, Nissan, Motorola, General Motors, and Whirlpool all have built multimillion-dollar plants in India to serve its many consumers as well as the vast export market. The government is predicting annual foreign investments to top thirty billion dollars. India's new consumers have heated up its automobile market, now the fourth largest in Asia. Ford, General Motors, and Japan's big three chalk up big sales each year. More than a third of the buyers are purchasing their first car. More than 90 percent spend less than fifteen thousand dollars for their vehicles, and India's Tata Motors is determined to bring that cost down with a five-passenger vehicle priced at twenty-two hundred dollars! Another Indian automobile company, Reva, offers Indians a two-passenger hatchback that runs on electricity. The environmental and economic concerns of the twenty-first century have enhanced the prospects of Indian automobile makers who have been concentrating on cheap, energy-efficient cars. Reva plans to market its electric automobiles in Europe and has already acquired European Economic Community certification.[42]

India's demographic dynamics make it competitive with China, where the one-child policy is shrinking the size of the next generation of workers. Not until 2030 will India nudge China out of first place in world population. Already its cohort of men and women, ages twenty to twenty-four, entering the job market in 2013, will be 116 million, compared with China's 98 million. Half the Indian population is under twenty-five; 40 percent under eighteen. In 1950, 29 percent of the world population lived in cities; in 2008 the figure was 60 percent, with India in the vanguard. Singh has committed billions to refurbish sixty-three Indian cities. Plans call for luring the poor in from the depressing outskirts of urban areas with decent living. Hyderabad has completed its urban renewal, and Calcutta and Bangalore have entered the blueprint stage. What makes these ambitious programs possible has been the 8.8 percent growth rate India has sustained for several years. Should it persist—a tall order—its one-trillion-dollar economy will double by mid-2016!

A Young Cohort of Indian Consumers

India is pressing close to the United States in having the world's top spenders; domestic consumption is 64 percent of Indian GDP, compared with 70 percent in the United States, 57 percent in Japan, 54 percent in Europe, and 38 percent in China. Retail lending now accounts for one-fourth of all credit extended by banks. Where China is a country of savers, India is one of spenders. In a nice folkloric touch to this contemporary phenomenon, banks hire drummers to serenade debtors who fall behind in their payments. They must be working overtime now, as India's debtors find themselves caught in a credit squeeze. At the same time, Indians save, their rate moving from 28 to 35 percent last year. The conservative policies of Indian banks keep their spending in check. Their wisdom became apparent when the global financial center collapsed in the West in 2008. Comparing themselves with the West, Indian banking leaders stressed their restraint: few home equity loans, no securitized mortgage investments, no subprime mortgages. No Indian banks have failed or received government bailout funds, but even the strong can get pulled down when they've tightly embraced others less prudent.[43]

Maybe moviemaking and consumption go together, for India has achieved world recognition for its films, its industry familiarly called Bollywood. Sports too have been drawn into the capitalism catch basin. None is more popular in India than cricket, whose world headquarters moved from its old Lord's Cricket Ground in London to Mumbai, no doubt the better to serve the multitudinous fans in India, Pakistan, and Sri Lanka. With a cohort of twenty-somethings gaining good incomes, Indians buy clothing, CD/DVD players, color TVs, air conditioners, and kitchen equipment at a fast clip. The new hyperrich are snapping up Chanel perfume, Piaget watches, Louis Vuitton bags, and Rossetti shoes, now available in their own stores.

The popularity of mobile phones has transformed retailing. As ardent spenders Indians want to get the best buy for the rupee and search the Internet for good prices. With such a promising market, the Finnish firm Nokia built a plant in India while the American firm Motorola, turned multinational, built the first global headquarters in India. In 1996 the *Forbes* billionaire list included three Indians; in 2006 there were twenty-three. They typically made their billions in telecommunications, wind energy, and a mix of information technology, synthetics, and textiles, along with oil and gas exploration and refining.

The biggest billionaire of all is Mukesh D. Ambani, whose father's company, Reliance Industries, has a finger in every Indian economic pie. Ambani is more than the wealthiest man in India; he is also a secular prophet and a Bill Gates–like doer. He envisions eliminating India's poverty within fifteen years and has suggested that Reliance build a new, more livable city across the harbor from his native Mumbai. The changing of the name of Bombay to Mumbai was a deliberate gesture to erase a lexical association with Britain. Ambani, whose family came from a merchant caste, exemplifies this spirit. Unlike the Brahmins of old who went to Oxford and adopted English tastes, Ambani prefers to speak his native tongue at home, loves the kind of Indian food that is sold on streetside carts, and relaxes with two or three Bollywood films a week.[44] Offering an entrepreneurial speedup to the sluggish pace of social reform in India, Ambani embodies the spirit of the New India, its back firmly turned against its socialist past.

Mahatma Gandhi and Mao Zedong—Two Men Cast Long Shadows over China and India

Because capitalism impinges so closely upon attitudes, values, habits—the stuff of culture—it is worthwhile comparing China and India in yet one more way. Both countries found their venerable traditions challenged by a charismatic leader in the late 1940s. Perhaps some of their responses to capitalism can be traced back to the impact of those two giants, Mahatma Gandhi and Mao Zedong. Gandhi headed the movement for India independence from Great Britain from 1913 to 1948, when a Hindu extremist assassinated him six months after India had reacquired its autonomy. Educated as a lawyer in London, Gandhi at twenty-four began a twenty-year stint in South Africa, which had a sizable Indian population in 1893. Outraged by the treatment of people of color there, Gandhi found his calling as an advocate for justice, a passion that landed him in prison on several occasions. He came to see civil disobedience and passive resistance as the best means for a suppressed people to build the solidarity and courage to overthrow their oppressors.

Gandhi dreamed of an India not only free of the British but liberated from the ugly clatter and soul-destroying exploitation of industrial societies like the one that the British had imposed. With ascetic habits, Gandhi inspired a powerful mix of love and admiration with a determination to prevail. His successor, Jawaharlal Nehru, succeeded in investing India's modern constitution with guarantees for human rights that reflected Gandhi's ideals. While the constitution recognized caste identities and the distinction between Hindus and Muslims, it corrected many unfair land laws and raised the status of women. Gandhi, who himself built on a long Indian tradition, stressed peaceful means of protest, a stance still lively in his country. He also bred a tolerance for India's diversity reflected in its twenty some political parties competing for authority today.

Mao came to power in China as the victor in a defensive war against Japanese occupiers and a protracted civil struggle with the Chinese Nationalists. The internal conflict began in the late 1920s, when he was in his thirties and lasted until 1949 with the creation of the People's Republic of China. Mao matured as a brilliant and ruthless general whose commitment to Communist principles dictated the course he followed when victorious. He masterminded a violent transformation of a traditional and, in some ways, very sick Chinese society. Once peace arrived, the Communist Party succeeded in eradicating prostitution, the exploitation of children, foot binding for women, and opium dens. Invested with totalitarian power, the party redistributed land and conducted a bloody suppression of "counterrevolutionaries." Mao and his associates also put into place a party structure, answerable to him, built up from the lowliest village through levels of command leading up to Chairman Mao.

While both India and China sought to ameliorate their countries' poverty by withdrawing from the international trade that seemed to have impoverished them, their experiences differed dramatically. India's people began an education in civic participation after independence, guided by Gandhi's self-effacing personal philosophy, whereas the Chinese people, while receiving many benefits from the state in health care and education, became objects of control. If Gandhi was an inspiration, Mao was an organizer. Despite the lingering bitterness from their colonial status, Indian men and women stayed closer to the Western world. They could much more easily become sophisticated consumers than the Chinese, who will need another decade or two to escape the numbing distortions and severe isolation that their totalitarian regime imposes upon them. The Indians, in a rather interesting twist of fate, have benefited from their caste system because the Vaishyas, the merchant caste, have had generations of experience in commercial enterprise. With a government tied in knots by its crosscurrents of influence and a caste deftly cutting a path toward global leadership, it's no wonder the Indians like to say that "our economy grows at night while the government is asleep."[45]

Each country has its liabilities, and India's are grave. While India's labor laws prevent exploitation, the country suffers from pervasive corruption, dangerous roads, frequent protests, violent attacks on religious minorities, abysmal sanitation, and chronic power shortages. Its financial system is stronger than China's state-owned banks, standing it in good stead during the 2008 financial meltdown.[46] The Chinese government can move more swiftly to solve social problems than the clogged democratic system in India, exacerbated by its diversity of religions and ethnicities. China shares many of India's problems: the profound poverty, the pervasive corruption, and the widening gap between rich and poor. Where Gandhi became a hero throughout the Western world, Mao was a global pariah. Working off these legacies will take some time.

A deeper problem to solve confronts the higher-status people of India and China: the ingrained contempt they show for the lowly of their society, especially peasants. An attitude beyond the ken of most Westerners, it runs deeper than mere prejudice, generating so much bitterness that leaders in both countries have addressed it specifically. The liberalization of politics began mitigating similar aristocratic mores in Europe in the eighteenth century. Like religious hostility or formal and informal caste systems, such ways of being in the world run athwart the homogenizing tendencies of capitalism. The open, prosperous societies that everyone in China and India seems to desire will wait in part on the cessation of indignities showered on poor country people.

Before the World Trade Organization's Doha talks collapsed in 2008, both India and China were invited to join a new group of seven industrialized nations, which will include the United States, the twenty-seven nations in the European Union, Brazil, Australia, and Japan. In the lingo of Wall Street investors, the BRICs, the emerging markets of Brazil, Russia, India, and China, are hot. In 2007 India, China, and Brazil produced the most millionaires, proof of their prosperity as well as of the unequal rewards of the capitalist system.[47] The downside of being hot emerged for the emerging markets in 2008, when foreign investors, short on cash, began withdrawing their money to cover their leveraged debts back home. India alone lost eleven billion dollars. They all experienced a double whammy in the shrinkage of demand for the exports that had fueled their economic growth and the contraction of foreign investment funds.[48] At least they are in the same boat as their customers.

Europeans and Americans have not yet fully taken in the meaning of Asia's arrival on the world economic scene. Not only has it moved the center of commercial gravity to the Orient, but more intriguingly, it has demonstrated the chameleon capacity of capitalism to adapt itself to sites far from its homelands. It doesn't seem that the Asian tyros are yet aware of their power either. The lingering orientation of China and India toward the United States is captured by the fact that together they own two trillion dollars in U.S. government securities. Since these yield practically nothing, economist Lawrence Summers has urged Asian leaders to put that money into a regional fund to finance infrastructural projects instead. Such action would be timely, for like their Western predecessors, India and China have polluted their way to economic development. Summers has also pushed the South Asian Free Trade Alliance to study ways that cooperation can enhance the competition that already exists.[49] India and China have made evident their entrance on the world economic stage during the past two decades. Just how the original capitalist nations of the West will adjust to their presence, their power, and their different political approaches adds excitement to thoughts about the future.

13

◆

OF CRISES

AND CRITICS

THE FULL MEANING of globalization in the twenty-first century hit home with the first worldwide recession. Revealing again the intoxicating mix of profit prospects and bad judgment that has precipitated panics in the past, the world's financiers constructed a rickety structure of derivatives and hedge funds based on American real estate mortgages. When housing prices tumbled in 2007, they brought the fancy new securities with them. Venerable firms went bankrupt, money became scarce, and millions of mortgage holders found themselves owing more on their houses than they were worth. Soon the trouble spread to the heart of the capitalist system, the financial center, where a liquidity crisis became one of solvency. Without a new bubble on the horizon to distract people from economic fundamentals, this strong dose of reality led to calls for a return to regulations and international cooperation to contain the damage.

Sometimes a cameo event acts like Tennyson's "flower in the crannied wall" and reveals a truth about a larger phenomenon. After the 2008 sequence of financial meltdowns, panic on the stock market, and a freezing of the flow of credit, an old news story from Cleveland made more sense. The city council in 2002 traced a blip in foreclosures to predatory lending practices, like charging high fees and repayment penalties along with ballooning interest payments. The council passed an ordinance to stop them. Toledo and Dayton followed suit. This jolted Ohio banks into action. They contested the ordinance in court and lobbied the legislature, which obligingly passed a law disallowing such ordinances. The Ohio Supreme Court reversed an earlier favorable ruling and disallowed the ordinances. Subsequently, the U.S. Office of the Comptroller of the Currency stepped in and ruled that not even states could pass legislation directed at national banks.[1] National and state power trumped local prudence. Nor was this an isolated example of legislatures' disproportionate willingness to protect businesses from their monitors.

The history of capitalism doesn't repeat itself, but capitalists do. The fact that rarely does anyone register surprise when a crisis arrives, even though few have done anything to prevent it, points to a quality that capitalism cultivates, an optimism that denies reality. The "spirit" of capitalism is that of the salesman who exudes confidence. When no one is in charge, and most participants are searching for new (and, if possible, easy) ways to make money, panics, crises, and meltdowns become inevitable. People worldwide can be counted on to seek out lucrative deals outside the patrolled precincts of regulation. When the good deals tank, governments rush in to fix what's wrong, with varying results.

Before the world recession of 2008–2009, the market's stumbles had grown ever more frequent and painful, starting with the crash of 1987, followed by the junk bond crisis of the late 1980s, the 1989 sinking of the savings and loan industry, the Japanese depression, the Asian fiscal crisis of 1997, the Long-Term Capital Management near default of 1998, the bursting of the dot-com bubble of 2000, the Enron and WorldCom debacle of 2001, climaxing with the rippling losses from the mortgage-based securities debacle in 2008. Mounting foreclosures, beginning in 2007, put the brakes on the subprime mortgage joyride, but the problems went deeper. China's great savings had made borrowing cheap. American consumers apparently decided to let the Chinese do the saving while they spent in a grand style. At the same time, low interest rates drove the managers of capital to seek new ways to get more for their money, even if they had to invent fancy stratagems to do so.

The trauma began with the failure of Lehman Brothers, an event that did not stir the U.S. government to act. The incredibly tight "sink-or-swim together" union of world financial institutions became apparent. So much so that the government quickly moved to save in succession Bear Stearns, its sponsored residential mortgage companies Fannie Mae and Freddie Mac, and the insurance company American International Group, while negotiating a fire sale of Merrill Lynch to the Bank of America. World-wide, governments acted quickly, if somewhat erratically, raising the hope that the lessons from the Great Depression of the 1930s and Japan's "lost decade" of deflation in the 1990s had left a residue of wisdom. The downside of a twenty-year run of high returns on capital unmistakably manifested itself, starting in New York and spreading to the major financial centers of London, Frankfurt, Hong Kong, and Tokyo. An autonomous nation, Iceland, verged on bankruptcy, leaving institutions that had invested in high-interest-yielding Icelandic bonds the poorer.

Bankers, whose caution in the nineteenth-century world of J. P. Morgan had mediated market development, became as risk happy as promoters of the latest Silicon Valley start-up. Enticed by the possibility of greatly increasing earnings, bankers began competing with one another on the basis of service fees. Unlike their predecessors who financed railroad construction in the nineteenth century, they invested in the securities they created for their customers, throwing caution to the wind in order to make loans with fewer assets as ballast. Corporations replaced partnerships, allowing executives to take more risks without assuming personal responsibility. In all this they were greatly aided by the repeal in 1999 of the Glass-Steagall Act of 1933, which separated commercial from investment banks and prohibited commercial banks from owning corporate stock. The go-go spirit of the 1990s also kicked in.[2]

The 2008 financial crisis had two underlying causes roiled by a wild card. The first predisposing cause was set in place in the late 1970s, when a recession stirred interest in eliminating the regulations that formed a legacy of the Great Depression of the 1930s. Writers began depicting capitalist enterprise as a Gulliver tied down by a thousand Lilliputian strings from environmentalists, safety monitors, and the like. Business people argued that an economy became robust when its participants had the freedom to act freely and quickly. This era of deregulation, associated with English Prime Minister Margaret Thatcher and President Ronald Reagan, was completed in the United States in 1999 with the Gramm-Leach-Bliley Financial Service Modernization Act, signed into law by President Bill Clinton.

A boon to banks, brokerage firms, insurance companies, and highfliers generally, the law permitted banks to merge with insurance companies and liberated investment banks from many of the restrictions that applied to regular commercial banks of deposits. The statute gave bank customers privacy protection. Far more important, it freed from oversight such esoteric investments as the multitrillion-dollar market for credit default swaps, a tricky instrument that investors used to hedge their bets on various securities. Perversely, these were developed to minimize and manage risk, when in fact they encouraged speculators to game the system.

Credit default swaps were a form of insurance that people took out to balance a possible downside to their investments. But others could also contract for a CDS if they thought a certain enterprise would fail, even without having an investment. It would be very much like taking out an insurance policy on a neighbor's house because his negligent smoking habits indicated that sooner or later the house would burn down. As an insurance company, AIG witnessed a rush of contracts from investors who wanted to insure their investments in securitized mortgages. With sophisticated computer models designed to estimate risk, this conservative firm plunged into the turbulent waters of collateralized debt obligations on its way to almost drowning. In a 2004 coda, the Securities and Exchange Commission unanimously voted to exempt America's biggest investment banks—those with assets greater than five billion dollars—from a regulation that limited the amount of debt they could take on.[3] The rest, as they say, is history.

While legislatures were busy deconstructing the regulatory system, an unusual amount of money was sloshing through global markets. Financial assets had been growing faster than real economic activity. High rates of saving among people in Asia's developing nations, combined with governmental efforts to stimulate their economies, had considerably reduced interest rates.⁴ Unhappy with rates in the 2 to 3 percent range, the mavens of finance began thinking up ways to increase that return. A boom in housing in the United States gave them the opportunity they were looking for. They contrived a dicey array of new financial investments. Bank mortgages were divided up and turned into derivative securities, a term that refers to assets with value derived from other assets. Soon these securitized mortgages passed from commercial to investment banks, which were not regulated, as were commercial banks. Investment banks repackaged and sold the securitized mortgages to investors or other banks. Lots of other individuals and institutions, looking for places to park their money, bought them too. Once commercial banks had sold their mortgages, they were free to write new ones in what became a jolly round of growth for those in the know. The actual mortgage payments from homeowners sustained the value of the securities. Alas, bankers underestimated the risks, which grew exponentially as the number and dubiousness of the mortgages increased. Even worse, foreclosure proceedings in 2009 uncovered widespread negligence in record keeping when some foreclosers could not provide proof of holding the mortgage.

For those playing the real estate market, mortgages offered a great scope for leveraging. If one bought a million-dollar house with a down payment of $100,000 and turned around and sold it for $1.1 million in a rising real estate market, he or she could recover the down payment plus another $100,000, doubling the initial investment. Leveraging is possible when you gain title to some object with a partial payment of it. To be successful, there must be an appreciation of value. Real estate prices in the United States enjoyed such a rise, nearly doubling between 2000 and 2006. Aptly called casino capitalism by Ralph Nader, mortgages showed the way toward securitizing any form of credit from automobile payments to credit cards.

Wanting to keep the good times going, financial institutions began issuing mortgages to people with risky credit records or insufficient income to make their payments. Banks and savings and loan companies lured customers with low down or no down payment offers. A whole new market for leveraging was tapped. The Federal Reserve Bank's downward pressure on interest rates also made home mortgages more appealing. Both Democratic and Republican administrations promoted homeownership as sound public policy. These additional buyers drove house prices up even higher. As more and more people with subprime credit records took out subprime mortgages, the risk grew exponentially. During the heyday of the housing market, many homeowners used the rising value of their property as a bank. Sharing in the financial sector's optimism, they took out home equity loans on the enhanced value of their houses. With these, they could pay for a child's college tuition, start a business, buy an SUV, or landscape the new home.

The unintended consequences of perfectly rational, individual decisions can help explain how the world's financial centers skidded into a trough in 2008. When Asian families decided to build nest eggs after their 1997 financial crisis, they didn't intend to stimulate American consumption with the cheap credit their savings created. When Republican and Democratic administrations endorsed homeownership as sound social policy, they didn't intend to set off a race among bankers to issue subprime mortgages so they could securitize them for eager investors. When CEOs at investment banks and hedge funds paid their star traders handsome year-end bonuses, they intended to reward and encourage superior performance. Totally unintended was the creation of a testosterone-driven competition so intense it kept at bay second thoughts, looking at the larger picture, or listening to naysayers. The notion of unintended consequences doesn't lend itself to the mathematical models favored by economists, but the freer the market system, the more widespread are individual initiatives that pull along in their train the unintended consequences of their actions. And when they converge, as they did in 2008, they can create unexpected consequences.

Risk taking is integral to capitalism, but it plays differently in the financial sector than it does in technology. Banks, like utilities, contribute most when they are dependable and efficient. Instead bankers became as ingratiating as used car salesmen. The cold shoulder they used to give to incautious borrowers turned into a warm welcome for all comers. Of course, if they never lent to risk-taking entrepreneurs, capitalism would suffer. Balancing stability with innovation eluded banks in the first decade of the twenty-first century. Investment banks even started buying the asset-based securities that they were selling to others, with disastrous results. Some say strategies of risk taking changed for bankers when their institutions went public, allowing them to bet on other people's money instead of their own. Year-end bonuses on performance furnished a further incentive to expand operations and became a major bone of contention in the public realm after the financial institutions came begging for government help to stay afloat. Those who didn't work on Wall Street considered bonuses running in the millions obscene. Nor were they impressed with the financial wizards' logic that they should profit handsomely from what they were able to sell for their company—or "eat what they killed," in insider lingo. They remained mute about what should be done when the kill roared back into life and brought their firms near bankruptcy.

We might dub this the world of virtual investment whose material reality was a stream of electronic messages issuing from some sixty thousand terminals around the world. Technological advances made possible the increasing volume of financial transactions. There was also some double duping, when mortgage salesmen encouraged people to assume mortgages they couldn't afford and financial firms talked pension fund managers and municipalities into buying their asset-backed securities without sharing information about the risk.

During the last ten years, financial services grew from 11 percent of our gross national product to 20 percent. Some otherwise sober men and women were able to leverage at a ratio of 1:30 for money invested, spreading risk without tracking it. The really daring investor would nest several forms of leveraging into a single investment vehicle. More damaging to the nation in the long run, physicists, mathematicians, and computer experts were drawn away from their original work to join the high-earning financial wizards. At least 40 percent of Ivy League graduates went into finance in the early years of the twenty-first century. With million-dollar annual incomes commonplace, Wall Street formed a tight little winners' circle where all the incentives were thrown on the take-more-risk side and positive disincentives discouraged caution or even candor.

Those working for the Securities and Exchange Commission feared offending the leaders of the major firms they hoped would hire them later.

Credit-rating agencies like Standard & Poor's and Moody's were similarly disinclined to lower the ratings of bank customers that took on too much risk. In retrospect, people who were making decisions affecting the economies of dozens of countries were sealed into a cozy club of high-fiving camaraderie where there was no tomorrow.[5]

The wild card in this scenario was psychological and endemic: the feeling of confidence that encouraged people—in this case institutional investors and hedge fund managers—to purchase the new asset-backed securities. In retrospect, their misperception of the risk seems bizarre. Pretty mindless during an upswing, optimism is contagious. Working the other way around, rumors and foolish public statements can cause a precipitous fall in confidence just about as easily as reports of disappointing earnings or turbulence in foreign markets. Whether upbeat or downbeat, these responses from traders and investors introduced a degree of risk that impinged on the whole global economy because of the easy access the world's investors had to these "good deals." One could add that the United States benefits from this selective blindness because of the world's indifference to the country's annual seven-hundred-billion-dollar trade deficit.

A Nobel Prize–winning chemist named Frederick Soddy had some ingenious observations to make about debt when he turned from chemistry to economics during the great bubble of the 1920s. People buy debt (i.e., lend money) because they want to realize more wealth in the future. The rub is that no one knows what will happen in the future. If I lend a farmer $100 in the expectation of getting back $110 when the harvest comes in, I am banking on good weather and no visit from locusts. If there are in fact more claims upon future wealth than can be redeemed, then some of those with claims on future earnings are going to lose out. The market in futures not only is volatile but must always cope with this uncertainty.[6] And in the case of the securitized mortgages, the number of claimants grew exponentially.

The American Dialect Society voted "subprime" the word of 2007.[7] During the euphoria over rising housing prices, the lexicon of global finance migrated out of Wall Street into daily newspapers, where you could find references to option adjustable interest rate mortgages, collateralized debt obligations, interest rate swaps, swaptions, and special purpose vehicles!

Hedge funds grew fivefold in the first decade of the twenty-first century, attracting managers of pension money, university endowments, and municipal investments, all now suffering with the retraction. Those people who ran hedge funds, established derivatives, and created option adjustable rate mortgages had built a house of cards with mortgage paper. Their initial success with rising house prices bred the "irrational exuberance" noted in an earlier bubble by the former Federal Reserve Bank president Alan Greenspan, himself a somewhat repentant opponent of regulation. Ignoring their conflicts of interest, credit rating agencies gave artificially high ratings to mortgage securities. Thus even those created to assess risk failed the system.

When house prices started to fall in late 2007, the securities they backed fell too. Like a boa constrictor, deleveraging—i.e., paying for securities bought on the margin—squeezed all along the financial line from bankers to insurers, hedge fund investors, and their institutional and private customers. Liquidity dried up; money became tight. Even legitimate business borrowers couldn't get loans. So bad were things that Goldman Sachs and Morgan Stanley sailed into the safe harbor of greater regulation and scrutiny by becoming commercial banks and leaving the shark-infested waters of investment banking. Of course they also gained access to government aid and lending sources.

Financiers who wanted a free hand are not alone responsible for the 2008 crisis. It also took public officials, from city councillors to members of Congress, mayors to presidents, to dismantle the regulatory system that had monitored financial firms. The U.S. government went from being a more or less neutral umpire of economic relations to an advocate of business interests. Changes in political campaigning promoted the collusion between economic and political leaders. With the emergence of television as the principal medium for election campaigns forty years ago, money—never negligible—took on a new importance. The expense of TV spots threw officeholders and their challengers into the arms of business interests. As slick Willie Sutton once explained, he robbed banks because that's where the money was. And that's why candidates of both parties went to the wealthy to seek contributions.

A toxic combination of greed and need—greed on the part of the high-flying engineers of finance and need from politicians to pay for their ever more expensive campaigns—made officeholders beholden to business executives who wanted government off their backs. The free market ideology dominating public discussions gave cover to those in government. Even so, after the passage of the Gramm-Leach-Bliley Act, some legislators still tried to limit the trade in derivatives. They accurately predicted the cascading effect of any downturn. Representatives proposed measures to combat predatory lending, like those the Ohio cities had passed, but the leave-enterprise-alone advocates blocked their efforts. When regulation has been discredited as it was in the 1980s, even those regulatory agencies left intact become faint of heart and inattentive.

Complacent administrative officials and legislators defended the relaxing of regulation on the ground that American bankers would have taken their money out of the country and built their securitized mortgage empires elsewhere. Competition, the elixir of capitalism, worked inexorably to promote risk taking. When more cautious bankers saw their rivals riding high, they wanted to do the same thing. Raining on a parade has never won popularity. Shorn of oversight, the banks' trade in credit default swaps ballooned from $900 billion in 2001 to $62 trillion in 2007.[8] Hedge funds grew in one decade from $375,000 to $2 trillion in 2008, plunging losses into the trillion-dollar column. The figures are hard to grasp, but not the dimension of the problem. Nor should consumers be let off the hook, if blame is to be assigned, for many Americans demanded easy credit and cheap mortgages.

As befits a litigious people, homeowners began sueing their banks, mortgage lenders, Wall Street banks, little banks, big banks, and those same banks' loan specialists. Even municipal governments got sucked into buying high-yielding shares of securities backed by mortgages, subprime and prime. Some as far away as Australia took investment banks to court for hiding the risks of the securities that they were selling. Such a respectable firm as General Electric, expanding into financial services, got hit with a suit from an insurance company for following fraudulent standards. Recent Supreme Court rulings have favored Wall Street, but that won't stop the march of people into lawyers' offices to seek retribution, if not full compensation.[9]

Housing prices did not need to decline very much before many home-owners owed more on their mortgages than their houses were worth. By 2009 more than one-quarter of all homes with mortgages—about thirteen million properties—were "underwater"; foreclosures averaged five thousand a day! Investors lost upward of four hundred billion dollars. Mindful that the Japanese government had not acted swiftly enough to stem the losses in its 1990 depression, the U.S. government struggled to get a handle on the recovery process and to speed the return of confidence. The Federal Reserve Bank and the Treasury Department at first offered seven hundred billion dollars for "troubled assets." "Bailout," with its strong suggestion of a sinking boat, lost favor as a term. Soon people were talking about stimulus, followed by promises of recovery. The new administration of President Barack Obama put in place the largest public works program since the Great Depression. All official efforts aimed at convincing ordinary market participants that the worst was over, or, as Franklin Roosevelt's 1932 campaign song had it, "Happy Days Are Here Again."

Meanwhile the long-brewing decline of the American automobile industry led to calls for infusions of taxpayers' funds. General Motors and Chrysler had run out of money, and Ford was barely limping along. The carmakers' intractable problems challenge one of economists' strongest convictions: that we can rely on the rationality of market participants. Enlightened self-interest should have whispered into the ears of Detroit leaders back in the 1970s that something was amiss when Hondas, Nissans, and Toyotas made their American debuts. Of course most people in Michigan "buy American," so they didn't see those natty new cars on the freeways of California and New York. Being large enough to control a whole region, the automakers' CEOs could indulge themselves in pipe dreams, responding to short-run tastes for gas-guzzling SUVs while exporting their innovative designs to showrooms abroad. In 1989 Michael Moore's popular film *Roger and Me*, mocked the studied myopia of GM's CEO Roger Smith after the layoff of fifty thousand auto workers in Moore's hometown of Flint. And there must have been regular reports on their dwindling market share. Such willful ignorance can't last forever. When all the sick chickens finally came home to roost in 2009, when both General Motors and Chrysler went into bankruptcy.

Among the woes of the heads of General Motors, Ford, and Chrysler, which employ 75 percent of the nation's some three hundred thousand auto workers, are their escalating payroll costs. When they went to testify before Congress in 2008, the head of the United Auto Workers of America went with them. This troubling entanglement of caring for present and retired workers is ironic because their predecessors had opposed national legislation for health insurance. Proposed in the 1940s, a bill would have funded the universal care through the Social Security Administration. Fearing that such a provision would undermine workers' loyalty, Detroit's leaders worked against the measure, pushing unions to fight successfully for their members' benefits at the bargaining table.[10] The fact that workers in American plants making Hondas and Toyotas didn't earn the equally high wages and benefits of Detroit's workers rankled with members of Congress and their constituencies. In an earlier time, the public might have wondered why those other workers weren't doing better. Three decades of slow wage growth and the success of low-wage employers like Walmart had effected a marvelous change in perceptions.

To counter these attitudes, labor leaders have awakened to the need to rebuild the solidarity that once existed between the public and organized labor. With the goal of representing a third of the American work force, as it did in its heyday in 1950, the AFL-CIO began a campaign explaining how a strong labor movement energizes democracy and keeps alive a moral commitment to living wages and decent working conditions worldwide. The facts on the ground back it up: Between 1978 and 2008 CEO salaries went from levels 35 times those of an average worker to 275 times. Nor have corporate heads been generous to their workers, as Henry Ford once was. Although the rate of American productivity has risen since 2003, wages have not, and benefits have declined in value.

Organized labor backs the Employee Free Choice Act, which Republicans blocked with a filibuster in the Senate in 2007. EFCA would protect workers' right to organize their plant once a majority of them had signed cards expressing their intent to form a union. Statistics indicate that one-quarter of all employers have illegally fired at least one person for union organizing, so unions consider EFCA essential to organizing new plants. Reports of flat wages coupled with escalating incomes in the top tenth of the top 1 percent of American earners have brought much of the public back to the union side. The disgrace into which laissez-faire economic theory fell during the fancy-free years that opened the twenty-first century bodes well for organized labor too, but it will have to contend with the countervailing force of shuttered shops and the monolithic opposition of American business.[11]

Missing warning signs of disaster apparently is a human trait found in capitalist and noncapitalist countries alike. In his study *Collapse*, Jared Diamond showed that failed societies invariably clung to their value systems long after they were dysfunctional.[12] The insistence that the market has its own self-correcting mechanism may be a fresh example of an old human failing. It certainly sounds now like whistling through the graveyard. Does each generation have to learn its own lessons? It would seem so. The post–World War II fiscal arrangements ushered in a quarter century of widespread prosperity in the capitalist homelands. Maybe it can be done again. The French president and the prime minister of Great Britain have called for a Bretton Woods agreement for the twenty-first century to rebuild the financial foundations of the world economy. For them evidently the accords hammered out in New Hampshire in 1944 represent a symbol of a shared appreciation of the clout of cooperation.

Although the center of the subprime mortgage debacle was in the United States, the meltdown of credit credibility spilled over the entire globe. The trouble brewing in lower Manhattan quickly reached cities and towns across the nation, not to mention foreign investors who took a ride with America's financial Evel Knievels. Even America's cockiest center of enterprise, Silicon Valley, felt the cascading effect of the credit crunch as orders dropped off, no small matter considering that computer and software sales account for half the capital spending of businesses in the United States. Normally awash in venture capital, the technology sector saw that dry up some as well.

When people who had borrowed against the rising value of their houses in the frenetic days of the real estate boom stopped spending, it hurt big and little exporters who counted on the dependable American consumer. Latin American leaders, often critical of the Goliath to the north, engaged in a bit of schadenfreude until they saw the looming danger in their own countries from collapse of the housing market in the United States. Like a booby trap with a trip wire that catches a walker unawares, this financial blowout caught everyone. Only India, saved by its conservative banking traditions, escaped relatively unscathed. The unexpected fragility of these securities—an oxymoronic term—that American banks were pushing worldwide left leaders of many emerging economies angry at the perpetrators of the debacle.

Globalization got another notch in its belt with the first worldwide Ponzi scheme, one that came a cropper at the end of 2008. Named after Charles Ponzi, the notorious swindler of the Roaring Twenties, such flimflams rely on enticing ever more people to invest in order to pay off those who have already bought into the fake firm. Buoyed by strong earnings, the shareholders then become informal salesmen of their remunerative investment. Bernard Madoff, a respected Wall Street financier, acknowledged that he had bilked fifty billion dollars from his clients, selling shares in one of his firms across a large swath of the world, including the United States, Canada, Europe, Middle Eastern countries, and China, before he ran out of new prospects.[13] So indifferent to its charge was the Securities and Exchange Commission that despite an insistent expert who told it repeatedly that the emperor Madoff had no clothes, it refused to investigate.

The dominance of the financial services industry in the last fifteen years is a classic case of the tail wagging the dog. Financial institutions developed initially to facilitate enterprise, but at the end of the twentieth century they became venture capitalists themselves. Stock markets, begun more than two hundred years ago, have acted as mediators between the public and publicly traded companies. Once the preserve of the wealthy, the stock market now serves thousands of institutions and millions of small investors. Banks too funneled funds into the production of goods and services. Power accrued to them. In the twenty-first century, financiers increasingly intruded into the affairs of the companies whose stock they traded and whose loans they negotiated. This shift of authority from company managers to debt holders had a profound impact on corporate decisions because of an emphasis on immediate gains. Shareholders have benefited from this—at least in the short run—while many values associated with strong firms have cratered.

If the goals of financial capitalism differ too much from those of enterprise generally, then the public suffers, as became apparent in 2008. When President Dwight Eisenhower chose General Motors CEO Charlie Wilson to be secretary of defense in 1953, Wilson made headlines by saying he thought: "What's good for the country is good for General Motors, and vice versa." Wilson got pilloried for that remark, made at his confirmation hearings, but there was sense in what he said. Then America's automakers were paying auto workers good wages and making consumers happy with their cars. The enormous profits to be made from the dexterous leveraging of paper transactions like mortgages pushed all the incentives into the short run, as have the complicated and generous CEO salaries of the early years of the twenty-first century. With hindsight, perhaps firms will put executive bonuses in escrow accounts to be paid after a spell of good years instead of a couple of flashy seasons.

The subprime mortgage collapse points up the difficulty of stabilizing the relentless revolution of capitalism because the past is a very imperfect guide to the future. Barney Frank, chair of the House Financial Services Committee, wryly commented that the surge of subprime lending was a kind of "natural experiment," testing theories about the radical deregulation of financial markets.[14] A whole new banking system materialized outside the safety net put in place in the Great Depression of the 1930s. Major concentrations of capital moved from conventional commercial banks that held deposits and lent money to investment banks that lent money through a veritable mangrove maze of lines of credit. Nor is this an anomaly. It is integral to capitalism that investors will seek new ways to make money, preferably free of regulation.

The time of reckoning finally arrived. The G20, formed in 1999 to give developing countries like Argentina, Brazil, Mexico, India, and China a chance to talk with the G7 industrial giants of France, Canada, Germany, Italy, Japan, Great Britain, and the United States met in São Paulo at the end of the tumultuous year of 2008. The finance ministers and central bank governors of the emerging economies called for cooperation in reconstructing the world's financial architecture. They stressed that the "rest" was no longer content letting the West carry on irresponsibly. Another meeting in Washington followed quickly. Protocol at the White

House state dinner gave some hint of the rest's success. Luis Inácio Lula da Silva, president of Brazil, sat on President Bush's right and Hu Jintao of China on his left. The times were again propitious, as they had been after World War II, for reaching international solutions to global instabilities.[15]

The new phenomenon of globalization made itself known in diverse ways, perhaps through the sight of a scarved elderly woman in Turkey using a cell phone or from TV images of Iranian youths dancing to American hip-hop or learning that some beautiful gerbera daisies were grown in Nigeria. For others, the recognition of our interconnectedness was more shocking and came in the form of a plant closing that supported a whole community like the Hershey Company in Hershey, Pennsylvania. As readers of this history know, global trade began in earnest in the sixteenth century with the arrival of spices from the East Indies and silver from the New World. Why then does globalization deserve our attention now? Because world communication and transactions have tied our lives together in ways unimaginable even fifty years ago. Governments have become more open, and their borders more porous. "The world is flat," as Thomas Friedman announced, by which he meant that people, money, and goods moved freely across the plane surface of the globe.[16]

Going well beyond telegraphy and telephones, the Internet links individuals, firms, and institutions instantly with messages, tables, photos, and spreadsheets. The incorporation of Asian nations into world markets made cheap imports available to the world's consumers. It also tied all these producers and consumers into the ups and downs of the international market. It hardly took the financial meltdown of 2008 to demonstrate that when the United States (or Germany or China) sneezes, the rest of the world gets a cold. The first decade of the twenty-first century also brought a lot of hype about global integration, typified by a two-page newspaper advertisement that IBM ran. Sharing the globalphilia of Friedman, the ad expatiated on the theme of a smarter world where sensors carry intelligent messages to cars, appliances, cameras, roads, pipelines, livestock, and medicine! To stress the point, IBM described its "holistic management approach that promotes business effectiveness and efficiency while striving for innovation, flexibility and integration with technology."[17] But intelligence and communication are not enough, as the recent financial fiasco demonstrated. Wisdom is required too.

Economists are now talking about something called moral hazard, a term that refers to the dangers of giving people the wrong incentives. It's a moral hazard for the government to bail out banks because bankers in the future will take foolish risks if they conclude that they will not have to pay for them. It's reminiscent of the expert who claimed that "capitalism without bankruptcy is like Christianity without hell."[18] A systematic means of controlling sin apparently is as necessary in economics as it is in religion. The phrase "moral hazard" itself suggests that market participants now realize that capitalism has an essential underpinning in social norms. People may say that virtue is its own reward, but most of us find that an insufficient return. We prefer vacationing, but because we must eat or we covet a higher standard of living, we are willing to work.

So there is something of a disconnect between what the market requires and what its participants want. We didn't see this for a long time because we as a society have been committed to the moral benefit of hard work. Only recently has an ethic of pleasure seeking become prevalent. And that's the problem. The free enterprise economy depends upon competition, sensible choices, and widely shared information, even as it rewards people who corner a market, trick others into foolish bargains, and use secret information to their own advantage. It's just possible that the real moral hazard today is that capitalism is battening off an older ethic taught by parents and teachers when there was an adult consensus about how to rear children to behave responsibly. If this set of values fades altogether, we will be bereft of the moral base of capitalism, which depends upon men and women's meeting obligations, managing resources prudently, valuing hard work, and treating others fairly.

The 2008 financial disaster was severe enough to reinstate regulations and a sense of caution among officeholders. It also changed the conversation in capitalist countries, and not a moment too soon. What is needed more than a new financial system is a legal overhaul. Capitalism can work pretty well to deliver on its promise of progress and prosperity when its participants have secured, as one expert detailed, "an effective legal system, a trusted judiciary, enforceable contract law, a disinterested civil service, modern bookkeeping, accurate property records, a rational system for tax collection, a successful educational system, clean police, clean politicians, transparent campaign financing, a responsible news media, and a widespread sense of civic responsibility."[19] Capitalism generates the wealth to pay for these social benefits. Whether the political will exists to secure them is now the question.

Capitalism's History Recapitulated

The origins of capitalism's flaws can be detected in its history, when things commercial moved from the periphery in premodern aristocratic societies to form the center of modern ones. Bargaining was as old as human association, but it had always been contained within the interstices of societies largely run by warriors. When Europeans traversed routes to the Indies, they found exotic Asian ports where they could buy silks and spices. Going in the other direction, they encountered a new world with two continents bracketing dozens of tropical islands. Lucrative trades sprang up, demonstrating that Europeans already had impressive savings to invest in foreign ventures.

The aristocracies that supported European monarchies in the sixteenth century looked down upon merchants because of their absorption with making money, but they liked the challenge of expanding European influence and power. They believed unquestioningly in human inequality. Some few were born to head diplomatic missions, serve the law or the church, advise kings, and lead armies; the remainder were the hewers of wood and drawers of water, not to mention the farmers and servants who lived lives of drudgery. As an urban group merchants fell somewhere in between these categories, respected for their skill and money but demeaned for their lack of distinguished family ties.

In the seventeenth century, in England at least, attitudes began to change as buying and selling things became more prevalent. When the primitive agricultural system yielded to improved techniques for raising food, larger harvests brought down food prices. At the same time, many of the farmers' children were no longer needed on the farm and moved into rural industries or left to pick up city trades or thicken the distribution networks of England's unified market. In the eighteenth century practical applications of scientific knowledge succeeded in getting steam to drain mine pits, power factories, and drive locomotives. These changes ran athwart the mores embedded in the laws, religion, and popular lore of the day. Proponents of economic developments marshaled arguments to justify the novel practices. They depicted the incipient capitalist system as natural, liberating, progressive, and rewarding. Once they secured belief for this view, capitalists had the ideological punch to disrupt settled communities and their values.

Scarcities continued to characterize Western societies in the eighteenth century because population began to grow in the 1730s and 1740s. Still, in cities buyers found objects of delight and usefulness, from maps and travel books to jewelry and clothing decorated with precious stones; exotic foods like sugar, coffee, and cocoa; and fascinating contrivances like eyeglasses, scientific instruments, and pocket compasses. The exultation at human inventiveness that had become part of the spirit of capitalism started to take hold of the public imagination. Invidious comparisons between the West and the rest of the world entered public discourse.

After the end of the seventeenth century, there were no more famines in England, and they became less severe elsewhere in Western Europe. The dreaded plague, which had revisited Europe with regularity since the Black Death of the fourteenth century also made an exit after its 1723 visit. That sense of life's precariousness that justified the invasive authority of fathers, magistrates, and kings would now slowly fade. Calls for greater political participation, religious toleration, and personal mobility grew louder as market participants acquired, or seized, the freedom to move outside the skein of social prescriptions. Short-term individual goals replaced old worries about the future. The aggregation of such decisions set prices and rates without anyone's taking responsibility for their consequences.

The celebration of the individual inventor—homo faber—gained ground as the initial experiments with steam turned into a revolution in production processes. The industrial era began in earnest in the nineteenth century, gaining momentum as it moved out from England to France, Germany, and the United States. By the end of the century the magic of the steam engine had been overtaken by the wizardry of electricity. Chemistry joined physics as a handmaiden to industry. Eager investors promoted a sustained search for new inventions, which led in time to organized research. This meant a constant delving into the qualities of the natural world and its elements, as they studied reactions to heat, cold, stress, compression, tension, and gravitational force. This work infused a wondrous quality into the material universe as it was replacing an earlier spirituality. Some called it the disenchantment of the world. While this constant bombarding of nature with questions began with natural philosophers, inventors came right behind them to commercialize their findings and diffuse their impact.

The social world that wound around the repetitions of each year's seasonal tasks and holidays morphed into one of constant variation. Change, always something to be feared, acquired a Janus-like quality. It could actually bring improvements; it could also obliterate long-standing ways of being in the world. To keep the economy developing required men and women to take risks, think innovatively, and accept changes that made their lives very different from those of their parents. New too was the idea of people's earning their place in society regardless of family origins. Social mobility, which seems so ordinary a concept to us, was an abomination in a society structured around the statuses of nobility, gentility, commoner, and servant—the dependent many and the independent few.

The ambition that played an essential role in inducing people to be more productive could be sustained only if there was room on the higher rungs of the social ladder. While statuses had supported stasis, striving promoted expectations of moving up and fears of moving down or being pushed there. Once uprooted from the old agrarian order, men and women learned crafts like shoemaking, worked in construction, formed the human ligaments of commerce, or were drawn into factory work. Two new classes emerged to take the place of the old ranks: those of workers and employers. Working with your hands was further distinguished from working with your brains. While these positions were open to all claimants as the old statuses were not, social mobility had its limits. But geographic mobility increased as farm people found work in rural industry and then in the cities. The more adventurous left Europe altogether to find a place and perhaps a fortune in South and North America. Capitalism benefited enormously from its association with political freedom, even as it created new forms of control. Factories replaced the home and the shop as work sites. Those who built, ran, and invested in them acquired power. Yet they held fiercely to the ideology of individualism, independence, and human rights that accompanied their rise to predominance.

Capitalist ideology battened off the concept of human nature. It specified rights as universal that prompted those dispossessed to agitate to enjoy the fruits of their labor and liberties. Yet the legal traditions of Europe distinguished sharply between the rights and privileges of masters and servants. Employers tried to maintain these old legal advantages, even as their employees saw themselves as the bearers of rights. Domestic consumption also became more important to capitalist economies. The supply side warred with the demand side. Producers wanted to keep wages low and hours long when making goods, but they needed to have customers well paid and interested in shopping when it came time to sell those goods.

The prospect of getting rich unleashed a rapacity rarely seen before in human society. Great wealth was to be made importing tropical plants like sugar, tobacco, tea, and cocoa to European consumers with purchasing power and addictive tastes. Rather than import these products from Asians and Africans, Europeans organized a system of plantation agriculture to raise these appetizing novelties in the New World. This trade was made possible because they could buy slaves by the millions from Africa and ship them to the Caribbean islands and Atlantic coasts of North and South America. The European exploitation of vulnerable people began with slavery in the sixteenth century and moved to on-the-site exploitation in distant countries, especially Africa in the nineteenth century. Then Germany and Italy joined Spain, Portugal, Great Britain, and France in building empires with capital investments directed to developing their colonies' natural resources. In treating colonial laborers and their societies as so many aspects of production, capitalists dehumanized their relations with the people outside their continent.

While the belligerent rivalries of Europe were very old, the wealth generated by capitalism changed the terms of engagement in the twentieth century, enabling the countries to sustain hostilities for years. When war broke out in 1914, no one expected this outcome. Most people thought it would end in months; instead it dragged on for four bloody years. Since the competition was in part over imperial holdings, far-flung colonies were dragged into the conflict. Two decades after World War I, the Second World War began. Perhaps no greater contrast has existed than that between the sense of accomplishment at the opening of the twentieth century and the despair that reigned when the Second World War ended in an explosion of ferocious energy in 1945.

The year 1900 opened with the marvels of the automobile, electric power, and reconfigured city centers dotted with skyscrapers. Life expectancy got longer, and public health measures checked the spread of diseases that had once ravaged populations. Four decades later war had killed millions of men and women, expelled millions of others from their homes, and utterly demolished thousands upon thousands of city blocks. Men and women who had been young for the First World War entered middle age chastened. Hard times promoted serious thought. After a second world war, capitalist nations recognized the need for cooperation and created templates for international organizations of lasting value.

Between the two world wars, Europe suffered a massive decline in commerce. Known as the Great Depression just as the First World War was originally known as the Great War, this sudden deceleration of the capitalist tempo left experts in a state of shock. Dozens of economies fell into shambles. Despite efforts at ameliorating the loss of jobs and savings, most government policies fell short. It took the massive spending of the Second World War to get the capitalist system humming again, a result that vindicated the theory of John Maynard Keynes. Keynes argued that private investments alone could not pull economies out of depression. Like the biblical reference to seven fat years followed by seven lean ones, capitalism has oscillated between good and bad times, though with less predictability. The pent-up demand after World War II and the great wealth that the United States was willing to spend to help in the recovery of Western Europe and then Japan led to a golden age of a quarter century. A generation later a new matrix for recession brought to an end the bounteous prosperity of the postwar era.

People began in the 1970s to take notice of the environmental toll taken by the accelerating levels of fossil fuel consumption, a fact driven home by the emerging power of OPEC, the association of oil-producing countries. Exercising something of monopoly power, OPEC voted a dramatic rise in oil prices, making noticeable several other problems in the homelands of capitalism. The most prominent was that for the first time rising prices did not signal a period of growth, but rather one of stasis or stagnation or, in the term of the hour, stagflation. The income equalizing of the postwar period reversed, followed by a four-decade-long stretch of the gap between low and high incomes in the United States. The mutually beneficial agreements among big business, big labor, and big government grew weaker. Organized labor, the beneficiary of depression despair and postwar growth, lost its purchase on the popular imagination. Stagflation also broke up the consensus that Keynesian solutions would work for all of capitalism's problems. As labor power waned, that of employers waxed.

While capitalist nations were taking in these troubling facts, capitalism moved into high gear with a cascade of new technologies that brought in the age of the computer, the transistor, and the Internet. Schumpeter's "perennial gale creative destruction" blew in with a new generation of ingenious devices. Every economic downturn gives critics a chance to draft obituaries for capitalism, but they underestimate the fecundity of capitalism in promoting ingenuity and turning novel prototypes into great cash cows.

Contemporary Capitalism and Its Critics

Gordon Gekko, the business antihero in the movie *Wall Street*, said that "greed, for lack of a better word, is good," but few agree. Alan Greenspan, for one, pointed to the dangers of an "infectious greed" while speaking to Congress in 1997 as chairman of the Federal Reserve Board. Nor is greed the only thing that people hold against capitalism. I've made a little list, and it includes such charges as responding to short-term opportunities to the neglect of long-term effects, dispensing power without responsibility, promoting material values over spiritual ones, commoditizing human relations, monetizing social values, corrupting democracy, unsettling old communities, institutions, and arrangements, and rewarding aggressive-ness and—yes—greed.[20]

Two other capitalist responsibilities have cast long shadows forward: intractable poverty and a deteriorating environment. While most of the world economies have been developing nicely, sixty years of effort by the First World to stimulate prosperity in many Third World countries has ended in disappointment. Experts are regrouping to test some novel approaches to animate stagnate economies and revive failed states. Think-ing more broadly, some think it's time to correct the flaws in capitalism instead of expecting another technological spurt to divert attention else-where. On the agenda for the new century is a multipronged effort to halt the environmental damage that a century of population growth, fossil fuel burning, water pollution, and various other human intrusions on the planet have caused.

Capitalism's critics fall into three groups. There are those who are offended by the vulgarity and ugliness that the pursuit of profit pro-motes. They don't like the surfeit of goods and the materialistic preoc-cupations of their fellow global citizens. This complaint usually comes from members of a social or academic elite. Others fight capitalism for the sins of a globalization that has enlarged the scope of the rich coun-tries' rapacity at the expense of the vulnerable poor. The multinational corporation is the bogey of the antiglobalization movement because it is seen as acting without social responsibility or sensitivity to human needs. Critics depict multinationals as octopuses whose tentacles cling to any profit-promising scheme, however dubious. A third group wants to work within the framework of capitalism to make the system more open, more fair, and as responsive to people as dollars. These latter seem the most interesting, if only because they are the most constructive in the fight against tenacious poverty and the misery and injustice that come with it.

Since the mid-1970s, developments in Korea, Taiwan, China, and India have lifted three hundred million people out of poverty. Millions of other men and women have moved themselves out of poverty by emigrating to more prosperous places.[21] For example, half a million Romanian immi-grants are now supplying the labor of the missing youths in an aging Italy.

And Italy is not the only European country losing population. France, Germany, Spain, and Greece all are dipping below the replacement rate.

Elsewhere, Middle Eastern oil fields, construction work, and domestic service in cities like Dubai are pulling workers, mostly young and male, from India and the Philippines. A wave of immigrants from Africa pushes its way through the European doorway of Spain every week. The remittances these expatriated workers send back home run to the hundreds of billions, but the cost of separation from home is cruelly high. Perhaps if global communication had not shown these men and women how the West lives, they wouldn't care, but they do know and want it. Still, without televised incitement, fifty-one million Europeans and two million Asians came to North and South America between the 1870s and 1930s, forty-nine million Southern Chinese and Indians migrated to Southeast Asia, and forty-eight million Russians and Chinese left home for Central Asia, Siberia, and Manchuria.[22]

The Problem of Poverty and Its Analyzers

Although "bottom billion" has not migrated out of Paul Collier's study of that name, it's an evocative label for those mired in poverty. Of the six billion people living today, one-sixth of them are in advanced capitalist economies, another four billion are in developing countries, and the remaining billion live in countries with stalled economies.[23] World Bank figures for 2005 indicate that 1.4 billion people live below the poverty line, earning less than $1.25 a day. Unlike the backward, underdeveloped Third World nations of yore, the bottom billion today live in particular countries—fifty-seven in fact—that are treading water while the world around them is swimming toward development, even during a world recession. They are not the BRICs (Brazil, Russia, India, and China), which have won attention as "emerging markets." Instead they are "failed states" that have begun to wear out the patience of philanthropists and test the imagination of aid organizations. Today more money is pouring into combating disease than into promoting economic change, evidence of a certain despair about development.

The fifty-seven states tethered to the bottom of the global economy are not like others in the world. They carry special burdens, which means that the conventional aid programs will not be effective with them. In his carefully analyzed study, Collier notes that the fifty-seven that have made no progress toward economic development have been plagued with bad governments, civil wars, landlocked locations, and, surprisingly, being resource rich. These conditions are often mutually enhancing. Natural riches like oil, ivory, or diamonds actually give the leaders of such countries abundant resources for bribery. The leaders don't need to court their people because they have the money to steal elections or buy off opponents.[24]

Civil war is another trap. Estimating that a typical one costs sixty-four billion dollars, Collier recommends military intervention in countries like Afghanistan and Somalia to rescue them from this trauma. Arguing that such interventions should last at least a decade in order to lay the foundation for sound government, he wants the intervening organizations to clarify their intentions through an international charter. Collier views neither trade nor aid alone as being of much help to failed states. Change must come from within, he maintains, but domestic reformers will succeed only with assistance from the industrialized world. Nor does he place faith in globalization per se because the entrance of India and China has made it much harder for latecomers to get into the world marketplace. A former official with the World Bank, Collier recognizes the tyranny of the already tried and urges a revitalized debate on the subject.[25]

The best ideas for tackling poverty have come from people, like Muhammad Yunus, Hernando de Soto, Amartya Sen, Frances Moore Lappé, Walden Bello, Raj Patel, and Peter Barnes, who want to use the strengths of capitalism in new ways to enhance everyone's life. This of course is what Marx wanted to do: build on the capitalistic base of wealth to provide for the entire society. He failed to foresee the danger of joining a society's economic and political power through state ownership of property. This consolidation of power ossified programs and created a ruling apparatus impervious to popular will. Yet the issue that Marx addressed persists: how to make the riches generated by capitalism increase the life chances of everyone, including the bottom billion.

Quite obviously what the poor lack is the magic of capital or even access to capital. There are now some ingenious ideas for changing this situation. Muhammad Yunus has come up with one of them. Born in British India in 1940, Yunus earned a Ph.D. at Vanderbilt University, where he taught nearby for three years in 1969–1972. The movement to create an independent Bangladesh lured him back home, where he began teaching economics at Chittagong University. Two years later reality came rushing at him in the form of a national disaster. With a terrible famine raging in Bangladesh, "it was difficult to teach elegant theories of economics in the university classroom," he recalled.[26] His contact with the villagers surrounding his campus convinced him that many poor people could pull themselves out of abject poverty if they could just lay their hands on a little money. Yet without collateral they could only borrow from loan sharks who charged as much as 30 percent interest.

Seeing women who made bamboo furniture pay such usurious rates to purchase their bamboo that they could never get their heads above water, Yunus thought of extending loans without collateral. He started with $27 from his own pocket and lent small amounts to forty-two women. It worked; they paid back their loans along with a reasonable interest rate. He next set up the Grameen (it means village) Bank in 1976 with a government loan. In 1983 the bank became independent. It grew from the village to the district to the nation as a whole. Grameen is now owned by its borrowers except for 10 percent the Bangladesh government owns. By 2007 it was lending $6.38 billion to more than seven million borrowers, inspiring hundreds of other microlending start-up institutions worldwide.

The Grameen Bank approached more women than men because they were the more likely to spend their earnings on their families. Yunus also recognized the need for creating support networks among the bank's clients. The bank wrote into their contracts mandatory weekly meetings so that groups of borrowers living near one another could gather to discuss their enterprises and share ideas. Participants in these groups also acted as coguarantors of repayment. The record of Grameen loans has been sensational with repayment rates above 90 percent. Radical leftists opposed the bank as an enticement into capitalism, and conservative clergy threatened female borrowers with denial of a Muslim burial. But nothing could stop the momentum of this effort. When he won the Nobel Peace Prize in

2006, Yunus donated half of his $1.4 million to start a company to make low-cost, highly nutritious food for the poor. Grameen's Village Phone Project has brought cell phones to 260,000 villagers in fifty thousand villages, many of whom rent out time on them. These have become a boon to urban day laborers who can now telephone their list of prospects rather than lose precious time traipsing all over town looking for their next job.

Today there are literally hundreds of microlending institutions working with one hundred million families on all continents. The largest private bank in India, ICICI, wants to take microfinance to a new level by cooperating with the Indian government and another one hundred partner organizations. Inspired by Yunus's example, ICICI has lent six hundred million dollars to three million customers. Its next project is to create a biometric identity card with one's credit rating encoded so a person could access credit at Internet kiosks or bank branches everywhere with the press of a thumbprint. Meanwhile Yunus has teamed up with Mexican telecom mogul Carlos Slim Hélu to bring microlending to Mexico in a big way. A contender with Warren Buffett and Bill Gates for the title of the world's wealthiest person, Slim has been a great benefactor. He has poured money into foundations, but as a monopoly owner of many sectors of the economy he is also part of the problem of Mexican poverty. He employs a quarter of a million men and women. Like Yunus, he has declared war on poverty and is turning his attention to helping fund Mexican health and education programs. "My new job," Slim says, "is to focus on the development and employment of Latin America." Critics ask if he intends to pay a working wage commensurate with the rest of North America.[27]

Yunus understands that one of the underpinnings of poverty is the widespread conviction that it is an ineradicable evil, like dying. "I firmly believe," he says, "that we can create a poverty free world if we collectively believe in it." In a poverty-free world, he says, "the only place that you would be able to see poverty is in a poverty museum."[28] Advocates for the poor are pushing against the same obstacles that eighteenth-century opponents of slavery confronted: acceptance of an evil because of its age and familiarity. It's hard to be outraged by a condition like poverty that's been around for millennia. That prevailing attitude once applied to slavery. Then, with remarkable suddenness, the idea of abolition aroused a cadre of reformers who successfully pushed against public complacency in less than a century. The legislature of Pennsylvania demonstrated in 1780 that an institution as old as the Bible could be abolished by statute. Northern states followed Pennsylvania's example, most of them providing for emancipation gradually according to the enslaved person's age.

"A house divided against itself cannot stand," Abraham Lincoln said on the eve of the Civil War. But the same Lincoln quoted scripture to say that the poor will always be with us. Thomas Robert Malthus's popular theory about population growth taught that poverty was the inescapable lot of the mass of men and women. Breaking through this penumbra of resignation has not proved easy. Almost two centuries ago the English radical William Cobbett denounced the cruelty of jobs that kept sober and industrious workers fully employed but did not pay them enough to feed their families. Cobbett's working poor have now attracted the attention of today's activists who have succeeded in getting more than a hundred cities in the United States to pass living wage ordinances for their employees and those working for firms with municipal contracts.

Amartya Sen, like Yunus, was born in what has become Bangladesh, but he emigrated to India after the partition of 1947. Sen has spent his adult life teaching at Cambridge, Oxford, and now Harvard. Awarded a Nobel Prize in economics in 1998, he has been both a moral force and an intellectual heavyweight in the fight against poverty or, more precisely, against the misconceptions of what causes poverty and what might relieve it. Sen has used his highly mathematical scholarly work to open the best minds in economics to new ways of thinking about the poor. Again like Yunus, an earlier Bengal famine, that of 1943, profoundly influenced his thinking. Studying this catastrophe, he discovered that people starved not because there was no food but because they couldn't buy it, owing to declining wages, rising unemployment, and faulty distribution.

Over time these reflections led Sen to develop the concept of social capabilities that are ends in themselves, not merely agents of economic development. More than social capital, they open up larger vistas. Education, for instance, may promote productivity, but more important, people have a broader perspective for making choices. Such capabilities could include women's being free to discuss contraception, which he found increases the possibility of their society's making it available to them.[29] The basic thrust of Sen's teachings is to see freedom as a positive force rather than discuss it as the absence of restraint. Governments must assume the responsibility, in his view, to make sure that their citizens have developed their potential. His emphasis has changed the way that aid and deprivation are evaluated. Many poor suffer because their governments fail to address their most basic needs, a neglect less likely to occur where freedom is respected, he says.

Hernando De Soto is another warrior in the fight against poverty. A Peruvian economist with strong connections to international banking and engineering firms, he now heads Peru's Institute for Liberty and Democracy. The institute concentrates on a different way to empower the poor: get them legal title to the land they occupy and the outfits they operate. De Soto has drawn attention to the informal economies worldwide where people cultivate land, improve their dwellings, and run businesses without having title to their property. This means that they can't use their property as collateral for loans, though the land may have been in their families for several generations. In De Soto's view, people choose to operate in the shadow economy because getting licenses to do business and title to land is usually an onerous and expensive task. Through his institute, De Soto has been able to eliminate dozens of restrictive registration and licensing laws, helping more than a million Peruvians and close to half a million firms gain legal title to their property. In Egypt, De Soto has counted seventy-seven procedures devised by thirty-one different public and private agencies necessary to complete before one can register even a lease for land. Having gained favor with the World Bank, De Soto is now sponsoring similar campaigns against bureaucratic restraint in El Salvador, Tanzania, and Egypt.

The best way to open opportunities to the children of the poorest in any society is to invest in public benefits like good schools, health care, parks, clean air, unpolluted water, effective police protection, and public art. Only in this way can some of the inequalities of very unlevel playing fields be addressed. This takes money or, more precisely, revenue. Peter Barnes has a number of ingenious ideas for raising money within the capitalist system. Barnes was one of the founders of Working Assets Long

Distance, an organization that combines telecommunications with liberal do-gooding like encouraging customers to buy worthy books, donate to environmental causes, and fire off letters to their congressional representatives. In *Capitalism 3.0*, Barnes explores the idea of "the commons," the things that we share like air, water, ecosystems, languages, and cultures. He makes a good case for including science, technology, and legal arrangements in our concept of the commons. Arguing that we need to cultivate our common wealth to balance private wealth, he stresses that what we own in common is much greater than we realize because we don't think about it, measure it, or exploit it.

One of our greatest shared assets is the legal instrument of incorporation. We own it; our legislatures dispense articles of incorporation; our courts adjudicate corporate issues. So why not exact some rent for this valuable privilege? After all, it enables firms to limit their liability and create a new entity, the corporation, endowed with rights and privileges. Barnes also proposes new institutions to manage common property, now rather sloppily run by various government agencies, subject to the whims of incoming administrations. Using the Alaska Permanent Fund as an example, he shows how it turned the windfall from state leases to oil companies into a public investment company paying yearly dividends to every resident. He sees the need for more of the already existing state land trusts. Nothing if not imaginative, Barnes imagines a public awakened to its great wealth starting an air trust, a watershed trust, a buffalo commons trust, a children's opportunity trust, and an airwaves trust. Like most reforms, the ones that Barnes advocates require that people break out of conventional ways of looking at things. In other words, they must innovate the way private entrepreneurs do.[30]

Feeding the world's hungry has inspired Frances Moore Lappé, Walden Bello, and Raj Patel, all of whom have written powerful studies of what's wrong with our efforts. Patel, a sociologist, worked at the World Bank, World Trade Organization, and the United Nations, experiences that turned him into an outspoken critic of organizations promoting globalization. Lappé achieved fame as the author of *Diet for a Small Planet*, which sold several million copies. In 1975, she launched Food First to educate Americans about the causes of world hunger. Like Sen, she has emphasized that world hunger is caused not by the lack of food but rather by the inability of hungry people to gain access to the food abundance that exists in the world. Contrasting the "thin democracy" of mere voting with a "living democracy" enriched by participants' wise choices of what to buy and how to live, she is a tireless advocate for the poor. Bello, a sociologist like Patel, has founded Focus on the Global South, a policy research institute based in Bangkok.

The spike in food costs has triggered an interest in the potato, whose virtues have been rediscovered. The United Nations declared 2008 "the Year of the Potato."[31] Its price has not soared like those of grain and rice because it is highly perishable and hence not suitable for export. It is favored more in the West than elsewhere, but food experts have been urging the world's poor farmers to plant them. Harvests ripen in fewer days with less land and fertilizer. Chinese production of potatoes rose 50 percent between 2003 and 2005. The fact that two of the most powerful newcomers to the world economy, China and India, must grapple with the prospects of famines means that the challenge of getting food to the hungry will not drop out of their minds, as it does so easily among the well fed.

These imaginative thinkers are not without critics. Opponents of De Soto's program to secure land titles for the poor say that this effort weakens collective tenures. The poorest squatters may even be evicted when others, less poor with better claims, register the land. They lament that the most able of the poor benefit to the detriment of the least able. The same argument could be lodged against microlending institutions like the Grameen Bank. Not all poor women have the talent to run their own operations even if reasonable loans were made available to them. This criticism calls attention to the fact that capitalism is a system of rewards. Those who do well in their market transactions prosper. In traditional societies, men and women inherited their status while command economies like those of the former USSR, Eastern Europe, China, and Cuba offered their people equality and guarantees of a certain standard of living. Neither traditional nor command economies were very good at creating wealth. They suffered through years of famine, even in the modern period, but they did respect shared human needs and put a brake on the incessant competition among their people.

There's actually a phenomenon called Yugonostalgia which is an expression of yearning for the days of leisure, fun, and equality once enjoyed in the Balkan states of the former Yugoslavia before its disintegration in 1989. As one sufferer from Yugonostalgia explained it, "in Yugoslavia, people had fun. It was a system for lazy people; if you were good or bad, you still got paid. Now, everything is about money, and this is not good for small people."[32] Those committed to the capitalist West want to scream, "But what about medical advances, great universities, laborsaving devices, easy global communication, and longer lives that hard work and deferred pleasure have brought us?" Worldwide life expectancy went from forty-eight years at mid-twentieth century to sixty-six years in 1999, and it's continuing to rise! Still, it would be nice to eat cake while keeping lazy ways too.

Signs of a Green Revolution

The Green Revolution is not philanthropic, but it is visionary in its plans for the future. Capitalism's voracious appetite for natural resources, especially oil, has led to the unthinkable: human beings making the atmosphere of their planet permanently inhospitable. It's a problem so profound that it was hard to take it seriously. The moment of truth and celebrity arrived when Albert Gore's movie *An Inconvenient Truth* won an Oscar, his book of the same name a Pulitzer, and his personal efforts a Nobel Peace Prize in 2007. Acceptance of the possibly monumental consequences of environmental degradation has been made difficult by the fear that it could not be solved in the usual way with new techniques. Or could it be?

Even though doubting Thomases continue to resist the idea of global warming, the elevated prices of oil in the first decade of the twenty-first century gave venture capitalists the push to move ahead on the technological front.[33] The Natural Resources Defense Council Action Fund has run ads explaining that "tackling global warming will generate a jobs program of epic proportions." The U.S. Senate has a Climate Security Act on its docket. The Russians have pioneered nuclear-powered civilian ships as icebreakers in the Arctic Circle. Nuclear power, never abandoned in

France, may get a second chance to replace oil elsewhere.

Rediscovering human power may also fight the battle of the bulging waistline. Municipalities in Europe are buying thousands of bicycles to place strategically around their cities for their citizens to pedal to their destinations. Most popular in France and Spain, sharing bikes joins old technology to new. Electronic cards and computerized bike stands let riders pick up and drop bikes with fees easily registered on their credit cards.[34] The green industry is finding cheap space for making the component parts of their wind machines and solar panels in the closed factories of the Rust Belt. Builders in Germany are constructing houses that use virtually no energy for temperature control. Venture capital is accumulating for the next round of fuel innovation. Detroit is getting serious about making electric cars. The broad reform and recovery plan of President Barack Obama made energy independence for the United States one of its goals. The adjustments are going to be wrenching. Still, the augmentation of artificial energy is absolutely essential if we are to confine evidence of poverty to museums.

Some Closing Thoughts about Capitalism

Capitalism is not a unified, coordinated system, despite that suggestion in the word "system." Rather it is a set of practices and institutions that permit billions of people to pursue their economic interests in the marketplace. There is no monolithic international corporate power, but many diverse players in the world market with, yes, a wide disparity in the influence that each wields. Among all the legitimate interests at play in the market are the less appealing opportunities to exploit legal loopholes, buyers' ignorance, and unexpected windfalls. Because of these and without coordination from any center, capitalists can cause serious damage, as the subprime mortgage meltdown abundantly proved. And it will not be the last panic. The dot-com bubble and the housing bubble had their forerunners in the South Sea Bubble of the eighteenth century and the tulip bubble of the seventeenth century. It's hard to believe that it won't happen again.

Capitalism's history suggests that democracy and capitalism might be decoupled because they generate values that are often in conflict. Democracy means majority rule with regular, contested elections; American and European democracies include the protection of civil and personal rights. Capitalism refers to investments in productive processes that may or may not rely on politically empowered participants. Capitalism is amoral while democracy is suffused with moral concerns about the well-being of the whole and the rectitude of leaders. Since capitalist growth depends upon innovation, and innovation upsets the status quo, the free market system regularly creates social problems that the government must address. "We, the people" then jars against "I, the individual." Capitalism relies upon technological wizardry to maintain its momentum, but applying new techniques requires stability in order to secure labor, supplies, customers, legal protection, and even peace. Democracy and capitalism go together nicely, but they often act like the couple that can neither live with nor live without each other.

A good deal more fraught with tension is the relationship between capitalism and equality, but its roots are entwined. The concept of equality as a prime social good emerged out of the Enlightenment. It found expression in the closing decades of the eighteenth century in the American Declaration of Independence and the French Revolutionary slogan of "Liberty, equality, and fraternity." Prior to that, the inequality that made some people dukes and others porters seemed as normal as the rising of the sun each morning. The Enlightenment thinking that undermined this acceptance of inequality owed much to capitalism, to the awe stirred by the human capacity to comprehend and harness natural forces for the benefit of all. The prosperity that the French espied across the Channel in England gave rise to the hope that the future would bring benefits, both tangible and intangible and previously unthinkable, to men and women, among them to be treated equally. Equality has remained more ideal than real, but an ideal with legs.

American economic leadership is now about one hundred and twenty years old. Since the middle of the 1880s the United States has had the world's largest economy, accounting for 25 percent of the whole, except during post–World War II decades, when its share totaled 50 percent! It will probably remain twice the size of China for the next two decades.

Unlike the other two great centers of wealth and dynamism—Europe and East Asia—the United States is geographically independent with vibrant market centers on coasts that front both the Atlantic and Pacific trade worlds.[35] Globalization, which the United States has pushed for at least a century, has succeeded spectacularly in creating many centers of influence and wealth. Perhaps because of this sponsorship, countries around the world consider America's leadership essential to recover the momentum behind its once expanding prosperity. Americans too are learning that what's good for a national economy is also good for a global one: competition, open access, and cooperative ventures. Nothing promotes growth more than having rich neighbors, as Adam Smith pointed out in his eighteenth-century classic *Wealth of Nations*.

Another eighteenth-century seer, James Madison, the so-called father of our Constitution, said something else pertinent to our times when he warned that the concentration of power in one branch of government is tantamount to despotism. The whole structure of the U.S. Constitution involves a balance of powers with additional checks on abuses (you remember those civics lectures on "checks and balances"). The danger of concentration is even greater if the two leviathans in our lives—the government and the economy—read off the same profit sheet. When government works hand in glove with the nation's businessmen, you can be sure that the market's own corrective mechanism will be disabled. Competition will then be muted, cronyism rampant, and inefficiency protected. The cash nexus between candidates for public office and wealthy donors, including labor unions, causes problems. Lobbyists have a field day with the quid pro quo of donations and favors. In the long run, raising small campaign donations from ordinary voters through the Internet may reduce politicians' dependence upon big-buck contributions. For the near future the convergence of good intentions with close encounters with disaster might revive some of the market's own self-regulating mechanisms. New and better regulatory systems are in the offing.

Schumpeter raised the possibility that capitalism was doomed because of its tendency to destroy the institutions that protect it.[36] The corruption of auditing firms in the 2008 mortgage collapse would be an example, as would be the way economic fluctuations undermine stable families needed to inculcate the discipline and respect for law that is essential to the market working well. But Schumpeter failed to take into account the different experiences market participants draw upon when making decisions. Their opinions differed when he wrote in 1942 from those that participants hold today or will have in another half century. People do learn from their mistakes. There is no reason to think that societies won't continue to modify and monitor their economies in pursuit of shared goals. A relentless revolution, yes, but not a mindless one.

NOTES

◆

CHAPTER 1. THE PUZZLE OF CAPITALISM

1. Simon Winchester, "Historical Tremors," *New York Times*, May 15, 2008.
2. Jared Diamond, *Guns, Germs, and Steel: The Fate of Human Societies* (New York, 1997). See also Gregory Clark, (Princeton, 2007).
3. David S. Landes, *The Wealth and Poverty of Nations* (New York, 1997); Alfred F. Crosby, Jr., *The Measure of Reality : Quantification and Western Society, 1250–1600* (New York, 2000), reviewed by Roger Hart, Margaret Jacob, and Jack A. Goldstone in the *American Historical Review*, 105 (2000): 486–508; Deepak Lal, *Unintended Consequences* (Cambridge, 1998). See also David Levine, *At the Dawn of Modernity: Biology, Culture, and Material Life in Europe after the Year 1000* (Berkeley, 2001).
4. Kenneth Pomeranz, *The Great Divergence: China, Europe, and the Marking of the Modern World Economy* (Princeton, 2000). The critical literature on this proposition is best covered in James M. Bryant, "The West and the Rest Revisited: Debating Capitalist Origins, European Colonialism, and the Advent of Modernity," *Canadian Journal of Sociology*, 31 (2006). See also David Landes, "East Is East and West Is West," in Maxine Berg and Kristine Bruland, eds., *Technological Revolutions in Europe: Historical Perspectives* (Northampton, MA, 1998), 19–38. For a more sympathetic response to Pomeranz, see P. H. H. Vries, "Are Coal and Colonies Really Crucial? Kenneth Pomeranz and the Great Divergence," *Journal of World History*, 12 (2001).
5. Jack A. Goldstone, "Efflorescences and Economic Growth in World History: Rethinking the 'Rise of the West' and the Industrial Revolution," *Journal of World History*, 13 (2002).
6. Karl Marx, *Contribution to the Critique of Political Economy* (New York, 1977 [originally published in 1859]).
7. Max Weber, *The Protestant Ethic and the Spirit of Capitalism*, trans. by Talcott Parsons (New York, 1958 [originally published in Germany in 1904–05]), 47–62.
8. Adam Smith, *An Enquiry into the Nature and Causes of the Wealth of Nations* (New York, 1937 [Modern Library ed.]), 306, 3, 13, and 328.
9. Joyce Oldham Appleby, *Economic Thought and Ideology in Seventeenth-Century England* (Princeton, 1978), 158–70, 199–216, 242.

CHAPTER 2. TRADING IN NEW DIRECTIONS

1. C. R. Boxer, *Four Centuries of Portuguese Expansion, 1415–1825: A Succinct Survey* (Berkeley, 1969), 14; Holland Cotter, "Portugal Conquering and Also Conquered," *New York Times*, June 28, 2007.

2. Alfred W. Crosby, Jr., *The Columbian Exchange: Biological and Cultural Consequences of 1492* (Westport, CT, 1972).

3. Leonard Y. Andaya, *The World of Maluku: Eastern Indonesia in the Early Modern Period* (Honolulu, 1993), 151; Sanjay Subrahmanyam, "Holding the World in Balance: The Connected History of the Iberian Overseas Empires, 1500–1640," *American Historical Review*, 112 (2007): 1367–68.

4. M. C. Ricklefs, *A History of Modern Indonesia* (Bloomington, 1981), 21.

5. Kenneth Pomeranz and Steven Topik, *The World That Trade Created: Society, Culture, and the World Economy*, 2nd ed. (Armonk, NY, 2006), 16–18.

6. Robert C. Ritchie, *Captain Kidd and the War against the Pirates* (Cambridge, 1986).

7. Christopher Hill, *The Century of Revolution, 1602–1715* (Edinburgh, 1961), 32; see also Joyce Oldham Appleby, *Economic Thought and Ideology in Seventeenth-Century England* (Princeton, 1978), 32–35.

8. Robert Brenner, *Merchants and Revolution: Commercial Change, Political Conflict, and London's Overseas Traders, 1550–1653* (Princeton, 1993).

9. C. R. Boxer, *The Dutch Seaborne Empire: 1600–1800* (New York, 1970), 43–44.

10. Lynn Hunt, Thomas R. Martin, Barbara H. Rosenwein, R. Po-chia Hsia, and Bonnie G. Smith, *The Making of the West: People and Cultures, a Concise History*, 2nd ed. (Boston, 2007), 494.

11. Daniel Defoe, *A Plan of the English Commerce: Being a Compleat Prospect of the Trade of This Nation, as Well as the Home Trade and Foreign Trade* (London, 1728), 192, as quoted in Charles Wilson, *The Dutch Republic and the Civilization of the Seventeenth Century* (New York, 1968), 20.

12. Wilson, *Dutch Republic*, 27.

13. Boxer, *Dutch Seaborne Empire*, 22.

14. Jan De Vries, "The Limits of Globalization in the Early Modern World," *Economic History Review* (forthcoming): 14.

15. Boxer, *Dutch Seaborne Empire*, 94.

16. Pomeranz and Topik, *World That Trade Created*, 80–83.

17. Holland Cotter, "When the Islamic World Was Inspired by the West," *New York Times*, March 28, 2008.

18. I am indebted to David Levine for this information.

19. Charles P. Kindleberger, *A Financial History of Western Europe*, 2nd ed. (New York, 1993), 173–76.

20. Dennis O. Flinn and Arturo Giraldez, "Cycles of Silver: Global Economic Unity through the Mid-Eighteenth Century," *Journal of World History*, 13 (2002): 391–427.

CHAPTER 3. CRUCIAL DEVELOPMENTS IN THE COUNTRYSIDE

1. Alfred W. Crosby, Jr., *The Columbian Exchange: Biological and Cultural Consequences of 1492* (Westport, CT, 1972).

2. Kenneth Pomeranz and Steven Topik, *The World That Trade Created: Society, Culture, and the World Economy*, 2nd ed. (Armonk, NY, 2006), 07.

3. Quoted in Andrew B. Appleby, "Diet in Sixteenth-Century England," in Charles Webster, ed., *Health, Medicine and Mortality in the Sixteenth Century* (Cambridge, 1979).

4. David Landes, *The Unbound Prometheus: Technological Change and Industrial Development in Western Europe from 1750 to the Present* (Cambridge, 1969), 15–16.

5. David Levine, *At the Dawn of Modernity: Biology, Culture, and Material Life in Europe after the Year 1000* (Berkeley, 2001), 333–37.

6. Thomas Robert Malthus, *An Essay on the Principle of Population* (London, 1798), 139.

7. E. A. Wrigley and R. S. Schofield, *Population History of England And Wales* (London, 1981); E. A. Wrigley, *Introduction to English Historical Demography from the Sixteenth to the Nineteenth Century* (New York, 1966), 96–159. See also Levine, *At the Dawn of Modernity*, 294–99.

8. Peter Laslett, *The World We Have Lost* (New York, 1965), 1. I have converted English currency to American dollars.

9. Fernand Braudel and Frank Spooner, "Prices in Europe, from 1450–1750," in Edwin E. Rich and Charles Henry Wilson, eds., *The Cambridge Economic History of Europe*, vol. 4 (Cambridge, 1967).

10. P. H. H. Vries, "Are Coal and Colonies Really Crucial? Kenneth Pomeranz and the Great Divergence," *Journal of World History*, 12 (2001): 4–5.

11. Robert Brenner, "Agrarian Class Structure and Economic Development in Pre-Industrial Europe," *Past and Present*: 68–72; Robert Brenner, "Property and Progress," in Chris Wickham, ed., *Marxist History-Writing for the Twenty-first Century* (Oxford, 2007). Brenner, more than any other contemporary scholar, prompted a debate on the role of agriculture in modern economic change.

12. T. H. Aston and C. E. Philpin, eds., *The Brenner Debate: Agrarian Class Structure and Economic Development in Pre-Industrial Europe* (Cambridge, 1985).

13. Wrigley, *Continuity, Chance, and Change: The Character of the Industrial Revolution in England* (Cambridge, 1988), 12–13.

14. Quoted in Joyce Oldham Appleby, *Economic Thought and Ideology in Seventeenth-Century England* (Princeton, 1978), 59–64.

15. Ibid., 130.

16. D. V. Glass, "Gregory King's Estimation of the Population of England and Wales, 1695," *Population Studies*, 2 (1950).

17. E. A. Wrigley and R. S. Schofield, *The Population History of England, 1541–1871: A Reconstruction* (London, 1981); Gregory Clark, "Too Much Revolution: Agriculture in the Industrial Revolution, 1700–1860," in Joel Mokyr, ed., *The British Industrial Revolution: An Economic Perspective*, 2nd ed. (Boulder, 1999), 238–39.

18. Thomas Culpeper, *Plain English* (London, 1673).

19. Robert C. Allen, "Economic Structure and Agricultural Productivity in Europe, 1300–1800," *European Review of Economic History*, 4 (2000), 6–8.

20. Brenner, "Agrarian Class Structure," 68–72.

21. Arthur Young, *Travels in France during the years 1787, 1788, and 1789* (Dublin, 1793), I:130.

CHAPTER 4. COMMENTARY ON MARKETS AND HUMAN NATURE

1. D. V. Glass, "Gregory King's Estimation of the Population of England and Wales, 1695," *Population Studies*, 2 (1950).
2. Locke Manuscripts, Cambridge University Library, Cambridge, England.
3. Boswell's *Life of Johnson*, ed. George Birkbeck Hill (Oxford, 1887), II:323.
4. Quoted in R. D. Collinson Black, "Smith's Contribution in Historical Perspective," in T. Wilson and A. S. Skinner, eds., *The Market and the State: Essays in Honour of Adam Smith* (Oxford, 1976).
5. E. A. Wrigley, "A Simple Model of London's Importance in Changing English Society and Economy 1650–1750," *Past and Present*, 37 (July 1967): 44–47.
6. *Puerta del Sol*, vol. 5, no. 6 (1994).
7. B. E. Supple, *Commercial Crisis and Change in England, 1600–1642* (Cambridge, 1959), 231–36.
8. *England's Treasure by Forraign Trade* (London, 1664 [originally published in 1622]), 218–19. Spelling has been modernized.
9. Benjamin Nelson, *The Idea of Usury: From Tribal Brotherhood to Universal Otherhood*, 2nd ed. (Chicago, 1969 [originally published in 1949]).
10. Ibid., 229ff, 74ff. See also Joyce Oldham Appleby, *Economic Thought and Ideology in Seventeenth-Century England* (Princeton, 1978), 63–69.
11. Timur Kuran, "Explaining the Economic Trajectories of Civilization: The Systemic Approach," *Journal of Economic Behavior and Organization* (2009, in press).
12. Appleby, *Economic Thought and Ideology*, 158–98.
13. Jan De Vries, "The Industrial Revolution and the Industrial Revolution," Paper presented at the Fifty-third Annual Meeting of the Economic History Association (June 1994): 257.
14. [Nicholas Barbon], *A Discourse of Trade* (1690), 15; [Dalby Thomas], *An Historical Account of the West-India Colonies* (London, 1690), 6, both quoted in Appleby, *Economic Thought and Ideology*, 169–71.
15. [Barbon], *A Discourse of Trade*, 15; [Sir Dudley North], *Discourses upon Trade* (London, 1681), 14; [John Cary], *An Essay on the State of England* (Bristol, 1695), 143ff., quoted in Appleby, *Economic Thought and Ideology*, 169–70.
16. Robert C. Allen, "The British Industrial Revolution in Global Perspective" (2006): 3–7, available on the Internet.
17. H-J. Voth, "Time and Work in Eighteenth-Century London," *Journal of Economic History*, 58 (1998): 36–37.
18. [Henry Layton] *Observations Concerning Money and Coin* (London, 1697), 12, quoted in Appleby, *Economic Thought and Ideology*, 237.
19. Appleby, *Economic Thought and Ideology*, 234.
20. Irwin Unger, *The Greenback Era: A Social and Political History of American Finance, 1865–1879* (Princeton, 1964), 38–40.
21. This and the previous paragraph have been drawn from Mark Dincecco, "Fiscal Centralization, Limited Government, and Public Revenues in Europe, 1658–1913," Paper given at the Van Gremp Seminar (UCLA, April 28, 2007), also available through scholar.Google.com.
22. Richard B. Sheridan, *Sugar and Slavery: An Economic History of the British West Indies, 1623–1775* (Baltimore, 1974), 436–37.

23. *Some Thoughts Concerning the Better Security of Our Trade and Navigation* (London, 1685), 4.

24. Jeff Horn, *The Path Not Taken: French Industrialization in the Age of Revolution, 1750-1830* (Cambridge, 2006), 51-53.

25. Elizabeth Fox-Genovese, *The Origins of Physiocracy: Economic Revolution and Social Order in Eighteenth-Century France* (Ithaca, 1976); Horn, *Path Not Taken*, 21, 30, 51-53.

CHAPTER 5. THE TWO FACES OF EIGHTEENTH-CENTURY CAPITALISM

1. These were the War of the League of Augsburg (1689-1697), War of the Spanish Succession (1702-1713), War of Jenkins's Ear (1739-1741), War of the Austrian Succession (1740-1748), Seven Years' War (1756-1763), War of the American Revolution (1777-1783), War of the French Revolution (1792-1800), Napoleonic Wars (1803-1815).

2. David Brion Davis, *Inhuman Bondage: The Rise and Fall of Slavery in the New World* (Oxford, 2006), 80; David Eltis, "The Volume and Structure of the Transatlantic Slave Trade: A Reassessment," *William and Mary Quarterly*, 58 (2001).

3. Peter Bakewell, *A History of Latin America*, 2nd ed. (2004), 153-57.

4. Kenneth Pomeranz and Steven Topik, *The World That Trade Created: Society, Culture, and the World Economy*, 2nd ed. (Armonk, NY, 2006), 88-89.

5. Arnold Pacey, *Technology in World Civilization: A Thousand-Year History* (Cambridge, 1991), 100.

6. Davis, *Inhuman Bondage*, 83-85.

7. Pomeranz and Topik, *World That Trade Created*, 104-07.

8. Richard S. Dunn, *Sugar and Slaves: The Rise of the Planter Class in the English West Indies* (Chapel Hill, 1972), 9-10.

9. Davis, *Inhuman Bondage*, 92-93.

10. Jan De Vries, "The Limits of Globalization in the Early Modern World," *Economic History Review* (forthcoming): 8.

11. Frank Tannenbaum, *Slave and Citizen: The Negro in America* (New York, 1947), 33.

12. See Chapter 2 for a fuller account of Virginia's tobacco boom.

13. Edmund Morgan, *American Slavery, American Freedom: The Ordeal of Colonial Virginia* (New York, 1975), 24-26.

14. Peter H. Wood, *Black Majority: Negroes in Colonial South Carolina from 1676 through the Stono Rebellion* (New York, 1974), 30-42.

15. Martha Schwendener, "Growing Up in the Caribbean, Inspiring Artists over the Centuries," *New York Times*, June 29, 2007; Pomeranz and Topik, *World That Trade Created*, 72-73.

16. Tannenbaum, *Slave and Citizen*, 48-54.

17. Carl N. Degler, *Neither Black nor White: Slavery and Race Relations in Brazil and the United States* (New York, 1971), 245-56; Davis, *Inhuman Bondage*, 120-21; Tannenbaum, *Slave and Citizen*, 10.

18. www.digitalhistory.uh.edu/black_voices_display.cfn?id-24.

19. Bryan Edwards, *The History, Civil and Commercial, of the British Colonies in the West Indies*, 5 vols. (London, 1810), 2:287-89, quoted by James Epstein, "Politics of Colonial

Sensation: The Trial of Thomas Picton and the Cause of Louisa Calderon," *American Historical Review*, 112 (June 2007): 714, n. 17.

20. Davis, *Inhuman Bondage*, 240–48.

21. Eric Williams, *Capitalism and Slavery* (London, 1944).

22. James M. Bryant, "The West and the Rest Revisited: Debating Capitalist Origins, European Colonialism, and the Advent of Modernity," *Canadian Journal of Sociology*, 31 (2006): 434; Joel Mokyr, *The Gifts of Athena: Historical Origins of the Knowledge Economy* (Princeton, 2002), 123.

23. David Levine, *Family Formation in an Age of Nascent Capitalism* (New York, 1977), 77–78, 146–47.

24. E. A. Wrigley, "A Simple Model of London's Importance in Changing English Society and Economy 1650–1750," *Past and Present*, 37 (1967): 48.

25. E. A. Wrigley, *Continuity, Chance, and Change: The Character of the Industrial Revolution in England* (Cambridge, 1988), 26–29, 32, 56.

26. Robert C. Allen, *The British Industrial Revolution in Global Perspective: How Commerce Created the Industrial Revolution and Modern Economic Growth*, forthcoming, April 2009, http://www.nuffield.ox.ac.uk/users/allen/unpublished/econinvent-3.pdf.

27. Mokyr, *Gifts of Athena*, 75, n. 72.

28. Margaret C. Jacob, *Scientific Culture and the Making of the Industrial West* (Oxford, 1997).

29. Margaret C. Jacob and Larry Stewart, *Practical Matter: Newton's Science in the Service of Industry and Empire, 1687–1851* (Cambridge, 2004), 38–41; Mokyr, *Gifts of Athena*, 44–45.

30. Jacob and Stewart, *Practical Matter*, 83–87; Joyce Chaplin, *The First Scientific American: Benjamin Franklin and the Pursuit of Genius* (New York, 2006), 29–33.

31. Allen, *British Industrial Revolution*, 10; Mokyr, *Gifts of Athena*, 68.

32. Chaplin, *The First Scientific American*, 29–33; Jacob and Stewart, *Practical Matter*, 95, 97; the quote is from p. 93.

33. Pacey, *Technology in World Civilization*, 111–12; Allen, *British Industrial Revolution*, 27.

34. Paul Collier, *The Bottom Billion: Why the Poorest Countries Are Failing and What Can Be Done about It* (Oxford, 2007), 82–84.

35. Allen, *British Industrial Revolution*, 28.

36. Eric Robinson and A. E. Musson, *James Watt and the Steam Revolution: A Documentary History* (London, 1969), 4–6.

37. Jack A. Goldstone, "Efflorescences and Economic Growth in World History: Rethinking the 'Rise of the West' and the Industrial Revolution," *Journal of World History*, 13 (2002): 363.

38. J. R. McNeill, *Something New under the Sun: An Environmental History of the Twentieth-Century World* (New York, 2000), 13, 315.

39. Neil McKendrick, "Josiah Wedgwood and Factory Discipline," *Historical Journal* (1961).

40. Pacey, *Technology in World Civilization*, 101.

41. Charles P. Kindleberger, *A Financial History of Western Europe*, 2nd ed. (Oxford, 1993), 193.

42. Pacey, *Technology in World Civilization*, 116.

43. A. E. Musson, "Industrial Motive Power in the United Kingdom, 1800–70," *Economic History Review*, 29 (1976): 415–17; Mokyr, *Gifts of Athena*, 131–40.

44. Walter G. Moss, *An Age of Progress?: Clashing Twentieth-Century Global Forces* (New York, 2008), 74–75.

45. Adrian J. Randall, "The Philosophy of Luddism: The Case of the West of England Woolen Workers, ca. 1790–1809," *Technology and Culture*, 27 (1986): 1–8; Mokyr, *Gifts of Athena*, 267; Jeff Horn, *The Path Not Taken: French Industrialization in the Age of Revolution, 1750–1830* (Cambridge, 2006), 96–101.

46. Raphael Samuel, "Workshop of the World: Steam Power and Hand Technology in Mid-Victorian Britain," *History Workshop*, no. 3 (1977).

47. Mokyr, *Gifts of Athena*, 87; Christine MacLeod, "James Watt, Heroic Invention and the Idea of the Industrial Revolution," in Maxine Berg and Kristine Bruland, eds., *Technological Revolutions in Europe: Historical Perspectives* (Northampton, MA, 1998), 96–98.

48. Mokyr, *Gifts of Athena*, 48, 65, 72.

49. Jan De Vries, "The Industrious Revolution and the Industrial Revolution," Papers Presented at the Fifty-third Annual Meeting of the Economic History Association (June 1994).

50. Adam Smith, *An Enquiry into the Nature and Causes of the Wealth of Nations* (New York, 1937 [Modern Library ed.]), 306, 3, 328.

51. Ibid., 13.

52. Thomas Paine, *Common Sense*, ed. Isaac Kramnick (London, 1976), 65–72, 228.

53. Lynn Hunt, *Inventing Human Rights: A History* (New York, 2007), 24–32.

CHAPTER 6. THE ASCENT OF GERMANY AND THE UNITED STATES

1. Manu Goswami, *Producing India: From Colonial Economy to National Space* (Chicago, 2004), 67.

2. J. R. Harris, *Industrial Espionage and Technology Transfer: Britain and France in the Eighteenth Century* (London, 1998), 10–12, 355–56.

3. Gregory Clark, "Why Isn't the Whole World Developed? Lessons from the Cotton Mills," *Journal of Economic History*, 47 (1987): 141–42, 149. See also Joel Mokyr, "Editor's Introduction: The New Economic History and the Industrial Revolution," in Joel Mokyr, ed., *The British Industrial Revolution* (Oxford, 1999), esp. 126–27.

4. Alfred D. Chandler, Jr., *Scale and Scope: The Dynamics of Industrial Capitalism* (Cambridge, 1990), 3; Goswami, *Producing India*, 41; Eric Hobsbawm, *The Age of Capital, 1848–1875* (New York, 1996 [originally published in 1975]), 40–41; W. D.Rubinstein, "Cultural Explanations for Britain's Economic Decline: How True," in Bruce Collins and Keith Robbins, eds., *British Culture and Economic Decline: Debates in Modern History* (London, 1990), 70–71.

5. Harold James, *A German Identity, 1770–1990* (London, 1989), 66.

6. C. Knick Harley's "Reassessing the Industrial Revolution," in Joel Mokyr, *The British Industrial Revolution: An Economic Perspective*, 2nd ed. (Oxford, 1999), 204–05. The figure is for 1820. Michael G. Mulhall, *The Dictionary of Statistics* (London, 1899), 420, puts the figure at 35.6 percent for Great Britain.

7. R. Allen, "Economic Structure and Agricultural Productivity in Europe, 1300–1800," in

European Review of Economic History, 4 (2000), 20; Angus Maddison, *Dynamic Forces in Capitalist Development* (Oxford, 1991), 32; Alan S. Milward and S. B. Saul, *The Economic Development of Continental Europe, 1780–1870* (London, 1973), 368; Thomas Weiss, "The American Economic Miracle of the 19th Century," *American Historical Association* (1994): 18.

8. Milward and Saul, *Economic Development of Continental Europe*, 388–96.

9. Ibid., 376.

10. Hobsbawm, *Age of Capital*, 193–94.

11. United States Bureau of the Census, *Historical Statistics of the United States: Colonial Times to 1957* (Washington, 1961), 7–11.

12. Edwin J. Perkins, *American Public Finance and Financial Services, 1700–1815* (Columbus, OH, 1994); John Majewski, "Toward a Social History of the Corporation: Shareholding in Pennsylvania, 1800–1840," in Cathy Matson, ed. *The Economy of Early America: Historical Perspectives and New Directions* (Philadelphia, 2006).

13. Noble E. Cunningham, Jr., *The Process of Government under Jefferson* (Princeton, l978), 107; and L. Ray Gunn, *The Decline of Authority: Political Economic Policy and Political Development in New York State, 1800–1860* (Ithaca, 1988).

14. Malcolm Rohrbough, *The Land Office Business: The Settlement and Administration of American Public Lands, 1789–1837* (Oxford, 1968), 48, as cited in Cunningham, *Process of Government*, 107. See also Arthur H. Cole, "Cyclical and Sectional Variations in the Sale of Public Land," *Review of Economics and Statistics*, 9 (1927): 50; Andrew R. L. Cayton, *The Frontier Republic: Ideology and Politics in the Ohio Country, 1780–1825* (Kent, 1986), 115–17.

15. Matthew Gardner, *The Autobiography of Elder Matthew Gardner*, Dayton, 1874), 69; Christopher Clark, "The Agrarian Context of American Capitalist Development" and Jonathan Levy, " 'The Mortgage Worked the Hardest': The Nineteenth-Century Mortgage Market and the Law of Usury," in Michael Zakim and Gary Kornbluth, eds., *For Purposes of Profit: Essays on Capitalism in Nineteenth-Century America* (Chicago, 2009).

16. John C. Pease and John M. Niles, *A Gazetteer . . . of Connecticut and Rhode Island* (Hartford, 1819), 6.

17. T. J. Stiles, *The First Tycoon: The Epic Life of Cornelius Vanderbilt* (New York, 2009), 90–95.

18. Thomas P. Hughes, *Human-Built World: How to Think about Technology and Culture* (Chicago, 2004), 35.

19. Henry L. Ellsworth, *A Digest of Patents Issued by the United States, from 1790 to January 1, 1839* (Washington, 1840); see also Kenneth Sokoloff, "Inventive Activity in Early Industrial America: Evidence from Patent Records, 1790–1846," *Journal of Economic History*, 48 (1988): 818–20.

20. Alexis de Tocqueville, *Democracy in America*, trans. and ed. Harvey C. Mansfield and Delba Winthrop (Chicago, 2000 [originally published 1835, 1840]), 386.

21. Olive Cleaveland Clarke, *Things That I Remember at Ninety-Five* (1881), 10–11. This was in 1802.

22. Bureau of the Census, *Statistical Abstract of the United States* (Washington, 1983). For slave fertility, see Robert Fogel and Stanley Engerman, eds., *Without Consent or Contract: The Rise and Fall of American Slavery* (New York, 1989), 149. See also Andrew

R. L. Cayton, "The Early National Period," *Encyclopedia of American Social History*, ed. Mary Kupiec Cayton et al., 3 vols. (New York, 1993), I:100.

23. Warren S. Thompson, "The Demographic Revolution in the United States," *Annals of the American Academy of Political and Social Sciences*, no. 262 (1949): 62–69; Andrew Cayton, "The Early National Period," 88.

24. Allen Trimble, *1783–1870 Autobiography and Correspondence* (1909), 74; Gershom Flagg, *The Flagg Correspondence Selected Letters, 1816–1854*, eds., Barbara Lawrence and Nedra Branz (Carbondale, 1986), 5–7; William J. Baumol, *Productivity and American Leadership* (Cambridge, MA, 1991), 34–35.

25. Arnold Pacey, *Technology in World Civilization: A Thousand-Year History* (Cambridge, 1991), 135–41.

26. Lynn Hunt, Thomas R. Martin, Barbara H. Rosenwein, R. Po-chia Hsia, and Bonnie G. Smith, *The Making of the West: People and Cultures, A Concise History*, 2nd ed. (Boston, 2007), 708.

27. John Majewski, *A House Dividing: Economic Development in Pennsylvania and Virginia before the Civil War* (New York, 2000), 111–40.

28. Joseph A. Schumpeter, *Capitalism, Socialism and Democracy*, 3rd ed. (New York, 1950), 83.

29. Maarten Prak, ed., *Early Modern Capitalism: Economic and Social Change in Europe, 1400–1800* (New York, 2001), 194ff; "Werner von Siemens," *Allgemeine Deutsche Biographie*, online version, vol. 55 (Historische Kommission bei der Bayerischen Akademie der Wissenschaften und der Bayerischen Staatsbibliothek, 2007): 203–13.

30. Colleen A. Dunlavy, *Politics and Industrialization: Early Railroads in the United States and Prussia* (Princeton, 1994), 202–05.

31. Clive Trebilcock, *The Industrialization of the Continental Powers, 1780–1914* (London, 1981), 44–46, 172–77; Stiles, *First Tycoon*, 82–85; Dunlavy, *Politics and Industrialization*, 38–41.

32. Trebilcock, *Industrialization of Continental Powers*, 173–74; Robert E. Wright and Richard Sylla, eds., *The History of Corporate Finance: Development of Anglo-American Securities Markets, Financial Practices, Theories and Laws*, 4 vols. (London, 2003), iv.

33. Timor Kuran, "Explaining the Economic Trajectories of Civilizations: The Systemic Approach," *Journal of Economic Behavior and Organization* (2009).

34. Caroline Fohlin, *Finance Capitalism and Germany's Rise to Industrial Power* (New York, 2007), 65–69.

35. Charles P. Kindleberger, *A Financial History of Western Europe*, 2nd ed. (Oxford, 1993 [1984]), 102–10.

36. Thorstein Veblen, *Capitalism, Socialism and Democracy*, 3rd ed. (New York, 1950), 83.

37. Trebilcock, *Industrialization of Continental Powers*, 40; Fohlin, *Finance Capitalism and Germany's Rise to Industrial Power*, 220–21.

38. Margaret C. Jacob, *Strangers Nowhere in the World: The Rise of Cosmopolitanism in Early Modern Europe* (Philadelphia, 2006), 76–77; Thomas K. McGraw, "American Capitalism" in Thomas K. McGraw, ed., *Creating Modern Capitalism: How Entrepreneurs, Companies, and Countries Triumphed in Three Industrial Revolutions* (Cambridge, 1995), 335.

39. Robert C. Allen, "The British Industrial Revolution in Global Perspective," (2006): 29 [available on the Internet]; Kenneth Pomeranz and Steven Topik, *The World That Trade Created: Society, Culture, and the World Economy*, 2nd ed. (Armonk, NY, 2006), 113.

40. Irwin Unger, *Greenback Era: A Social and Political History of American Finance, 1865–1879* (Princeton, 1964), 13–20.

41. Mark Twain and Charles Dudley Warner, *The Gilded Age* (New York, 1873).

42. Stephen Mihm, *A Nation of Counterfeiters: Capitalists, Con Men, and the Making of the United States* (Cambridge, MA, 2007), 69–74.

43. Wright, *History of Corporate Finance*, 1:iv; Timothy W. Guinnane, Ron Harris, Naomi R. Lamoreaux, and Jean-Laurent Rosenthal, "Putting the Corporation in Its Place," *Enterprise and Society*, 8 (2007): 690–91.

44. Kindleberger, *Financial History of Western Europe*, 196.

45. Wright, *History of Corporate Finance*, I: x–xxvii.

46. McGraw, "American Capitalism" in McGraw, ed., *Creating Modern Capitalism*, 315–16.

47. Guinnane, Harris, Lamoreaux, and Rosenthal, "Putting the Corporation in Its Place": 698.

48. Trebilcock, *Industrialization of Continental Powers*, 54, 64–66.

49. Walter A. Moss, *An Age of Progress?: Clashing Twentieth Century Forces* (New York, 2008), 58–59.

50. Jeffrey A. Frieden, *Global Capitalism: Its Fall and Rise in the Twentieth Century* (New York, 2006), 6–7, 14–19, 42–43.

51. A striking exception to this generalization can be found in Colleen Dunlavy and Thomas Weisskopp, "Myths and Peculiarities: Comparing U.S. and German Capitalism," *German Historical Bulletin*, 41(2007).

52. Henry James, "The German Experience and the Myth of British Cultural Exceptionalism," in Bruce Collins and Keith Robbins, eds., *British Culture and Economic Decline* (London, 1990), 108.

53. Steve N. Broadberry, "How Did the United States and Germany Overtake Britain?: A Sectoral Analysis of Comparative Productivity Levels, 1870–1990," *Journal of Economic History*, 58 (1998): 375–76.

54. Margaret C. Jacob and Larry Stewart, *Practical Matter: Newton's Science in the Service of Industry and Empire, 1687–1851* (Cambridge, 2004), 126–27.

CHAPTER 7. THE INDUSTRIAL LEVIATHANS AND THEIR OPPONENTS

1. T. J. Stiles, *The First Tycoon: The Epic Life of Cornelius Vanderbilt* (New York, 2009).

2. Ibid., 279.

3. Harold C. Livesay, *Andrew Carnegie and the Rise of Big Business* (Boston, 1986).

4. Daniel Yergin, *The Prize: The Epic Quest for Oil, Money, and Power* (New York, 1991), 39–42.

5. Jeffrey Fear, "August Thyssen and German Steel," in Thomas K. McGraw, ed., *Creating Modern Capitalism: How Entrepreneurs, Companies, and Countries Triumphed in Three Industrial Revolutions* (Cambridge, 1997), 185–226; Clive Trebilcock, *The Industrialization of the Continental Powers, 1780–1914* (London, 1981), 61–62.

6. J. R. McNeill, *An Environmental History of the Twentieth-Century World* (New York, 2000), 24–25.

7. Jean-Christophe Agnew, "Capitalism, Culture and Catastrophe: Lawrence Levine and the Opening of Cultural History," *Journal of American History*, 93 (2006): 783

8. Jose C. Moya, "A Continent of Immigrants: Post Colonial Shifts in the Western Hemisphere," *Hispanic American Historical Review*, 86 (2006): 3–4; Stephen Nicholas and Deborah Oxley, "The Living Standard of Women during the Industrial Revolution, 1795–1820," *Economic History Review*, 46 (1993): 745–49.

9. Geoffrey Barraclough, ed., *Times Atlas of World History* (London, 1992), 208–09.

10. Adam Mckeown, "Global Migration, 1840–1940," *World History*, 15 (2004): 156.

11. Moya, "A Continent of Immigrants," 3–4.

12. Trebilcock, *Industrialization of Continental Powers*, 32; Alan S. Milward and S. B. Saul, *The Economic Development of Continental Europe, 1780–1870* (London, 1973), 142–45.

13. David Khoudour-Casteras, "The Impact of Bismarck's Social Legislation on German Emigration before World War I," eScholarship Repository, University of California; http://repositories.edlib.org/berkely.econ211/spring2005/, 4–45; Trebilcock, *Industrialization of Continental Powers*, 65–77; Hubert Kiesewetter, *Industrielle Revolution in Deutschland, 1815–1914*, Neue Historische Bibliothek (Frankfurt, 1989), 90.

14. Thomas Weiss, "U.S. Labor Force Estimates and Economic Growth, 1800 to 1860," in R. Gallman and J. Wallis, eds., *The Standard of Living in Early Nineteenth Century America* (Chicago, 1992), 8–10; Lee A. Craig and Thomas Weiss, "Hours at Work and Total Factor Productivity Growth in 19th-Century U.S. Agriculture," *Advances in Agricultural Economic History*, 1 (2000): 1–30; Weiss, "American Economic Miracle": 20.

15. Nelson Lichtenstein, *State of the Union: A Century of American Labor* (Princeton, 2002), 4; Karen Orren, *Belated Feudalism: Labor, the Law, and Liberal Developments in the United States* (Cambridge, 1992); Irwin Unger, *The Greenback Era: A Social and Political History of American Finance, 1865–1879* (Princeton, 1964), 22.

16. Mark Twain and Charles Dudley Warren, *The Gilded Age* (New York, 1973); Upton Sinclair, *The Jungle* (New York, 1906).

17. Walter G. Moss, *An Age of Progress?: Clashing Twentieth-Century Global Forces* (New York, 2008), 3–12.

18. Lisa Tiersten, "Redefining Consumer Culture: Recent Literature on Consumption and the Bourgeoisie in Western Europe," *Radical History Review*, 57 (1995): 116–59.

19. Lisa Jacobson, *Raising Consumers: Children and the American Mass Market in the Early Twentieth Century* (New York, 2004).

20. Price F. Fishback and Shawn Everett Kantor, "The Adoption of Workers' Compensation in the United States, 1900–1930," *Journal of Law and Economics*, 41 (1998): 305–308.

21. Alfred D. Chandler, Jr., *Scale and Scope: The Dynamics of Industrial Capitalism* (Cambridge, 1990), 70ff, 167–70, 218–36, 375ff, 430–34.

22. Rosanne Curriaro, "The Politics of 'More': The Labor Question and the Idea of Economic Liberty in Industrial America," *Journal of American History*, 93 (2006): 22–27.

CHAPTER 8. RULERS AS CAPITALISTS

1. Thomas Pakenham, *The Scramble for Africa: White Man's Conquest of the Dark Continent from 1876 to 1912* (New York, 1991), 18–74; Adam Hochschild, *King Leopold's Ghost: A Story of Greed, Terror, and Heroism in Colonial Africa* (New York, 1999), 26–33.

2. Tim Jeal, *Stanley: The Impossible Life of Africa's Greatest Explorer* (New Haven, 2007), 230.

3. Pakenham, *Scramble for Africa*, 15, 22.

4. Ibid., 71–87.

5. Kenneth Pomeranz and Steven Topik, *The World That Trade Created: Society, Culture, and the World Economy*, 2nd ed. (Armonk, NY, 2006), 108–09.

6. Debora Silverman, "'The Congo, I Presume'": Tepid Revisionism in the Royal Museum of Central Africa, Tervuren, 1910/2005," Paper given at the annual meeting of the American Historical Association, January 2–6, 2009.

7. Geoffrey Barraclough, ed., *The Times Atlas of World History*, rev. ed. (London, 1984), 238–41.

8. Pomeranz and Topik, *World That Trade Created*, 130–32.

9. Jonathan Holland, ed., *Puerto del Sol*, 13 (2006): 4: 61–62; 14 (2007): 38–40.

10. Walter G. Moss, *An Age of Progress?: Clashing Twentieth Century Forces* (New York, 2008).

11. Hannah Arendt, *The Origins of Totalitarianism* (New York, 1951).

12. Jared Diamond, *Guns, Germs and Steel: The Fates of Human Societies* (New York, 1999), 56–57.

13. Lynn Hunt, *Inventing Human Rights: A History* (New York, 2007).

14. Kazushi Ohkawa and Henry Rosovsky, "Capital Formation in Japan," in Kozo Yamamura, ed., *The Economic Emergence of Modern Japan* (New York, 1997), 208.

15. F. G. Notehelfer, "Meiji in the Rear-View Mirror: Top Down vs. Bottom Up History," *Monumenta Nipponica*, 45 (1990): 207–28.

16. W. G. Beasley, *The Modern History of Japan*, 2nd ed. (New York, 1973), 156–57, 311, 120–31; Notehelfer, "Meifi in the Rear-View Mirror," 222–26; E. Sydney Crawcour, "Economic Change in the Nineteenth Century" and "Industrialization and Technological Change, 1885–1920," in Yamamura, ed., *Economic Emergence of Modern Japan*, 34–41, 53–55; Thomas K. McGraw, Introduction to Thomas K. McGraw, ed. *Creating Modern Capitalism: How Entrepreneurs, Companies, and Countries Triumphed in Three Industrial Revolutions* (Cambridge, 1995), 1.

17. Kaoru Sugahara, "Labour-Intensive Industrialisation in Global History: The Second Notel Butlin Lecture," *Australian Journal of Economic History*, 47 (2007): 134, n. 24; Ohkawa and Rosovsky, "Capital Formation in Japan," in Yamamura, ed., *Economic Emergence of Modern Japan*, 214–15; Mark Elvin, "The Historian as Haruspex," *New Left Review*, 52 (2008): 88.

18. Yamamura, ed., *Economic Emergence of Modern Japan*, 34–41, 53–55.

19. Beasley, *Modern History of Japan*, 134–49.

20. Constance Chen, "From Passion to Discipline: East Asian Art and the Culture of Modernity in the United States, 1876–1945" (UCLA dissertation, 2000).

21. Yamamura, ed., *Economic Emergence of Modern Japan*, 112.

22. Jon Halliday, *A Political History of Japanese Capitalism* (New York, 1975), 82–91.

23. Ibid., 112.

24. Alfred D. Chandler, Jr., *Scale and Scope: The Dynamics of Industrial Capitalism* (Cambridge, 1990), 226–29.

25. Mary A. Yeager, "Will There Ever Be a Feminist Business History?," in Mary A. Yeager, ed., *Women in Business* (Cheltenham, 1999), 12–15, 33–34.

26. Duncan K. Foley, *Adam's Fallacy: A Guide to Economic Theology* (Cambridge, 2006), 9.

27. Thomas K. McGraw, "American Capitalism," in McGraw, ed., *Creating Modern Capitalism*, 327–28.

28. Alfred D. Chandler, Jr., and Stephen Salsbury, *Pierre S. du Pont and the Making of the Modern Corporation* (New York, 1971), 591–600.

29. Charles S. Maier, "Accounting for the Achievements of Capitalism: Alfred Chandler's Business History," *Journal of Modern History*, 65 (1993): 779–82.

30. Chandler, Jr., *Scale and Scope*, 74–78, 21; Colleen Dunlavy and Thomas Weiskopp, "Myths and Peculiarities: Comparing U.S. and German Capitalism," *German Historical Bulletin*, no. 41 (2007):18–19; Naomi Lamoreaux, *The Great Merger Movement in American Business, 1895–1904* (Cambridge, 1895), 2–5.

31. Peter Barnes, *Capitalism 3.0: A Guide to Reclaiming the Commons* (San Francisco, 2006), 20–23.

32. Miguel Cantillo Simon, "The Rise and Fall of Bank Control in the United States, 1890–1939," *American Economic Review*, 88 (1998): 1079–83; Vincent P. Carosso, *Investment Banking in America: A History* (Cambridge, 1970), 496–99; Ronald Dore, William Lazonick, and Mary O'Sullivan, "Varieties of Capitalism in the Twentieth Century," *Oxford Review of Economic Policy*, 15 (1999): 104.

33. McGraw, "American Capitalism," 322–25.

34. John M. Kleeberg, "German Cartels: Myths and Realities," http://www.econ.barnard .columbia.edu/~econhist/papers/Kleeberg_German_Cartels.

35. Chandler, Jr., *Scale and Scope*, 492.

36. Dore, Lazonick, and O'Sullivan, "Varieties of Capitalism in the Twentieth Century," 104.

37. James, *A German Identity*, 57.

38. Charles P. Kindleberger, *The World in Depression, 1919–1939*, rev. and enlarged ed. (Berkeley, 1986), 291.

39. Jeffrey Fear, "August Thyssen and German Steel," in McGraw, ed., *Creating Modern Capitalism*, 191; Clive Trebilock, *Industrialization of Continental Powers, 1780–1914* (London, 1982), 63–64.

40. Henry James, "The German Experience and the Myth of British Cultural Exceptionalism," in Bruce Collins and Keith Robbins, eds., *British Culture and Economic Decline: Debates in Modern History* (London, 1990), 108–11.

41. Richard B. DuBoff, *Electric Power in American Manufacturing, 1889–1958* (New York, 1979), 17, 100–01.

42. Lee Iacocca, "Builders & Titans," *The Time 100* (New York, 2000). Available also at www.time.com/time/time100/builder/profile/ford.

43. James P. Womack, Daniel T. Jones, and Daniel Roos, *The Machine That Changed the World* (New York, 1990), 30–31.

44. Moss, *Age of Progress?*, 38, 62; Lynn Hunt, Thomas R. Martin, Barbara H. Rosenwein, R. Po-chia Hsia, and Bonnie G. Smith, *The Making of the West: People and Cultures: A Concise History*, 2nd ed. (Boston, 2007), 881.

45. Thomas K. McGraw and Richard S. Tedlow, "Henry Ford, Alfred Sloan, and the Three Phases of Marketing," in McGraw, ed., *Creating Modern Capitalism*, 269.

46. Kindleberger, *The World in Depression*, 43.

47. William Berg, "History of GM," http://ezinearticles.com/?The-History-of-GM---General-Motors&id=110696.

48. Pomeranz and Topik, *World That Trade Created*, 97–100.

49. Daniel Yergin, *The Prize: The Epic Quest for Oil, Money, and Power* (New York, 1991), 58–63.

50. Ibid., 110-11.
51. Simon, "Rise and Fall of Bank Control": 1077-93.

CHAPTER 9. WAR AND DEPRESSION

1. Rondo Cameron, *A Concise Economic History of the World: From Paleolithic Times to the Present* (New York, 1989), 347-50.
2. Charles Kindleberger, *A Financial History of Western Europe*, 2nd ed. (New York, 1993), 308-13.
3. Alan S. Milward and S. B. Saul, *The Economic Development of Continental Europe, 1780-1870* (London, 1973), 128, 130, 142-68.
4. Walter G. Moss, *An Age of Progress?: Clashing Twentieth-Century Global Forces* (New York, 2008), 42.
5. W. G. Beasley, *The Modern History of Japan*, 2nd ed. (New York, 1973), 161-63; Jon Halliday, *A Political History of Japanese Capitalism* (New York, 1975) 84-86.
6. Kozo Yamamura, ed., *Economic Emergence of Modern Japan* (New York, 1997), 123-37.
7. Charles P. Kindleberger, *The World in Depression, 1929-1939* (Berkeley, 1986), 119.
8. Lizbeth Cohen, *Making a New Deal: Industrial Workers in Chicago, 1919-1939* (New York, 1990), 102-03, 213-35.
9. Jack Garraty, *The Great Depression* (New York, 1987), 23; Cameron, *Concise Economic History of the World*, 356-60.
10. Garraty, *Great Depression*, 75-77.
11. John Maynard Keynes, *The General Theory of Employment, Interest and Money* (London, 1930).
12. Paul Krugman, "Franklin Delano Obama?," *New York Times*, November 10, 2008.
13. Richard Overy, "About the Second World War," excerpted from Charles Townshend, ed., *The Oxford Illustrated History of Modern War* (New York, 1997), available at englishuiuc.edu/maps/ww2/overy, 10.
14. Bill Gordon, "Greater East Asia Co-Prosperity Sphere," www.wgordon.web.wesleyan.edu.; Beasley, *Modern History of Japan*, 256-57.
15. Geoffrey Barraclough, ed., *The Times Atlas of World History*, rev. ed. (Maplewood, NJ, 1985), 280-81.
16. Beasley, *Modern History of Japan*, 268-76.
17. Mark Harrison, "Resource Mobilization for World War II: The U.S.A., U.K., U.S.S.R., and Germany, 1938-1945," *Economic History Review*, 2nd ser., 12 (1988): 175.
18. Overy, "About the Second World War," 6.
19. Ibid., 10.
20. Ibid., 4.

CHAPTER 10. A NEW LEVEL OF PROSPERITY

1. Jeffrey A. Frieden, *Global Capitalism: Its Fall and Rise in the Twentieth Century* (2006 [paperback ed., 2007]), 287; Charles Kindleberger, *A Financial History of Western Europe*, 2nd ed. (New York, 1993), 453.

2. Elizabeth Borgwardt, *A New Deal for the World: America's Vision for Human Rights* (Cambridge, 2005), 14–15.
3. Kindleberger, *Financial History of Western Europe*, 453.
4. Cameron, *Concise Economic History of the World*, 371–78.
5. Frieden, *Global Capitalism*, 278; N. R. R. Crafts, "The Golden Age of Economic Growth in Western Europe, 1950–1973," *Economic History Review*, 48 (1995): 429–30; Angus Maddison, *Dynamic Forces in Capitalist Development: A Long-Run Comparative View* (Oxford, 1991), 164.
6. Diethelm Prowe, "Economic Democracy in Post–World War II Germany: Corporatist Crisis Response, 1945–1948," *Journal of Modern History*, 57 (1985): 452–58.
7. Paul L. Davies, "A Note on Labour and Corporate Governance in the U.K.," in Klaus J. Hopt et al., eds., *Comparative Corporate Governance: The State of the Art and Emerging Research* (Oxford, 1999), 373; Martin Wolf, "European Corporatism Must Embrace Change," *Financial Times*, January 23, 2007.
8. Maddison, *Dynamic Forces in Capitalist Development*, 274–75; Frieden, *Global Capitalism*, 289.
9. John Gillingham, "The European Coal and Steel Community: An Object Lesson," in Barry Eichengreen, ed., *Europe's Post-War Recovery* (Cambridge, 1995), 152–53, 166.
10. Barry Eichengreen, "Mainsprings of Economic Recovery," in ibid.: 6–21.
11. Cameron, *Concise Economic History of the World*, 377–78.
12. H. Bathelt, C. Wiseman, and G. Zakrzewski, "Automobile Industry: A 'Driving Force' behind the German Economy," wwwgeog/specialist/vgt/Englisih/ger, 2.
13. Mary Nolan, review of Hans Mommsen, *Volkswagenweck and seine Arbeiter im Dritten Reich, International Labor and Working Class History*, 55 (1999): 149–54.
14. Maddison, *Dynamic Forces in Capitalist Development*, 151; Cameron, *a Concise Economic History of the World*, 329–30.
15. James F. Hollifield, *Immigrants, Markets, and States: The Political Economy of Postwar Europe* (Cambridge, 1992), 4–5.
16. Maddison, *Dynamic Forces in Capitalist Development*, 128; Russell Shorto, "Childless Europe: What Happens to a Continent When It Stops Making Babies?," *New York Times Magazine*, June 29, 2008.
17. Robert Higgs, "From Central Planning to the Market: The American Transition, 1945–1947," *Journal of Economic History*, 59 (1999): 611–13. The wonderful list of government measures is Higgs's.
18. Tom Lewis, "The Roads to Prosperity," *Los Angeles Times*, December 26, 2008.
19. Nelson Lichtenstein, *State of the Union: A Century of American Labor* (Princeton, 2002), 76–80; Nelson Lichtenstein, "American Trade Unions and the 'Labor Question': Past and Present," in *What's Next for Organized Labor: The Report of the Century Foundation Task Force on the Future of Unions* (New York, 1999), 65–70.
20. Frieden, *Global Capitalism*, 261–62; Higgs, "From Central Planning to the Market": 600.
21. Kindleberger, *Financial History*, 413–17.
22. Louis Hyman, "Debtor Nation: How Consumer Credit Built Postwar America" (Ph.D. dissertation, Harvard, 2007); Karen Orren, *Corporate Power and Social Change: The Politic of the Life Insurance Industry* (Baltimore, 1974), 127–31.

23. Alfred D. Chandler, Jr., *Inventing the Electronic Century: The Epic Story of the Consumer Electronics and Computer Industries* (New York, 2001), 27–30.

24. Vanessa Schwartz, "Towards a Cultural History of the Jet Age," Paper presented in Paris, November 13, 2008.

25. Walter G. Moss, *An Age of Progress?: Clashing Twentieth Century Forces* (New York, 2008), 2–23.

26. Clark Kerr, *The Uses of the University* (Cambridge, MA, 1963).

27. Kenneth Flamm, "Technological Advance and Costs: Computers versus Communications," in Robert W. Crandall and Kenneth Flamm, eds., *Changing the Rules: Technological Change, International Competition, and Regulation in Communications* (Washington, 1989), 15–20.

28. Rowena Olegario, "IBM and the Two Thomas J. Watsons," in Thomas K. McGraw, ed., *Creating Modern Capitalism: How Entrepreneurs, Companies, and Countries Triumphed in Three Industrial Revolutions* (Cambridge, 1997), 352.

29. *Public Papers of the Presidents of the United States* (Washington) Dwight D. Eisenhower Papers (Washington, 1960) 1035–40.

30. J. R. McNeill, *Something New under the Sun: An Environmental History of the Twentieth-Century World* (New York, 2000), 149, 168–69, 178–80.

31. Olegario, "IBM and the Two Thomas J. Watsons," 349–93.

32. Ibid., 350–54.

33. Chandler, *Inventing the Electronic Century*, 91; Emerson W. Pugh, *Memories that Shaped An Industry: Decisions Leading to IBM System/360* (Cambridge, 1984), 187–90.

34. Olegario, "IBM and the Two Thomas J. Watsons," 378–79.

35. Ibid., 366–70.

36. Robert Korstad and Nelson Lichtenstein, "Opportunities Found and Lost: Labor, Radicals, and the Early Civil Rights Movement," *Journal of American History*, 75 (1988): 786–96.

37. Stephen F. Rohde, *Freedom of Assembly* (New York, 2005), 33–38; Frieden, *Global Capitalism*, 299–300.

38. Roger Lowenstein, "The Prophet of Pensions," *Los Angeles Times Opinion*, May 11, 2008.

39. *New York Times*, June 18, 2008.

40. Crafts, "Golden Age of Economic Growth in Western Europe," 433.

41. Joseph A. McCartin, "A Wagner Act for Public Employees: Labor's Deferred Dream, and the Rise of Conservatives, 1970–1976," *Journal of American History*, 95 (2008): 129–31; Tami J. Friedman, "Exploiting the North-South Differential: Corporate Power, Southern Politics, and the Decline of Organized Labor after World War II," *Journal of American History*, 95 (2008): 323–48.

42. Frieden, *Global Capitalism*, 344.

43. Olegario, "IBM and the Two Thomas J. Watsons," 356.

44. Maddison, *Dynamic Forces in Capitalist Development*, 148.

45. Cameron, *Concise Economic History of the World*, 394.

46. Maddison, *Dynamic Forces in Capitalist Development*, 155–167.

47. Daniel Yergin, *The Prize: The Epic Quest for Oil, Money, and Power* (New York, 1991), 601–909.

48. Ibid., 590–91.

49. Barbara Weinstein, "Presidential Address: Developing Inequality," *American Historical Review*, 113 (2008): 15.

50. Kaoru Sugihara, "Labour-Intensive Industrialisation in Global History," *Australian Economic History Review*, 47 (2001): 122.

51. Joyce Appleby, "Modernization Theory and the Formation of Modern Social Theories in England and America," *Comparative Studies in Society and History*, 20 (1978): 260; Crafts, "Golden Age of Economic Growth in Western Europe," 434; Barbara Weinstein, "Developing Inequality," *American Historical Review*, 113 (2008): 6–8.

CHAPTER 11. CAPITALISM IN NEW SETTINGS

1. Sheldon L. Richman, "The Sad Legacy of Ronald Reagan," *Free Market*, 10 (1988): 1.

2. Milton Friedman, "Noble Lecture: Inflation and Unemployment" and Gary Becker, "Afterward: Milton Friedman as a Microeconomist," in *Milton Friedman on Economics: Selected Papers* (Chicago, 2007), 1–22, 181–86.

3. Edward Perkins, "The Rise and Fall of Relationship Banking," www.Common-Place .org, 9:2 (2009).

4. Andrew Ross Sorkin, "A 'Bonfire' Returns as Heartburn," *New York Times*, June 24, 2008.

5. Thomas K. McGraw, Introduction to Thomas K. McGraw, ed., *Creating Modern Capitalism: How Entrepreneurs, Companies, and Countries Triumphed in Three Industrial Revolutions* (Cambridge, 1995), 1.

6. Ronald Dore, William Lazonick, and Mary O'Sullivan, "Varieties of Capitalism in the Twentieth Century," *Oxford Review of Economic Policy*, 15 (1999): 105; Randall K. Morck and Masao Nakamura, "A Frog in a Well Knows Nothing of the Ocean," in Randall K. Morck, ed., *A History of Corporate Governance around the World: Family Business Groups to Professional Managers*, National Bureau of Economic Research Report (Chicago, 2007), 450–52.

7. Yutaka Kosai, "The Postwar Japanese Economy, 1945–1973," in Yamamura, ed., *Economic Emergence of Modern Japan*.

8. Ibid., 138–39, 185.

9. Ian Buruma, "Who Freed Asia?," *Los Angeles Times*, August 31, 2007; W. G. Beasley, *Modern History of Japan*, 2nd ed. (New York, 1973), 286–87.

10. Beasley, *Modern History of Japan*, 290–93, 303–07, 311–14; Jon Halliday and Gavin McCormack, *A Political History of Japanese Capitalism* (New York, 1978), 195–203; Normitsu Onishi, "No Longer a Reporter, but a Muckraker within Japan's Parliament," *New York Times*, July 19, 2008.

11. Kosai, "Postwar Japanese Economy," 181–89.

12. Rondo Cameron, *A Concise Economic History of the World: From Paleolithic Times to the Present* (New York, 1989), 375, 392; James P. Womack, Daniel T. Jones, and Daniel Roos, *The Machine That Changed the World* (New York, 1990), 11.

13. Womack, Jones, and Roos, ibid., 159–68.

14. Ibid., 240–45; Ralph Landau, "Strategy for Economic Growth: Lessons from the Chemical Industry," in Ralph Landau, Timothy Taylor, Gavin Wright, eds., *The Mosaic of Economic Growth* (Stanford, 1996), 411–12.

15. Kosai, "Postwar Japanese Economy," 198; Nick Bunkley, "Toyota Moves Ahead of G.M. in Auto Sales," *New York Times*, July 24, 2008.

16. Jeffrey R. Bernstein, "Japanese Capitalism," in McGraw, ed., *Creating Modern Capitalism*, 473–74.

17. Ibid., 477–78; Kosai, "Postwar Japanese Economy," 192–93; E. S. Crawcour, "Industrialization and Technological Change, 1885–1920," in Yamamura, ed., *Economic Emergence of Modern Japan*, 341; Womack, Jones, and Roos, *Machine That Changed the World*, 54.

18. Alfred D. Chandler, Jr., *Inventing the Electronic Century: The Epic Story of the Consumer Electronics and Computer Science Industries* (New York, 2001), 35–40.

19. Ibid., 45–48.

20. Walter G. Moss, *An Age of Progress?: Clashing Twentieth Century* (New York, 2008), 44; Rowena Olegario, "IBM and the Two Thomas J. Watsons," in Thomas K. McGraw, ed., *Creating Modern Capitalism*, 355; Chandler, Jr., *Inventing the Electronic Century*, 136–37.

21. Ben Marsden and Crosbie Smith, *Engineering Empires: A Cultural History of Technology in Nineteenth-Century Britain* (New York, 2005), 99; Chandler, Jr., *Inventing the Electronic Century*, 137.

22. Olegario, "Two Thomas J. Watsons," 383.

23. Chandler, Jr., *Inventing the Electronic Century*, 35–40; Lee S. Sproul, "Computers in U.S. Households since 1977," in Alfred D. Chandler, Jr., and James W. Cortada, eds., *A Nation Transformed by Information: How Information Has Shaped the United States from Colonial Times to the Present* (New York, 2003), 257.

24. Emerson W. Pugh, *Building IBM: Shaping an Industry and Its Technology* (Cambridge, MA, 1995), 314; Chandler, Jr., *Inventing the Electronic Century*, 140–41.

25. Ibid.

26. Ibid., 170–75.

27. Alex MacGillivray, *A Brief History of Globalization: The Untold Story of Our Incredible Shrinking Planet* (New York, 2006), 267.

28. David Carr, "Google Seduces with Utility," *New York Times*, November 24, 2008.

29. Kenneth Flamm "Technological Advance and Costs," in Robert W. Crandall and Kenneth Flamm, eds., *Changing the Rules: International Competition, and Regulation in Communications* (Washington, 1989), 28; Marsden and Smith, *Engineering Empires*, 100–1.

30. "Tech Hot Spots," Silicon.com (2008).

31. William S. Broad and Cornelia Dean, "Rivals Visions Differ on Unleashing Innovation," *New York Times*, October 16, 2008.

32. Olegario, "Two Thomas J. Watsons," 381.

33. Chandler, Jr., *Inventing the Electronic Century*, 233–34.

34. Brenton R. Shlender, "U.S. PCs Invade Japan," *Fortune*, July 12, 1993.

35. Chandler, Jr., *Inventing the Electronic Century*, 211–12; Michael C. Latham, *Modernization as Ideology: American Social Science and "Nation-Building" in the Kennedy Era* (Chapel Hill, 2000).

36. Richard A. Stanford, "The Dependency Theory Critique of Capitalism," Furman University Web site.

37. Barbara Stallings, "The Role of Foreign Capital in Economic Development" in Gary

Gereffi and Donald L. Wyman, eds., *Manufacturing Miracles: Paths of Industrialization in Latin America and East Asia* (New York, 1990), 56–57.

38. Stephen Haggard, "The Politics of Industrialization in the Republic of Korea and Taiwan," in Helen Hughes, ed., *Achieving Industrialization in East Asia* (Cambridge, 1988), 262–63.

39. Ian Buruma, "Who Freed Asia?," *Los Angeles Times*, August 31, 2007.

40. Robert Wade, "The Role of Government in Overcoming Market Failure in Taiwan, Republic of Korea, and Japan," in Hughes, ed., *Achieving Industrialization in East Asia*, 157–59.

41. Seiji Naya, "The Role of Trade Policies in the Industrialization of Rapidly Growing Asian Developing Countries," in Hughes, ed., *Achieving Industrialization in East Asia*, 64.

42. James Riedel, "Industrialization and Growth: Alternative Views of East Asia," in Hughes, ed., *Achieving Industrialization in East Asia*, 9–13.

43. Chandler, Jr., *Inventing the Electronic Century*, 212–15; David Mitch, "The Role of Education and Skill in the British Industrial Revolution," in Joel Mokyr, ed., *The British Industrial Revolution* (Oxford, 1999), 277–78.

44. Nancy Birdsall, "Inequalitiy Matters: Why Globalization Doesn't Lift All Boats," *Boston Review* (March–April 2007): 7–11.

45. Amelia Gentleman, "Sex Selection by Abortion Is Denounced in New Delhi," *New York Times*, April 29, 2008.

46. Choe Sang-Hun, "South Korea, Where Boys Were Kings, Revalues Its Girls," *New York Times*, October 23, 2007.

47. Robert W. Crandall and Kenneth Flamm, "Overview," in Crandall and Flamm, eds., *Changing the Rules*, 114–29; Tony A. Freyer, *Antitrust and Global Capitalism* (New York, 2006), 6–7.

48. Dick K. Nanto, "The 1997–98 Asian Financial Crisis," CRS Report for Congress, February 6, 1998 (www.fas.org/man/crs/crs-asia2), 5.

49. "The Time 100," *New York* (2000).

50. Thomas L. Friedman, *The World Is Flat: A Brief History of the Twenty-first Century* (New York, 2005), 128–39; Nelson Lichtenstein, "Why Working at Wal-Mart Is Different," *Connecticut Law Review*, 39 (2007): 1649–84; "How Wal-Mart Fights Unions," *Minnesota Law Review*, 92 (2008): 1462–1501.

51. Kenneth Pomeranz and Steven Topik, *The World That Trade Created: Society, Culture, and the World Ecoomy, 1400 to the Present* (Armonk, NY, 2006), 260.

52. Robert Pollin et al., *A Measure of Fairness: The Economics of Living Wages and Minimum Wages in the United States* (Amherst, 2008).

53. Nelson Lichtenstein, "American Trade Unions and the 'Labor Question': Past and Present, *What's Next for Organized Labor: The Report of the Century Foundation Task Force on the Future of Unions"* (New York, 1999); Steven Greenhouse, *The Big Squeeze: Tough Times for the American Worker* (New York, 2008), 289–301.

54. Robert Brenner, *The Economics of Global Turbulence: The Advanced Capitalist Economies from Long Boom to Long Downturn, 1945–2005* (London, 2006).

55. Charles R. Beitz, "Does Global Inequality Matter?," in Thomas W Pogge, ed., *Global Justice* (Oxford, 2001), 106, quoted in Barbara Weinstein, "Developing Inequality," *American Historical Review*, 113 (2008): 2.

CHAPTER 12. INTO THE TWENTY-FIRST CENTURY

1. Kenneth Pomeranz and Steven Topik, *The World That Trade Created: Society, Culture, and the World Economy, 1400 to the Present* (Armonk, NY, 2006), 263; Joseph E. Stiglitz, "Capital Market Liberalization, Globalization, and the IMF," *Oxford Review of Economic Policy*, 20 (2004).

2. Justin Yifu Lin, "Lessons of China's Transition from a Planned Economy to a Market Economy," *Distinguished Lectures Series*, no. 16 (2004): 30; Jonathan Holland, ed., "Top Manta: la pirateria musical en Espana," *Puerto del Sol*, vol. 11, no. 5 (2003): 15–18; Stephen Mihm, "A Nation of Outlaws," *Boston Globe*, August 26, 2007.

3. Tina Rosenberg, "Globalization," *New York Times*, July 30, 2008.

4. Jeffrey A. Frieden, *Global Capitalism: Its Fall and Rise in the Twentieth Century* (New York, 2007), 166–67, 467–70.

5. Kenneth Pomeranz, "Chinese Development in Long-Run Perspective," *American Philosophical Society Proceedings*, 152 (2008): 83–84.

6. Barry Naughton, *The Chinese Economy: Transitions and Growth* (Cambridge, 2007), 82, 222.

7. Ibid., 217–19.

8. S. Shuming Bao et al., "Geographic Factors and China's Regional Development under Market Reforms, 1978–98," *China Economic Review*, 13 (2002): 90, 109–10; Lin, "Lessons of China's Transition": 2; Naughton, *Chinese Economy*, 222.

9. Lin, "Lessons of China's Transition": 29.

10. Wing Thye Woo, "Transition Strategies: The Second Round of Debate" (2000): 10.

11. Siri Schubert and T. Christian Miller, "Where Bribery Was Just a Line Item," *New York Times*, December 21, 2008.

12. Naughton, *Chinese Economy*, 79; Philip Huang, *The Peasant Family and Rural Development in the Yangzi Delta, 1350–1988* (Stanford, 1990); Philip Huang, *The Peasant Economy and Social Change in North China* (Stanford, 1985).

13. C. V. Ranganathan, "How to Understand Deng Xiaping's China," in Tan Chung, ed., *Across the Himalayan Gap: An Indian Quest for Understanding China* (1998).

14. Pomeranz, "Chinese Development in Long-Run Perspective": 90–92.

15. Naughton, *Chinese Economy*, 202–3, 398.

16. Pomeranz, "Chinese Development in Long-Run Perspective": 95.

17. Edward Wong, "In Major Shift, China May Let Peasants Sell Rights to Farmland," *New York Times*, October 11, 2008.

18. Naughton, *Chinese Economy*, 161.

19. David E. Bloom et al., "Why Has China's Economy Taken Off Faster than India's?" (June 2006), available on the Web; Kenneth Pomeranz, "Why China's Dollar Pile Has to Shrink (Relatively Soon)," *China Beat Blog*, http://thechinabeat.blogspot.com/2008/01/why-chinas-dollar-pile-has-to-shrink.htmlp, January 19, 2008.

20. Woo, "Transition Strategies": 10; Ranganathan, "How to Understand Deng Xiapeng's China."

21. James Fallows, "China Makes, the World Takes," *Atlantic Monthly* (July–August 2007); Ching-Ching Ni, "The Beijing She Knew Is Gone; In Its Place, the Beijing She Loves," *Los Angeles Times*, August 3, 2008.

22. Donald Clarke, Peter Murrell, and Susan Whiting, "The Role of Law in China's Economic Development" and Fang Cai, Albert Park, and Yohui Zhao, "The Chinese Labor

Market in the Reform Era," in Loren Brandt and Thomas G. Rawski, eds., *China's Great Economic Transformation* (New York, 2008), 172–73, 390–91; Robert Brenner, *The Economics of Global Turbulence: The Advanced Capitalist Economies from Long Boom to Long Downturn, 1945–2005* (London, 2006), 324–26; Emily Hannum, Jere Behrman, Meiyan Wang, and Jihong Liu, "Education in the Reform Era" and Alan Heston and Terry Sicular, "China and Development Economics," in Brandt and Rawski, eds., *China's Great Economic Transformation*, 233, 40.

23. Naughton, *Chinese Economy*, 422–23, 107–10, 478–81; Keith Bradsher, "Qualifying Tests for Financial Workers," *New York Times*, December 26, 2008.

24. Hannum, Behrman, Wang, and Liu, "Éducation in the Reform Era" and Heston and Sicular, "China and Development Economics," 233, 40; Amy Chua, *World on Fire: How Exporting Free Market Democracy Breeds Ethnic Hatred and Global Instability* (New York, 2005), 3–7.

25. D. S. Rajan, "China: Tibet-Indian Ocean Trade Route—Mixing Strategy, Security and Commerce," *South Asia Analysis Group*, Paper No. 1546 (2005); Somini Sengupta, "After 60 Years, India and Pakistan Begin Trade across the Line Dividing Kashmir," *New York Times*, October 22, 2008.

26. Lin, "Lessons of China's Transition": 16; Jeffrey D. Sachs and Wing Thye Woo, "Understanding China's Economic Performance," *Journal of Policy Reform*, 4 (2000): 18; Woo, "Transition Strategies": 10, 12, 23; Sachs and Woo, "China's Economic Growth after WTO Membership," *Journal of Chinese Economic and Business Studies*, vol. 1, no. 27 (2003): 27; Albert G. S. Yu and Gary H. Jefferson, "Science and Technology in China," in Brandt and Rawski, *China's Great Economic Transformation*, 320.

27. Qiu Xiaolong, *Death of a Red Heroine* (New York, 2000), 135, 308.

28. J. R. McNeill, *Something New under the Sun: An Environmental History of the Twentieth-Century World* (New York, 2000), 107.

29. Mark Magnier, "Bribery and Graft Taint Every Facet of Life in China," *Los Angeles Times*, December 29, 2008.

30. Barry Naughton, "China: Which Way the Political Economy?," Paper delivered at the UCLA Brenner Seminar, April 9, 2007.

31. Lin, "Lessons of China's Transition": 3. The opinion expressed is that of Grzegorz W. Kolodko.

32. Parag Khanna, "Waving Goodbye to Hegemony," *New York Times Magazine*, January 27, 2008.

33. Manu Goswami, *Producing India: From Colonial Economy to National Space* (Chicago, 2004), 46–53.

34. Ibid., 224–26, 233.

35. Pranah Bardhan, "What Makes a Miracle?: Some Myths about the rise of China and India," *Boston Review* (January–February 2008); Heston and Sicular, "China and Development Economics," 31.

36. *Los Angeles Times*, July 7, 1973, Part 1:6.

37. Somini Sengupta, "A Daughter of India's Underclass Rises on Votes That Cross Caste Lines, *New York Times*, July 18, 2008.

38. Bardhan, "What Makes a Miracle?": 11–13; Amartya Sen, *Development as Freedom* (New York, 1999), 149–51, and "An Elephant, Not a Tiger: A Special Report on India," *Economist*, December 13, 2008, 6.

39. Naughton, *Chinese Economy*, 154–57, 196.

40. McNeill, *Something New under the Sun*, 219–21.

41. Naughton, *Chinese Economy*, 497; Mira Kamdar, *Planet India: The Turbulent Rise of the Largest Democracy and the Future of Our World* (New York, 2007), 143–48, 160, 179–85; Somini Sengupta, "India's Growth Outstrips Crops," *New York Times*, June 22, 2008.

42. Kamdar, *Planet India*, 112–16.

43. Ibid., 192–94, 102, 116–17; Jeremy Kahn, "Booming India Is Suddenly Caught in the Credit Vise," *New York Times*, October 24, 2008; Joe Nocera, "How India Avoided a Crisis," *New York Times*, December 20, 2008.

44. Kamdar, *Planet India*, 102, 107, 124; Anand Giridharadas, "Indian to the Core, and an Oligarch," *New York Times*, June 15, 2008.

45. Gurcharan Das, "The Next World Order," *New York Times*, January 2, 2009.

46. Keith Bradsher, "A Younger India Is Flexing Its Industrial Brawn," *New York Times*, September 11, 2008.

47. Alexei Barrionuevo, "For Wealthy Brazilian, Money from Ore and Might from the Cosmos," *New York Times*, August 2, 2008.

48. Kahn, "Booming India Is Suddenly Caught in the Credit Vise."

49. Heather Timmons, "Singing the Praises of a New Asia," *New York Times*, April 19, 2007.

CHAPTER 13. OF CRISES AND CRITICS

1. Michael Hirsch, "Mortgages and Madness," *Newsweek*, June 2, 2008.

2. Robert O'Harrow and Brady Dennis, "Credit Ratings Woes Sent AIG Spiraling," *Los Angeles Times*, January 2, 2009.

3. "Agency's '04 Rule Let Banks Pile Up New Debt, and Risk," *New York Times*, October 3, 2008.

4. Willaim Greider, *One World Ready or Not: The Manic Logic of Global Capitalism* (New York, 1996), 316, 310–11.

5. Erik Lipton and Stephen Labaton, "A Deregulator Looks Back, Unswayed," *New York Times*, November 17, 2008.

6. Michael Lewis and David Einhorn, "The End of the Financial World as We Know It," *New York Times*, January 3, 2009.

7. I am indebted to Erid Zensy for introducing me to Frederick Soddy and his study *Wealth, Virtual Wealth, and Debt* (London, 1926).

8. Jack Rosenthal, "On Language," *New York Times Magazine*, September 8, 2008: 18.

9. Vikas Bajaj, "If Everyone's Finger Pointing, Who's to Blame?," *New York Times*, January 22, 2008.

10. Nelson Lichtenstein, *State of the Union: A Century of American Labor* (Princeton, 2002), 125–28.

11. Peter Dreier and Kelly Candaele, "Why We Need EFCA," *American Prospect*, December 2, 2008.

12. Jared Diamond, *Collapse: How Societies Choose to Fail or Succeed* (New York, 2005).

13. Diana B. Henriques, "Madoff Scheme Kept Shipping Outward, Crossing Borders," *New York Times*, December 20, 2008

14. Paul Krugman, "A Catastrophe Foretold," *New York Times*, October 28, 2007. Four

people—Doris Dungey, Nouriel Roubini, Brooksley Born, and John Bogle—clearly saw what was wrong with the prevailing financial incentives. See Bogle, "The Case of Corporate America Today," *Daedalus*, 136 (Summer, 2007).

15. Alexei Barrionuevo, "Demand for a Say on the Way Out of Crisis," *New York Times*, November 10, 2008.

16. Thomas L. Friedman, *The World Is Flat: A Brief History of the Twenty-first Century* (New York, 2005); Jeffrey A. Frieden, *Global Capitalism: Its Fall and Rise in the Twentieth Century* (New York, 2006 [paperback ed., 2007]), 293ff; Robert W. Crandall and Kenneth Ramm, eds., *Changing the Rules: Technological Change, International Competition, and Regulation in Communications* (Washington, 1989), 10.

17. *New York Times*, November 17, 2008.

18. Dick K. Nanto, "The 1997-98 Asian Financial Crisis," CRS Report for Congress, February 6, 1998 (www.fas.org/man/crs/crs-asia2): 5.

19. Claire Berlinski, "What the Free Market Needs," *Los Angeles Times*, October 21, 2008.

20. "Modern Market Thought Has Devalued a Deadly Sin," *New York Times*, September 27, 2008; Steven Greenhouse and David Leonhardt, "Real Wages Fail to Match a Rise in Productivity," *New York Times*, August 28, 2006.

21. Tina Rosenberg, "Globalization," *New York Times*, July 30, 2008.

22. Adam Mckeown, "Global Migration, 1840-1940," *Journal of World History*, 15 (2004): 156.

23. Paul Collier, *The Bottom Billion: Why the Poorest Countries Are Failing and What Can Be Done about It* (Oxford, 2007).

24. Ibid., 9, 42-45, 79-84.

25. Ibid., 185-89.

26. www.iht.com/articles/ap/2006/12/10/Europe/EU_Gen_Norway.

27. http://losangeles.broowaha.com/article.php?id=962.

28. Mira Kamdar, *Planet India: The Turbulent Rise of the Largest Democracy and the Future of Our World* (New York, 2007), 118-19; www.iht.com/articles/ap/2006/12/10/Europe/EU_Gen_Norway.

29. Amartya Sen, *Development as Freedom* (New York, 1999), 204, 282-65.

30. Peter Barnes, *Capitalism 3.0: A Guide to Reclaaiming the Commons* (San Francisco, 2006), 65-78, 135-52.

31. Elisabeth Rosenthal, "To Counter Problems of Food, Try Spuds," *New York Times*, October 25, 2008.

32. Dan Bilefsky, "Oh, Yugoslavia! How They Long for Your Firm Embrace," *New York Times*, January 30, 2008.

33. Deepak Lal, *Reviving the Invisible Hand: The Case for Classical Liberalism in the Twenty-first Century* (Princeton, 2006), 214-19.

34. Elisabeth Rosenthal, "European Support for Bicycles Promotes Sharing of the Wheels," *New York Times*, November 10, 2008.

35. Fareed Zakaria, "Is America in Decline? Why the United States Will Survive the Rise of the Rest," *Foreign Affairs*, 87 (2008): 26-27; Parag Khanna, "Waving Goodbye to Hegemony," *New York Times Magazine*, January 27, 2008.

36. Joseph A. Schumpter, *Capitalism, Socialism and Democracy*, 3rd ed. (New York, 1950), 61.

INDEX